# Islam and Christianity

# Islam and Christianity

*Theological Themes in Comparative Perspective*

## John Renard

UNIVERSITY OF CALIFORNIA PRESS
*Berkeley · Los Angeles · London*

University of California Press, one of the most distinguished university presses in the United States, enriches
lives around the world by advancing scholarship in the
humanities, social sciences, and natural sciences. Its
activities are supported by the UC Press Foundation and
by philanthropic contributions from individuals and institutions. For more information, visit www.ucpress.edu.

University of California Press
Berkeley and Los Angeles, California

University of California Press, Ltd.
London, England

Library of Congress Cataloging-in-Publication Data

Renard, John, 1944–.
  Islam and Christianity : theological themes in
comparative perspective / John Renard.
      p.   cm.
  Includes bibliographical references and index.
  ISBN 978-0-520-25508-1 (cloth, alk. paper)
  ISBN 978-0-520-26678-0 (pbk., alk. paper)
    1. Islam—Relations—Christianity.   2. Christianity
and other religions—Islam.   3. Islam—Doctrines.
4. Theology, Doctrinal.   I. Title.

BP172.R462   2011
297.2'83—dc22                              2010023443

Manufactured in the United States of America

19  18  17  16  15  14  13  12  11
10  9  8  7  6  5  4  3  2  1

This book is printed on Cascades Enviro 100, a 100% post
consumer waste, recycled, de-inked fiber. FSC recycled
certified and processed chlorine free. It is acid free, Ecologo
certified, and manufactured by BioGas energy.

*In grateful memory of*

*my parents*
*George (1911–2009) and Virginia (1915–2006)*

*and*

*Richard J. McCarthy, SJ (1913–1981),*
*who dedicated his professional life*
*to understanding and sharing the riches*
*of Islam's theological traditions*

# Contents

# Preface

Recent world events have countless Americans and Europeans entertaining dire thoughts about the future of "civilization." While many conjure up "Islamic" threats to a world in which the existence of "secular" societies is under siege, many more seem persuaded that Islam represents an ideology programmatically oriented to exterminating "Christian" civilization and its sociopolitical protégé, the State of Israel. Scholars, journalists, think tanks, and pundits have produced a vast array of publications addressing various facets of this so-called clash of civilizations and the attendant "threat analysis" aimed at unmasking the sinister designs of the world's Muslims. Conspicuously rare amid the burgeoning catalogue of books on Islam and the West/Christianity are attempts to present straightforward comparisons between the explicitly "theological" themes that arguably form the core of the various subcommunities that have historically comprised Christendom and Islamdom.

It has long been commonplace to observe that Islamic tradition, like that of Judaism, pays more attention to orthopraxy than to orthodoxy. Such broad characterizations are of limited utility, however, and can give the mistaken impression that "theology" plays no significant role in the history of Islamic thought. Though it appears that concerns with creed and "orthodoxy" have occupied Christian thinkers more consistently than they have their Muslim counterparts, theological images, themes, questions, and problems have been very much in evidence throughout the history of Islamic religious thought from the very outset.

Small books about large topics invariably face a daunting array of limitations. Here are some of the most significant challenges that arise in a comparative study of theological themes in Christian and Islamic traditions. First, both traditions extend over vast expanses of time, space, and culture, and this volume represents a very selective overview. Even if one could credibly claim anything like consistency in theological developments in any centuries-old global tradition, selecting samples from the countless important figures and themes would be virtually impossible. But—and this is the second enormous hurdle—despite intraconfessional claims to the contrary on both sides, the worldwide Christian and Muslim communities have both in fact been comprised of multiple subcommunities. Christians and Muslims alike might prefer to imagine that "real" Muslims or "true" Christians have never varied in the faiths they profess, but a striking diversity of views on virtually every significant theological question has been a major feature of both traditions. A relatively short survey such as this therefore confronts the thorny question of which of the many "Christianities" and "Islams," all with their prominent spokespersons and great interpreters, to proffer as representative of the traditions. I do not attempt, furthermore, to describe "contemporary" Christianities or Islams, though I do seek to acknowledge in broad overview the vast sweep of historical developments down to our day. For reasons of space, simplicity, and the limitations of my own academic background, I lean toward characterizing source materials from "classical" or "middle" periods of history. In short, what I present here is in no way intended to characterize a normative version of either Islamic or Christian traditions, but to provide a selective overview of major theological themes in both.

That diversity in turn leads to a third challenge, namely, the choice of criteria for intertraditional comparability. Here it is crucial to observe an important difference between formal and functional comparisons. A fairly obvious formal comparison between Islamic and Christian traditions would be a pairing of foundational sacred texts, the Qur'ān and the New Testament. Both are "books" and, from a phenomenological perspective, ought to be comparable to that extent. From a functional perspective, however, the two scriptures play very different roles in the two theological traditions. As the presence of the word of God in book form, or "inlibration," the Qur'ān functions more as a theological counterpart to the Christian understanding of Jesus as God's Word made flesh in the "incarnation." The New Testament, as the words of Jesus, could then be paralleled with the Hadith, authoritative gatherings of the words and deeds of Muhammad. This in turn presupposes that one posits a similar function for Muhammad and Jesus, as foundational figures of the two traditions. Some would argue, to the contrary, that the apostle Paul functioned more credibly as a counterpart to Muhammad in "institutionalizing" the new faith communities as distinctive traditions. In the course of this volume, I will attend to such distinctions as needed.

I want to underscore that such comparative accommodations are in no way meant to suggest that Muslims have thought of Christ as Logos or of the *injīl* as analogous to the sayings of Muhammad, or that Muslims typically draw such comparisons as these (though, in fact, some have). All comparisons and analogies, implicit or forthright, I suggest only as possible ways of making links between two very different families of religious traditions.

A fourth challenge is that in a book of this size that attempts to encompass a subject of such vast scope through a selection of diverse themes, it is all but impossible to root each theme adequately in its rich and complex historical contexts. As a result, the reader must understand in advance that the juxtaposition of structurally similar features in Christianity and Islam—for example, exegetical traditions, development of analogous institutions such as educational systems, or structures of intentional community—does not imply a simple one-to-one correspondence across traditions. Many differences, from the subtle to the mutually incompatible, remain to be acknowledged and discovered by further exploration into the themes laid out in these chapters. In short, *caveat lector:* general structural parallels or analogies suggested here are in no instance meant to imply point-for-point correspondence, let alone that the Islamic and Christian faith traditions are variants of one another.

A related challenge has to do with the difficulty of marshaling evidence and illustrations evenhandedly. Though it has been my overarching desire to do just that, I have not always succeeded. Disparities in this respect are in no way programmatic or deliberate, but merely ad hoc evidence of my limited ability to juggle with perfect dexterity and symmetry such a vast array of data. My choices as to the level of historical detail to be provided have turned on a compromise as to the book's primary audience. In the end I decided to aim at the broad middle readership of those seeking to enhance a beginning interest in the subject. I apologize in advance both to specialists who find the occasional provision of clusters of names and dates unnecessary and to readers new to the field who may find such data daunting at least initially.

Last, but perhaps most importantly, I am presuming to challenge, and perhaps frankly redefine, regnant assumptions about what constitutes "theology" as a mode of interpretation of disparate religious traditions. I begin the process by stretching the range of the adjective "theological" beyond the intellectual or academic exercise of probing foundational sources for the purpose of articulating elements of a given "creed" and ultimately defining one community of belief in distinction to another. I use the term "theological" to include the broad panoply of texts and images and the various modes of interpreting them; ways of reasoning and analysis of human "religious" experience; modes of expression, whether verbal or visual, of that experience; and the host of institutional and cultural developments that have formed the settings and contexts for all such interpretation, processing, and expression. The essential pivot is the clear association of some sort of divine impetus with all of the above. In no way do I wish to diminish the importance of theology as a key religious and academic discipline, but merely to set that activity in the broadest possible context, apart from which its relevance cannot be fully assessed. If the discipline of "theology" is a walled city, stoutly defended, visible from afar but accessible only to the elite, the "theological" is the surrounding landscape, with its towns, villages, and farms, which stretches to the horizons and on which the citadel depends for its sustenance.

## ANGLE OF APPROACH, STRUCTURE AND INTENT

As a specialist in Islamic studies, with a focus on medieval religious texts in Arabic and Persian, I have been absorbed for over thirty-five years with religious questions raised by Muslim authors. Prior to doctoral studies in the Islamic tradition, a master's degree in biblical studies and a master of divinity program of theological education leading to ordination as a Roman Catholic priest of the Society of Jesus (Jesuits) provided a broad familiarity with Christian sacred sources and theological disciplines. Several years ago I decided to combine the two streams of study. There have been more than a few books comparing large religious themes in Islam and Christianity, but very few that have sought to provide an overview of similarities and differences in the two traditions in the more limited field of explicitly *theological* themes. At the same time, an emphasis on themes expands the scope of the book beyond the confines of the relatively narrow category of theology as an academic religious discipline. An underlying structural conviction here is that one can identify very broadly analogous trends in Christian and Islamic theological traditions. Before there were disparate theological systems, there were evolving schools of thought; those "schools" in turn evolved alongside the identification of diverse theological positions in creedal formulations, and creedal statements codified elements of the faith community's master narrative.

I view the overall project through the frame of "theological dialogue." Though it is not pointedly *about* theological dialogue, this exploration presupposes that such an intertraditional conversation is both desirable and possible, but that it needs to occur against a broader backdrop than generally available until now. As a working definition, I propose that theological dialogue begins with the assumption that the traditions of both (or all) interlocutors are rooted in experiences of, and insight into, a divinely initiated connection with humankind and the "world." We have considerable historical data about a wide variety of examples, however halting or ill intentioned or unsuccessful, of Christian-Muslim theological dialogue beginning over thirteen centuries ago. In practical terms, theological dialogue turns on an identification of concepts and values essential to characterizing the overall relationship between two faith traditions or communities. A community's place in the political scheme of things in a given region and time has historically had a profound influence on the choice of themes. Theologies have always been fraught with political implications, and few political systems have been entirely free of theological resonances. On the basis of that de facto selection of target themes, interlocutors assess the issues from the perspectives of their own traditions and make conclusive judgments about the "truth" of the other.

One could theoretically look through such a frame of reference from both sides. In the interest of space and desire for relative simplicity, I have chosen to do so from the Christian perspective only. Two short bookend pieces set the framework of theological dialogue. A prologue looks back at four key historical "models," from very early in Islam's history down through the twentieth century. An epilogue looks to the future with suggestions as to one possible method and several motives for pursuing theological dialogue in generations to come. Inside the frame, an introduction and nine chapters propose a variety of themes as the vocabulary for a language of comparison and contrast.

In the introduction, I set the overall structural context by suggesting an expansive model for understanding the broad purview of theological issues in both traditions. The main parts then explore a complex of four "dimensions" informed and defined by those theological concerns. Historical dimensions are the focus of the first two chapters, which discuss comparable categories in five areas: sacred sources and their interpretation; theological interpretations of history, especially with respect to the definition of protocommunities; evolving criteria of membership in the community; conversion and global mission; and eschatology, including end-time scenarios.

Chapters 3 and 4 address creedal dimensions, including the emergence of formal creeds and varieties of theological thought, with specific focus on themes of revelation and the nature of God. Institutional dimensions come to the fore in chapters 5 and 6, which explore questions of authority and law. The final three chapters, on ethical and spiritual dimensions, examine a variety of topics, including sources, methods, and themes in theological ethics, the role of imitation of the founding figure, and the overarching theme of social responsibility; and prayer, piety, and mysticism and the role of exemplary religious figures in inspiring the believer.

In brief notes introducing each of the four main parts, I identify the specific aspects of the theological "disciplines" described in the general introduction that figure most prominently in the chapters of each part. Each chapter's title signals its own overarching theological theme, and each chapter concludes with a brief summary of the theological principles suggested by the data, with specific reference to the comparisons and contrasts they imply.

A concern for pedagogical utility undergirds the structure of the volume. The scope of the subject is exceedingly broad, and many readers may be only marginally familiar with the major figures and themes. To accommodate the subject and audience, I have organized the order and content of the main sections as a series of verbal overlays, much the way an anatomy textbook might provide visual transparencies that overlay the vascular, neural, and muscular systems on an image of the human skeleton. Thus I am able to refer in later sections to elements laid out previously in different contexts, the better to orient readers in their tour of the subject's expansive terrain. A glossary of technical terms is also provided as an aid to readers. In the glossary and throughout the text and notes, I have opted for a simplified form of transliteration for Arabic names and technical terms, using macron, ayn, and hamza to assist with basic pronounciation.

Let there be no mistake about the pretensions of this volume: the subject matter is clearly so broad and complex as to preclude any ultimately satisfying and satisfactory, let alone definitive, outcome by a single author in a single small book. As for my interpretation of sources, I claim no scholarly originality here. The raw material of this volume arises, to put it bluntly, out of a survey of surveys. To the extent that the scope of comparison and the structuring of its numerous themes may be original in its conception, I hope that the text may occasionally challenge readers by tweaking their default settings on the subject. I seek to offer an occasion for considering the connecting points among the various Christianities and Islams, as well as their numerous irreducible differences, from what I hope will prove a fresh perspective.

As for my method, I do not propose to undertake specific point-for-point comparisons of questions of doctrine or history. My general purpose is to limn out, through a juxtaposition of broadly similar features in the histories of Islam and Christianity, a master argument that comes unassumingly down to this: the preponderance of historical data suggests that Islam and Christianity are, after all, not as incompatible as many readers might once have thought.

. . .

By way of acknowledgments, I want first to salute Hugh Goddard for his pathfinding work in Muslim-Christian "theological dialogue." I read his excellent *Christians and Muslims: From Double Standards to Mutual Understanding* (Surrey: Curzon, 1995) soon after its publication, and since then his example has encouraged me to undertake what I hope is a successful attempt to extend and broaden at least slightly his pioneering work. Although the present text and his overlap somewhat—occasionally and fortuitously in structure and, almost inevitably, in some details of thematic content—they cover very diverse territories in historical and textual sources, frame the larger issues distinctively, proceed from varying presuppositions, and suggest different conclusions.

I thank Saint Louis University for a Summer Research Award and a Faculty Research Leave in the fall of 2008 to devote full time to writing. My thanks also to Lisa-Marie Duffield for help in initial stages of gathering resources; Robert Porwoll for special assistance through the summer of 2008; Chih-Yin Chen for her extensive work in spring and fall 2009 on refining early drafts, finalizing revisions, and constructing the glossary; Sarah Swaykus for helping in indexing; and for critique by students in a graduate medieval seminar in spring 2009: Andrew Bangert, Marilyn Kincaid, Jonathan King, Erick Moser, Scott Shoger, and Eric Wickman. I thank also the members of the fall 2009 honors seminar "Islam and Christianity: An Interdisciplinary Approach" for their insightful comments on a semifinal draft: Nicole Bisel, Caroline Brand, Carole Dobbins, Rachel Dratnol, Laura Henry, Alexis Lassus, Robin Lund, Laurel Marshall, Kate Maxwell, Hannah Moore, Latasha Morris, Madalyn Robb, Katarina Semkiu, and Kristen Wegener.

For their thoughtful comments on earlier drafts I thank David Bertaina, Frank Nichols, and Debra Majeed; and I am grateful to David Vishanoff for his suggestions regarding final draft revisions. I have also benefited from the critique and suggestions of anonymous readers solicited by the Press and send along my thanks here belatedly and indirectly. I am most grateful to Ahmet Karamustafa for his extensive comments on the entire early text and his ongoing willingness to let me run test-pieces by him; and I am particularly indebted to David Johnston for his generous engagement with the project from the earliest, very rough drafts through the final revisions. And I wish to express my gratitude to Reed Malcolm, Kalicia Pivirotto, Cindy Fulton, and the editorial staff of the University of California Press for their high-level professional work and commitment to excellence in academic publication. Special thanks also to Marian Rogers for a superb copyediting job.

Scriptural citations throughout represent my adaptations of the Revised Standard Version of the Bible, in consultation with the Hebrew and Greek texts; and of various widely used English versions of the Qur'ān, especially that of Abdullah Yusuf Ali, with reference to the Arabic text. The prologue and the epilogue represent an expanded version of a plenary address delivered to the Catholic Theological Society of America in San Antonio in 1993.

Finally, as always my profound gratitude to my beloved Mary Pat for her constant patience, support, and wise counsel through it all.

# Prologue

*Christian-Muslim Theological*
*Dialogue in Retrospect*

Four historical models of Christian theological engagement with Islam represent a broad spectrum across which Christian theologians have accounted for the church's relationships with Islamic thought as they have perceived it. The four are the polemical, the Scholastic, the Christian-inclusivist, and the dialogical.

## JOHN OF DAMASCUS AND THE POLEMICAL MODEL

John of Damascus (c. 655–750), sometimes called the last of the classical church fathers, is a fine example of a polemical model. His message to Muslims is that he hears what they are saying and finds that he must take serious account of their rationale, if largely in self-defense and in reaction against a hostile claim. For John, it is clear that what Muslims are reported to hold does not comport with the truth and must therefore be condemned and revealed for the distortion it represents. John instinctively regards Islam as a competitor, either as a Christian heresy or as an upstart heathen creed. His basic assumption is that there is a right belief, and all other belief systems are to be defined in relation to that norm. John's theological worldview did not arise out of a vacuum.

Before taking a closer look at John of Damascus, a bit of historical context will be useful. A number of seventh- and eighth-century Middle Eastern Christian treatments of Muhammad and Islam are surprisingly positive. The earliest account, Armenian bishop Sebeos's *History of Heraclius* (finished c. 661, the year of the commencement of the Umayyad dynasty), is remarkably generous, attributing to Muhammad a thorough knowledge of Mosaic law and acknowledging a general moral uprightness in his teaching. As such, his account represents, in John Moorhead's view, "not merely a re-telling of what the Arabs believed concerning the status of their religion, but an implicit endorsement of the status they claimed for it." Moorhead attributes Sebeos's few negative comments to political rather than theological interests. An anonymous Nestorian monk writing within the next ten years or so likewise acknowledges firm biblical precedent for Islam and the Prophet. About a century later we find the Monophysite Pseudo-Dionysius of Tell-Mahre virtually applauding Muhammad's solid stance for morality and monotheism, and against idolatry.[1]

A number of documents from the seventh and eighth centuries do indeed roundly condemn Muslims and their Prophet on theological grounds. For example, some argue that Muslims do not worship the true God, because they do not acknowledge the divinity of Jesus. But it will perhaps come as a surprise that as late as the twelfth century generally positive assessments of Islam by Middle Eastern Christian theologians seem to outnumber the blanket condemnations. A twelfth-century Jacobite patriarch of Antioch named Michael the Syrian represents one of the latest such evaluations. Were these authors expressing their true convictions, or merely sugar—coating their opinions in fear of their Muslim rulers? Moorhead argues that because they wrote not in Arabic, but in Syriac, Armenian, and Coptic, they would surely have felt free enough to be straightforward.

But what of John of Damascus, whose family served the Umayyad caliph in the administration of Damascus and whose own grandfather and father had risen to high rank in fiscal and military matters? Daniel Sahas observes:

> Studying John of Damascus as a real person, living and reasoning with his own people and with the Muslim settlers in his home city . . . discloses one of the most serious originators of the Muslim-Christian dialogue; a pioneer mind of distinguishing qualities, such as personal objective knowledge and sensitivity, which one finds generally missing from later Christian representatives. . . . [His example allows one to] trace the origins of some of the grossest misunderstandings which have shaped the attitude of one religion toward the other.[2]

The decree of the Iconoclastic Synod of 754, ironically, condemned John not only for his iconolatry, but for being "Saracen-minded" (*sarrakenophroni*), slapping him with a total of four anathemas. The epithet had been applied to a number of famous iconoclasts, including Leo III, which was more readily understandable, since he seemed to be acting in sympathy with the iconoclastic preferences of the caliph Yazid II; but why was John labeled a Saracen sympathizer? Evidently because the synod's constituents regarded John's background as tainted by his living among Muslims. John's grandfather, already a high official in Byzantine administration of the province of Syria, had been involved in negotiating the surrender of Damascus to Khālid ibn al-Walīd and his army (636). He extracted promises of security for all the inhabitants of Damascus except, apparently, for the representatives of Byzantium. The citizens of Damascus were not sorry to see the end of Byzantine rule. John's father later inherited the position; John himself rose high in the Umayyad administration, serving as secretary—chief adviser, according to one interpretation—to the caliph 'Abd al-Mālik (684–705), the man who commissioned the Dome of the Rock in Jerusalem. A celebrated legend tells how the emperor Leo III, angered by John's resistance to his iconoclastic policies, contrived to raise the caliph's suspicions against John. According to that story, the plot worked. John was ousted and headed for the monastery of St. Sabas near Jerusalem. It seems likely, however, that John actually left of his own accord, although 'Abd al-Mālik's immediate successors were increasingly hostile to Christians.[3]

Within John's major theological work, *Fount of Knowledge,* is a section entitled "On Heresies," including a segment dedicated to the Ishmaelites. Most of the hundred heresies merit only a few lines, but the portion on Islam takes up four and a half Migne columns.[4] In Daniel Sahas's words,

> [John] presents the facts about Islam in an orderly and systematic way, although not at all complimentary; he demonstrates an accurate knowledge of the religion, perhaps higher than the one that an average Muslim could possess; he is aware of the cardinal doctrines and concepts in Islam, especially those which are of an immediate interest to a Christian; he knows well his sources and he is at home with the Muslim mentality . . . not inflammatory of hatred, neither grandiloquent and full of self-triumph; it is an essay on Islam, in a book of Christian heresies. In this simple fact lies its significance and its weakness![5]

Another important work, whose content is attributed to the Damascene Father but whose written form comes from a Melkite bishop named Theodore Abū Qurra (c. 720–825), contains a dialogue-disputation between a Muslim and a Christian. The document provides an excellent glimpse into major issues of importance in the eighth-century Middle East, namely, whether God's omnipotence leaves any scope for human freedom, the meaning of the term "word of God," and whether Islam constitutes a definitive prophetic revelation. These themes prompt further intriguing questions about the degree to which Muslim and Christian thought had already begun to interpenetrate in shaping divergent views of parties within both communities. To what extent does the dialogue represent actual Muslim views, and to what extent does it represent John's attempt to demonstrate clear differences between Christian and Muslim positions? From the very early eighth century, around the same time as the Damascene dialogue, Muslims had heatedly debated these same problems among themselves. The Christian argues for human self-determination in the interest of preserving God's justice, while remaining unconcerned that the position appears to compromise God's power. For his part, the Muslim argues for God's omnipotence and is willing to settle for the appearance of the inability of human beings to choose freely.

In the matter of the word of God, we find another interesting point of both convergence and divergence. Mainstream opinions on both sides consider the Word uncreated, but for very different reasons and with different consequences. Both find themselves defending highly paradoxical conclusions, but, ironically perhaps, the Muslim and Christian positions are closer on this question than on that of divine power and human choice. At this point the interreligious issue is not a narrowly christological one as such, but a question of how God communicates to humanity. Disputes about the matter within the Muslim community had the same political implications as debate about the first question. John's distinction between Word (Christ) and words (scripture) of God more or less parallel the Muslim distinction between God's eternal Speech and the Qurān as book.[6]

In sum, John of Damascus offers an example of as positive an approach to Islam as any apologist or polemicist has produced. He did, to be sure, condemn Islam on theological grounds. He regarded Islam as a Christian heresy chiefly because of its denial of the central doctrines of redemption and the divinity of Christ. But at no time does John distort Muslim theological positions; on the contrary, he shows a remarkably thorough knowledge of Islamic sources and intellectual developments of his time. John seems quite intent on informing his Christian readers about Islamic beliefs and practice, not to inflame them against their Muslim neighbors. As Daniel Sahas concludes, "What distinguishes John as a Christian interlocutor in the Muslim-Christian dialogue is that he was motivated to refute Islam as, primarily a theological heresy and as a 'false' religious tradition, whereas later Byzantine writers were involved in anti-Muslim polemics which, more often than not, had political dimensions and support."[7] A major problem with John's contribution remains his characterization of Islam as a heresy, reducing it solely to its relation to Christianity.

## THOMAS AQUINAS AND THE SCHOLASTIC MODEL

Thomas Aquinas is a prime exponent of a "Scholastic" model. He defines Islamic thought not precisely as Islamic but as an intellectual endeavor, not always negatively, in relation to other intellectual endeavor. The model's basic assumption is that there is a right belief, and while appeal to scripture will not persuade unbelievers, one can martial rational arguments to demonstrate the superiority of that system. The Scholastic model attempts to establish an objective criterion—namely, reason rather than revelation—from which to proceed. Thus does this model advance somewhat beyond the older view of Islam as outright heresy, by viewing the contributions of Islamic thinkers not so much in relation to Christian theological doctrine as in relation to their intellectual credibility, attempting to take them seriously on their own terms in light of reason's objective critique.

Thomas presents two faces with respect to his views of Islam. The first, evidenced largely in the *Summa Contra Gentiles,* seems to articulate what many before him and since have felt but seldom said publicly or in print. He does not shrink from hurling his share of vituperation at Muslims, and especially at Muhammad.[8] Here it is most uncharacteristic of Thomas that he relies on hearsay or unreliable tertiary sources in his characterization, not of Islamic thought, but of the venality of Muhammad and the gullibility of his followers. The false prophet seduced the gullible with promises of carnal pleasure, filled their minds with naive fabrications, and forbade them to read the Christian scriptures lest they show him up for a liar. What truth Muhammad did purvey amounted to little more than what any reasonable mind might acquire unaided.

It is puzzling that Thomas says such things even though he was clearly aware that Muslims were monotheists who believed their Prophet had brought a scripture in many ways similar in content to those of Christianity and Judaism. He knew further that Muslims believed that their scripture and prophet abrogate all previous dispensations, and that Muhammad never claimed proof through miracles. Thomas also knew how Muslims regarded Christian beliefs in the incarnation, redemption, Eucharist, and Trinity. He may have had access to John of Damascus's work and probably learned much about Islam from Peter the Venerable's (d. 1156) *Summa of the Entirety of the Saracen Heresy,* some of whose weaknesses Thomas merely reproduces.[9] Thomas more than likely had met few if any Muslims, and his membership in the mutual denigration society to which so many Muslims and Christians have belonged over the centuries is a testimony to the insidious corrosive power of popular bigotry and fear of the other. We can scarcely claim to have advanced very far beyond that.[10]

On the other hand, we find Thomas evidently persuaded that a number of Islamdom's greatest intellectuals called for a more refined response. In the *Summa Theologiae* he maintains a posture of professional decorum in his assessment of important positions of Muslim intellectuals of note, such as Ghazālī (Algazel, d. 1111), Ibn Sīnā (Avicenna, d. 1037), and Ibn Rushd (Averroes, d. 1198). To them he says in effect: I take you seriously as a contributor to human thought, I believe I understand what you are saying, and I think you are asking many of the right questions. But you have gone too far in some respects and not far enough in others.

Thomas responded notably to the well-known conclusions of the great philosophical theologians on such crucial cosmological matters as the creation of the world, but the theme that is perhaps most relevant here is that of the status and function of prophetic revelation—a theme also of interest to such remarkable Jewish theologians as Rabbi Moses bar Maimon (Maimonides, d. 1204). A study by Juan Casciaro, *El dialogo teologico de Santo Tomas con musulmanes y judios: El tema de la profecia y la revelacion* (The Theological Dialogue of Saint Thomas with Muslims and Jews: The Theme of Prophecy and Revelation), surveys the questions of the *Summa's Secunda Secundae* (Second Part of the Second Part) on prophecy with a view to assessing the influence of Muslim thought (and that of Maimonides specifically among Jewish scholars). The study categorizes Thomas's conclusions variously as largely borrowed, borrowed and partly refuted, profoundly influenced, influenced to a lesser but still measurable degree, or independent. Casciaro observes that about two-thirds of Thomas's material relates directly or indirectly to earlier speculations of Muslims and Jews. Quantitatively speaking, more than half of Thomas's texts on this subject find important correspondences in Islamic and rabbinic literature, much in the form of opinions shared by Maimonides and one or more of the Muslim thinkers.[11] There is much more extensive direct citation in Thomas's earlier works concerning the subject, especially in the *De Veritate* and *Summa Contra Gentiles*.

Thomas shared Peter the Venerable's quest for a rational basis on which to engage Muslims in discussion. Indeed, the conviction that Muslims were after all worth talking to on those grounds elevates both Peter and Thomas well above most of their contemporaries. The intriguing case of Francis of Assisi (d. 1226) is another remarkable exception, but for very different reasons.[12] Thomas remained steadfast in his belief that the purpose of discussion was to persuade people of the truth of Christianity, and to that extent his approach shares much with the polemical model. Here, however, it is essential to emphasize that Thomas goes a major step further in the seriousness with which he views his adversaries' positions.[13]

## HANS KÜNG AND THE CHRISTIAN-INCLUSIVIST MODEL

In the post-Vatican II era, Hans Küng has been working out what one might call a Christian-inclusivist model. He says to the Muslim: I think I understand what you are saying and why, and I am convinced that the future of the world depends on our continuing to listen critically but non-judgmentally to each other. Küng's explicit motive for approaching inter-religious dialogue is that world peace demands religious peace, religious peace demands dialogue, and dialogue demands understanding.[14] This model sees Islam as a religious tradition, not so much because of its validity even within its own orbit, as because it is ultimately better for us all if Christians can learn to account for Islam as both intellectually and theologically too important to ignore.

Küng's basic assumption is that a global plurality of religious systems is an undeniable and probably permanent fact. We must find a way of getting along but without attempting to homogenize, lest anyone recoil at the insinuation that absolute truth claims have to be relinquished. Comparison of doctrinal positions is not a thing of the past, for the approach still begins with Christian doctrine as the standard of truth; but debate over who is right must be replaced by the conviction that understanding is preferable to dominance. Küng's method involves comparison of formal doctrinal categories, with Christianity as the norm and standard. But whereas the Scholastics and apologists were responding to an Islamic impulse that had come toward them, Küng (and others who share his convictions at least in general) has decided to move toward Islam.

Küng places the theological encounter with Islam within the context of Christian engagement with several non-Christian traditions. He enlists the help of scholars, none adherents of any of those traditions, to lay out the theological frameworks in each instance. Noted German expert on Islamic theological sources Josef van Ess provides the "Islamic perspectives," to which Küng offers as "a Christian response" his rendition of the Christian perspective.

The discussion is divided into four segments: prophecy and revelation as the Islamic view of Muhammad and the Qur'ān; Sunni and Shi'i views of history as an approach to issues of state and law; images of God and humanity and a discussion of mysticism; and Jesus in the Qur'ān as a starting point for a treatment of Islam's attitudes to other religious traditions. Van Ess's treatment is excellent and highly informative. In each instance, Küng frames the issues in decidedly Christian terms, asking in effect whether a Christian can regard Islam's interpretations of revelation, salvation, and prophethood as measuring up. He asks such questions as whether Islam is a way of salvation, whether Muhammad was a prophet, whether the Qur'ān is the word of God—all as though a Christian should be in a position to answer them objectively, or indeed as though anyone could do so. Apart from the use of Christian doctrine as standards of truth, there lurks in the background the implicit canonization of the Renaissance and the Enlightenment as definitively formative of an intelligent approach to religious matters. And it has become a truism to say that the Islamic world has yet to experience either of these baptismal realities.[15]

To his enormous credit, Küng articulates as clearly as any Christian scholar to date what is really at stake here, and he then goes a step beyond that. His statement about the prophethood of Muhammad exemplifies his position:

> The New Testament doesn't bid us reject in advance Muhammad's claim to be a true prophet *after* Jesus and in basic agreement with him. Naturally, the relationship between Jesus the Messiah and Muhammad the Prophet has yet to be explained in detail. Still, the simple recognition of Muhammad's title of "prophet" would have momentous consequences, especially for the message he proclaimed, which is written down in the Qur'an.[16]

Also very important in the present context is what Küng has accomplished in his monumental work *Islam: Past, Present, and Future.* Adapting Thomas Kuhn's "paradigm change" model, Küng authored his sweeping analysis of Islamic historical developments "to help people engage in dialogue in this decisive transitional phase towards a new relationship between the civilizations, religions and nations."[17] One could debate the degree to which his use of the "paradigm change" model succeeds methodologically. In the final analysis, however, Küng has walked to the edge of what Paul Knitter has aptly dubbed his "theological Rubicon"—taking the fearsome step of crossing over toward the shores of genuine pluralism might place him in the company of theologically unsavory characters.[18] Küng's major work on Islam well exemplifies the kind of broad background that both assumes an expansive definition of what qualifies as "theological," and must inform all our discussion of theological dialogue.

## KENNETH CRAGG AND THE DIALOGICAL MODEL

Anglican bishop Kenneth Cragg, whom many consider the unofficial dean of church-affiliated Islamicists, has ventured midway across the theological Rubicon. He uses the metaphor of language translation to describe what he calls "inter-theology"—one must learn to translate accurately by conceptual, rather than verbal, equivalence. Cragg takes the best in Küng's approach and puts it at the service of serious theological dialogue. Referring to the plurality of truth claims represented by the various traditions, he notes:

> Theology's first task . . . is to interrogate this diversity of self-legitimation, its own and that of others, and seek what might establish between us the sort of *bona fide* relationship which does not exempt its own credentials from engagement with the other. Otherwise, the closed-shop nature of what, in most religions, purports to be of universal relevance, will persist and harden. In practice we concede the givenness, the there-ness, of other faiths in the world scene and their immense liabilities for society and the future. How then do we do so theologically?[19]

Cragg's model arguably strives for more genuine mutuality than does Küng's. Where Küng seems still to be reacting and comparing doctrinal concepts one for one, Cragg seems to be inviting and seeking broader concepts within which both parties can comfortably identify their respective doctrines.

Where can one find important theological cross-references with Islam? Cragg offers two modes of association: by more or less direct analogy and by subtle indirection. The more direct kind of cross-reference sees functional parallels in the two traditions and builds on their similarities. For example, Cragg suggests the shared Muslim and Christian celebration of God's greatness makes them both "theologies of Magnificat," rooted deeply in the formative experiences of their foundational figures. Here one must first look for parallels, not between Jesus and Muhammad, but between Mary and Muhammad. Muhammad also affirmed in almost the same terms Mary's conviction that God's "mercy is upon those who stand in reverent awe" of God. Like Mary, Muhammad experienced and proclaimed the grandeur of God, marveled at the mystery of God's ongoing involvement in human affairs, and reveled in the profusion of divine largesse. Recalling the root Semitic affinity between the words for "mercy" and "womb," Cragg suggests further cross-reference in attitudes toward the mystery of birth. Numerous Qur'ānic texts celebrate the divine fertility as manifest in countless natural revelatory "signs on the horizons." All fecundity, the Qur'ān insists, both reminds humankind of God's mercy and instills a profound awe.[20]

A more difficult mode finds connection less in evident parallels than in issues on which Islam and Christianity appear to have agreed at some point but later diverged significantly because of the dynamics of a doctrinal logic based on divergent assumptions. Cragg builds his "inter-theology" on less obvious grounds in his discovery of intriguing christological cross-overs. Qur'ān 4:172, "The Messiah would never shrink from being servant of God," calls to mind Philippians 2:6–8's startling affirmation of Jesus' refusal to avoid servanthood by claiming a son's privilege. To the Islamic way of thinking, the issue is precisely the other way around: a servant would never claim to be a son. For Christians, only a Son can render the ultimate and necessary service, namely, redemption; for Muslims, service of God rules out the higher honor of filiation. Cragg notes that theological relations are characterized by such cross-connections over a wide range of issues. "The contra-Christian animus of Islam has Christian criteria, just as there are, one might truly say, Islamic reasons for continuing Christian!"[21]

Pursuing this oblique line of argument, Cragg allows himself to be carried along on the current of God's transcendence rather than risking the undertow of Trinity and incarnation. The interconnection via God's transcendence goes like this. Both traditions affirm the divine sovereignty, even as both insist on God's responsibility for, and hence affinity with, creation and humanity through a covenant. Both teach the centrality of humanity's willing acknowledgment of God's sovereignty in grateful surrender, which by definition cannot be coerced. The God of Islam, like the God of Christianity, "has been willing to incur the most heinous of all repudiations, namely that his creatures may refuse His Lordship. We cannot make sense of *Shirk* [associating partners with God] and also see divine sovereignty as at all costs immunised from human rejection. Nor can we see that sovereignty as so unsure as to create, not creatures, but automata, not men but only non-volitional subjects."[22] But it is at the point of the possibility of human denial of that transcendence that Islam and Christianity part company. For Christians that possibility requires the redemption; for Muslims it calls for a new prophetic dispensation.

. . .

Against this broad historical panorama of Christian-Muslim theological dialogue, an overview of how the various theological subdisciplines have evolved in the two traditions will in turn set out the conceptual tools needed for further discussion of theological themes in "four dimensions."

# Introduction

*Theological Themes and Subdisciplines*

Islamic and Christian theologies developed over vast expanses of time and space, were rooted in a host of cultural and linguistic contexts, and have generated enormous libraries of works in dozens of languages and employing numerous methodologies. We are approaching here an immense and complex subject, but before delving into some of the more specific "dimensions" of this involved story, an overview of the major contours of the topic will be helpful. Here I will organize the material in two main sections, each dedicated to one of the two major traditions. In chapters 1–9, I will, by contrast, offer basic thematic comparison by juxtaposing Islamic and Christian perspectives in each of several subtopics.

## OVERVIEW OF CHRISTIAN THEOLOGICAL THEMES AND SUBDISCIPLINES

Theological curricula vary from one Christian denomination to another, but a general characterization of the main outlines of contemporary theological subject matter and methodologies will be of use in this context. I have organized the overview under four principal headings: Biblical and Exegetical Theology, History and Theology, Systematic Theology, and Practical/Pastoral/Public Theology.

### Biblical and Exegetical Theology

Three major themes lie at the foundation of theological reflection on Christian sacred texts. First, the question of what precisely comprised the "canon" of revealed scripture was a major concern that early Christians discussed and fought over for many generations. Second, even before early Christian authorities had agreed on a definitive scriptural canon, exegetes had begun to explore a variety of interpretative methods. Third, exegesis both turns on a host of important theological presuppositions concerning the nature of the biblical revelation and gives rise to further theological conclusions. Here we are talking about theologies of the Bible and biblical theology. I begin with a brief description of these three themes.

A fundamental question in Christian theological study of scripture concerns exactly what belongs in the Bible. Discussions about what constitutes the canon of scripture began among Jews long before the time of Christ. But what Jewish scholars decided some two millennia ago about the Hebrew scriptures, Christian scholars did not regard as the final word on the shape of the Old Testament. Jewish scholars included under the three divisions of Torah, Nevi'im, and Chetuvim (known collectively by the acronym TaNaCh), respectively, the five books of Moses, the Prophets, and the Writings.[1] A total of thirty-nine "books" completed the Judaic canon. Christian scholars faced a dual challenge as they considered matters of canonical criteria, for they needed to decide not only what their version of the Old Testament would encompass, but which of the many competing texts of the early Christian era qualified for inclusion in what would become the New Testament.

Eventually, all the main branches and denominations of Christianity agreed on a single set of twenty-seven books of their uniquely Christian sacred text: four Gospels, Acts of the Apostles, the book of Revelation, and twenty-one "Epistles" or Letters, traditionally ascribed to a total of eight different inspired authors (Matthew, Mark, Luke [Gospel and Acts], John [Gospel, Revelation, and three Letters], Paul [fourteen Letters], Peter [two Letters], James and Jude [one Letter each]).

Deciding on the final contents of the Old Testament was more complex and contested among the major segments of Christianity. All Christian denominations agree on the Torah, the main Historical Books (which the Protestant traditions generally call the Lesser or Former Prophets), the principal Prophetic Books (known to most Protestants as the Greater or Latter Prophets), and most of the "Writings" that comprise what the majority of Christians call the Wisdom literature. A set of fifteen works known as the Apocrypha, including the two-volume book of Maccabees, is often printed as an appendix to the thirty-nine canonical books in "ecumenical" versions of the Bible. Catholic Bibles, by contrast, call these works "deuterocanonical" and incorporate nine of them into their sections of Historical (five), Wisdom (two), and Prophetic books (two).[2]

Christian exegetes have been engaged since the earliest generations in the complicated enterprise of interpreting the sacred texts. The story is complex and intriguing. Very early on, exegetes began discussing a variety of levels of meaning, or "senses," of scripture. In more recent times, very few Christian denominations continue to emphasize a "literalist" interpretation in the conviction that the text's sacred meaning was revealed complete and invariable, and that its authority and import are universal and timeless. Far more widely accepted modes of interpretation begin with the presupposition that God works in and through history and that one must always read holy writ with attention to diversity of literary genres and authorial intent. In other words, God inspired the biblical authors precisely as their times and circumstances required. As a result, those who interpret the sacred text must continue to take into consideration the historically conditioned nature of the sources as they uncover their meaning for changed circumstances.[3] The so-called historical-critical method is the result of these concerns.[4]

Finally, "biblical theology" means at least two very different things in Christian thought over the centuries. First, it can refer to the theological implications and themes of the text of the Bible—that is, reading the Bible precisely as a theological document. For Christians who start from the fundamental principle of direct divine authorship of every word in Old and New Testaments (generally a minority of "evangelicals" worldwide), biblical theology generally presupposes the perfect consistency of the whole. An underlying methodological principle, therefore, is that apparent contradictions within or between individual biblical books are precisely that—apparent—and it is the task of exegetes to find a way to "harmonize" them in view of the overall message. For those who approach the study of the Bible from the perspective of the historical-critical method (or some variation of it), the notion that individual biblical authors were "inspired" and responded within a variety of historical and cultural contexts is the governing principle. From this point of view, one finds in the sacred text multiple theologies embodied in the divergent interpretations of the many inspired authors.

Secondly, biblical theology can refer to the labors of early modern and contemporary Christian exegetes, whether of a more conservative or the avowedly historical-critical method, to articulate integrated theological interpretations of the sacred text—that is, theologies of the Bible. Such works as Gerhard von Rad's now-classic *Old Testament Theology: The*

*Theology of Israel's Historical Traditions,* for example, represent the results of historical-critical method, offering a synthesis of the various theologies discernible in large segments of the Bible (such as the Hexateuch—that is, Torah plus Joshua; the Historical Books; Prophets, or Wisdom literature).[5]

## History and Theology

Christian theological traditions encompass a wide range of historical approaches and methodologies. One can speak, for example, of histories of theology (accounts of the whole sweep, or studies of important periods, of theological developments and works), theologies of history (theological interpretations resulting in various master narratives of the larger meanings of Christian "salvation history"), and historical theology ("the genetic study of Christian faith and doctrines," or, sometimes more broadly, "all those theological and paratheological disciplines whose method is historical").[6] Whatever the specific perspective one chooses, a look at a periodization of the sort commonly built into Christian theological curricula will be useful here.

*Early Church through Late Antiquity (1–800 C.E.).* All of the first Christian century comprises the New Testament and apostolic era. Beginning with the life of Jesus,[7] the period witnessed the composition of all of the now-canonical books of the New Testament. But, in addition, those seventy or so years after the death of Jesus also saw a gradual but significant growth of the Christian community beyond Palestine and into other provinces of the Roman Empire and surrounding regions. By around 100 C.E., Christian communities had been rooted throughout the eastern Mediterranean rim, well into Asia Minor, in parts of Greece, and as far as Rome.

Much of second-century Christian theology was articulated by writers known since early modern times as the apostolic fathers and the apologists. Late in the New Testament period the former group, including most notably bishops Ignatius of Antioch (c. 35–107), Clement of Rome (fl. c. 96), and Polycarp of Smyrna (c. 69–155), articulated the new faith of their local communities.[8] Between about 120 and 220 C.E., the apologists turned their energies to defending the new tradition and presenting it to outsiders. They were particularly concerned with describing it in terms congenial to Hellenistic philosophy and responding to criticism from Jews. Among the most influential apologists were Justin Martyr (c. 110–65) and Tertullian of Carthage (c. 160–225).[9]

Major Christian thinkers as late as the thirteenth century were named "Fathers of the Church," but the honorific has come to be associated almost exclusively with key figures of the second through eighth centuries. The heritage of this so-called patristic (from the Latin *pater*, "father") period includes a variety of genres, from sermons to treatises to exegetical commentaries, mostly in Latin, Greek, and Syriac (a Semitic language related to Aramaic). Christology and Trinitarian doctrine were hallmarks of the classical patristic age, and it was largely through the medium of the "ecumenical council" that the Fathers promulgated the results of their work. Predominantly biblical imagery used by the earliest generations of Christian thinkers to describe the Christ (Shepherd, Messiah, High Priest, Lamb, Servant of God) gradually gave way to the more philosophical concepts associated with the notion of the divine *logos* (word).

As they combated the various "heretical" responses to christological questions (such as the argument of the "Docetists" [from the Greek *dokeo*, "to seem, appear"] that Jesus' humanity was only an "appearance"), the Fathers elaborated on the coequal interrelationships among God the Father, Christ the Son, and the Holy Spirit, with the divine humanity of Jesus as the centerpiece. "Spirit Christologies," like that of Cyprian of Carthage (200–58), focused on the key role of the Spirit's entering into Mary and becoming clothed in human flesh. Some, such as Clement of Alexandria (150–215) and Origen (185–254), developed "Logos Christologies" centered on how the divine Word became "incarnate," while others, such as the Cappadocians Gregory Nazianzen (330–90) and Gregory of Nyssa (c. 335–95), concentrated on how two "natures" could coexist in the one "person" of Christ.[10]

Beginning at Nicaea in 325, a series of seven major church councils have been acknowledged as authoritative by all Christian denominations. Defining the patristic era generally, three councils in Constantinople, two in Nicaea, and one each in Ephesus and Chalcedon (all in Asia Minor, present-day Turkey) issued formal statements as the theologians clarified the fine points of doctrine.[11] Many historians consider John of Damascus (c. 655–750), who lived and worked under Muslim rule in the new Umayyad capital, the last of the classical church fathers.

*Medieval Theology (800–1500).* Periodizations variously begin the age of medieval theology as early as Augustine (354–430) or Gregory the Great (540–604), but I use the end of late antiquity and the age of the last "classical" Fathers, so that the Middle Ages span the years from 800 to 1500 C.E. Developments in theology during the Carolingian age include influential work by John Scotus Eriugena (810–77) on integrating Platonic concepts into Latin Christian thought, and in sacramental theology by Rabanus Maurus (784–856) and Paschasius Radbertus (785–860).[12] The tenth and eleventh centuries saw major changes in the growth of monastic theology, with the establishment of independent monasteries such as Cluny (910) and other powerful Benedictine foundations. Many of the most important theologians, such as Anselm of Canterbury (1033–1109), Bernard of Clairvaux (1090–1153), Peter the Venerable (1100–56), and the Victorines Hugh (1096–1141) and Richard (1100–73), were prominent members of religious orders.[13]

By the mid-twelfth century, the beginnings of Scholasticism appeared in the work of Peter Abelard (1079–1142), Peter Lombard (1100–60), and Alexander of Hales (1170–1245). Along with the founding of new mendicant orders during the early thirteenth century (most notably the Dominicans and Franciscans), Albert the Great (1200–80), Thomas Aquinas (1225–74), and Bonaventure (1221–74) marked the flowering of "High Scholasticism" with their treatises on nearly every facet of systematic theology.[14]

During the fourteenth and fifteenth centuries, exponents of mystical spirituality such as Meister Eckhart (1260–1327), John Ruysbroeck (1293–1381), Orthodox monk Gregory Palamas (1296–1359), and Catherine of Siena (1347–80) developed new genres of theological literature, including some in vernacular languages. Dante Alighieri's (1265–1321) celebrated spiritual epic, *The Divine Comedy,* gave poetic expression to both mystical and Scholastic theology. Meanwhile, traditional Scholastic methodologies began to move in new directions under the influence of Duns Scotus (1264–1308), William of Ockham (d. 1347), and Nicholas of Cusa (c. 1400–64). Early stirrings of reform movements also took root with the impetus of John Wycliffe (1329–84) and John Hus (1369–1415).[15]

*Reformation: Protestant and Catholic (1500–1650).* With his call for a return to "interior religion" based on scripture and the fathers of the church, Erasmus of Rotterdam (1466–1536) arguably paved the way for Martin Luther's (1483–1546) much better-known reformist document, the "Ninety-five Theses" of 1517. But Luther did not act alone. Other branches of the larger Reformation movement owe their genesis to Ulrich Zwingli (1484–1531), John Calvin (1509–64), and Anglican theologian Richard Hooker (1554–1600), while yet another competing reformist development evolved in the various Anabaptist movements led by Thomas Müntzer (1490–1525) and Menno Simons (1496–1561), among others.[16]

In the wake of "Protestant" responses to a variety of issues, the Christian community that would come to be identified as Roman Catholicism responded with renewed efforts at internal reform that had begun arguably during the fifteenth century or even earlier. Fearing "conciliarism," the devolution of power away from the papacy, later medieval popes hesitated to convene reforming councils. When at last Lateran V was convened in 1512, it passed important legislation against simony, concubinage, and usury, but the outcomes failed to respond adequately to the need for change.[17] Some attribute critical impetus in Catholic reform to the rise of new orders such as the Capuchins (Franciscan roots) and the innovative "active" order of the Society of Jesus (or Jesuits), founded by Ignatius of Loyola (c. 1491–1556).

A major consolidation of Catholic response to the emerging Protestantism occurred in the immensely influential Council of Trent (1545–63). Catholic zeal for ongoing reform moved the popes to introduce the disciplinary methods of the Spanish Inquisition through other regions of Europe, and to institute the "Index of Prohibited Books" to counter the spread of Protestant reformist teachings.[18] Still more violent policies were enacted in service of the Catholic Reformation, and the period is traditionally said to have ended with the Peace of Westphalia at the end of the Thirty Years' War in 1648.

*Early Modern Theological Developments (1650–1900).* Major developments between the end of the Thirty Years' War and the First Vatican Council (1869–70) occurred most notably in the theological subdiscipline of ecclesiology (theology of the church). This is not surprising, given the momentous effects of the Catholic and Protestant Reformations on the "sociology" of Christendom.[19] Questions concerning the nature and extent of papal authority gradually crystallized in growing discussion on the matter of infallibility. These debates were spurred on by conflicting claims among emerging "national" authorities who claimed priority in regulating regional church matters over papal assertion of universal authority. Over against national movements such as Gallicanism, the Ultramontanists ("beyond the mountains") argued for the primacy of centralized universal papal authority as the only antidote to revolutionary instability in Europe.[20] Alongside debates on papal authority, noteworthy developments were occurring in the theology of grace, spurred by the spread of Jansenism through the seventeenth and eighteenth centuries.[21]

Early modern times saw continued exploration and colonization, often in the name of Christ, and a flourishing of global missionary movements by various Christian denominations. Meanwhile, Protestantism continued to spread in new forms, such as German Pietism, exemplified by Count Zinzendorf (1700–60) and his initiation of the Moravians, and Methodism under the leadership of John Wesley (1703–91), bringing to North American Christianity the Great Awakening.[22]

*Contemporary Theology (1900–Present).* Vatican Council I's most significant legacy for Catholicism was arguably the further definition of "infallibility" in connection with a reassertion of "papal primacy." Both questions had earlier been raised most notably at the Council of Constance in 1415. With definitive reformulations of both matters of authority, the "modern" Catholic Church would devote considerable attention during the early twentieth century to combating the challenge of "modernism." A loosely organized movement of late-nineteenth/early-twentieth century scholars, modernists were concerned with informing Catholic theology with a fuller accounting of a changing world. Most importantly here, they advocated early approaches to what would become the "historical-critical" method of biblical scholarship, moving theological method beyond reaffirmation of medieval Scholasticism, and reexamination of long-accepted assumptions about the origins of Christianity.

Vatican I (1869–70) was the twentieth ecumenical council acknowledged by the Catholic Church, and the first convened in over three centuries. By contrast, Vatican II (1962–65) opened less than a century later amid a pervasive atmosphere that it was time to reevaluate the position of the church in the contemporary world. As during the early modern period, one could argue that ecclesiology was the focal point of theological endeavor. A concomitant of this focus was an "ecumenical" movement among Christian denominations generally, along with an acknowledgment that Christians must attend to the relationships of their global tradition with the roughly 70 percent of humanity that is not Christian. Theologians—notably Thomas Aquinas—had long been seriously acknowledging the work of Jewish and Muslim thinkers. With Vatican II, the beginnings of a more deliberate "interreligious dialogue" came to the fore.[23] In the late twentieth century, major systematic theologians such as Karl Barth (1886–1968), Rudolf Bultmann (1884–1976), Karl Rahner (1904–84), Hans Urs von Balthasar (1905–88), and Bernard Lonergan (1904–84) further refined the tools of contemporary theological method. They dealt with the ever secularizing trend and the philosophical complexity since the Enlightenment. Each of them had to take into consideration Kantian and Hegelian idealism, historical criticism and positivism, while keeping a balance between faith and reason.[24]

## Systematic Theology

Theologians since the very early Christian centuries have been refining ways of saying the ineffable, conceptualizing the inconceivable. As they hammered out the precise differences between "orthodox" and "heretical" doctrine, the Fathers, Scholastics, Reformers, and countless others filled vast libraries with their often highly technical and recondite work. Their chief concerns have revolved around attempts to understand the reality of God in relation to humankind and the physical world; the human condition in relation to God and the end of life; and humanity's earthly home and role in representing the Creator as stewards of creation. Subdisciplines of systematic theology sometimes go by the names constructive, foundational, fundamental, or dogmatic theology.

Earlier sections (on biblical and historical theology) have referred in various ways to themes that have developed over the centuries into the subdisciplines in the theological specialization, based on philosophically informed reflection on those themes. Within the larger category of systematic (or constructive) theology, Christians have included a variety of methodologies and themes. Foundational concerns form the basis of systematic treatments in general. In particular, most major Christian denominations now divide their systematic theological reflection into several categories. Christology evolved as a theological theme early in the patristic period, developed into a "subject" in later patristic and medieval Scholastic treatises, and has remained an important subject in theological curricula in Christian education. Early Christian theologians debated for centuries in search of the clearest and most accurate ways to describe their understandings of the mystery of Christ. Perhaps the greatest challenge was the paradoxical perfect blend of humanity and divinity, eternity and historicity, in the one person, Jesus the Christ. How can one best understand a God at once utterly transcendent and unambiguously immanent—both beyond human limitation and intimately involved in the human condition? One underlying reason for the complexity of christological language is that the early theologians faced the daunting challenge of explaining their faith to a broader public in which the dominant conceptual frameworks were those of Hellenistic philosophy.[25]

Study of the Holy Trinity also became a vital feature in theological reflection on the nature of God, with a study called pneumatology devoted to understanding the role of the Holy Spirit. A related theme, sometimes known as charitology, is the study of how divine grace (*charis*) figures in the lives of believers, but the theme is typically integrated into courses on Christology and/or Trinity. Theologies of the church, known technically as ecclesiology (from the Greek *ekklesia*, "assembly"), have also been important in most branches of Christianity, as have studies of the "last things" (death, judgment, heaven, hell, and the "end of time"), known as eschatology. Some church groups may refer to this study with terms such as "apocalyptic theology."

Two subdisciplines largely exclusive to Roman Catholicism and the Orthodox Churches are sacramental theology and Mariology. Study of the sacraments, numbering seven for Catholics and typically two (baptism and the Lord's Supper or Eucharist) for most other communities, seeks to explain the role of sacred ritual in the life of the church. Mariology focuses on the role of Mary, Mother of Jesus, her place as *mediatrix* (female mediator) in salvation history and popular piety, and systematic analysis of her function as "Mother of God." Orthodox churches, along with Roman Catholicism, have long referred to Mary as the *Theotokos*, "God Bearer," as a principal tenet in their systematic theological formulations.[26]

Finally, some include in the category of systematic theology the subdisciplines of apologetics—the science of argument for one position and against those of dissenting groups or individuals; polemics—literature designed to attack opposing theological positions and factions; and heresiology—the study of positions and factions judged unacceptable, that is, heretical or schismatic, along with the literature of heresiography.

*Practical/Pastoral/Public Theology*

Most major Christian denominations further identify the need to reflect on the sources of their traditions in relation to the kinds of moral responsibility and behavior expected of their members. Many church seminary curricula feature courses in theological ethics, or, as Catholics call the field, moral theology. This subdiscipline is methodologically distinct from philosophical (or "rational") ethics in that theological ethics derives its fundamental principles explicitly from scripture. Though the conclusions of theological ethics may coincide with those at which moral philosophers might arrive, their starting points are generally quite different. Some Christian groups identify this subject as a part of "practical theology," others as "pastoral theology."

Whatever the label, we are dealing here with efforts to respond to the experiential dimensions of religious practice. Pastoral counseling, for example, presupposes a familiarity with theological aspects of scripture and tradition that address daily concerns of countless Christians as they confront a host of personal and family stresses. Finally, some Christian denominations make a special place for the subdiscipline of homiletics (formal preaching), which implies its own hermeneutical orientation toward the sacred sources. As a branch of pastoral theology, homiletics focuses on helping believers apply scriptural revelation to deeper understanding of their personal relationships with God, and practical solutions to daily challenges to their own faith convictions.

Some denominations, including Roman Catholicism and the various Orthodox communities, have also developed complex systems of liturgical theology, sometimes situated under the larger rubric of "systematic" theology. Finally, a subdiscipline most important for Roman Catholics is the study of canon law. The term refers to a complex system of ecclesiastical rules and regulations that originated at the Council of Nicaea (325), were expanded further through the patristic age, and were formally systematized in medieval times with the Decree of Gratian (1140).[27]

## OVERVIEW OF ISLAMIC THEOLOGICAL THEMES AND SUBDISCIPLINES

Muslim scholars long ago delineated a group of religious disciplines as "indigenous" as distinct from "imported." Some sources distinguish between "traditional" or inherently Islamic approaches (*naql*) and "rational/ intellectual" approaches (*'aql*), often indicating a decided bias toward the former category. The authentically "Islamic" specializations included various aspects of the study of the sacred text of the Qur'ān; scholarship and textual criticism of the body of literature enshrining the words and deeds of Muhammad (the Hadith); and the sciences of *sharī'a,* or "revealed law" generically understood, including the subdisciplines of applied law (*fiqh*) and the principles of religious law (*usūl al-fiqh*).

Among the non-Islamic intellectual disciplines, traditional scholarship identifies especially the Greek sciences, including medicine and philosophy, with an emphasis on all methods of rational inquiry as distinct from more restricted study of the sacred sources. This latter category would therefore include the kind of rational or systematic theology long known by the name *kalām,* "discourse." Here I will summarize some of the main concerns and methodological considerations that have informed Muslim theology and theologically oriented scholarship.

### Qur'ān and Tafsīr

The Qur'ān itself sounds a note of caution concerning any form of idle speculation or the quest for knowledge that is either "useless" or by definition available only to God. Addressing the "People of the Book," the Qur'ān asks: "Why do you argue about things of which you have no knowledge? God [alone] possesses knowledge of those things, while you do not" (3:66). Nevertheless, Muslim scholars from the earliest days were keenly aware of the need to apply all the investigative tools available to them to the task of interpreting the sacred text.[28]

By the early seventh century C.E., Arabs already possessed a rich tradition of refined rhetorical and literary development of the Southwest Semitic tongue known as Arabic, especially in the form of sophisticated poetry. Since the Qur'ān was delivered through Muhammad in the Arabic language, one must assume that his contemporaries generally understood the vocabulary and idioms in which the message was couched. Even so, early sources (especially the Hadith and primitive historical documents) suggest that the Prophet's listeners did not always comprehend the content of the message. Scholars in the first post-Prophetic generations turned to a ready source of comparative linguistic data, namely, the tradition of pre-Islamic Arabic poetry. They began to elaborate for the first time the principles of Arabic grammar in service of arriving at a more precise meaning of the Qur'ānic text. In addition, early historians of the Muslim community became convinced that one could not fully understand individual texts without first knowing the context in the life of Muhammad and the proto-community in which the texts were revealed. This led to the development of the exegetical concept of circumstances of the revelation (asbāb an-nuzūl).

Compared to the Bible's centuries-long evolution, plural authorship, and complex process of canonical validation, the textual history of the Qur'ān may seem relatively simple and straightforward. It came into being over less than a quarter-century, through the agency or mediation of a single individual, and is known to the world's Muslims in what is essentially a single version. Recent scholarship has begun to discover important twists and turns in that history, suggesting that it was likely more complex than Muslim tradition would have it; but much more research needs to be completed to make further specific comment useful at this point.[29]

Suffice it to say for the present that the Qur'ān (Recitation) consists of some 6,200 verses (depending on how they are numbered) arranged in 114 segments known as sūras. Traditional accounts say that though some of the texts were written down on materials such as palm fronds or large animal bones, the first "official" full text was the so-called 'Uthmānic Codex produced by the third caliph, 'Uthmān, in 653. I will return to this problematic scenario in chapter 1. The arrangement of the 114 suras is idiosyncratic in that relative length, rather than theme or chronological order, became in effect the single most important criterion. In some instances, thematically related chapters were clustered together. After the brief seven-verse opening chapter, *al-Fātiha* (The Opening), comes the longest chapter, *al-Baqara* (The Cow). With a few notable exceptions (such as the 227-verse *ash-Shu'arā'*, "The Poets," sura 26; and the 182-verse *as-Sāffāt*, "Those Ranged in Ranks," sura 37), the chapters proceed in descending order of length. Most of the briefer chapters appearing in the latter quarter of the text are generally dated to the Meccan period (610–22), as are various longer suras positioned earlier in the book.

## Theological Aspects of the Qur'ān

Reading the Qur'ān more or less chronologically reveals what amounts to a development, or at any rate a relatively consistent change, in theological themes. Earlier texts, especially "very early" and "early" Meccan material (c. 610–15), emphasize social-ethical concerns against a backdrop of inevitable moral accountability at the end of time. Muhammad's initial preaching did not focus explicitly on the need to eradicate all forms of polytheism, hammering away instead at the responsibility of society's better-off members to look after those struggling to survive: widows, orphans, the elderly, the ill, and travelers. Theological concerns gradually began to shift toward a critique of the prevailing polytheistic orientation of Mecca's dominant Quraysh tribe, combined with a steady condemnation of the complicity of Quraysh leadership in the commercial exploitation of Mecca's ritual center, the Ka'ba, and of religious allegiances in general.

Allusions to previous prophets, and eventually more substantial prophetic narratives and exempla, grew into a staple of Muhammad's preaching, together with implicit parallels between the rejection of God's earlier messengers by the people to whom they had been sent, and Muhammad's rejection by elements of Meccan society. Along with increasing attention to the concept of divine transcendent oneness (*tawhīd*) came an elaboration of the central features of Muslim devotional life that would come to be known as the Five Pillars: profession of faith, fasting during Ramadan, ritual prayer, and alms-giving, to be joined later by the practice of pilgrimage to the Ka'ba. After the Hijra, or migration to Medina in 622, the situation of the young Muslim community changed dramatically. No more the beleaguered minority, the Muslims emerged as the dominant polity in Medina. The longer and less poetic Medinan texts of the Qur'ān reflect those changes, showing increasing concern for the practicalities of family life and community discipline.

It is especially important that later revelations suggest a shift from the earliest texts' emphasis on eschatological themes to the role of prophets since the beginning of creation and underscore Muhammad's place within that revelatory dispensation. This broadened context of revelation is, one could argue, the Islamic analogue to the Christian (and Jewish) notions of "salvation history." There is a pervasive sense of continuity with the earlier divine disclosures, tempered by reminders that the Qur'ānic revelation, while not new in the greater scheme of things, is a needed corrective to prior prophetic communications unheeded or corrupted by their recipients. The theme of "prophetology" is at the theological heart of the matter in this context.[30]

Perhaps the single most consistent underlying theological theme (whether explicit or implied) in Muhammad's preaching is the central implicit concept of a tri-level progressive divine revelation through a multiplicity of signs (āyāt, plural of āya). Revelation occurs in creation, in the soul of the individual, and in the verses of the Qur'ān. Two key texts refer to God as "showing signs on the horizons" and "within your/their very selves" (41:53; 51:20–21). Numerous other texts have God speaking of "our signs," typically in reference either to people's grateful acknowledgment of them or unbelievers' stubborn rejection or blindness. Moreover, the scripture continually refers to itself as composed of "signs," since the same term (āyāt) also means "verses." In other words, God's revelation is available to all of humanity in a variety of ways, from the marvels of creation to the workings of the divine power within the individual heart and soul to the text of the revealed scripture. One cannot, therefore, plead ignorance because one is not technically or formally a "Muslim," since evidence of the one transcendent deity is all around. The concept of a primordial covenant undergirds this theologically: according to Qur'ān 7:172, God called all yet unborn souls to witness, asking: "Am I not your Lord?" All replied in unison: "Yes, to that we testify." God then reminds them that their testimony rules out any chance to claim at judgment that they were unaware of the bigger picture.

For present purposes, the equivalence of "sign" and "verse" requires further explanation, for it is intimately connected with the Qur'ān's claim to divine authority. From a linguistic perspective, the scripture's use of the term āya, at least in the earlier suras, underscores the divine origin of the text. Since the substance of Muhammad's preaching is not only *about* revelatory signs, but is in fact itself among those signs, listeners ought not lightly dismiss the message. Furthermore, the text suggests, these sign-verses are not the first of their kind. They are part of a long history of such prophetic revelations that have taken the form of scrolls (*suhuf*), sacred texts that moved from the recitation of previous prophets into the sacred books (*kutub*) delivered to specific communities.[31]

## Muslim Traditions of Exegesis

Questions about the meaning and applicability of the sacred text as Muhammad preached it over roughly the last twenty-two years of his life abounded among the community of believers. Muhammad's ad hoc responses to such questions comprised an essential resource for the young community. Many of the Prophet's allocutions were in effect early examples of scriptural exegesis, pointing out the less obvious implications of texts as questioners brought their concerns and confusion to him. After Muhammad's death, many of the earliest expositors from among his Companions (first-generation Muslims) would explicate the import of his responses still further by clarifying the specific situation in which (according to their recollection) Muhammad made specific comments on one or another revelation. The result is therefore a kind of layered commentary, with the Hadith collector providing the immediate context of Muhammad's commentary on the Qur'ānic text.[32]

After Muhammad's death, tradition has it, the Muslim community's most trusted exegetes were a select group of the Companions of the Prophet, who were in turn succeeded by the next generation, the Followers. Among the earliest written commentaries (*tafsīr*) were typically short works from the early eighth century whose style tended toward paraphrasing the sacred text quite straightforwardly. With the passage of time, commentaries grew more complex and sophisticated, with the introduction of linguistic and philological methods leading the way. But with the evolution of schools of religious legal methodology, commentators again resorted more deliberately to "tradition" (i.e., the Hadith) for their exegetical guidance. As jurisprudents became more engaged in exegesis, some commentaries took on a more explicitly legal cast, while theological debates from the mid-ninth century on gave rise to exegetical works geared to defending the positions of the systematic and dialectical work of the theologians. At the same time, developments in "mystical" thought resulted in yet another formative type of exegesis that favored Qur'ānic references to the divine-human connection. Finally, alongside of the various distinctively "Sunni" approaches to scriptural interpretation, Shi'i exegetes searched the sacred text for references to the unique qualities and characteristics of the imams. Mystical and Shi'i exegesis typically employs metaphorical interpretation far more liberally than the other types of commentary.[33]

## Hadith, Sacred Biography, and Historical Considerations

Second in authority only to the Qur'ān is a body of literature enshrining the words and deeds of Muhammad. Known generically as the Hadith (Sayings, Traditions), this extensive treasury of Prophetic lore evolved gradually from a purely oral tradition into a considerable library of multi-volume works. For several generations, the Muslim community resisted any temptation to consign the Hadith to writing, perhaps in part at least out of a concern that the Prophet's own words not be confused with the already-written words of God that comprised the text of the Qur'ān. By about the early ninth century, however, concern was mounting among Muslim scholars that continuing to rely solely on the memory of successive generations, each passing on to the next the sacred burden of its recollective powers, was a policy increasingly prone to failure.

An important methodological concern in Hadith scholarship from the start was the emphasis on the reliability and veracity of the transmitters themselves. Their credibility was in effect more important than the content of the "texts" they were attributing to the Prophet. Since generations of Muslims were the custodians of the tradition, it became standard practice to begin citations of Prophetic utterances with a rehearsal of the names of every individual in the chain of transmitters (*isnād*). When Muslim scholars began the daunting task of amassing a definitive collection of Hadith to commit to writing, they confronted the complex challenge of distinguishing authentic sayings from inauthentic. Instead of beginning with the body (*matn*) of a given Hadith, they sifted through the names of the transmitters credited with preserving the saying. Reasoning that the chain could be only as strong as its weakest link, the scholars looked for names of individuals known for their tendentious views or, in some cases, downright dishonesty.

To aid subsequent generations of Hadith specialists, the early scholars developed a crucial research tool—the biographical dictionary. Eventually this "science of men" (*'ilm ar-rijāl*) catalogued thousands of transmitters, evaluating each person according to a scale of reliability and veracity. Building on this research, compilers of major written compendia of Hadith categorized every saying recorded by locating it on that scale. In addition to the criterion of individual veracity of transmitters, the scholars also took into account the relative preponderance of attestation of each saying. So, for example, Hadith transmitted by a larger number of trustworthy reporters were judged "stronger," whereas a saying attested by only a single transmitter of even the highest credibility received a lower rating (such as *hasan gharīb*, "good, but rare"). The enormous attention lavished on establishing a reliable corpus of Hadith implies an underlying conviction of the huge responsibility of the community of believers in handing on the tradition.

In addition, there is considerable material in the content of the Hadith that is of theological import, both explicit and implicit. One need only scan the tables of contents of the great compendia to get a sense of the areas of greatest concern to the protocommunity. Some of the major collections, such as the late ninth-century works of the central Asian scholars Bukhārī (d. 870) and Muslim (d. 875), employed a thematic organizational principle. Large sections dedicated to traditions about faith, ritual purity, the Five Pillars, marriage and divorce, the lofty moral qualities of Muhammad and his Companions, personal prayer and the remembrance of God, and eschatological topics provide essential data for the study of theological themes.[34]

A distinctively Islamic version of prosopography (writing on personalities) called 'ilm ar-rijāl played a central role in the discipline of Hadith studies. This intense interest in the stories of transmitters is an important link in the development of the historical disciplines of biography, chronography, and history (ta'rīkh).[35] Very early in the Islamic era, Muslim scholars began to fashion versions of the life story (sīra) of the Prophet. Ibn Ishāq (d. 767) wrote the first major "biography" of Muhammad, and Ibn Hishām (d. 833) produced an extensively revised and expanded version of the work within two generations. In a manner reminiscent of the Gospels of Matthew and Luke, Ibn Hishām begins with a substantial genealogy that traces the Prophet back to Adam. He notes that he has constructed his narrative out of a patchwork of "reports" preserved by a host of transmitters, and observes that the result provides lessons for the discerning, and mercy, guidance, and encouragement for all believers.[36] This and later accounts of Muhammad's exemplary life were in a way an extension of the sections on the "excellent qualities" (fadā'il) of the Prophet and his Companions that had become a standard feature in Hadith collections.

Meanwhile, other Muslim authors were reflecting on large questions concerning the religious implications of God's dealings with humankind through time, musing about how faith can inform understanding of the divine purpose of history and of God's plans for the human race. Some discerned a central paradigm not unlike the pattern that undergirds the "Deuteronomistic History" of the Bible's Historical Books (Joshua, Judges, Samuel, and Kings): covenant, betrayal, and redemption.[37] By the late ninth and early tenth century, Muslim authors were developing the important new genre of the "universal history."[38] In general, they nested their accounts of the full sweep of "salvation history"—that is, the story of

God's prophets from Adam to Muhammad—amid narratives of the other cultural and religious contexts and post-Prophetic Muslim dynasties up to the author's time.[39]

Another important historical genre is the "tales of the prophets," limited to narratives of God's emissaries. Works by Tha'labī (d. 1036) and Kisā'ī (fl. c. 1200) were the earliest and most influential in the genre, setting the pattern for many later variations on the theme.[40] Elements of yet another explicitly religious genre of Islamic biography, hagiography (sometimes called *adab al-manāqib*, "literature of extraordinary achievements"), also implicitly took their cue from the practice of including sections on the "virtues and excellent qualities" of the Companions of the Prophet.

Above all, the Hadith function as the primary source of Muslim knowledge about the Prophet's life and relationships, his values and behavior. Muslims often refer to the record of this ultimate human model of a paradigmatic Muslim life as the *sunna* (exemplary conduct). As extensive and detailed as this written compendium of the *sunna* may be, even in tandem with the Qur'ān, it does not account for all the religious and ethical concerns for which Muslims have held themselves accountable. Very soon after the death of Muhammad, the expanding young Muslim community began to encounter circumstances that required new ways of interpreting and implementing the divine word and the Prophetic example. These needs led to the emergence of Islamic religious law as a distinct set of disciplines.

### Sharia: The Complex of Revealed Law

One of the earliest forms of Qur'ānic exegesis grew out of a concern to anchor all manner of religiously acceptable behavior in the divinely revealed Word. Although the Qur'ān is clearly not primarily a legal document, many of the Medinan suras (622–32) deal in some detail with matters of individual and community discipline. Just as some early Muslim scholars became specialists in Hadith collection and criticism, others focused on what would become the core of Islamic religious law. Muslims most often use the term *sharī'a* (from a root that originally connoted the path to the oasis, or main road) to refer to the whole complex of divinely ordained behavior incumbent on believers.

When Muslims speak of religious scholars (*'ulamā'*, sg. *'ālim*, "those who possess traditional knowledge [*'ilm*]"), they are generally referring to individuals with special training in matters of *sharī'a* in general. But in practice this typically means expertise in religious law in the narrower sense of *fiqh* (positive law, from a root meaning "deeper understanding") and *usūl al-fiqh* (jurisprudence, or "principles of law"). Serious specialists in Islamic law must of course be well grounded in the disciplines of Qur'ān, exegesis, and Hadith. But scholars have rarely, if ever, studied Islamic law in general. They must, in addition, pursue more focused education in the methodology of one of the four historic schools (*madhāhib*, sg. *madhhab*) of Sunni law or one of the two main Shi'i law schools.

Beginning in the late seventh or early eighth century, Muslim administrators entrusted with regulating the life of local communities that arose in the wake of Islamic conquest of the central Middle East and North Africa became in effect the first Muslim legal specialists. Governors appointed by early caliphs (successors to Muhammad) in turn appointed judges or magistrates (*qādī*) whose task was to adjudicate a host of everyday disputes, from resolving conflicts over property and distribution of inheritance to meting out punishment for criminal acts. The job of a judge was almost impossibly broad, but gradually became more restricted, and before long, cases tried by magistrates were limited to the religious equivalent of "civil" rather than criminal law. Criminal cases were more and more relegated to authorities higher up in the caliphal administrations. Early judges were expected to make complex legal decisions through relatively independent processes of legal opinion, but before long the *qādī*'s job was limited to applying the decisions that had evolved as standard solutions and were codified in books of *fiqh*. Here, in brief, is the story of how legal administration developed in this direction.

By the early ninth century, a variety of distinct schools of legal methodology were taking shape in the Arab Middle East. Most died out long ago, but the four still-extant Sunni schools were named after the renowned scholars credited with "founding" them, though these individuals were more precisely eponyms. The Hanafī school was named after Abū Hanīfa (d. 767) of Kufa (Iraq); the Mālikī after Mālik ibn Anas (d. 795) of Medina; the Shāfi'ī after Muhammad ibn Idrīs ash-Shāfi'ī (d. 820), who was born in Ghaza and died in Egypt; and the Hanbalī after Ahmad ibn Hanbal (d. 855) of Baghdad. These *madhāhib* represent the evolution of religious jurisprudence into a systematic discipline that would become the foundation of legal administration. All four schools were in agreement concerning the primacy of the Qur'ān and Hadith as "sources" of all religious law. Principal differences in their evolving methodologies turned on the relative importance they accorded to methods for deciding questions not explicitly covered in either the sacred scripture or the sayings of the Prophet.

Two principles emerged as essential ingredients in jurisprudence. First, scholars agreed generally that the actual practice of a local or regional community could solve disputed questions, on the conviction that Muslims acting in good faith were implicitly seeking to follow the *sunna* of Muhammad. One could thus arrive at a legal benchmark by determining the consensus (*ijmāʿ*) embodied in the behavior of a given community. As local communities became larger and more complex, and establishing large-scale consensus became impracticable, the principle was revised to mean the *ijmāʿ* of religious scholars. In the case of questions that did not receive attention in either Qurʾān or Hadith and did not correspond clearly with "actual practice" among Muslims, the principle of analogical reasoning (*qiyās*) was drafted into service.

A rough equivalent of argument from precedent, analogical reasoning establishes a link between an already settled matter judged to be legally analogous to the "new" problem. One might make a very simplified analogy with a contemporary dilemma in medical ethics. Prior to the advent of life-sustaining technology such as the mechanical ventilator, no one had faced the terrible decision of when, or whether, to remove life support. With no clear guidance from either scripture or tradition, and no precedent in the previous practice of any community, legal ethicists had recourse to analogical reasoning. Deliberate killing is wrong, but is the removal of life support from a patient with no hope of survival without mechanical intervention the same as murder? Here the question of intent comes to the fore, and if the removal of life support is decided apart from primary intent to kill, it might be judged an ethical course.

In the early history of Islamic jurisprudence, a legal scholar (*faqīh*, pl. *fuqahāʾ*, from *fiqh:* [possessor of] "deep understanding") with the highest levels of understanding in the interpretation of the sources and in deciding the most difficult cases was accorded the highest authority. His task was to exercise independent investigation (*ijtihād*) in searching the sources for answers to complex questions, and such a scholar was known as a *mujtahid,* one who "exerted himself" in legal scholarship. Traditional Sunni accounts hold that the "door of *ijtihād*" closed around the year 900, so that thereafter jurists were expected merely to rule by appeal to the positive law already decided in manuals of *fiqh.* That account, however, is heavily polemical in intent and may not accurately reflect the historical reality across the board. New questions did not magically cease to arise in 900, and reports of *ijtihād*'s demise turned out to be exaggerated.

Shiʿi law was evolving alongside of the Sunni *madhāhib* and continued to feature a prominent role for the *mujtahid,* reserving an important place for ongoing *ijtihād* in the elaboration of positive law. In the largest of the Shiʿi communities, known generally as the Twelvers, the term Jaʿfari often serves as a generic reference to all Shiʻi law, but it actually developed into more than one school. In modern times, Iranian and Iraqi Shiʻi religious scholars articulated two principal legal methodologies, the Usūlī and the Akhbārī. The Usūlīs, also known as Mujtahidīs, emphasize the principles of law (usūl) and the role of the mujtahid, insisting that believers choose a living jurist as a source of imitation (marjaʻ-i taqlīd). There have typically been several "sources of imitation" at any one time, allowing some flexibility and variety of authoritative views. By contrast, the Akhbārī school emphasizes the ability of individual believers to interpret the traditions (akhbār) of Muhammad and the imams without necessary recourse to the pronouncements of scholars.

Finally, Muslim thinkers continued to debate the relative demerits of taqlīd, uncritical acceptance of the opinions of previous authorities. Judges were early on limited to repeating the judgments that constituted "established" law, but scholars in other religious disciplines argued that taqlīd was a danger to the growth of—perhaps even a death warrant for—a vibrant Islamic tradition.[41]

*Themes in Islamic "Systematic" Theology (Kalām)*

If the Qurʼān is not primarily a legal document, it is just as clearly not technically a "theological" treatise, but it bristles with themes that begged for theological commentary. Just beneath the legal and practical surface of conclusions elaborated by Islam's early exegetes and jurisprudents, a variety of more subtle questions of a more theological nature began to emerge. One of the problems that arose as early as the late seventh century was the relationship between divine and human authority. Hasan al-Basrī's (d. 728) letter supporting the Qadarīya argument for a measure of free will and moral responsibility displeased the caliph. If free will trumped divine predestination in practical terms, the caliph would be fully accountable for his reprehensible deeds and unable to take moral refuge in absolute divine predetermination of events.

More importantly, Islam's expansion out of the Arabian Peninsula into the central Middle East and westward across North Africa and eastward as far as the Indus River by 711 raised new issues even beyond those concerning the regulation of Muslim community discipline in new social and cultural contexts. Mesopotamia and adjacent Middle Eastern regions had long since been fertile ground for imported intellectual and scientific traditions, particularly of Hellenistic origin. Jewish rabbinical academies and Christian monasteries and schools had already begun to integrate Greek philosophical thought and medicine. Scholars in what are now the nations of Lebanon, Syria, Israel/Palestine, Iraq, and Jordan had begun the work of translating Greek philosophical and medical texts into Syriac. Not long after the Muslim Abbāsid caliphate (750–1258) established its capital in the newly founded city of Baghdad, Muslim scholars became engaged in this seminal intellectual and cultural interchange as well. Early in the ninth century, caliphs Hārūn ar-Rashīd and al-Ma'mūn facilitated debate among scholars from various traditions and funded large-scale translation efforts to render Syriac texts into Arabic.

As chapter 4 will describe in greater detail, early ninth-century Baghdad's intellectual ferment marked the genesis of the first serious Islamic schools of dialectical, rational, or systematic theology. Of those schools, that of the Muʿtazila was the most important and influential. Over the subsequent century and a half, responses to the rationalist Muʿtazila formulations took the shape largely of tradition-based thinking, especially that of Ahmad ibn Hanbal, and attempts to integrate rationalist methodologies into ways of thinking more acceptable to traditionalists than those of the Muʿtazila.

By the mid-tenth century, major proponents of *kalām* ("discourse," by extension "dialectic") had published important systematic treatises that would establish the groundwork and patterns for works of subsequent scholars. Two "schools" of systematic theology that would come to exercise enormous influence across central Islamdom began to emerge. The Ashʿarī school, named after former Muʿtazila Abū 'l-Hasan al-Ashʿarī (d. 935), arose in Iraq as an attempt to balance the concerns of the traditionalist Hanbalīs with the use of rational analysis. Meanwhile, Ashʿarī's central Asian contemporary Māturīdī (d. 944) took a slightly less conservative tack. In general, the major theological schools worked hand in glove with particular Sunni law schools. So, for example, Ashʿarī theologians were typically either Mālikī or Shāfiʿī in law, while Māturīdī and Muʿtazilī theologians were generally aligned with the Hanafī law school.

A survey of major tenth- and eleventh-century Ashʿarī and Māturīdī systematic treatises suggests that the following topics and questions were emerging as matters of fundamental importance in *kalām*. Various treatises begin by establishing an epistemological framework that characterizes the discipline as their authors defined it. Here they describe the methodological presuppositions and pitfalls of rational inquiry and delve into the nature of knowledge, both human and divine, underscoring the limitations of the former and the unaccountable, inscrutable infinity of the latter.[42] Some include sections on basic concepts in what one could call theological metaphysics, describing the essential differences between contingent and uncreated realities. Against that backdrop, the theologians typically launch into extended and detailed analyses of the divine will and a host of other attributes.

God's relationships with his creation form another major topic, followed by the nature of divine revelation through prophets, prominently featuring the mission of Muhammad. Some works include significant sections on the nature of the Qur'ān in this context. Eschatological themes comprise yet another more or less standard segment of major treatises, some authors injecting such topics as repentance and intercession. Most important works also analyze theologically critical aspects of the doctrine of the "imamate," with a host of implications for religiously legitimated authority as embodied in political institutions. In addition, polemical responses to the views of competing or "heretical" factions and non-Muslim groups alike sometimes receive considerable attention.[43]

Polemical material in the history of Islamic theological literature developed beyond the briefer accounts of unacceptable opinions that were a feature in classical systematic treatises. Heresiography arguably became a subgenre of theological literature, and a number of major systematicians produced large-scale works on the subject.[44]

## Pastoral and Mystical Theology

Finally, many influential Muslim authors over the centuries have produced important works in what one might label "pastoral" or "mystical" theology. Beginning as early as the eighth century, authors began to reflect on the interface between psychology and spirituality. Most works in this genre suggest strong influence of early Sufi psychology, which analyzed patterns in people's affective responses to their experience of the divine initiative in their inner lives. Tenth- and eleventh-century theorists developed intricate typologies designed to assist spiritual seekers in identifying their interior movements as part of a larger pattern of progress along a "spiritual path" back to God.[45]

Abū Hāmid al-Ghazālī's (d. 1111) *Revitalization of the Religious Disciplines* is perhaps the most influential and widely read work of its genre. In forty "books" divided into four quarters, Ghazālī leads seekers gradually from the most basic levels of awareness and desire for repentance on through increasingly challenging and subtle experiences of the divine-human connection. Some works are less oriented toward a graduated pedagogy, diving instead right into analyses of the "science of hearts" that presuppose considerable acumen.

In addition to a considerable body of prose works in pastoral/mystical theology, Muslim poets, typically identified as Sufis, have produced an extensive literature of didactic poetry in a dozen major languages. Jalāl ad-Dīn Rūmī (d. 1273) is perhaps the best known of Islam's great mystical poets, and much of his didactic and lyrical poetry is now available in English translation.[46] But this vast literary-theological tradition is also richly represented by a host of other brilliant poets who wrote in Arabic, Persian, Turkish, and a dozen major regional languages, especially of South and Southeast Asia.[47]

# PART I

# Historical Dimensions

*Interpreting God's Communication and Divine
Engagement in Time and Space*

In the field of religious studies, the term "history" can embrace a wide
variety of topics and themes. In the following two chapters, an exploration
of five features of the vast histories of Islam and Christianity will bring to
the fore the diversity of "Islams" and "Christianities." First, at the heart
of both communities we find not only bedrock figures who embody the
"tradition," but foundational texts as well. These "sacred scriptures" have
been the object of intense scrutiny and interpretation, or exegesis (from
the Greek *ex-hegeomai,* "to lead or draw out"), since the earliest generations. The varieties and concerns of exegesis are an integral tributary to the
historical evolution of tradition. Second, both faith traditions formulated
quasi-canonical versions of how their original communities came into
being, and of the embodiment of key values that have come to constitute
their ethical and organizational or structural core—the wellsprings of
authority. The theological disciplines (as described in the introduction)
most at issue here are the two traditions of scriptural exegesis, and the
religious/theological interpretation of history that runs deep in both traditions. For Muslims, the latter includes a heavy dose of prosopography
(study of important individuals), particularly in service of evaluating the
credibility of sayings attributed to Muhammad and his Companions.

Third, both religious traditions emphasized "true doctrine" (in very
different ways) but have also shown considerable interest in the makeup
of the "authentic community." Christians and Muslims alike have elaborated criteria by which one might distinguish "true" believers from "false."

Fourth, Islam and Christianity have spread historically across the entire globe and now comprise roughly half the human race between them. Both have also promoted vigorous missionary efforts and continue to proselytize, often apparently in direct competition with each other. Finally, the two traditions have developed remarkably similar views about the end of history, heralded in both by revelatory and disturbing signs and events. As in chapter 1, here again the dominant disciplinary tools are those of the theological interpretation of history, now with an increased emphasis on the respective traditions' conviction of their divinely ordained mission of growth and expansion.

A word about the final section in chapter 2, on the "end of history." I chose to locate this section here, rather than in chapter 1's consideration of "theologies of history," in order to suggest a shared closure for both traditions of theological interpretations of history. Chapter 4 will address the more individual creedal aspects of eschatology, the "last things" (death, judgment, heaven, hell). In the present context I will limit consideration to events of more cosmic moment that are part and parcel of each community's understanding of "history."

# CHAPTER I

# Sacred Sources and Community Origins

Two major theological themes occupy this chapter. First, at the heart of the formation, reception, and history of interpretation of their sacred texts, the Christian and Muslim traditions exhibit several noteworthy similarities as well as important differences. Though both came eventually to revolve around a unique sacred text, the Muslim community grew even as the scripture was being revealed. For the Christians, the multiauthored New Testament was relatively delayed, by contrast, in its formation as a unified canon. Second, the earliest communities of Christians and Muslims bore very different relationships to their sacred sources but also showed some intriguing analogies in the ways the core circles of original adherents related to their founding figures.

## SCRIPTURE, EXEGESIS, AND TRADITION

As the two largest "Peoples of the Book," Christians and Muslims are keenly aware that their traditions are rooted in authoritative sacred texts. Both global communities have also generated complex histories of scriptural interpretation. In both traditions, exegesis begins with, and within, the primary revealed texts themselves. In this section I will outline the principal varieties and histories of exegetical methods in the two traditions and conclude with a look at the "historical" implications of how the respective scriptures talk about the "foundational figures" Jesus and Muhammad.

Both Christian and Islamic traditions have long histories of explicit awareness of the challenge and delicacy of interpreting communications believed to be of divine origin, whether as product of "inspiration" or as the mediation of the very words of God. This awareness begins with the sacred texts themselves, in the ways they incorporate, or allude to, previous "books" as well as in their more explicit comments on the limits of human interpretation and the inherent differences in various types of sacred communication.

## Varieties of Christian Exegesis

Christian traditions of exegesis begin with the twenty-seven "books" of the New Testament.[1] The "inspired" authors of the New Testament works found themselves at an exegetical crossroads of sorts. As Jews, they were heirs to already well-established methods of Jewish exegesis. But as members of the fledgling Christian community, they recognized the need to reorient their interpretation of the Hebrew scriptures so as to make clear how and to what degree the new faith distinguished itself from ancient Jewish beliefs. The crux of the matter lay in a dramatic departure from Jewish messianic expectations, which Christians regarded as being fulfilled in Jesus of Nazareth. In other words, for Jewish-Christians the long wait for the Messiah was over, but for their Jewish brothers and sisters it was not. This fulfillment required a new mode of interpretation for the texts of the Hebrew scriptures long thought to refer to the expected Messiah, as well as a reorientation of formerly nonmessianic texts the better to reflect the characteristics that Christians now associated with the long-awaited deliverer.[2]

Elements of continuity linking Jewish and Christian exegesis included a variety of methods, as evidenced by the ways New Testament texts cite the Hebrew scriptures. Verbatim quotation can be qualified by "thus fulfilling the words of . . . [followed by a quotation of an Old Testament text]" or simply by citing an Old Testament text and assuming that readers would recognize the allusion, as when Mark 15:34 cites Psalm 22:2. Near quotes appear often, with or without contextualizing comment, as in Matthew 11:2–5. In addition, many New Testament texts allude to more ancient scriptural texts, clearly referring to the literal sense but further clarifying the text's meaning for Christians. For example, all three Synoptic Gospels (Matthew 27:35, Mark 15:24, and Luke 23:34) allude to Psalm 22:18's reference to dividing by lot the garments of a "type of Christ." Finally, the Gospel of John and the Pauline Letters often quote or allude to Old Testament texts in ways that clearly move well beyond a literal sense by "spiritualizing" the meaning (as, for example, John's prologue and Romans 16:25–26, both reminding readers of the connection between the Old Testament and the "hidden meaning" of it, revealed in Christ).[3]

Jewish exegetical methods employed by New Testament authors include allegorical readings of Old Testament narratives, such as Galatians 4:21–31's reinterpretation of the various elements of the story of Abraham. Sarah and Hagar represent the two covenants (old and new), Isaac and Ishmael free persons and those still under the Law respectively, and places such as Sinai refer to eschatological concepts such as the New Jerusalem. Line-by-line commentary, known as *pesher,* occasionally appears, as when Romans 10:5–13 provides a Christian rereading of each verse of Deuteronomy 30:12–14, showing how each is actually a reference to Christ. In short, the Pauline Letters give solid evidence of early "typological" thinking, that is, discerning precursors (types) of New Testament figures or truths in the Old; but beyond that one might also see Paul's distinction between "letter" and "spirit" as a precursor of Christian exegetical concepts of "historical" (i.e., more literal) and "allegorical" interpretation.

Traces of the "Seven Hermeneutical Principles of Rabbi Hillel" occur in various guises throughout the New Testament. One of the last rabbinical "pairs of teachers" (along with Shammai), Hillel is credited with systematizing a set of guidelines for scriptural interpretation.[4] One of those principles, the "light and heavy," argues that if a given action is acceptable in a clearly serious and highly restrictive setting, it is surely acceptable in a far less momentous situation. Mark 2:23–28, for example, has Jesus referring to the account in which David and his hungry men ate bread from the Temple's ritual supplies (1 Samuel 21:1–16). Implicitly applying the principle of the "light and heavy," Jesus responds to those who criticized his followers for eating grain on the Sabbath (thus violating the prohibition of labor on the holy day). If David could eat even from the sacred and therefore forbidden ritual offerings of the Temple (the heavier case), Jesus argues, there is clearly no problem with the apostles nibbling on some grain that has obviously not been consecrated for ritual use (the lighter case).

As for the specific purposes of New Testament authors, use of the Hebrew scriptures to assert that an ancient prophecy has been fulfilled in the life of Jesus is among the most prevalent methods. Few details of the life of Jesus go unsupported by Old Testament texts. Many allusions to the Old Testament are meant to establish unshakable historical bases for certain Christian practices, including apparent departures from ancient Jewish prescriptions. Arguments both for and against circumcision based on Old Testament texts appear. For example, Acts 15:16–18 cites Amos 9:11–15 (God will rebuild the fallen house of David) as proof that circumcision should not be required of new converts; but Galatians 3 cites Habakkuk 2:4 (life comes through faith and not through the Law) to bolster the Pauline case for the supersession of the Jewish law (which mandates circumcision).[5] Conversely, some New Testament texts (John and Hebrews in particular) also validate "new" ideas or beliefs by reframing Old Testament references as "prefiguring" imperfectly the reality of Jesus. So, for example, while Israel is the "vine" and God's people fed on the "bread" of desert manna, Jesus is the "true" vine and the "true" bread (Isaiah 5:7; Exodus 16:11–31; John 15:1–5, 6:35, 41).

In short, New Testament exegesis functions largely to characterize the relationships between the old and new dispensations. In some cases the point is that the new flows directly from the old (prophecy fulfillment); in others, that the new builds on the old by deepening its underlying themes (allegorical and typological); and in still others, that the New Testament reading represents a dramatic rupture with the Old (supersession, as in Hebrews 10, with its dual argument that Jesus supplants Moses and that Jesus' sacrifice renders all subsequent sacrifice nugatory and the Temple obsolete).

During the second Christian century (known variously as the post-apostolic period or the period of the apostolic fathers), exegetes continued to refine methods and varieties of interpretation. The basic structure of the "Muratorian Canon" of the New Testament was not formalized until around 180 C.E., and it was in 367 that Athanasius first listed the canon as now accepted. Early interpreters therefore continued to focus largely on further exegesis of the Old Testament. Apostolic Father Justin Martyr (110–65) argued for the identity of "letter and spirit" in the interpretation of scripture, and saw witness to "Christ as Logos" as the key criterion of scriptural authenticity in the process of canonization. Typological interpretation was a staple, so that, for example, Justin read Old Testament references to "wood" as "types" of the cross of Christ.[6] Drawing on Paul in Romans and Galatians, Irenaeus (130–200) advanced this typological method with his concept of recapitulation, whereby New Testament figures "renew" the Old Testament. Hence, for example, Christ is the "new Adam," Mary the "new Eve."[7] Later second-century figures such as Tertullian of Carthage and Clement of Alexandria further developed the concept of the New Testament as an allegorical fulfillment of the Old Testament. Tertullian, however, remained more conservative in his appeal to allegorical exegesis, using evolving church teaching as his touchstone. Clement espoused a more individualistic approach based on what the individual's own faith moves him or her to discern in scripture.[8]

Origen of Alexandria further refined Clement's methods of allegorical interpretation, so that by the mid-third century, the Pauline distinction between letter and spirit had blossomed into a tripartite exegetical model (the historical, the typological, and the spiritual sense).[9] It is likely that the Alexandrian Jewish exegete Philo (c. 20 B.C.E.—c. 50 C.E.) influenced Origen in this regard. In turn, Basil of Caesarea (330–79), Gregory Nazianzen, and Gregory of Nyssa taught the superiority of images to mere words as the foundation for a further development into what came to be called the "four senses of scripture." On the basis of the work of these Cappadocian Fathers, exegetes came to refer to the four levels of meaning as follows: *historia* ("What God and Fathers did"), yielding a typological interpretion; *allegoria* ("Where our faith is hid"), resulting in a spiritual interpretation; *tropologia* ("Rules for daily life"), or ethical interpretation; and *anagogia* ("Where we end our strife"), reading texts for their eschatological meanings.[10] So, for example, one might understand texts about "paradise" variously as referring to the garden of Eden (historical), Christ and the church (allegorical), the realm of the four cardinal virtues (tropological), and the heavenly reward at the end of time (anagogical). By the same token, references to Jerusalem would mean the Holy Land, the church, the soul of the believer, and the heavenly city, respectively.

Subsequent major early exegetes like Augustine, Jerome (345–420), Theodore of Mopsuestia (350–428), and Gregory the Great went on to argue for varying emphases on the respective "senses" of scripture.[11] Ephraem of Syria (d. c. 373) and other Syriac-writing exegetes of the central Middle East are of particular importance in this context, as their work arguably set the stage for the exegetical writings of Islam's earliest Qur'ān commentators.[12]

Over the course of late antiquity and the Middle Ages, Christian exegetes further refined the interpretative options. The story of the last millennium and a half is too long and complex to retell in detail. Here a few general characterizations concerning major developments must suffice. During early medieval times major figures such as Alcuin (735–804) and John Scotus Eriugena continued the quest to reconcile exegesis with the Neoplatonic concept of emanation (as in the increasing materialization of spiritual realities) and integrated exegesis into the traditional schema of liberal education. A favored system identified quadripartite patterns everywhere, from the Gospels to the seasons, cardinal directions, ages of the world, and cardinal virtues. In the reforming monasteries and emerging universities of twelfth- and thirteenth-century Europe, exegetes further refined a full range of traditional hermeneutical styles, from the strictly literal to the highly symbolic. Earlier emphasis on the link between scripture and prayer yielded to a more academic approach to exegesis as a topic for university lecturers.

During the later Middle Ages (thirteenth and fourteenth centuries), exegesis took second place to the emergence of Scholastic systematic theology, but early Reformers such as Wycliffe and Hus again tilted the scale in favor of scripture study. Martin Luther, John Calvin, and other sixteenth-century Reformers revitalized exegesis further by reorienting the principles of patristic hermeneutics. No longer would church teaching be the decisive criterion in how to read the sacred text. Now holy writ would become the authoritative commentator on itself. As a result, Reformation exegetes emphasized finding the "spirit in the letter," severely limiting the use of allegory, in the interest of adapting scriptural preaching to an age of exploration and discovery.

In the early modern and modern periods, changing political, social, and cultural dynamics played a major role in shaping exegetical theology and hermeneutics. With the rise of nation-states, for example, the church's relationships with political power shifted dramatically. In more recent times, increased consciousness of the decisive influences of race and gender has given rise to heightened awareness of how cultural and social dominance can skew interpretation in favor of those already at the top of the power pyramid.[13] With that much too brief summary of an enormously complex subject, we must move on to the Islamic side of the story.

*Muslim Traditions of Exegesis*

Unlike the New Testament, the Qur'ān does not specifically "quote" earlier scriptures. It does, however, make multiple allusions to figures and narratives that appear in both Old and New Testaments. Early Muslim exegetes also made considerable use of narrative material called *Isrā'īliyāt* (stories about the people of Israel), a practice roughly analogous to New Testament allusion to Old Testament stories. In other words, much Qur'ānic narrative material has what one might call "biblical resonances." At the same time, the Muslim scripture evidences a variety of distinctive hermeneutical principles. First, Muslim tradition assumes that explicit citation of what Jews and Christians acknowledge as authoritative versions of their sacred texts is not only unnecessary but would lead to serious error. Behind this assumption lies the concept of tampering (*taḥrīf*), according to which any perceived discrepancy between biblical and Qur'ānic texts and accounts is traceable to deliberate interference by Jewish or Christian scholars.[14]

Second, the concept of abrogation (naskh) arises from the notion that God revealed his word gradually as a concession to the inability of humankind to receive and absorb all of the divine truth at a stroke. As a result, exegetes interpret texts of the Qur'ān that may appear at first glance to contradict each other as sequential rather than mutually incompatible.

Following upon the need to distinguish "abrogated" texts from "abrogating" revelations, Muslim exegetes have insisted from very earliest times on the importance of identifying as precisely as possible the historical context of every Qur'ānic text. Naming these occasions of revelation (asbāb an-nuzūl) gave rise to the practice of labeling each sura of the Qur'ān with an acknowledgement of its location in the original order in which the texts were revealed to and through Muhammad. Not unlike the Christian concept of context in the life of Jesus (Sitz im Leben), the circumstances of revelation anchor the text in the concrete setting of the early community and life experience of the Prophet. A key methodological difference, however, is that the Christian exegetical principle arose centuries later with the historical-critical method rather than out of a concern to anchor a text explicitly in an already established chronology.

The Qur'ān itself makes a fundamental distinction between two ways of understanding the scripture's texts. According to sura 3:7, "He it is who has revealed the Scripture to you. Some of its verses [or "signs"] are categorical in meaning [muhkamāt]. They are the mother [i.e., essence] of the Book. Others are open to interpretation [i.e., metaphorical or allegorical, mutashābihāt]. Those whose hearts harbor ill will pursue its metaphorical verses in their desire for disharmony and [esoteric] interpretation [ta'wīl]. None but God knows the inner meaning."[15] Even though the text seems rather obviously to warn Muslims away from presuming to read God's mind, Muslim interpreters began very early to develop an extensive exegetical literature, for the Qur'ān itself leaves relatively open the question of which verses belong to which category.[16]

Soon after the death of Muhammad, leading Companions (first-generation Muslims) noted for their unique knowledge and understanding of the Prophet's Qur'ānic recitations embarked on what would become a massive, centuries-long project—unfolding the multiple meanings of the sacred text. As early as the seventh century, a seminal exegete named Ibn 'Abbās (d. 688) suggested that the Qur'ān had four facets: tafsīr (possibly a literal dimension), known to scholars; an "Arabic" aspect, clear to native speakers; a legal or ethical aspect, embodied in its commands and prohibitions; and *ta'wīl,* perhaps a symbolic meaning, known only to God (but another reading of 3:7, based on a variant in punctuation, suggests that this meaning may also be known to "those firmly rooted in knowledge"). This quadripartite model arguably reflects Jewish and/or Christian influence, but the important point is that the first Muslim specialists acknowledged the complexity of interpreting the sacred text. There is considerable variety in the ways various exegetes define the levels of meaning discernible in Qur'ānic verses.

Beginning in the eighth century, Muslim commentators began producing various forms of *tafsīr,* mostly fragmentary notes rather than full-scale commentaries. The simplest, such as that of Mujāhid (d. 722), were those that largely paraphrased Qur'ānic texts, using synonyms for certain key words, as in "Lord, that is, master." In addition, narrative commentaries, somewhat after the fashion of Jewish *midrash,* explained by telling stories based heavily on ancient regional lore and relying very little on the Hadith. Muqātil ibn Sulaymān (d. c. 767), from northeastern Persia, was among the most influential in the genre.[17] Whereas the paraphrastic type hewed closely to the Qur'ānic text, the narrative type often departed considerably from the sacred words. Finally, a form of legal exegesis took specific topics of mandatory religious behavior as its organizing principles, rather than following the order of the scriptural text itself. Most works of this genre confined themselves to ferreting out, for example, how one ought to perform ritual prayer or pilgrimage or deal with questions of family and inheritance. Some legal works, like that of Qatāda (d. 736), specialized in the juristic implications of *naskh* (abrogation), sorting out in which instances a requirement mentioned in one text might have been superseded or nullified by a variation revealed in a later text.

By the early ninth century, commentators had begun to apply sophisticated grammatical and linguistic disciplines to the study of the sacred word. Grammatically oriented exegetes, such as Ibn Qutayba (d. 889), were especially interested in the increasingly important theological themes of the Qur'ān's "inimitability" and "excellent qualities." Here the commentators were moving more obviously toward drawing theological implications from their analysis: though one can apply the rules of grammar to the text, that very application leads to the conclusion that this is no ordinary literary work. During this phase of exegetical development, an increasingly important feature was recourse to the Hadith with a view to mining their explicitly exegetical content.[18] The result is generally called *tafsīr* based on "tradition" rather than on "individual opinion." Over the next several centuries, major exegetical works of this kind included the massive multivolume opus of Tabarī (d. 923) and somewhat shorter works by Fakhr ad-Din ar-Razi (d. 1209), Thaʿlabī (d. 1036), Ibn al-Jawzī (d. 1200), Ibn Taymīya (d. 1328), Nasafī (d. 1310), and Ibn Kathīr (d. 1373), to name only a few—representing the varying perspectives of different Sunni schools of religious legal methodology. Some legal scholars during the eleventh through fourteenth centuries wrote more explicitly juristic commentaries, focusing almost exclusively on fine points of law.

Meanwhile, as the many examples of "mainstream" exegesis appeared in considerable profusion, exegetical works of a more specialized kind were also being produced. Some commentaries keyed in on aspects of the sacred text related directly to God's nature and attributes. Members of two schools of thought in particular, the Muʿtazilī and the Ashʿarī, were largely responsible for such "theological" commentaries, the earliest dating from the ninth and tenth centuries. Primary later examples are the works of the Muʿtazili Zamakhsharī (d. 1144) and Fakhr ad-Dīn ar-Rāzī (d. 1210). Some commentaries also came from more "sectarian" environments, with the intent of providing scriptural support for the secessionist tendencies of the Kharijites (discussed below) and for the distinctive theological flavors of the various Shiʿi groups. In the latter instance, a bias of exegetes was to look for references that could be taken to refer allegorically to members of the "House" (i.e., Family) of the Prophet. For example, the famous "Verse of Light" (24:35) likens God's cosmic illumination to a niche within which there is a lamp within which there is a glass shining like a star. A Shiʿi exegete might identify the lamp as Muhammad and the glass as the first imam, Ali, thus suggesting both the imam's intimacy with the Prophet and access to revelatory illumination.[19] Yet another thread in early exegetical literature was discussion of problematical scriptural texts (majāz al-Qurʾān). Finally, beginning as early as the eighth century, some commentators began producing works of "mystical" exegesis, with a preference for texts that suggested God's immanence and the possibility of a close relationship between human lover and divine Beloved.

In more recent times, Qurʾānic exegesis has expanded somewhat both in genre and in method. Some modern works have been oriented to the use of a broad educated public rather than merely to specialists, and some more thematically structured works gather texts on related themes and comment on them together. Methodological developments have gone in several important directions. Some interpreters have taken their stand in an Enlightenment perspective, while others begin with the assumption that the Qurʾān embodies the roots of all modern science, if only one knows how to read it properly. More daring exegetical approaches involve a literary study of the sacred text. It is the use of a variety of "historical-critical" methods, however, that has caused the greatest stir, much as those methods raised enormous controversy among Christian biblical scholars less than a century ago. It is hardly surprising that these more recent studies have generated considerable debate, and even open hostility, with so much at stake. Muslims are not the first to face the challenge of working through such daunting paradigm shifts.[20]

### Jesus and Muhammad in the Scriptures

Christian and Islamic sacred texts function very differently as sources on the two traditions' "founding" figures, Jesus and Muhammad, as "historical" personages. Christians of various denominations, from the most conservative wing of Evangelicals to a small percentage of Catholics, lean toward more literal interpretation of the biblical record. Evident contradictions among the four Gospels (and elsewhere) concerning the chronology and events in the life of Jesus pose no major problems. The hermeneutical key in this approach is that scripture is the result of verbal inspiration and inerrancy in all details, though most Evangelicals now speak in terms of "what the Bible affirms," thus allowing somewhat greater scope for interpretation. As for the degree to which the New Testament presents a reliable account of the actual life of Jesus, it is likely that most Christians simply presume the sources' historical accuracy.[21] Others, however, acknowledge forthrightly the relatively limited degree to which one can rely on the New Testament record for "factual" data about the final years of Jesus' life. But in general Christians agree at a minimum that the most important New Testament texts are in some way "about" the Messiah and represent to some (debatable) degree the sayings and deeds of a historical figure called Jesus of Nazareth.[22]

From the New Testament, Christians glean far more about Jesus' life story than the Qur'ān affords Muslims about the earthly career of Muhammad. Muslims in general do not consider the Qur'ān a primary source about the life of Muhammad as such. For Muslims, the source that provides the most direct familiarity with the Prophet is the Hadith, with their manifold references to a host of details of Muhammad's life, as well as insight into his personal likes and dislikes.[23]

Both traditions, on the other hand, have at least roughly analogous attitudes to the "transhistorical" prerogatives of Jesus and Muhammad. Integral to the sacred legitimacy of both figures is the concept that their comings were presaged in earlier scriptures. As I have suggested above,

Christian "sightings" of Jesus in the Hebrew scriptures both determine exegetical styles and vary with the type of exegesis employed. Muslim exegetes have also discerned proleptic references to the Prophet Muhammad in both Old and New Testaments. The Qur'ān itself provides a cue, with God speaking to Moses about "those who follow the Messenger [i.e., Muhammad] whom they find mentioned in [their own] Torah and Gospel" (7:155–57). In Deuteronomy 18:15, for example, Moses assures his people that God "will raise up for you a prophet like me from among you." That "new Moses," according to some Muslim sources, is none other than Muhammad. In a Muslim reading of an Old Testament text attributed to Isaiah (21:6–7), the prophet reports that he saw two riders approaching, one riding a camel and the other a donkey. For some Muslim interpreters, the camel rider is Muhammad, and Jesus is his companion.[24] The preeminent New Testament text in this connection is from the Gospel of John. There Jesus promises his apostles that after Jesus himself departs, God will send them another "advocate" (parakletos, John 14:16). Muslim exegetes have argued that Christian scholars have misread the Greek word, inserting the wrong vowels. A correct reading would be periklutos—not "advocate," but "highly praised one," the root meaning of the name Muhammad. Jesus is therefore actually predicting the advent of the final prophet, not the "Holy Spirit," as Christians would have it. The problem, from the Christian side, is that none of hundreds of ancient manuscripts of John show this "alternative" spelling.[25]

## THEOLOGIES OF HISTORY: INTERPRETING A FAITH COMMUNITY'S MASTER NARRATIVE

In both pristine traditions, communities of belief coalesced around the conviction that God had blessed them specifically as a people with a divinely revealed source of guidance. Emerging largely from Jewish roots, the earliest Christians knew the Old Testament as their sole sacred scripture at first. It was not until several generations had passed that the New Testament had evolved sufficiently to claim center stage as a unitary authoritative text. For the early Muslims, by contrast, the link between community identity and its own sacred scripture was strikingly more immediate and concrete. There the community took shape around the focal point of the Qur'ān, even as the future "text" emerged piecemeal and orally in Muhammad's preaching. This important divergence of experience suggests significant theological differences in the ways the two traditions interpreted the unfolding of their original core communities. For Muslims the Qur'ān speaks the words of God, whereas for Christians it was the Christ who was the Word. The Muslim source that presents the closest analogue to the New Testament is the Hadith: both emerged only considerably later as complete texts, and both are regarded as divinely revealed but articulated in the words of human beings—Muhammad and the New Testament authors, respectively.

Many of the world's major faith traditions have given birth to detailed and complex narratives of the origins and development of their communal identities. Master narratives, especially in the Abrahamic traditions, embody and arise out of theological interpretations of the community's history. Such interpretations are characteristic of highly structured, symbol-laden, even stylized, retrospective readings of the "data" of the community's earliest sources. A fully formed communal narrative may give the impression of an organizational structure in place since the very beginning. In reality, tidy systematic representations invariably develop over generations of reflection on the sources. Only gradually do they develop the institutional structures taken for granted by subsequent generations of believers. In the case of both Christianity and Islam, one can discern a distinctly theological thread running through and integrating their retrospective interpretations of that early formation. This section will explore some of the dynamics behind conceptions of idealized primordial faith communities, including the evolution of early notions and structures of authority, constructions of gender and women's roles in those communities, and the de facto role of criteria of individual authority and ranking within both early traditions.

## Christian Apostles and Disciples

A key narrative of Christian origins centers on the gradual formation of a core group of "apostles" around Jesus. Perhaps the most striking feature of the larger story are gospel accounts in which Jesus "calls" each of the first twelve followers. Their stories depict variations on the theme of "conversion," a conversion not obviously away from Judaism but toward a new orientation centered on spreading the message of Jesus. The Teacher then "sent" the apostles (from the Greek *apostellein*, "to send") by commissioning them as a group and dispatching them on their individual teaching missions (Matthew 10:1–15, Mark 6:7–13, and Luke 9:1–16). The original twelve included Simon Peter, Andrew, James the greater, John the brother of James, Philip, Bartholomew, Matthew, Thomas, James the lesser, Thaddeus (aka Jude), Simon the Canaanite, Judas Iscariot, and Matthias (who was chosen to replace Judas after he committed suicide; Acts 1:23–

26). The number twelve reflects the ancient Jewish construction of the people of Israel as composed of "twelve tribes," though the apostles' roles were never associated with the territorial home turf long connected with those twelve tribes.

According to a comment attributed to Simon Peter (Acts 1:21–22), the crucial criterion of apostolic authenticity was having "witnessed" the resurrection of Christ. In other words, early texts identify the original apostles as men who knew Jesus personally. Very early on, however, Christian tradition added to the list of apostles the names of two of the earliest Christian "missionaries," Paul of Tarsus (in southeastern Anatolia) and Barnabas of Cyprus. In the process of this accommodation, the criteria for official "apostleship" were implicitly broadened. Paul argued that he was eminently qualified for the rank by virtue of his dramatic conversion experience in which he "saw" the Lord (esp. 1 Corinthians 9:1; see also Galatians 1:1; 2 Timothy 1:1). Barnabas, for his part, introduced Paul to the twelve apostles in Jerusalem, assuring them that they need not fear Paul because of his former persecution of Christians, for he had been commissioned by Jesus in a vision (Acts 4:26–27). New Testament texts suggest that, with the exception of Peter, the role of apostle was eventually supplanted by the office of bishop (*episkopos,* "overseer"; see 1 Timothy 3:1–7; Titus 1:7–9), governing the earliest Christian communities as they arose around the eastern end of the Mediterranean.[26]

In addition to the apostles, early Christian sources identify a larger core group of "disciples." Initially numbered at seventy-two, the disciples (Greek *mathetai,* "learners") harkened back to the group of seventy elders appointed by Moses as his inner circle during the Exodus (Exodus 24:1; Numbers 11:16). In Luke 10:1–24, Jesus gathers and commissions the Seventy-Two and sends them out in twos to prepare various local communities for Jesus' arrival there (see also Mark 6:7). Some interpreters see the apostles as forerunners of church hierarchical leaders, and the disciples as foreshadowing the eventual development of a clerical class.[27] A larger group of 120 "apostles and elders" (*presbyteroi*) are said to have attended the Council of Jerusalem in the year 49 (Acts 15).

From within this larger cadre yet another specialized cohort of Christians emerged in response to the perceived need to address specific social and material concerns within the protocommunity—the deacons. Complaints from Gentile converts that their widows were not receiving adequate food assistance prompted the apostles to have the community choose seven outstanding men for special service. Though they are not called deacons (*diakonoi,* "those who serve at table") explicitly in that context, the seven have traditionally been identified as the first deacons. The apostles named Stephen, Philip, Prochorus, Nicanor, Timon, Parmenas, and Nicholas of Antioch to the new office and commissioned them formally by "laying hands on them" (Acts 6:1–7). Long before Luke wrote Acts, Paul refers to "bishops and deacons" as separate offices (Philippians 1:1) and lists the characteristics required of a deacon (1 Timothy 3:8–13). Some scholars decline to see the origins of the diaconate in the appointing of the "seven," preferring to understand their role as that of liturgical assistant to the bishop at the "table" of the Eucharist.[28]

Within a generation or two after the death of Jesus, Christians had developed the notion of "apostolic succession." This technical term refers to the unbroken continuity of leadership and authority from Jesus, via the originally commissioned apostles, and down through those whom they and the disciples evangelized (this according to a Catholic interpretation, at least). Other specific, if not always clearly defined, functions within the proto-Christian community include prophets, evangelists, pastors, and teachers (Ephesians 4:11). Diverse gifts characterized the various categories: speaking in tongues, interpreting tongues, working miracles, and discernment of spirits (1 Corinthians 12:4–11).

All was not sweetness and light among the earliest Christian leaders, however. The New Testament addresses frankly the significant disagreements as to what elements of Jewish practice ought to be carried over into the new community. Peter and Paul had a head-on confrontation over the applicability of Jewish customs, such as circumcision and dietary restrictions, to Gentile Christians (Galatians 2:11–14). Paul himself decries the tendency to split into interest groups based on loyalty to the individual who first introduced a local community to the gospel (1 Corinthians 1:10–12, 3:4–10). John's letters call insistently for efforts to maintain unity in the church, as do important early fathers such as Ignatius of Antioch and Clement of Rome, with their concern for safeguarding the community's apostolic and catholic character.[29]

Alongside the various groups of men in leadership positions, women also played very important roles among the earliest Christians. Mary, Mother of Jesus, is only one—albeit a central one—among many women mentioned in the New Testament, both in the Gospels and Acts, and in the Pauline Letters. Mary's genealogy remains something of a mystery, but, according to Luke's gospel, she was betrothed to a man named Joseph, "of the house of David." The much older Elizabeth, wife of the priest Zechariah and mother of John the Baptist, was a "kinswoman" of Mary's. Luke parallels the aged and "barren" Elizabeth's miraculous pregnancy with Mary's even more wondrous virginal conception. Luke further draws analogies between Mary and Hanna, mother of the prophet Samuel (1 Samuel 2:1–10). Elizabeth, too, like Hanna, became pregnant under unusual circumstances. When she realized that she would have an extraordinary child, she broke into a song of thanksgiving, as does Luke's Mary (Luke 1:1–2:57). An ancient prophetess named Anna was one of two sage figures who acknowledge the wondrous nature of Mary's child (Luke 2:36–40).[30]

The Gospels describe Jesus' relationships with women, some brief encounters and some more extended. John's gospel uniquely recounts one of Jesus' most striking, and no doubt controversial, interactions in the story of the Woman at the Well. This woman was socially marginal and unapproachable on three counts: her gender (a woman alone at a well conversing with a strange man) and her ethnicity and religious adherence (she was a Samaritan; John 4:7–42). Jesus' relationship with Mary Magdalene is perhaps the most widely discussed, and she was the first to visit the empty tomb and see the risen Jesus (John 20:11–18). Women figured prominently as witnesses to Jesus' crucifixion, death, and interment, as well as to the empty tomb and postresurrection appearances (Matthew 27:55–56, 61, 28:1–10; Mark 15:40, 15:47, 16:1–9; Luke 23:27–28, 49, 55, 24:1–10). Luke and John devote especially noteworthy attention to women in their two Gospels and the Acts. Luke 8:3 describes a small group of women dedicated to supplying the material and financial needs of Jesus and his apostles. In addition to featuring Mary, Mother of Jesus, and Mary Magdalene, Luke's Gospel notes prominently the healing of more than a few women from intractable diseases (Luke 4:38–39, 8:1–3, 43–48, 13:10–17); and he alone tells of the role of the elderly widow Anna, a "prophetess" who gives thanks in the temple at the presentation of the child Jesus (Luke 2:36–40). More importantly, in his "second volume," the Acts of the Apostles, women were among the earliest converts in many regions (Acts 16:12–40) and were noteworthy for hosting church meetings in their homes (Acts 12:12–17). John's gospel brings five women or clusters of women unmistakably to center stage: in addition to Jesus' mother, Mary Magdalene, and the Samaritan woman, Martha and Mary (sisters of the Lazarus Jesus raised from the dead) play a major scene together, as do the women at the foot of the cross (John 2:1–11, 8:1–11, 4:1–30, 11:1–44, 12:1–8, 19:25–27).[31]

The Apostle Paul's missionary endeavors put him in touch with several remarkable women. At least one, Phoebe, was a deaconess; and Paul singles her out for her assistance in his ministry (Romans 16:1–2). Paul also mentions by name as "workers in the Lord" such other women as

Tryphaena, Tryphosa, and Julia and refers to the mother of Rufus as Paul's own "mother" as well (Romans 16:1–16). Paul points out that his colleagues Priscilla and her husband, Aquila, were apostles as well as missionaries (Romans 16:3). Paul commends sisters Tryphaena and Tryphosa, likely Gentile converts and former slaves, as "working hard in the Lord" in a way that he reserved for missionaries and local church leaders, and he charges Christians to be subject to their authority.[32] He notes prominently the role of Timothy's grandmother Lois and mother, Eunice, in nurturing Timothy in the true faith (2 Timothy 1:5). Lydia, a Jewish businesswoman who dealt in luxury textiles, stands out as the first convert in her region of Asia Minor. Lydia may have been a leader of a group of women who gathered for prayer, perhaps in the absence of enough local Jewish men to form a synagogue quorum. In any case, during her conversion, she did not shrink from speaking with strange men in public or from offering Paul and his fellow missionaries hospitality in her home.[33] Perhaps the most intriguing reference to a woman among the proto-Christians occurs in Romans 16:7. That text appears to identify a certain Junia, probably a freed slave, as "an apostle." The text links Junia with a man named Andronicus, and the early fathers of the church unanimously identified Andronicus's partner as a woman. It seems that scribes during the Middle Ages, for whom the concept of a female apostle was simply unthinkable, turned the feminine name into its masculine counterpart, Junias.[34]

### The Earliest Muslims: Muhammad's Companions and Followers

Muslims have long known their tradition's earliest stalwart and exemplary figures as the Companions (sahāba) of the Prophet.[35] The Companions included, naturally, the elect cadre of first converts to Islam but eventually embraced a much broader variety of people. Beneath the retrospective listing of Companions that began to take shape some seventy to eighty years after Muhammad's death (632) lies a skein of interrelated criteria that characterize an authentic Companion.[36] In addition to having "seen" the Prophet, Companions were ranked first in terms of chronological order in conversion (the earliest known as the sābiqūn, "predecessors"). Other criteria included, for example, accompanying Muhammad in the Hijra to Medina (622), fighting in the battle of Badr (624), participation in the treaty of Hudaybiya (628), or presence among the early converts in Medina known as the Prophet's Helpers (ansār). A host of other qualifications, mostly related to pinpointing the date of conversion, include participation in the battles of Uhud and the Ditch, for example, and relatively late conversion to Islam during Muhammad's visit to Mecca after the Muslims reclaimed it in 630. These were such signal events in the life of Muhammad and the early community that participation in them became roughly analogous to the presence of leading first-generation Christians at major moments in Christ's life.

An important early genre of hagiography (writing about exemplary or holy figures) in Islamic religious literature focuses on the excellent qualities or lofty virtues (*fadā'il*) of the Companions. Among the ethical and spiritual hallmarks of the group are intimate relationship with the Prophet, steadfastness in faith, absolute fairness and evenhandedness in all dealings, and intense devotion and piety. The Companions enjoy such an elevated place in Islamic tradition that casting the slightest aspersion on any of them has long been condemned as sinful. At the pinnacle of the de facto hierarchy of Companions are the "Ten Recipients of Good News" (*'ashara mubāshara*), who enjoyed the signal blessing of knowing that they would enter paradise. Most prominent among the ten are the four immediate successors to the Prophet in leadership of the Muslim community, the Rightly Guided Caliphs (Abu Bakr, 'Umar, 'Uthmān, and 'Alī)—this according to the Sunni interpretation of history, about which I will say more shortly. The additional six merited membership in the top rank as a result of their closeness to the Prophet in various ways. Whenever Muslims mention the name of a Companion, it is traditional to add "May God be pleased with him."[37]

A number of women formed a group of particular importance among the Companions, beginning with the Prophet's wives and one of his daughters. Muhammad's first wife, Khadīja, and his daughter Fātima are ranked among the four "most perfect" women in history (along with Jesus' mother, Mary, and Āsiya, the martyred wife of the pharaoh in the time of Moses). Tradition lauds Khadīja as Muhammad's first and most steadfast confidant during the early experiences of revelation, encouraging the Prophet not to doubt his experience nor be discouraged by what he thought he was "hearing" during his periods of prayerful solitude. As Mary was, in Muslim tradition, the "finest of her age," so too was Khadīja. A Hadith indicates that, like the uppermost of the Companions, Muhammad informed Khadīja that she was destined for paradise. Another of the Prophet's more important wives was 'Ā'isha, who is credited with transmitting an unusually large number of Hadiths. Muhammad's daughter Fātima played a crucial role in the early history of the Muslim community, but especially in the Shi'i perspective, since she was the wife of the first imam (spiritual leader in the line of the Prophet), 'Alī, and the mother of the second and third, Hasan and Husayn. Fātima's place in Shi'i tradition is analogous in some ways to that of Mary in Christian tradition.[38]

Muhammad's wives are known by the honorific title "Mothers of the Believers" and stand out as paragons of piety and wisdom for all subsequent generations of Muslims. Though none are mentioned by name in the Qur'ān, the sacred text speaks of them as perhaps the single most important group or "class" of people in the early community. In fact, the Qur'ān (33:50) further explicitly categorizes Muhammad's wives according to a set of criteria based on the historical circumstances under which God sanctioned the Prophet's unions with them (not unlike the various subcategories of Companions mentioned earlier). So, for example, some women were taken as prisoners of war, some were from families that offered a dowry, some were maternal or paternal cousins, and others offered themselves to the Prophet.

Tribal lineage and pedigree bore important social and political implications in early seventh-century Mecca, and many of Muhammad's thirteen formally acknowledged marriages cemented significant inter- and intratribal alliances. Fewer than half of the Prophet's wives belonged to the principal Meccan tribe, the Quraysh, and none of them were from Muhammad's own clan (within the tribe), the Banū Hāshim. The rest came from other tribes, two were Jewish, and one an Ethiopian Christian. Scripture endows the wives as a group with dignity surpassing that of all other women, but they also carry unique responsibilities and are expected to hew to higher ethical standards. As members of the early Muslim community, therefore, these women served not only as pillars of the Prophet's family, but as exemplars of ideal behavior.

Beyond their moral and spiritual nurturance as "Mothers of the Believers," a still broader symbolic function in the overall revelatory scheme of the scripture is similar to that of the wives of earlier prophets from Adam on. "Actors in Qur'ānic history, they function as images, or metaphorical extensions, of that historical reality which God revealed to His Prophet."[39] The Qur'ān does not name any of the earlier prophets' wives, though Muslim exegetes were careful to supply proper names to all of them in their commentaries.[40]

A Hadith is evaluated for authenticity and credibility on the strength of each of the personalities listed among its transmitters, and no transmitter is credited with greater veracity and reliability than a Companion. Ranking of early Muslim notables is not limited to the Companions but embraces subsequent generations known as the Successors (tābi'ūn; also "Followers") and the Successors of the Successors. The term salaf, "ancestors in faith," eventually became a convenient way of referring to the collectivity of paradigmatic Muslims.

## Caliphs and Imams: Divergent Narratives of Muslim Primal History

Upon the death of Muhammad in 632, the young Muslim community faced what some have called a "constitutional crisis," concerning the manner of choosing a successor to the Prophet. According to what would become the majority view, Muhammad had not named a successor but had indicated instead a preference that the elders of the community select a *khalīfa* (vice-gerent) from among their peers. The selection process favored Muhammad's already elderly father-in-law Abū Bakr. Meanwhile, a minority faction within the community argued that Muhammad had indeed designated by name a successor, his cousin and son-in-law 'Ali. 'Ali's "partisans," the *shī'a,* insisted that the Prophet had appointed him to serve in the office of general guardianship (*walāyat al-'āmma*) at Ghadīr Khumm when they were returning from Muhammad's final pilgrimage to Mecca, in 632. Those who supported Abū Bakr's caliphate denied the validity of 'Ali's counterclaim, and the Shi'a responded by arguing that Abū Bakr and his two immediate successors, 'Umar and 'Uthmān, were usurpers.[41]

Those in the majority called themselves the "People of the Sunna and the Assembly" (*ahl as-sunna wa'l-jamā'a*), on the grounds that they were following the express wishes of the Prophet with its communitarian implications. But the minority partisans of 'Ali developed the central concept that a legitimate successor must be, first, designated explicitly by his predecessor and, second, come from the family of the Prophet. Out of these two principles of leadership there developed a distinctively Shi'i conception of the imamate. According to what became the majority position from among the various Shi'i groups that emerged over the next several centuries, God would raise up twelve imams from the Prophet's family. Their role would be to function both as successors to Muhammad and as guardians (*walī*) of the whole community. As tenth-century Shi'i theologians read their community's history, the eleventh imam designated his successor, and shortly after the former's death in 873, the twelfth imam went into the "Lesser Concealment." For the next seventy years or so, the final imam communicated to his faithful followers through a series of four representatives. When the fourth *wakīl* died, around 945, without having designated a successor, the twelfth imam entered into what is known as the Greater Concealment.[42] This theological interpretation of early Muslim history developed further in the elaboration of a distinctively Shi'i eschatology, to which I will return at the end of chapter 2.

. . .

One major procedural similarity worth highlighting is that exegetes in both traditions devised and employed a variety of modes of interpreting the sacred text. The intellectual and textual histories of both communities suggest further that segments of the communities favored and emphasized one or another of those exegetical styles (such as the legal, mystical, or pastoral) and used them to further underscore their various central purposes and messages. A larger common theme in the scriptural foundations of Islam and Christianity is that the sacred texts and their exegetical histories both reflect and construct Muslim and Christian understandings of their traditions' relationships to previous dispensations in the process of explaining divergences from previous revelations.

Early Christians in effect expanded their scriptural canon while simultaneously reinterpreting the Old Testament to such a degree that the New Testament superseded it. Islam likewise acknowledged the existence of earlier Jewish and Christian scriptures and regarded its own as superseding the earlier revelations, but for different reasons. Instead of understanding the Qur'ān as an addition that still accorded exalted status to prior revelations in their current form, Muslims developed the concept of alteration/tampering by Jews and Christians to explain the de facto irrelevance of the earlier texts. In addition, the concept of abrogation shored up the definitive status of the new scripture as a vehicle for God's progressive revelation. In other words, both early Christians and Muslims confronted the problem of contradictory scriptures but solved them in rather different ways: Islamic revelation corrects and replaces entirely previous but corrupted revelations, while the Christian New Testament fulfills the Jewish revelation. Put another way, whereas the eternally existent Qur'ān embodies a perfect and self-sufficient revelation, the Christian canon retains the Old Testament as integral to the tradition while according the New Testament a more perfect status.

There are in addition a number of important specific differences between the two traditions. From the Christian perspective: first, the final shape of the New Testament, with its variety of literary genres and plurality of human authors, suggests an important principle concerning divine communication. Here God "inspires" multiple individuals, including prominently two not originally from the inner circle of apostles (on which more in part 2 in this volume), and entrusts them with communicating the divine message from diverse points of view. Second, beneath the rich variety of methods and styles of exegesis that evolved in Christian history lies the fundamental concept of divine/scriptural "inerrancy." God makes no mistakes in what or how he communicates, but exegetes and theologians are still left with the vexing problem of how and to what degree human interpreters must apply nonliteralist (or symbolic) hermeneutics in order to explain apparent contradictions in scripture.

From the Islamic perspective: by contrast, God entrusts formal "revelation" to only one class of human representatives, his prophets. Until the "final" (and therefore universal) revelation to Muhammad, God had delivered a message fashioned for each community in its own language. While earlier prophets had access to various kinds of "miraculous" power to establish the veracity of their revelations, the inimitability of the Qur'ān itself is Muhammad's sole proof of his prophethood. Throughout the process of the scripture's unfolding, the concept of abrogation undergirds the theological principle of progressive revelation, by which God is continually tailoring the message to the limited but evolving capacities of its addressees. Finally, as suggested above, Islamic tradition teaches that had Jews and Christians not "tampered" with their own scriptures, God would not have needed to intervene yet again with a corrective message in the form of the Qur'ān.

Both traditions affirm the finality of their unique scriptural revelations, and yet both scriptures also hint at their own inability to contain the whole of God's communication:

But there are so many other things that Jesus did; were every one of them to be recorded, I suppose that the world itself could not contain the books that would be written. (John 21:25)

If all the trees on earth were pens and all the oceans ink, with seven more seas besides, they would not suffice to record the words of God. (Q 31:27; see also 18:109)

The theological implication is that God continues to clarify the message by shaping human community through history, and both traditions read their early histories in particular through that theological lens.

The earliest components of the New Testament appeared a quarter-century after the death of Jesus, and the last some fifty years after that. The Qur'ān was "complete" with the death of Muhammad, while the sayings of the Prophet (Hadith) continued to evolve as a literary corpus for several centuries. Both traditions speak of levels of interpretation or meaning. Christian views of four levels of meaning in scripture—historia, allegoria, tropologia, and anagogia—are very roughly analogous to Islamic notions of ordinary commentary (*tafsīr*), linguistic or grammatical explication, legal or ethical meanings, and esoteric or mystical interpretation (*ta'wīl*).

As in the first Islamic generations, the earliest Christians formalized oral traditions considered authoritative for the interpretation of faith. Initially, both Christianity and Islam entrusted the continued teaching of their fledgling communities to groups of followers (apostles, Companions) who were close to the principal teachers (Jesus, Mohammad), rather than to a single successor. But after their founders' deaths, both traditions gradually evolved more institutionalized structures. On the Muslim side, this comparative view emphasizes the Qur'ānic tradition "There is no clergy in Islam," though there are important variations in the Shi'i tradition. Even so, by the second Islamic century, formal ranking of Muslim authorities had become essential for authenticating the growing body of Hadith. With respect to the exercise of power within the community, it was none other than the first converts and closest Companions of the Prophet who managed the early conquests and thus became the first political rulers in a nascent empire. By contrast, though the bishop of Rome wielded some quasi-political power even in early times, formal investiture of Christian leaders with civil authority was not common until after Constantine.

Finally, a noteworthy difference in the construction of gender has to do with the relationships between exemplary women and the foundational figure. Christian tradition interprets Jesus' choice not to marry as a sign of his complete dedication to the church as its "spouse," thus effectively diminishing the range of female authority roles in Christian institutional history. The more intimate link of Muhammad's wives and daughters to the foundational figure, by contrast, may suggest a somewhat broader influence, at least in the life of the early community.

In chapter 2 we turn to more detailed evidence of how Christians and Muslims have interpreted their respective histories in light of their sacred sources and communal foundations.

CHAPTER 2

# Development and Spread

Chapter 1 traced two large formative themes in the histories of Islam and Christianity. In their respective histories of exegesis, the traditions exhibit the immense richness and variety of ways in which Christians and Muslims have approached their sacred sources. Narratives enshrining persons and events regarded as essential foundations of the traditions represent their earliest implicitly theological constructions. The present chapter moves beyond the foundational texts and early history to examine the gradual internal differentiation and external expansion that have made Islam and Christianity truly global faith communities.

## COMMUNITIES, PLURALISM, AND THE FAITH TRADITIONS

Diversity in interpretation of sacred texts is only one of many types of evidence of theological variety in the two traditions. Questions of authentic membership in their respective communities of faith have been important concerns for both Christian and Muslim sources since very early in their histories. I begin here with a look at some of the earliest ways of distinguishing authentic members of the faith communities from those who do not belong.

### Who Is a "Christian"?

As the Acts of the Apostles indicates, the earliest followers (the "disciples") of Jesus were first called Christians in the city of Antioch, near Syria's

Mediterranean coast (Acts 11:26). These first missionaries considered themselves responsible for spreading the core teachings of Jesus beyond the original Jewish matrix in which the Teacher had begun to disseminate his message. Since virtually all of the earliest disciples were themselves Jews, questions naturally arose early on about the degree to which the missionaries should emphasize—or allow—ritual and conceptual continuity between the old and new. These questions emerged in increasingly sharp relief as the young Christian community's outreach introduced the teachings of Jesus to communities either not previously Jewish or already long shaped by Hellenistic culture. Mission to the Gentiles, non-Jews, with all the attendant challenges of introducing unusual concepts to a public unfamiliar with biblical traditions, became the larger purpose of the early Christian leadership.

A faction called the Judaizers played a formative role in the definition of the early Christian community. Among the divisive issues that confronted the earliest Christians were questions about the persistence of Jewish practices associated with Mosaic law. These questions included both the degree to which non-Jewish converts ought to be required to subscribe to Mosaic ritual prescriptions (e.g., can one eat meat offered to idols, or of animals killed by strangulation?) and initiatory rites such as circumcision. At the heart of the matter was the complex process of characterizing relationships between Jewish and Gentile converts to the new faith tradition.[1]

Christian theologians call "ecclesiology" the dimension of their faith traditions that seeks to define the global and historical community as a "church." For some, the topic includes aspects of practical governance often dubbed church polity. Tradition came to identify the Universal Church formally as "one, holy, catholic, and apostolic." A distinctively Christian feature in this context is the sacramental character of formal membership signified by the ritual of baptism. Rituals of election or spiritual legitimation were integral to the Jewish religious life of Jesus' time. Indeed, sanctification by water was the hallmark ritual of the ministry of John the Baptist (whom Christian tradition sometimes identifies as the last Old Testament prophet). A key rite of passage that launched Jesus' own public ministry was his acceptance of baptism at the hands of John. Patristic authors, beginning with the Apostolic Fathers, discussed various sacramental dimensions of baptism. They generally agreed that the ritual forgave sins, sealed individuals as members of the body of Christ, and brought the baptized into union with the death and resurrection of Jesus. Christians discerned in the ritual "types" of baptism in such biblical moments as the flood, crossing the Red Sea, and the ablutions of the Old Law. Most importantly, baptism symbolized the individual's reception of the Holy Spirit. Christian authors were of various minds as to how (immersion or pouring) and when (in infancy, youth, or adulthood) one ought to be baptized; whether converts from heretical sects needed to be rebaptized; and to what extent symbolic baptisms of blood (martyrdom) or profound repentance (desire) sufficed for salvation.

During medieval times, Scholastic theologians further debated such questions as baptism's validity if conferred by a faithless minister, the nature of the "character" imprinted on the soul, who qualifies as a potential minister of the sacrament, and whether baptism ever needs to be repeated. Protestant reformers differed on the necessity and efficacy of the sacrament. Luther insisted that baptism permanently removed sinfulness, while Calvin argued that baptism assured pardon only for the elect, and Zwingli dismissed it as a mere symbol of membership in the Christian community.[2]

As chapter 3 will discuss further, the need for explicit formulations of essential elements of belief became apparent to religious leaders both Christian and Muslim as fissures began to appear in their protocommunities. In the Greco-Roman milieu in which Christianity emerged, the term *hairesis* originally denoted merely a "position" or "view" with little or no negative theological connotation. Though New Testament texts (e.g., Acts, Peter, and 1–3 John) hint at a variety of early divisions, not until the second Christian century did the term evolve into a designation of "incorrect position" or "heresy," as the term is more commonly used now.

Even in the New Testament we find evidence of significant areas of disagreement and open dispute as to how to define the new Christian community over against the parent traditions of Judaism and the surrounding environments so profoundly shaped by Hellenistic culture and Roman rule. During the second Christian century, the earliest distinct groups espousing views that would soon be attacked as unacceptable came to be known collectively as Gnosticism.[3] Emphasizing the centrality of privileged arcane knowledge (*gnosis*) as the key to salvation, these factions inspired a host of responses from the church's earliest theologians. These apologists and apostolic fathers countered the theological elitism of the gnostics with elaborate arguments reframing "true *gnosis*" by identifying it variously with Christ himself (Ignatius of Antioch), knowledge of the name of Jesus (Justin Martyr), the fullness of Christian sacramental/ritual life (Irenaeus, 130–200), or the result of contemplation of the mystery of Christ in sacred scripture (Clement of Rome and Origen). Authentic *gnosis*, Irenaeus argued, is the heart of Christian truth, while the "heretics" are in fact "pseudo-gnostics." Along similar lines, Clement of Alexandria

(150–215) identified Hellenistic philosophy as a helpful propaedeutic to *gnosis,* which is in turn both cause and result of love *(agape).*[4]

Central features in early Christian theology were the dual (divine/human) nature of the person of Christ and the triune reality of God. Several dozen major third-, fourth-, and fifth-century Latin-, Greek-, and Syriac-writing figures of the eastern Mediterranean basin gradually evolved formulations of Christology and Trinitarian theology that were incorporated into various creedal statements. In the course of these same centuries, a host of groups identified with unacceptable explanations of christological and Trinitarian intricacies were formally anathematized in the proceedings of a series of "ecumenical councils"—that is, they were condemned as heretical and formally deemed to be outside the "true church."[5] Part 2 of this volume will provide further detail about the particulars of these and other ingredients of "true belief" as Christians have articulated them.

## Who Is a "Muslim"?

The Qur'ān's earliest message was heavily oriented toward forming the consciences of Muhammad's listeners, summoning them to a heightened awareness of the demands of social justice. Only gradually did the content of the Prophet's preaching develop a sharper focus on explicitly "Islamic" theological concepts. A key element in the evolution of the Qur'ānic distillation of critical features of Muslim identity was the notion that *islām,* "surrender to God," was not a novel characteristic but a hallmark of the spiritual lives of all true servants of God—indeed, of all created beings—since Adam. Qur'ānic preaching thus built on the exemplary stories of the earliest *muslims* (those who surrender), emphasizing in particular the paradigmatic surrender of Abraham, Moses, and Jesus. These ancestors in faith thus model the critical quality of a healthy relationship to God.[6]

Among the Qur'ān's more specific references to the identity of "believers" are a number of fairly straightforward descriptions of their characteristics. Several essential features characterize believers according to their responses to the divine initiative in their lives. They "feel a tremor in their hearts" when they hear mention of God and his "signs"; they perform the ritual prayer and give freely (to the needy) of what God has given them. Fulfilling their covenant (*'ahd*) with God, believers stand in reverent awe before God and have a healthy fear of their moral accountability. They persevere in patience and in the hope of eternal reward. Believers are humble in prayer, modest, and dedicated to trustworthiness in all their personal relationships. Foremost among believers are those who are the first to perform every good work. They conduct their responsibilities in consultation with others of their community and refuse to allow injustice to take root among them. (See, e.g., 8:2–4, 13:20–24, 23:1–11 and 57–61, 42:36–39). Perhaps one of the more concise descriptions of the piety of believers occurs in the "Verse of Righteousness" (*Āyat al-birr*, 2:177):

> Righteousness does not consist in whether you face east or west [in prayer]. The righteous person is the one who believes in God and the Last Day, in the angels and the Book and the prophets; who, though he loves it dearly, gives his wealth away to his kinfolk, to orphans, to the destitute, to the traveler in need and to beggars, and for the redemption of captives; who attends to his prayers and renders the [religiously stipulated] alms.

Above all, true Muslims are those who "do not obscure truth with falsehood or conceal the truth when [they] are fully cognizant of it" (2:42). A fundamental distinction is made therefore between truth tellers and truth concealers (*kāfirūn*).

Muslim tradition developed distinctive ways of understanding the meaning of a community of belief. One could argue that the Qur'ān is marginally more concerned with making distinctions between authentic belief and various forms of unbelief than the New Testament, although the latter does draw relatively clear contrasts between unbelievers and believers. The Qur'ān contrasts the new dispensation heralded by the revelation delivered through Muhammad with the previous age of ignorance (*al-jāhilīya*) characterized by wholesale rejection of God's revelatory signs. The term *kāfir(ūn)*, from a root meaning "to cover," came to be a basic way of referring to "unbelievers" and would in time become commonly used in a verbal form meaning "to anathematize" or "declare [someone] an unbeliever" (*takfīr*). An equally important concept in the Qur'ān is wandering in error (*dāl*) away from the straight path (*sirāt al-mustaqīm*), perhaps the most common way of referring to those who stray from the truth whether in ignorance or out of malice. But the scripture also uses several other important terms to describe religiously unacceptable attitudes and actions. One of the most common semantic clusters are references to "forgery" (*farā*) and "fabrication" (*kadhaba*) in order to deny God's signs (e.g., 16:101–106).

I referred earlier to the development of a Shi'i theology of history and now turn briefly to other important implications of the earliest Sunni/Shi'i divide. 'Ali, claimed by the Shi'a as the legitimate successor of the Prophet, finally acceded to power as the generally accepted caliph in 656 after the murder of ʿUthmān. This marked the onset of the "first *fitna*" (trial, dissension, civil war), as ʿAli set up his base of power in the garrison city of Kufa in Iraq. Muʿāwiya was governor of Syria and a cousin of ʿUthmān. Convinced that ʿAli had been at least complicit in ʿUthmān's murder, Muʿāwiya confronted ʿAli's army at Siffin on the Euphrates in 657. When the battle ended in a stalemate, ʿAli agreed to an arbitrated settlement, thus precipitating what was arguably the first important Muslim theological dispute. A faction among ʿAli's supporters refused to abide by any such negotiated arrangement and announced that they would secede. The seceders (*khawārij*) were henceforth known as the Kharijites, "Those Who Depart." They argued that ʿAli had reneged on his original purpose of avenging the Shiʿa for the injustices done them by the murdered ʿUthmān. In their view, ʿAli, had forfeited the right to be considered a true Muslim, opting to rule as a kind of dictator rather than as "first among equals." Claiming that their uncompromising insistence on divine justice made them the only true Muslims, the Kharijites continued to fight with those who rejected their extremist criteria for membership in the community of believers.[7]

During the post-Prophetic era, several theological concepts came into more common usage. If the traditions established under Muhammad were the norm of good Muslim belief and behavior, any innovation (*bidʿa*) was suspect, although not necessarily to be judged "heretical." Individuals or groups considered out of step with accepted tradition might be known as errant or deviant (*dāll*), and early heresiographers categorized as "sectarian" members of groups (*firaq*) whose views on God's transcendent unity, divine providence and justice, God's promise of reward and threat of punishment, and the divine communication to humankind through prophets diverged from what was emerging as a norm. Some accused of freethinking (*zandaqa*) those who did not conform to that standard. Those who pushed the boundaries still further, to the point of causing a theological uproar and fomenting fragmentation or "schism" in the community might be known by a moniker such as "corrupters" (*fāsiqūn*). Anyone who associated a partner with God was guilty of idolatry (*shirk*) and known as a *mushrik*, while people guilty of general unbelief (*kufr*) merited the title *kāfirūn*. People who took the extreme step of separating themselves from the community generally came to be known as *khāriji* (pl. *khawārij*, "those who secede") in the pejorative sense of the term. Others were accused of apostasy (*radd*) or irreligion (*ilhād*), while those who pretended to be believers in public but resorted to treachery behind the scenes were hypocrites (*munāfiqūn*).[8]

## GLOBAL MISSION AND CONVERSION

Three of the world's major faith traditions have spread over large areas of the world at least in part as a result of a missionary thrust that developed fairly early in their histories. Though Buddhism failed to take firm root in the land of its origin, India, the teachings of the Enlightened One gradually spread through Central, East, and Southeast Asia, where (with the exception of Indonesia, arguably) Islam and Christianity have enjoyed far less success. The nature of the initial impetus to large-scale dispersion, as well as the dynamics of the dispersal, varies among the three traditions. One could argue that it was not the Buddha himself who mandated a missionary thrust, but a third-century B.C.E. monarch, King Ashoka, who set a missionary effort in motion after converting to Buddhism. The Jesus of the Gospels, on the other hand, appears to commission his core followers explicitly to "go out and make disciples of all nations, baptizing them in the name of the Father and of the Son and of the Holy Spirit" (Matthew 28:19). Muhammad, for his part, preached with the conviction of one whose revealed message "came down" as a universal corrective to the long-corrupted revelations delivered by earlier prophets to Jews and Christians (among other then-defunct communities that had been punished for rejecting the prophets God had sent to them).

However, the widely accepted narrative that names Islam as the faith tradition uniquely and invariably spread "by the sword" throughout its history needs to be reconsidered. This now broadly accepted narrative rests largely on the poorly attested assumption that Muslim forces engaged in their wars of conquest entirely, or almost exclusively, for religious motives, when in reality their motives (not unlike those of the Crusaders) were almost certainly quite diverse. In addition, this narrative ignores both the historical reality that Islam was spread in many parts of the world (e.g., Southeast Asia) peacefully by unarmed missionaries, and the well-documented record of Christian conquests linked to winning souls for Christ, for example, in the Americas.

Attempts to characterize the spread of the two most truly global of the world's faith traditions are fraught with difficulty, perhaps the greatest of which is the sheer expanse of the subject both chronologically and geographically. A close second is the dearth of reliable detailed sources about both the quantitative and the qualitative aspects of the story. Polemical accounts, both from within and outside the respective communities, typically portray the positive aspects of the originating source and the negative, even catastrophic and barbaric, features of the competition. Richard Bulliet has made an important contribution in his *Case for Islamo-Christian Civilization*, arguing that medieval Christendom and Islamdom were more alike than mutually incompatible in the ways in which they co-opted large pieces of the global real estate. In both instances early conversion to the community was very gradual, as the new religious culture filtered down from the conquering administrators to the broader population. There is no doubt that in later centuries the armies of the two traditions came to blows with increasing regularity and dire consequences, but irenic mercantile and cultural relations remained far more the rule than the exception. A genuine parting of the ways did not commence in earnest until the sixteenth century, not for ideological reasons, but because of "accidents of history."[9]

## Christianity as a Global Faith Community

Christianity did not emerge as a clearly defined new entity when the first followers of Jesus began to fan out across the landscape of Palestine's three provinces—Judea, Samaria, and Galilee. Virtually all of the original apostles and disciples were Jews, and it is quite impossible to discern a point at which the emerging faith community ceased being Jewish and became something uniquely and recognizably Christian. Perhaps, one could argue, the definitive change had not come to pass even thirty years after the death of Jesus, when the earliest wider missionary initiatives were well under way with Paul's travels across the eastern Mediterranean world initiating new Gentile members into the fold. Some historians suggest that in any case Paul, not Jesus, deserves the credit for "founding" Christianity.[10] Others point to the reticence of the followers of Jesus to grieve the Roman destruction of the temple in Jerusalem in 70 C.E. Perhaps the litmus test was the "Christian" refusal to support Bar Kochba's rebellion in 132–35 C.E. against Roman intentions to replace the temple with a shrine to Jupiter.[11] Whichever events one identifies as the juncture at which Christianity severed its umbilical cord to Judaism and began to stand alone as a movement or institution, it seems clear that its spread across the Roman Empire was impressive but hardly meteoric.

Christian communities took root in various social and cultural contexts. Northward through Greek-speaking Asia Minor (present-day Turkey) and westward across Latin-speaking eastern and central Europe, Christians appeared in all the major population centers by the mid-second century. By the early third century, churches arose as far west as Spain. To the south and west, Christian groups developed in Egypt and across North Africa as far as Tunisia. In addition, important but little-appreciated church groups became established at the eastern end of the Mediterranean, in the land of Christianity's origins. For nearly two and a half centuries, beginning in 64 C.E., Christians were subject to persecution under Roman rule. Increasing in extent and fury, ten local or regional persecutions culminated in two empire-wide attempts to wipe out the impertinent citizens who stubbornly refused to worship the divine emperor. Murderous campaigns by Decius (250) and Diocletian (303), separated by intermittent periods of official toleration, not only failed to eradicate Christianity, but appear in fact to have hastened its growth through conversions.[12]

According to traditional accounts, the conversion of the emperor Constantine (c. 288–337) definitively turned the tide in favor of Christianity, and the Edict of Milan (313) officially ended the era of imperial persecution. It was Constantine who convened the first of the "ecumenical councils" at Nicaea (present-day Iznik, Turkey) in 325, seeking to solidify Christian unity as the official creed of the empire.[13] A century on, Sasanian ruler Yazdegerd I put an official end to persecution of Syrian Christians (409), thus opening the way for important growth of the church in the central Middle East.[14] Chapter 3 will explore further the doctrinal implications of Nicaea and subsequent major councils; suffice it to say here that Constantine's dream of theological as well as political peace proved elusive as individual teachers and factions with diverse doctrinal views continued to assert themselves. Meanwhile, Christian churches multiplied across western Europe and the British Isles, as well as throughout the eastern Mediterranean basin.

Divisions within the larger Christian community that remain significant to this day began to solidify in the fourth and fifth centuries. Eastern churches formerly but inappositely referred to as "Nestorian," as well as Monophysite ("one [divine/human] nature" in Christ, rather than two distinct divine and human natures), Jacobite, and Armenian churches, played major roles in the eastern Mediterranean; and the Monophysite Coptic and Ethiopian (or Abyssinian) churches took solid root in Egypt and the Horn of Africa.[15] By the late eighth century, widening fissures were beginning to separate Roman Latin from Eastern Greek Christianity. According to traditional reckoning, the "official" breach between Roman and Orthodox communions occurred in 1054.

Throughout the Middle Ages, important developments transformed the shape of European Christianity. Beginning in 800, when Charlemagne symbolically picked up the mantle of Constantine by proclaiming himself

Holy Roman Emperor (with the complicity and juridical cooperation of the papacy), issues of church and state bedeviled civil and religious rulers. When they were not busy establishing or consolidating their own hold on power, they were struggling to prevent their religious or secular counterparts from claiming more for themselves. When the religious and secular leaders were not contending with each other, they were often enough engaged in putting down disruptions within their own spheres—heretical movements or invasions from outside. Beginning in 1096, the Crusades comprised a series of major efforts that united religious and secular authorities in common cause against the infidel Muslims for the express purpose of liberating the Holy Land for the church.[16]

One could argue, however, that the three most significant developments that reshaped premodern Christendom were the Protestant and Catholic Reformations; the sixteenth-century drive for exploration, conquest, and conversion in the New World; and the massive global missionary efforts that followed. As the Ottoman Empire was entering one of its largest periods of expansion, including serious assaults on eastern Europe, ferment within the European church was steadily building toward far-reaching reform movements. Martin Luther was the most celebrated of the Protestant reformers, but he was not alone. His 1517 protest against papal authority and pervasive clerical structure, along with a lengthy list of what Luther regarded as corrupt practices and theological distortions, spearheaded the fragmentation of the church into what would become multiple "Protestant" churches. As suggested in the introduction to this volume, the period of the Catholic Reformation saw the Roman Catholic Church's mobilization against what it regarded as forces of disunity.

Massive missionary thrusts into the Americas sent Catholic priests along with royal armies to claim souls for Christ as the troops claimed land and resources for their monarchs. In less than two centuries, much of the indigenous population of Central and South America had become at least nominally Catholic, while missionary efforts in North America proceeded more slowly. Catholic evangelists, particularly as represented by the Jesuits, labored with much less overt success in South and East Asia. Major exceptions were regions such as the Philippines, where the political control of European colonial powers (such as Spain) propelled Catholicism's spread. One could argue that the faith took root more readily in populations historically identified with indigenous religious traditions and not previously influenced by the more "established" faiths, as China and Japan were. By the nineteenth century, Christian communities had begun to grow across virtually the entire globe.[17]

*Islam, Umma, and Caliphate*

As for the question of whether Islam as a faith was actively and ordinarily "spread by the sword," intriguing (though still very tentative) archaeological and archival research suggests otherwise. It seems clear, on the one hand, that Muslim forces gained military and administrative control over a very large expanse of territory by the year 711, advancing to Spain at the western extreme and the Indus River to the east. The pace of conversion to Islam appears to have gone much more slowly than political subjugation to Muslim armies. Well over a century after Muhammad's death (632), the population of Iran (conquered in 653) appears to have been around 10 percent Muslim, while about the same time the populations of much of the central Middle East (Greater Syria and Iraq) were no more than 20 percent Muslim. Not until 850 did Persia's Muslims number around 50 percent of the population. And 250 years after that, on the eve of the First Crusade, the population of the central (Arab) Middle East evidently remained less than 50 percent Muslim. These figures suggest the need for a reassessment of how people who were themselves Muslims imposed their political and military dominance over a large area in the space of little over a century, and why their conquests were not always inseparable from mass conversion. Much more work remains to be done on the history of Muslim missionary endeavors that did not occur at sword point.[18]

From the earliest days, Muslims referred to the collectivity of believers as the *umma*, from a root that connotes an exemplary or paradigmatic reality. The initial spread of Muslim rule from the Arabian Peninsula into the central Middle East and thence to North Africa and Iran may indeed have envisioned an expansion of the Umma. But before the Umma as such could grow, mechanisms of rule and administration had to be set into motion after the conquest of the new territories. Initially, the first three of the "Rightly Guided Caliphs" (Abū Bakr, 'Umar, 'Uthmān) ruled from Medina; and when Sunni Muslims finally acknowledged 'Ali's claim to the caliphate in 656, he would rule from his already-established seat of power in the Iraqi garrison town of Kufa. Not until the Umayyad family overthrew 'Ali in 661 and established its new capital at the ancient city of Damascus in Syria did Muslim rule formally move to embody its wider designs in the larger political symbolism of claiming a cultural and political center outside of Arabia. By the year 711, the Umayyads had extended Muslim dominion from Spain to northwestern India, and they would maintain reasonably solid control over much of that realm for nearly ninety years, until a rival clan undermined them and brought them down.

From their newly founded capital of Baghdad, deliberately sited near the once-glorious Sasanian capital of Ctesiphon, the Abbasid caliphs ruled at least nominally from 750 to 1258. Though they claimed unitary, centralized caliphal rule across the length and breadth of Umayyad lands and then some, their grip on the distant reaches of the empire began to loosen within but a few generations. Even before the founding of Baghdad, survivors of the Umayyad family had set themselves up as an independent emirate in Cordova, Spain. At both the western and the eastern extremities of the empire, provincial governors began to declare their effective independence from Baghdad early in the ninth century. By the mid-tenth century, the power behind the throne in Baghdad was in fact a major Twelver Shi'i family, the Buyids, who wielded their influence for over a century. Around that same time, two rival caliphates had proclaimed themselves rulers of the universal Muslim community—the Umayyad caliphate of Cordova (929) and the Fatimid Isma'ili (Shi'i) caliphate ensconced in its newly founded capital of Cairo (969). Though many of the principalities and governorates across nominally Abbasid Islamdom continued to include the name of the caliph in Baghdad in the Friday prayer, it was largely empty symbolism that masked de facto independence in the provinces.

By the mid-eleventh century, the Saljuqid Turks had swept across western Asia from their ancestral homes in central Asia. Capturing Baghdad in 1055, they soon diminished the role of the caliph still further by establishing the parallel institution of the sultanate, where all the serious political power rested, thereby effectively reducing the caliph's function to ceremonial leadership as "commander of the faithful." Though the office of caliph survived nominally and ceremonially in many subsequent political regimes, down through the Ottoman dynasty's early twentieth-century demise, the concept of a seamless union of religious and secular authority vested in a single institution never truly functioned as once envisioned by some Muslim rulers—or as various contemporary extremist groups imagine themselves resurrecting it.

As the unitary caliphate succumbed to political fragmentation, and regional Islamic dynasties multiplied from the inside, other sociopolitical entities brought under Muslim rule territories not previously within the bounds of the Abbasid caliphate even at its greatest extent. In the wake of the initial Turkish incursion by the Saljuqids came other waves of Turkic and other groups from central Asia westward across the Middle East, culminating in the sack of Baghdad by the Mongols in 1258. Around that same time, Muslim rule in what are now Afghanistan and Pakistan expanded to include the northern third of India, and trade ventures brought Muslim missionaries to Southeast Asia. As Islam took root, peacefully as a rule, in Malaysia and Indonesia during the fourteenth and fifteenth centuries, Muslim rule extended to nearly two-thirds of India.

Meanwhile, back in the central Middle East, the emerging Ottoman dynasty began to threaten what was left of the rapidly shrinking Byzantine Empire. From their origins as the leading tribe of a Turkic confederation that had gathered in Anatolia (formerly Asia Minor) since the late eleventh century, the Ottomans grew into a serious regional power. After surrounding the Byzantine capital of Constantinople inexorably for 150 years, the Ottomans successfully besieged the city and captured it in 1453. Over the next century or so, the Ottoman sultans gradually claimed for themselves much of the former Byzantine Empire, and then some, expanding into the Balkans and parts of eastern Europe. By 1492, with the end of the Catholic reconquest of Spain, Muslim regimes and far-roving missionaries had planted the seeds of Islamic communities in large areas of sub-Saharan Africa.

With the Sunni Ottomans approaching the zenith of their power, a new "gunpowder empire" established itself in Iran and proclaimed Twelver Shi'ism the creed of the realm. From 1501 until the early 1700s the Safavid dynasty flourished between the Ottomans to the west and the Sunni Mughals to the east. Last and most important of a series of Muslim regimes in South Asia, the Mughals controlled much of India, including what are now Pakistan and Bangladesh, ceding power to the south to a succession of Deccani sultanates. Not long after Safavid power had waned, Mughal rule began to succumb to factionalism within and the British from without. By the late eighteenth century, the combined pressures of reviving Hindu regimes and growing British influence had taken a serious toll on Mughal power.

Despite well over five hundred years of Muslim rule in the Indian subcontinent, the current population of the region remains overwhelmingly Hindu. With the exception of the black Africans who had been Muslim in their homelands before being enslaved (about one in six according to some estimates), Islam remained largely unrepresented in the Americas until the twentieth century. Today, roughly 1.6 billion people identify themselves as Muslims, thereby comprising about a fifth of the world's population. Of that total, some 80 percent are Sunni, with the remaining minorities composed chiefly of Twelver and Ismā'īlī Shi'is, and various other groups who consider themselves Muslims but are not always recognized as such by the majority (including, for example, Alawis and Ahmadiya).[19]

## THE END OF HISTORY: APOCALYPTIC THEMES

Chapter 1 began with theological constructions of the origins of the two now-global traditions. At the opposite end of history, Muslims and Christians share remarkably similar scenarios about how history will come to a close. Christian and Muslim views of history have one major overarching feature in common: time has a more or less discernible beginning, a more measurable middle, and a loosely predictable end. In addition, the traditions share various significant forms of apocalyptic imagery as well as associated theological implications, but there are also important differences. Here are some of the prominent themes.

Apocalyptic scenarios appear in both the Old and New Testaments. Ezekiel and the book of Daniel, along with the New Testament's book of Revelation (the Apocalypse of John) are among the most striking examples of the genre, which is characterized by arcane visions and vivid imagery. Freestanding works of Jewish and Christian apocalyptic literature were generated mostly from about 200 B.C.E. to 200 C.E., with elements of important themes appearing in a few earlier Old Testament texts. In general, the "seer" (or author) announces that he has witnessed a revelatory vision, with angels delivering a heavily encoded message about the future. The revelation often couches the coming conflict of worldly and heavenly powers in allegorical terms.

Various texts of the Old Testament refer indirectly to the elusive theme of the "Day of the Lord (or Yahweh)," which seems to have originally referred to times when Israel was victorious in its divinely mandated conquests of the Land. But when the concept is first described explicitly in the scripture, the prophet Amos (Amos 5:18–20) portrays it rather grimly as a time when the manifest power of God would judge Israel for its unfaithfulness. Some prophetic texts (such as Isaiah and Zephaniah) tend to interpret the concept in apocalyptic terms as a reference to the end of time.[20] They feature the fearsome aspects of the Day as a time of darkness and cosmic cataclysm. Later prophets (such as Joel and Zechariah), however, revive the earlier more positive, triumphal characteristics of the Day: on that Day, Israel will again be victorious over its enemies, and Jerusalem will be restored as the heart of Zion.

The Gospel of Luke (17:24, 30) refers to the "Day of the Son of Man," with christological resonances associated with the incarnation. Elsewhere in the New Testament, the "Day of God" appears in apocalyptic garb with its allusions to a final battle between good and evil (e.g., 2 Peter 3:12; Revelation 16:14). Finally, the Pauline Letters speak of the "Day of Jesus Christ" (e.g., 1

Corinthians 1:8; 2 Corinthians 1:14; Philippians 1:6, 10, 2:16) on which Christ will appear in glory as judge of all humankind. Expectation of the imminent dawning of the "Day" posed a practical problem for early Christians, with Paul eventually reframing his warnings to include the caution that no one can predict the moment of its advent. For Christians, however, it is the final book of the New Testament, Revelation, that represents the pinnacle of apocalyptic literature.[21] A fine example of apocalyptic imagery, referring to part of the author's "vision," comes from the book of Revelation:

> Then I saw another mighty angel coming down from heaven, wrapped in a cloud, with a rainbow over his head, and his face was like the sun, and his legs like pillars of fire. He had a little scroll open in his hand. And he set his right foot on the sea, and his left foot on the land, and called out with a loud voice, like a lion roaring; when he called out, the seven thunders sounded. And when the seven thunders had sounded, I was about to write, but I heard a voice from heaven saying, "Seal up what the seven thunders have said, and do not write it down." And the angel whom I saw standing on sea and land lifted up his right hand to heaven and swore by him who lives for ever and ever, who created heaven and what is in it, the earth and what is in it, and the sea and what is in it, that there should be no more delay, but that in the days of the trumpet call to be sounded by the seventh angel, the mystery of God, as he announced to his servants the prophets, should be fulfilled. (Revelation 10:1–7)

Privileged access to arcane symbolism, astonishing signs in nature, and the in-breaking of the power of the next world into this are characteristics of the genre in both Old and New Testaments.

Some of the most arresting apocalyptic texts in the history of Middle Eastern religious literature occur in the earlier suras of the Qur'ān. They function as reminders of ethical responsibility in view of an impending accountability, an arresting summons to attend to the reality of a dimension of human existence that transcends the cramped confines of individual lives in this world. Unlike the best-known of the biblical texts, the Qur'ānic apocalyptic episodes tend to be relatively short, explosive, poetically potent allusions to striking conditions that could obtain only in a universe on the verge of cataclysmic dissolution. These texts typically employ a series of "temporal" or "conditional" clauses, building in intensity and culminating in a denouement that resolves the mounting tension with a hard truth that will come to pass at the moment of final accounting. The following is a good example of this intriguing rhetorical device:

> When the sun is folded up,
> And when the fading stars fall away,
> And when the mountains disappear,

And when camels ten months pregnant are abandoned,
And when free-roaming creatures are corralled,
And when the oceans turn to tidal waves,
And when the souls (of all people) are divided (between good and evil),
And when the baby girl buried alive is asked
    For what sin she was murdered,
And when the Scrolls are unrolled,
And when the heavens are revealed,
And when the infernal conflagration blazes,
And when the Garden (of Paradise) becomes closer . . .
THEN will the individual know the import of his or her deeds. (Q 81:1–14)

Among the most important concepts shaping the Qur'ān's use of apocalyptic themes are *as-sā'a*, "the Hour (of judgment)," and *amr*, variously glossed as "divine sovereignty" or "fulfillment of God's command." Features of the "Hour" include its imminence, inevitability, sudden arrival at a time known only to God, and accompaniment by such signs as the "splitting of the moon" and earthquake. Most people are in deep denial of the reality of the Hour. As with the Hour, the arrival, or return, of God's *amr* will also be marked by (unspecified) signs, suddenness, and desperation for the naysayers.[22] Qur'ānic calls for apocalyptic awareness and a sense of the imminence of "the Hour" are reminiscent of New Testament author Paul's insistence that the end of time was near. Apocalyptic themes did not remain a staple of Muhammad's preaching, yielding in later Qur'ānic revelations to more mundane concerns that arose as the Muslim community grew into a distinct polity in Medina.

These themes do, however, appear in various forms in the Hadith literature, particularly in the subgenre traditions of discord (*ahādīth al-fitan*). As Paul found himself needing to adjust the sense of expectation as the end failed to materialize, so one gets a sense that the keen warning of the Qur'ānic texts gave way to the Hadiths of discord in which "signs of the Hour" are a key theme. Here the sense of imminence is somewhat muted, and anxious believers enjoy a bit of a reprieve even as they keep a wary eye for telltale changes around them.[23] The sayings typically describe dire conditions that will characterize a future time during which the Muslim community will experience severe trials and testing (*fitna*). Though these specific traditions focus on discord within the Muslim community rather than on cataclysms expected at the end of time, sections on *ahādīth al-fitan* in some of the Hadith collections include sayings of a more cosmically apocalyptic import. Themes of greatest significance here include narratives about the return of the guided one (*mahdī*), Jesus, and the Antichrist (*dajjāl*).[24] Subsequent Muslim authors and commentators continued to imbue these and other shorter Qur'ānic texts, as well as stories gathered in Hadith collections, with deeper apocalyptic significance. Exegetical works in particular were responsible for expanding on the apocalyptic imagery of many Qur'ānic texts and Hadiths, such as the enigmatic references to Gog and Magog.[25]

With these considerations of apocalyptic concepts, we begin to make a transition to the concerns of part 2, "Creedal Dimensions." In both traditions, articles of faith relating to the more personal, individual aspects of eschatology play a greater role in creedal formulations than apocalyptic interpretations of sacred history. Before moving on, however, a summary of the varieties of theological interpretations of sources and history will be helpful.

. . .

Both the Christian and Islamic traditions evidence a spectrum of fundamental orientations to the interpretation of their sacred texts and histories: idealist, traditionalist, realist, and personalist. As it is impossible to characterize adequately in a few words such complex ways of thinking, I propose these four orientations not as neatly discrete styles, but as amorphous and often overlapping perspectives.[26]

The idealist reading of religious history, whether Christian or Muslim, regards the period associated with the origins or founding of the new community of faith as a watershed of revelation and an idealized time in which foundational wisdom and practice existed in their purest form. After the death of the founding figure, whether Jesus or Muhammad, spiritual entropy began to set in, and the community underwent a steady deterioration and disconnection from the original teaching. After a period characterized by increasing distortion of the sources and lack of direction, reformers arise, inspired anew with a zeal for the halcyon days of pristine truth, and effectively write off the intervening centuries as a total loss. There have been many variations on this theme. Some Protestant reformers argued that the great fathers of the church were the last credible witnesses to the authentic tradition prior to the sixteenth century, and dispensed with a millennium of wayward thinking. The Church of Jesus Christ of Latter-day Saints, also known as Mormons, developed an even more radically selective reading of history, discarding everything between the Apostle Paul and the revelation to the prophet Joseph Smith (1805–44)—a lacuna of over seventeen centuries. Some Christian groups, known variously as Dispensationalists, Supersessionists, and Christian Zionists, look to an overturning of the old order and seek to foster ideal conditions for the cosmic conflicts that signal the end of time.[27]

Radical modern and contemporary reform groups within the larger Muslim community have in an analogous fashion sought to reaffirm the lifetime of the Prophet Muhammad as a paradigmatic "golden age." Within a generation or so the faith became so diluted and encrusted with layers of misinterpretation that only by jettisoning over twelve hundred years of history can one hope to recover the true spirit of the original revelation. Generally allied with a literalist interpretation of the Qur'ān, radical reform-oriented Muslim groups typically require serious political activism of their members. Here change typically means "returning" to the group's vision of a long-lost authenticity. The universally and eternally valid sacred sources must be enacted as "literally" as necessary to recover that vision.

A much more pervasive orientation in both Christian and Muslim theologies, however, requires far less drastic historical surgery. Still regarding the period of the founding figure as unique and seminal in many ways, the traditionalist perspective does not lead to the conclusion that the faith community completely lost its bearings over subsequent generations. Many Christian and Muslim readings of their histories discern periods of decline and renewal, but they choose to own the "whole story" as the record of God's dealings with a people who have needed constant reminders of their waywardness, and a chance to return to the path. This less selective reading of history reflects, arguably, the approach undergirding the religious education of the overwhelming majority of both Christians and Muslims. I am not suggesting that large masses of people enjoy the luxury of thinking at leisure about history in these terms, but only that this generally uncritical orientation at least implicitly informs the thinking of those who teach and preach to the majority. An overall temper of conservatism and/or "fundamentalism" (in a very general sense) goes hand in hand with a preference for political quietism. Stability in religious values trumps change, which some regard as capitulation to ephemeral cultural trends. Revelation abides somehow in its "original" spirit but does not mandate an overturning of the social order.

The realist approach regards history and change itself as critical ingredients in the unfolding understanding of the core meaning of the religious tradition. At the heart of this orientation—call it pragmatic, modernist, progressive, rationalist or adaptationist, perhaps—is the conviction that God works through, not in spite of, history. The Revealer in fact tailors revelation to the times and cultural circumstances, so that all divine communication is historically conditioned. Interpreters of the ancient sources face the daunting challenge of translating them into terms consonant with conditions vastly different from the contexts in which they first appeared.

Finally, there have been numerous movements across the length and breadth of both Christendom and Islamdom founded and sustained on the centrality of a charismatic personality. One could, of course, claim that both traditions arose from the teachings of a charismatic figure; but in both cases, majorities of Christians and Muslims have considered themselves members of larger institutional systems in which individual authority is subsumed into a higher level of organization and administration—even if not centralized, as in Roman Catholicism. In the history of Christianity, such groups have typically been rather short-lived, with religious orders arguably a notable exception within various Christian groups (Catholic and Orthodox in particular). Within the larger Muslim community, Shi'i Islam and the traditional Sufi orders suggest the personalist orientation, with the imam or Sufi shaykh as the ultimate recourse and teaching authority.

Cutting across the four orientations in both traditions, Christian and Islamic apocalyptic visions are similar in several respects. Both warn of the dissolution of the cosmos, the end of time, and an Antichrist figure. Both visions also adapted over generations when the "Day of the Lord" or the "signs of the Hour" failed to materialize. Though both foresee trials and testing in the end-time, Islamic traditions describe them more pointedly as signs of dissension within community than do Christian views.

# PART II

# Creedal Dimensions

*Faith and the Development of Theology*
*as a Religious Discipline*

Very early in their respective community histories, Christians and Muslims began preserving their core beliefs in narratives that enshrined signature characteristics of God's dealings with them as a unique community. Sayings and deeds of their foundational figures as exemplars of the ideal response to the divine initiative formed a second essential theme in these stories. These accounts represent the origins of "narrative theology" in the two traditions, the first major theme in chapter 3. But with the passage of generations and the growth of the communities, the pristine narratives of faith were no longer suitable for encompassing the increasing complexities introduced by both internal diversity and external engagement with new cultural and ethnic influences. A new method of specifying details that distinguished among various interpretations of core beliefs took the form of relatively brief summaries, or creedal formulations, as discussed in the latter part of chapter 3.

"Narrative theology," which will play a secondary role in later chapters of this volume as well, requires a bit of explanation here. Theological study is an inherently interdisciplinary affair, as the importance of narrative theology exemplifies very well. In both traditions the art of recounting God's initiatives on behalf of his people has deep roots in scripture, as well as in the cultures from which Christianity and Islam arose. Far more than "just stories," these primary pedagogical narratives are the product of serious theological reflection. They both emerge from, and expand upon, a fundamental set of beliefs about the divine-human connection. As such these accounts share with "myth" truly so-called the ability to put into words what believers cherish as ultimately ineffable in their hearts, and what theologians have eventually gotten around to couching in more technical language.

Chapter 4 explores that further development of the languages of faith. Historical studies reveal that a divergence of views on various essential elements of creed increasingly manifested itself in identifiable subcommunities in both traditions. Some of these variant views gave rise to splinter groups or subcommunities. Some further crystallized into the beginnings of "schools" of theological opinion about issues that went on to become the main concern of more elaborate systematic thought. Here the theological disciplines of historical interpretation and systematic theology come to the fore as primary tools of inquiry.

# CHAPTER 3

# From Story to Creed

Elements of the content of belief play important roles in both Christianity and Islam, though they have functioned differently in the two traditions. It is not necessarily a question of ceding priority to what people think about their faith—over, say, how they feel or what they do about what they believe. But the histories of both traditions give ample evidence that Christians and Muslims have devoted a great deal of attention and energy to conceptualizing and communicating the details and mechanics of belief. Here I will explore several of the more important ways in which influential sources and interpreters have articulated what Muslims and Christians believe, and why.

Creedal dimensions in both the Christian and the Islamic traditions include four areas of particular importance. First, early examples of "narrative theology" are an important form of expression of belief in both traditions. Fundamental intuitions and convictions about God, creation, and humanity typically take shape first in stories that give voice to often complex worldviews. Second, among the earliest technical statements of belief are summary formulations called "creeds." It may be helpful to think of creedal statements as distillations of a faith community's master narratives. Chapter 4 will take up the third and fourth ingredients, namely, the emergence of systematic approaches to creedal elaboration and the differentiation into various schools of theological thinking.

In this chapter I have included somewhat more material from the Islamic tradition than from Christian sources. Two assumptions have prompted this choice: first, that most readers will come to the subject with less background on Islamic themes than on Christian materials and will benefit at this juncture from slightly more detail on the former; and second, that sources for the Islamic themes in question here are in any case still less widely available to the reading public.

## NARRATIVE THEOLOGY

In chapter 1, I introduced the concept of an evolving master story at the heart of both Christian and Muslim theologies of history. In addition to stories of community origins, both traditions have also articulated prime narratives that enshrine the earliest summaries of the core teachings of the faith. Here I explore the evolution of those narratives as prologue to the crafting of more formal creedal statements.

### Narrative and Scripture

In both Christian and Islamic traditions, arguably the earliest and least appreciated variety of theological discourse is narrative theology. In the introduction I described examples of scriptural theologies, ways of understanding the specific theological themes and concerns inherent, if not explicit, in the sacred texts (as distinct from theologies of scripture, which discuss the larger issues of the evolution, contents, and authority of sacred texts). Scriptures are, in general, not intended to be read as manuals of theology, but that does not mean they are not fraught with theological significance. For Christians, this implies that, for example, the individual New Testament inspired authors—particularly the four Evangelists, Matthew, Mark, Luke, and John—each have a unique perspective on the life of Christ.[1] Though some interpreters over the centuries have sought to downplay the apparent disparity of views by harmonizing the four Gospels, Christians have come to appreciate the value of the four perspectives as prime examples of narrative theology. For example, while the three Synoptic Gospels (Matthew, Mark, and Luke) follow generally similar outlines of the life of Jesus, only Matthew and Luke include genealogies and infancy narratives. They also frequently arrange events in the life of Jesus in slightly different orders, and each has a distinctive narrative flavor or tone. Luke emphasizes the universality of the message; Matthew, writing for a Jewish audience, structures his work in five parts redolent of the five books of Moses; while Mark's much briefer account depicts a Jesus very much on the move from community to community.[2] Finally, John has Jesus make three annual pilgrimages to Jerusalem rather than one as in the Synoptics—a curious implied variation in the length of his public life.

An example of New Testament narrative based on the Jewish tradition of midrashic exegesis is Matthew's account of the flight into Egypt (Matthew 2:13–15) and the follow-up story of Herod's slaughter of the innocents (Matthew 2:16–18). Though only Matthew includes these two brief narratives, many Christians choose to believe that they reflect actual historical occurrences—not that attestation in only a single source need in itself cast doubt on their historicity. From the perspective of narrative theology, however, it is essential to take into account that both stories bear the unmistakable stamp of *midrash,* arising out of reflection (*derash*) on, and designed to explain the true meaning of, certain scriptural texts—Old Testament texts in this instance, cited by an author writing for a Jewish audience.

After Matthew tells the story of Joseph's taking Mary and Jesus into Egypt, he notes that the "event" occurred "to fulfill what the Lord had spoken by the prophet [Hosea 11:1], 'out of Egypt I called my son [Israel].'" Matthew then tells how Herod contrived to slay all male children born in the previous two years around Bethlehem, thus "fulfilling" the words of Jeremiah (31:15) describing the wailing of Rachel over the deaths of her children. The pertinent question here, as always, is not whether such an interpretation casts doubt on the historicity of the actions that Matthew describes, but what theological presuppositions and principles underlie and emerge from Matthew's narrative tactics. Matthew is clearly concerned with connecting the beginnings of Jesus' life with the prophetic message of the Hebrew scriptures, a purpose manifest in Matthew's genealogy of Jesus as well (Matthew 1:1–17, which differs significantly from Luke's genealogy, 3:23–38), and in the way the five-part structure of his gospel evokes thoughts of the Pentateuch.[3]

Other forms of New Testament narrative theology use diverse literary devices and strategies. Christians early on began to characterize the kernel of their faith as a "proclamation," or *kerygma*. Explicit formulations of the essential elements of the new message are at the heart of the "speeches" delivered particularly by Peter, Stephen, and Paul in Acts of the Apostles. Luke, author of Acts, uses the literary device of the public address in a host of varying contexts, and delivered by these early Christian leaders, as summaries of the main outlines of the early Christian narrative of "salvation history." Stephen's defense (Acts 7:2–53), after he was hailed before the high priest on charges of blasphemy, is perhaps the most detailed example of the genre.

The principal ingredients of the kerygmatic narrative begin with a "historical prologue" designed as a reminder of God's covenants with Abraham and Moses and the liberation of God's people from slavery in Egypt and into the promised land. Under David and Solomon, God fashioned a people around worship in the temple and through the prophets announced the coming of a Righteous One. But the Jewish people rejected that expected Messiah, Jesus, and delivered him over to be killed. Though some of the briefer speeches leave out detailed references to the Old Testament, an essential feature of most of the speeches is the failure of the Jewish community to recognize the identity of Jesus as the Messiah promised through the prophets of the Hebrew scriptures. Above all, the speeches emphasize that these deniers were responsible for the death of the Just One, whom God raised from the dead, and who continued to appear to the early followers. It was this risen Jesus who sent the Holy Spirit as the gift of his ongoing presence among them, and who commissioned his followers to go out and baptize in his name.[4] These kerygmatic summaries expand, in effect, on the creedal capsulizations that took the form of "covenant treaty formulae" in the Hebrew scriptures, remnants of which appear in texts like Joshua 24:2–27.[5]

Here I need to explain my rationale for arguing that narrative *kerygma* was indeed the stepping-stone to early "systematic" theological reflection. It is well documented that Paul's letters, many of which develop theological themes beyond simple narrative, in fact predated the writing of the Gospels and Acts. But both the Pauline corpus and the later Gospels derive from a common earlier *kerygma*. Luke begins his gospel by reminding Theophilus that "many have undertaken to compile a narrative of the things accomplished among us," and that the work at hand will provide "an orderly account" of things he has already heard in a more haphazard manner (Luke 1:1–3). Hebrews also alludes to the Lucan themes, noting that the message "was declared at first by the Lord, and it was attested to us by those who heard him" (Hebrews 2:3). In addition, Paul often assures his readers that his message is authentic precisely because he has received it from earlier custodians of the *kerygma*. Paul prefaces his summary account of the Lord's Supper by reminding the Corinthians that he is handing on to them what he received from the Lord (1 Corinthians 11:23–32). Moreover, Paul was at pains to emphasize that his apostolic commission was further authenticated by his seeking and receiving a commission from Peter and James in their capacity as representatives of the original Jerusalem community (Acts 9:26–30; Galatians 2:1–10).

A scripture-related category of literature generated during the early

Christian centuries also deserves mention here. So-called apocryphal literature represents a fascinating array of perspectives on important theological themes, though many were at length judged unacceptable for inclusion in the canon of the New Testament. Some articulate tendentious views eventually pronounced marginal or even heretical, but they nevertheless preserve an essential record of themes of interest to many people active in the process of refining what Christians would eventually proclaim consistent with true belief. Major apocryphal narrative genres mirror those of the canonical New Testament, including most notably gospels and Acts of the Apostles dating mostly from the late first to early third centuries. Among the gospel forms are some that closely parallel widely acceptable theological positions, while some, such as the celebrated Coptic-language Gospel of Thomas, represent heterodox views such as those of various gnostic factions. In the genre of Acts of the Apostles are works generally ascribed to, or about, individual apostles (unlike the New Testament version's collective approach). These range in content from obvious retellings of canonical accounts to highly embellished, imaginative, and romanticized versions.[6]

Narrative content in the Qur'ān prompts a very different set of questions and potential conclusions. The Islamic scripture emerged as more of a unitary document, rather than the product of multiple authors, and Muslims generally regard the text as God's own speech. That said, the Qur'ān uses numerous brief narrative passages in a variety of ways. One way in which the Qur'ān is strikingly different from Christian scriptural narrative is that the Qur'ān includes no accounts about Muhammad himself (with the possible exception of cryptic allusions later identified with his visionary experience). Stories of the pre-Islamic prophets and their unbelieving peoples comprise by far the single largest category of narrative content. References to prophetic mission and message emerge as an important teaching device, especially later in the Meccan period. In fact, the phenomenon of a succession of individual prophets provides the subtext of narrative theology in the Qur'ān. God's ongoing communication through prophets is itself the master narrative. But, with the notable exception of Joseph, most of the scripture's references to prophetic narratives are relatively brief and meant as moral examples punctuating the Prophet's preaching. The story of Joseph in sura 12 is a remarkable departure from the Qur'ānic pattern in this respect. Aside from only one other brief mention (40:34), this chapter is the only account of Joseph in the whole book. Entirely dedicated to one prophet, it relates his story as a single literary unity. Perhaps the best way for Christian readers to approach the Qur'ān is to read the biblical account of Joseph (Genesis 37–50) and then read sura 12.[7]

Though the Qur'ānic account has naturally provided the most widely known version of the Joseph story throughout Islamdom, other variants demonstrate the importance of the story far from the land of Islam's Arabic roots. Wherever the story has been told, elements that represent regional influences have made their way in. The Malay counterpart, called the *Story of Joseph* (*Hikayat Yusof*), includes a number of biblical details not found in the Qur'ānic account. It uses the biblical name Potiphar where the Qur'ān uses 'Aziz, and calls his wife Asnath instead of Ra'il or Zulaykha (as later Islamic texts usually call her). In the Malay version the brothers tell Jacob his beloved son has been devoured by a tiger rather than by a wolf.[8]

Uniquely Muslim prophets whose stories appear piecemeal in the Qur'ān include Sālih sent to Thamud, Hūd sent to 'Ād, Shu'ayb sent to Midian, and Dhū 'l-Qarnayn, an unnamed mysterious character traditionally identified by exegetes as none other than Iskandar, or Alexander the Great. Other prophets of particular Qur'ānic importance include Adam, Noah, Abraham, Isaac, Isma'il, Jacob, Jonah, Khidr, Moses, David, Solomon, Zakariya, John (the Baptist), and Jesus. Many of these are, of course, major biblical figures but play different, nonprophetic roles in Jewish and Christian understanding.[9]

Finally, an important change in the pattern in Qur'ānic narrative of the prophets appears upon comparison of Medinan texts to Meccan texts. The earlier texts tend to emphasize the role of the earlier prophets as preachers whose message their peoples reject, thus mirroring Muhammad's experience of rejection in Mecca. By contrast, Medinan texts depict pre-Islamic prophets as lawgivers, thus providing a paradigm for Muhammad's own changing role in governing the community in Medina.

*Narrative in Postscriptural Texts*

Beyond the scriptural theologies expressed in narrative form, both traditions enshrine narrative theological expressions in various postscriptural texts. Within the Christian tradition, much early scriptural exegesis was cast in narrative form (arguably under the influence of Jewish midrashic writing). Important patristic writings, in genres very different from exegetical texts, have further refined narrative approaches to theological themes. A fine early example of patristic narrative theology is Gregory of Nyssa's *Life of Moses, or Concerning Perfection in Virtue*. Gregory employs three elements in the biblical story of Moses as a framework within which to describe the spiritual quest and progress of the individual soul's unfolding relationship to God. Zeroing in on the "spiritual sense" of scripture, Gregory describes God's progressive self-revelation to Moses under three metaphors: light (in the Burning Bush and the Pillar of Fire by night), an intermediate state (symbolized by the Pillar of Cloud that led by day), and darkness.[10]

Some of the more theologically astute observers of the human condition have also been gifted poets. Major theological storytellers include the likes of Dante Alighieri and John Milton (1608–74). Dante's monumental religious epic *The Divine Comedy* holds a mirror to the dominant Christian beliefs and worldview of his age, as did Milton's *Paradise Lost* and *Paradise Regained* during the Reformation era. As Dante wanders through a trilevel world beyond, the Roman poet Virgil is his guide amid the nether regions of hell and purgatory, and the beloved Beatrice becomes his psychopomp through the upper reaches of paradise. Milton's elegant epic pair addresses the wellsprings of cosmic injustice and explored the hidden meanings of Satan's temptation of Christ in the desert. Both Dante and Milton became embroiled in political and theological disputes and spent much of their adult lives living on the fringes of "orthodoxy," but their masterworks were nonetheless enduringly eloquent compendia of theological themes.[11] Chapter 8 will reprise the essential role of narrative theology in the context of hagiography, and mystical literature and spirituality. Resources on these and countless other Christian "classics" are widely available in English translation. Because comparable Islamic sources remain far less accessible, the following section provides greater detail.

Like no category of Christian theological literature, sayings of the Prophet function uniquely as both a "divinely revealed" and a "postscriptural" source, and thus this crucial source merits special attention here. The Hadith literature does not take the form of a self-consciously theological project but does include many theological themes in narrative form. Unlike the Qur'ān, the Hadith do contain material about Muhammad's daily life, and in often striking detail—his dislike for certain foods, his ways of dealing with people, for example. Much more important for present purposes are the brief narratives that reveal deeper themes and concerns of the early community. Sections in the major Hadith collections most likely to contain theological themes are those on God's transcendent unity (*tawḥīd*); faith (*īmān*); the virtues or excellent qualities of Muhammad and his Companions, and of the Qur'ān (*faḍā'il*); virtuous behavior (*adab*); God's dominion over human affairs (*qadr*); the active remembrance of God (dhikr); piety/asceticism and the softening of hearts (zuhd, ar-raqā'iq); repentance (tawba); and eschatology (al-qiyāma [the resurrection], al-janna [the garden], an-nār [the fire], al-fitan [end-time strife], as-sā'ah [the Hour]).

Accounts often describe interchanges between the Prophet and interlocutors, whether members of the Muslim community or outsiders bent on confrontation. Sometimes Muhammad is the one posing the question: a Companion named Mu'ādh ibn Jabal was once riding behind the Prophet when Muhammad asked him if he knew what claim God has over his servants and what claim servants have on God. After Mu'ādh replied that God and his Messenger know best, Muhammad went on to explain that God's claim on his servants is that they worship God and him alone, while the servants' claim on God is that God not punish an individual who does not worship other than God. When Mu'ādh asked whether he should spread that consoling message to the community, the Prophet forbade him to do so, lest people not yet fully schooled in the meaning of "worship" conclude that merely professing their fidelity to God was sufficient to merit them a heavenly reward.[12]

A subgenre of Hadith features Muhammad's Companions, much as the Acts of the Apostles spotlights Jesus' principal disciples. One brief exchange with interesting theological implications finds a Muslim in search of advice confessing to a Companion named Hudhayfa ibn al-Yamān that he fears that he may become a hypocrite (munāfiq)—virtually a technical term for fair-weather supporters of the Prophet who profess their loyalty in public only to undermine Muhammad's designs behind his back. People relied on Hudhayfa for advice on this topic, for Muhammad had designated him as the community's expert on the subject. Hudhayfa reassures the questioner he needn't worry, for hypocrites do not fear hypocrisy.[13]

Countless such stories deal with a full range of theologically significant questions, including intercession, individual prayer, acts of kindness, asking forgiveness from God, and criteria for heavenly reward. Chapter 1 indicated the importance of the Hadith in which the Prophet responds to inquiries as to the meaning of certain Qur'ānic texts, so that the Hadith functions in effect as an exegetical commentary. Some of the more interesting sayings are cast in the form of a dream or vision, which then forms the core of a larger teaching Hadith. One day one of Muhammad's Companions, Sa'īd ibn Jubayr, asked whether any of his friends had seen a shooting star (a good omen) the night before. Husayn said he had, but confessed that he had been awake not because he was keeping prayerful vigil, but because he had been stung by a scorpion. When Sa'īd asked what

Husayn did about it, he replied that he had recourse to a charm, since he had heard that Muhammad had said that charms are useless except against the evil eye or scorpion sting.

Saʿīd responded, however, that according to another report from the trusted Companion Ibn ʿAbbās, charms were nevertheless a serious problem. According to a Hadith from Ibn ʿAbbās, Saʿīd went on, Muhammad recalled that he had once "seen" several prophets, one of whom had a small group of people with him, another with only a few, and a third with no companions. Then the Prophet saw a large throng brought toward him, and he imagined it to be his own community, but was told that this crowd was in fact Moses and his community. He was then instructed to gaze out to the horizon, where stood an enormous gathering. This, Muhammad was informed, was his community—including seventy thousand strong destined to enter paradise effortlessly. Muhammad returned home after recounting this "vision." The people gathered outside his house speculated among themselves as to what one could possibly assure someone of eternal reward without suffering or accountability. Muhammad emerged, and they asked him to clarify, so he told them that those were people who neither practiced charms or omens nor encouraged others to do so, but trusted completely in God alone. At that, someone in the crowd stood and asked Muhammad to assure him of membership among the elect, and he did; then another man made the same request and was granted his wish.[14]

Parables or similitudes (*mathal*, pl. *amthāl*) form another noteworthy subgenre of narrative in the Hadith literature. Muhammad fashions an analogy to describe the nature of the knowledge and guidance with which God sent him, one whose general contours are reminiscent of the New Testament parable of the Sower, only using the metaphor of various types of soils' receptivity to nurturing rain. Good ground soaks up the rain readily and produces much verdure. Terrain above cisterns, on the other hand, collects the water so that people and livestock can drink from it. Some land is simply barren, however, and neither produces growth nor gathers water. Just so, some people truly understand Muhammad's message, others receive the message and pass it along to others, while still others pay the message no heed.[15] Two other parables also use water imagery, in a different way. One tells of Muhammad going to a cistern in advance of his people so that they would then follow him and receive a drink after which they would never thirst again. A variation on the first describes Muhammad's cistern (the wellspring of the revealed message) in detail: it is so large that it would take a month to travel around its circumference; its water is silver, it emits the fragrance of musk, and the vessels that surround it are like stars.[16]

Other parables use very different imagery. In one, a person kindles a fire to which moths and other insects are attracted; they would all perish in the flames if not for the efforts of Muhammad, though some fall in spite of his attempts to protect them with his teaching.[17] According to another, Muhammad likened the prophetic revelation to a beautiful house that inspires admiration in all who view it. They invariably notice, however, that one brick is missing in a corner, and remark on the house's incompleteness. That brick is, of course, Muhammad, who at last perfected the edifice.[18] One of the more unusual parables likens Muhammad "and the message with which God sent [him]" to an agitated man who arrived before a people, announcing that he had seen an advancing army. If they would save themselves, they must run for their lives. Some took his advice and escaped under cover of night. Some, alas, dismissed the warning of this "naked herald" and stayed in their camp, where the assault troops slaughtered them as they slept. These two groups represent people who accept Muhammad's preaching, and those who rebel and reject the Prophet.[19]

Key theological themes in the Hadith cover an intriguing variety of topics, many of which eventually became grist for the mill of systematic theologians. The historical nexus between the process of formal validation of the Hadith in the major ninth-century collections and the emergence of major theological schools during the ninth and tenth centuries is complex and in its relative infancy as a subject of critical academic investigation. Nevertheless, one can conclude that at least in very general terms the correspondence between the most prominent theological themes in the Hadith and the questions taken up by the main proponents of kalām suggests important mutual influences.

Chapter 2 alluded to the importance of the Hadith on apocalyptic themes. The following are several more of the most important theological themes discussed in the Hadith. Short sections on the divine names appear in some Hadith collections, emphasizing simply the importance of those names in prayer, and without the kind of analysis one finds in theological works. Though ancient Muslim tradition, beginning with the Qur'ān, insists on equality among God's prophets, many Hadiths raise questions about the relative ranks among the various prophets, with specific concern for the ultimate superiority of Muhammad, and of his faith community over the others. Most of the major Hadith collectors feature "miracle" stories under various headings, particularly that of the "virtues" of the Prophet and his predecessors and Companions. Some collections include separate sections on the meaning of seeing Muhammad in dreams, and whether human beings will be capable of ocular vision of God in the next life. Questions of prophetic intercession (*shafāʿa*) at the final judgment also find a place.[20]

As in the history of Christian theological literature, postprophetic Muslim authors have produced scores of literary works very much in the genre of narrative theology. Among the dozens of important examples, here is a tiny sampling. An influential prose genre, the imaginative narrative (*hikāya*), became an important vehicle for reflection on significant theological themes, especially in Arabic and Persian. Ibn Sīnā (d. 1037, aka Avicenna), from Bukhara (now in Uzbekistan) in central Asia, is best known as a prominent Muslim philosopher. His talents were not limited to crafting philosophical treatises in the more technical sense, however. Ibn Sīnā also wrote three short prose works, and Shihāb ad-Din Suhrawardī (d. 1191) contributed important works in the genre. Themes in this "visionary recital" genre tend toward journey imagery in which the hero or seeker embarks on a quest through the cosmos.[21]

Other narrative forms choose more down-to-earth settings. Major Muslim didactic poets through the ages have fashioned stories into one of the most effective teaching devices for conveying theologically significant content. Master storytellers all, authors like Sanāʾī (d. 1131), Saʿdī (d. 1292), and Rūmī (d. 1273), expand on Qurʾānic or other traditional tales already known to their readers or fashion anew imaginative scenarios in the form of fables or vignettes designed to teach some theological or ethical truth. Rūmī, for example, sometimes uses an animal fable as a setup for another (sometimes historically anchored) story in which he draws out a theological point. In his didactic masterwork *The Spiritual Couplets* (*Masnavī-yi maʿnavī*), Rūmī retells a tale from the widely popular *Kalila and Dimna*, about a lion and the animals he held captive in his web of intimidation. After losing too many of their ranks to the lion's regular dinner raids, the animals offered to save the lion the trouble of the hunt by sacrificing one of their own daily. At first the lion king argued that he would prefer to rely on his own efforts. To persuade the lion that trust in God and their promises was preferable, the captives told him the story of a man who bribed Solomon to carry him to Hindustan (on his carpet) to escape death, only to have death meet him there. The lion saw their point, and the animals fulfilled their grim contract until the hare's turn came. He asked the others to let him try a trick to confound the lion with God's own wisdom of choosing the weak to best the mighty. With their reluctant consent, the hare arrived late at the angry king's throne and explained that he had been en route with a second hare when another lion snatched it despite their warning that he would only incur the wrath of a more powerful competitor. Determined to eliminate the trespassing predator, the king ordered the hare to take him to his alleged adversary. The hare jumped on the lion's back and took him to a well; looking down, the lion saw his enemy, and when he leapt in to attack it, the hare escaped.

Pointing out that such is the price for denying God's providence, Rumī continues to riff poetically on the themes of the futility of trying to circumvent God's designs through one's own stubborn choices, God's gift of wisdom to the apparently weak and insignificant, and the folly of relying on one's own rational cleverness. Rumī, master of the frame tale, then segues into a more historically anchored anecdote. He explains that the victorious hare returns to exhort his fellow captives that their challenge now is to struggle against their own inward base tendencies. The brave hare illustrates this new theological point by telling a story of his own, about a Byzantine emperor who sent an ambassador to the caliph 'Umar. When the emissary inquires at Medina where he might find the caliph's palace, the citizens inform him that the caliph's abode is a spiritual refuge discernible only to the pure of heart. After wandering about town, the ambassador spots 'Umar under a palm tree and approaches as a humble seeker. 'Umar responds kindly to his questions about the spiritual life, and Rumī is again off into metaphorical musings on how the wise understand the balance between God's absolute power and human moral freedom and responsibility.[22] Living during the thirteenth century, Rumi was quite familiar with issues that had exercised the minds of systematic theologians for centuries already, but he preferred to address them in a less formal and more entertaining setting. We will return to the central theme of God's determination of events in chapter 4.

## THE EVOLUTION OF CREEDAL FORMULATIONS

### Christian Creeds

Three Christian creedal formulae have been prominent as summaries of the faith in many denominations and have been used in ritual or liturgical settings to varying degrees. First, the Apostles' Creed, so-called because it is believed to reprise authentic apostolic teachings, may represent an expanded version of a formula dating back to the earliest Christian generation.[23] In twelve "articles," the creed goes as follows:

> I believe in God, the Father almighty,
> Creator of heaven and earth;
> And in Jesus Christ, His only Son, Our Lord,
> who was conceived by the Holy Spirit,

Born of the Virgin Mary,
Suffered under Pontius Pilate,
Was crucified, died, and was buried.
He descended into hell;
The third day he rose again from the dead;
He ascended into heaven,
Sits at the right hand of God, the Father almighty;
From thence he shall come to judge
the living and the dead.
I believe in the Holy Spirit,
the holy Catholic Church;
the communion of saints,
the forgiveness of sins,
the resurrection of the body,
and life everlasting. Amen.[24]

During the early patristic Age, Christian theologians expended a great deal of energy and attention on the articulation of correct doctrine in the process of ruling out unacceptable, or heretical, interpretations of ancient sources and tradition. The role of the first ecumenical councils in anathematizing errant views in turn led to the elaboration of creedal statements aimed more at doctrinal clarity than the earlier kerygmatic summaries. These new creeds sought to provide minicompendia of essential beliefs with an integrated set of affirmations that clearly corrected the mistaken beliefs of various heretical groups. One such patristic age text is known as the Athanasian Creed, though it was probably written, or at least revised, by Ambrose (d. 397) rather than by Athanasius (d. 373) and has been attributed to a variety of other Fathers as well. Likely written between 381 and 428 (during the Apollinarian controversy but before the Nestorian and Eutychian disputes), the Athanasian Creed has a noteworthy feature in common with the early Muslim creeds in that it retains very prominent condemnations of incorrect doctrinal views. Various Protestant churches, including Episcopalian/Anglican and Lutheran, have used the creed in liturgical contexts, and Roman Catholic tradition has ensconced the text into parts of its Liturgy of the Hours (or Divine Office).[25]

More widely used by Christian denominations, especially Roman Catholicism, the latter of two "Nicene" Creeds dispenses with the harsh anathemas of the Athanasian and expands on the basic articles enunciated in the Apostles' Creed. It was incorporated officially into the Roman liturgy early in the eleventh century, after many years of liturgical use on a regional basis. This formulation includes all of the affirmations of the Apostles' Creed, and in virtually the same order, but it adds in the context of its first reference to the three persons of the Trinity that the "Son" is "one in being with the Father"—that is, of the same substance (homoousios). Toward the end, after what would have approximated the conclusion of the Apostles' Creed, the text also adds another pointed reference to the relationship among the persons of the Trinity: "Holy Spirit, the Lord, the giver of life, who proceeds from the Father and the Son. With the Father and the Son he is worshipped and glorified. He has spoken through the Prophets." The Nicene Creed thus underscores several key issues in Christology and Trinitarian theology hammered out during the earlier church councils.[26]

## Muslim Creeds

Arguably the earliest Islamic creedal summaries appear in Qur'ānic texts that enjoin Muslims to believe in God and his Messenger (Muhammad), in the Qur'ān and the sacred texts given to his predecessor prophets, and in God's angels, scriptures, and the day of judgment (4:136; see also 2:285). Elements of the most basic profession of faith, the shahāda, abound in the sacred scripture, affirming the transcendent unity of God and the "Apostleship" of Muhammad, but the text also elaborates on the second element fairly often. Prophetic revelation is the bedrock of the Islamic creed, and an extended version of that element in this more basic statement of belief goes like this: "Proclaim: We believe in God, and what was revealed to us and to Abraham, Ismāʿīl, Isaac, Jacob, and the Tribes, and what was given to Moses and Jesus, and what was given to [all] the prophets from their Lord. We make no distinction among them." (2:136; also 3:84).

The famous "Hadith of Gabriel" reinforces these summaries and expands on them. In this tradition, an unidentified young man approaches Muhammad, sits down before him, and begins to interrogate him about the fundamentals of the religion of Islam. The questioner, traditionally identified as Gabriel, asks the Prophet in turn to explain the meaning of the terms islām, īmān, and ihsān. In the first category, Muhammad puts the so-called Five Pillars (affirmation that there is no deity but God and Muhammad is his Messenger, ritual prayer, alms, Ramadan fasting, and pilgrimage). Faith (īmān) moves a step beyond the basic attitude of surrender (islām), and the Hadith describes the core elements of its content. To the five items mentioned in the Qur'ānic summaries (God, his Messengers, his books, his angels, and the last day), the Hadith adds explicitly a sixth implicit in the general concept of the last day, namely, the "measuring out." It also describes (here under the heading of ihsān, "doing what is beautiful") an apocalyptic theme characterizing the end of time, that of "the

Hour," in which all things humankind has become accustomed to will be definitively overturned. *Ihsān* accordingly has a strong ethical quality, reminding one to behave "as if God saw me, even if I do not see God."[27]

Further elaborations of the fundamentals of the Muslim creed were gradually hammered out as more technical formulations during the century or so after Muhammad's death. Known by the term *'aqīda* (pl. *'aqā'id*), early creedal formulations are not so much professions of faith that function liturgically (as do several Christian creeds and the Muslim *shahāda*) as they are summaries of theological positions adopted by famous scholars or schools of thought. Creeds therefore tend to include statements meant to respond as correctives to misconceived (or even malicious) articulations of core beliefs, as was the case with various Christian creedal statements. In other words, they function rather as proclamations to the world beyond the core of "true believers" that those who hold otherwise are on notice that they have in effect situated themselves outside the community. They are, one might say, low-key polemics for anathematizing unbelievers. Beginning around the mid-tenth century, various authors began producing more detailed accounts in the emerging genre of heresiography.

Most of the important early creeds date from between about 900 and 950. A useful example of the genre is the very brief so-called Fiqh Akbar I (or "Greater Learning"). All of its ten articles are clearly responses to disputed questions, and since neither the transcendent oneness of God nor the prophetic mandate of Muhammad was among those, even these most foundational tenets receive no mention here. Here is the text of this creed, with brief explanations inserted at each article:

1. We do not regard any person as unbeliever on the grounds of sinfulness, and we do not deny that such a person has faith. (Here the creed is responding explicitly to the cramped ecclesiology of the Kharijites, who dismissed all serious sinners as unbelievers devoid of faith.)

2. We command the acceptable and condemn what is hateful. (This underscores Islam's inherent ethical activism and condemns the quietism of the so-called Jabrīya. The latter argued that since God alone has the power to act, human beings are subject to moral compulsion [*jabr*], and one need not condemn behavior in which humans have no free choice.)

3. What affects you could not have passed you by, and what passes you by could not have affected you. (One of the creed's more enigmatic assertions counters the Qadarīya belief that human beings possess the capacity [*qadar*] to affect the events of their lives through pri-

mary agency and "free will." On the contrary, says the creed, God foreordains all things, and everything occurs exactly so—there are no humanly devised alternatives, no "what-ifs." Important political implications were among the key concerns behind the article: a ruler, for example, cannot be held solely responsible for an action or a policy that might otherwise betoken evil intent or corruption.)

4. We do not reject any of God's Messenger's Companions, nor do we give priority to any one of them. (Here and in article 5, the creed seeks to clarify questions associated with important differences between Sunni and Shi'i interpretations of early Islamic history, concerning the question of legitimate succession to the Prophet.)

5. Concerning the matter of [the conflict between] 'Uthmān and 'Ali [as to succession to leadership], we defer to God who is aware of the inmost hidden meanings of things. (Again steering a neutral course on contested matters of community governance, the fifth article refers to the outcome of the first *fitna,* the conflict that arose between 'Uthmān, third of the Rightly Guided Caliphs in Sunni reckoning, and 'Ali. The creed thereby seeks to avoid further dissension and recrimination as to guilt in the murder of 'Uthmān, which many Sunni sources blamed on 'Ali's supporters.)

6. Understanding of religion is preferable to understanding in acquired learning and law. (In the final five articles, questions of religious knowledge and faith come to the fore. Article 6 offers insight into the priority of matters of faith over expertise in religious and legal disciplines.)

7. Diversity of opinion [among religious scholars] is a sign of God's mercy to the community. (Some later theorists would clarify the assertion by insisting that this applied only to legal questions and not to doctrinal or theological issues.)

8. Anyone who accepts in faith all that one is expected to hold, but remains agnostic as to whether Jesus and Moses are among [God's] Messengers is an unbeliever. (Commentators on the creed provide precious little insight as to why fashioners of the statement would have considered this a necessary addition.)

9. Anyone who asserts that he does not know if God is in the heavens or on the earth is an unbeliever. (Around the time of this creed, however, the notion that God abides neither in heaven nor on earth but cannot be contained in any place became a standard theologi-

cal distinction. In fact, it may be that this article was meant as a critique of the "spiritualizing" tendency behind the notion of divine omnipresence.)

10. Anyone who asserts that he knows nothing of the suffering of the grave is a member of the Jahmīya who are bound for eternal punishment. (A small, little-understood faction, named after Jahm ibn Safwān [d. 746], held positions on the nature of the deity that were probably more influential, and controversial, than their eschatology. Traditional beliefs implicitly affirmed here include the notions that the newly interred deceased will be interrogated by two no-nonsense angels, Munkar and Nakīr, and will experience a frightening sense of confinement.)[28]

Later *'aqā'id* became increasingly more detailed in their definitions of articles of faith and exhibit varying polemical orientations, depending on the errors they sought to expose.

Some of the creeds were not addressed to the wayward among those who claimed to be Muslims, but fulfill a less polemical, more basic catechetical function as a guide to correct belief rather than a critique of error. These works, in turn, paved the way for more systematic treatises by representatives of what would become the principal "schools" of Islamic systematic theology (*kalām*). In the next chapter, a brief overview of how some of the main theological themes developed will provide essential background for an appreciation of the historical unfolding of these schools and their major exponents.

. . .

An important theological principle in the narrative heritages of both faith traditions is the conviction of active divine providence, reaching back to the origin of human history and pervading the "present" of the early periods of the two communities' formation. On a more broadly cultural level, both traditions have likewise fostered creative and imaginative theologically fecund works of narrative art. Islam and Christianity use narrative theology in rather distinctive ways. Christianity's earliest uses of narrative theology occur in scripture itself, and chiefly either in the form of extended accounts of the life of Jesus or as a link to pre-Christian sacred history. By contrast, Islamic narrative theology in more extended forms (with a few exceptions, most notably the story of the prophet Joseph) is far less evident in the Qur'ān than in the Hadith. Qur'ānic allusions to prophetic narratives are generally piecemeal, and neither there nor in the

Hadith do we find any extended comprehensive narratives of the life of Muhammad.

Additional attention accorded here to the theological themes and narrative genres of the Hadith follows from my identification of the Hadith as "postscriptural." The implicit argument here is that while the major Hadith collections derived their authoritative status from an exhaustive canonical vetting, they are very different from the apocryphal texts eventually culled from the Christian scriptures. One could argue that, as the record of the founder's words and deeds, the Hadith are formally and thematically analogous to the New Testament, but their function remains unique to Islam in that they are not on the same level theologically as the Qur'ān. The formation of the Hadith literature shares with the shaping of the New Testament a multiplicity of individuals involved in compiling the various "authoritative" collections, but Muslim tradition never formally proclaimed a single unified "canon" of the Hadith as Christians did with the New Testament texts (in addition to the "six" main collections, dozens of others remain useful and important).

Both traditions rely to a certain extent on historical narrative as revealed in their sacred scriptures—and while the Gospels were a novel and unique literary genre, they retained some similarity to the historical books of the Old Testament in narrating special events, whereas the Qur'ān is presented as the direct speech of God. Although there are narrative elements, the Qur'ān is not an account of God's action among humankind; it is God's own account, so to speak.

Both great traditions began to refine specific points of belief particularly in response to views increasingly identified as theologically eccentric, whether willfully so or not. To that end, both traditions generated a variety of early creedal formulations, but only within Christianity did these creeds come to play a formal role in ritual. Also by way of contrast, Christian creeds have typically focused explicitly on affirmative matters of doctrine, whereas their Islamic parallels function rather more reactively and thus tend to frame issues in terms of at least implicit rejection of unacceptable positions. One could suggest, in other words, that Christian creeds are statements of faith, intended for internal use within the core community, while their Islamic parallels are theological summaries and clarifications intended to distinguish core community beliefs from those espoused on the periphery. Finally, though both traditions produced multiple creedal formulations, none of the more numerous Muslim creeds achieved the authoritative and definitive status of the major Christian creeds.

# CHAPTER 4

# The Emergence of
# Theological Disciplines

As narrative has morphed into creed, creedal formulations have historically often given impetus to developments in systematic theology as an intellectual religious discipline. They have evolved in complexity and sophistication through the early and middle periods of the two traditions' histories. In the story of both Christian and Islamic thought, systematic thinking became an essential vehicle for theological content as the faith communities expanded into new cultural, social, intellectual, and linguistic contexts and adapted accordingly the language and logic in which they communicated their creeds. In the section that follows, I will briefly discuss a few of the many major doctrinal themes that emerged and how Christian and Muslim thinkers began to confront and sort out the problems and questions that arose. Then I will explore, again in summary fashion, some of the more influential "schools" of systematic theology that first addressed those problems comprehensively, and the role of their most important theologians.

## EMERGING THEOLOGIES: EARLY
## PROBLEMS AND QUESTIONS

Creedal statements provide important hints as to the earliest theological problems with which the early generations of Christian and Muslim scholars struggled, and to some of the contending interest groups within the larger communities of believers. Here I will expand on those hints, interweaving themes from both great traditions where appropriate.

Christian authors began to engage in the rudiments of systematic theology during the patristic period. Church fathers were not simply inclined toward speculation as such, but the intellectual climate of Hellenistic culture presented early Christian thinkers with an important challenge: how to translate the essential concepts of a faith tradition rooted in a reinterpretation of Semitic sources and culture into terms adaptable to the spread of Christianity to a Greco-Roman Gentile world. The initial transcultural evolution of basic Christian concepts had begun with the writing of the Greek New Testament. There we see traces of an already complex process in which the Greek-writing authors, working a generation or two (or perhaps longer) after the death of Jesus, recast the teaching of the Aramaic-speaking Jesus and his early followers in Hellenistic molds.[1] Early Christian theologians began defining essential themes in a variety of historical and cultural contexts as Christian communities appeared across the eastern Mediterranean basin. Muslim scholars similarly first confronted thorny theological issues as Arab conquests facilitated Islam's spread beyond the Arabian Peninsula into parts of the Byzantine Empire.

## Images of God and Models of Revelation

To understand the spirit of a faith tradition, an appreciation of the power and symbolic influence of prevailing images of God is essential. Members of a given faith community seem generally inclined to assume that the people in the next row for Friday mosque prayer or those sitting just down the pew in church conceive of God much as they themselves do. Though this may be true in a very general way, many Christians and Muslims might be surprised, perhaps shocked, at the nuances and diversity that characterize images of God represented within a local community or even a given family. In fact, a Christian attending services on Sunday could conceivably share more in his or her personal experience of God with a Muslim stranger who worships on Friday across town than with fellow Christians. For example, a given Christian may conceive of God as more judgmental and severe than a Muslim who believes that God's mercy always takes precedence, as many Muslims do—a reality quite contrary to the assumption now common among many non-Muslims that the deity Muslims worship must surely be a dark, despotic tyrant.

Under the circumstances, it is hardly surprising that there is a wide spectrum of views and disagreements among Muslims and Christians with respect to the question "Do Muslims and Christians worship the same God?" Many Christians and Muslims would answer in the negative. In fact, some Muslims insist that translations of the Qur'ān should retain the Arabic word *Allāh* rather than translating it as "God," precisely because of the significant theological differences in the traditions with respect to how they define or describe the supreme reality. Many Christians are similarly convinced that "this Allāh" is decidedly not "their" God. One striking peculiarity in all of this is that if asked whether they claim the "God of the Old Testament" as their own, many, if not most, Christians would reply in the affirmative while in the next breath denouncing "Allāh" as an alien deity. What is odd about this state of affairs is that perceived incompatibilities between Allāh and Christianity's triune God incarnate in Jesus are arguably no more problematic from a personal spiritual perspective than those between the God of the Old Testament and the "Christian" God.

The "Throne Verse" is one of the most important Qur'ān ic texts on the divine reality. Its imagery clearly emphasizes God's perfect transcendence, and its references to the heavens and the divine throne have made the text the most popular choice as an inscription around the domes of mosques:

> God: there is no deity but He; the Living, the Everlasting. Neither slumber nor sleep overcomes Him. To Him belongs all that the heavens and earth encompass. Who can intercede with Him, except by his leave? He knows all that surrounds [created beings], while they can grasp nothing of what He knows, except as He chooses. His Throne stretches across heaven and earth; sovereignty over them tires Him not, for He is the Exalted, the Magnificent. (Q 2:255)

Christianity and Islam share a number of important features in their models of divine revelation. These shared aspects include several basic presuppositions about God and humanity. One is that human beings are incapable of discerning fully the ultimate truths without divine assistance. Another is that God has been actively engaged in human history, supplying the needed aid in various forms—most notably in the form of individuals commissioned to guide humanity toward the divine truth. A third important theme is the conviction that human beings do not always attend to that guidance, preferring instead to reject the divine initiative and any human beings sent to announce it. Fourth, both traditions exhibit an implicit conviction that divine disclosure is a process, a progressive unfolding accommodated to humanity's limited capacity for receiving and acting on the ultimate truths. Finally, both Christian and Islamic models of revelation presuppose that though God never ceases to engage humankind with reminders of the message, there is a temporal limit to "formal revelation" in the sense that Jesus and Muhammad represent the definitive message.

On the other hand, both traditions have articulated those presuppositions in often very different ways. Christian conceptions of revelation begin with Old Testament images of a God engaged intensely in communication with a long line of individuals chosen for their aptness to receive and pass along the message, notwithstanding glaring faults and limitations. Images of this revealing God span a wide spectrum: walking and chatting with Adam in the garden; instructing Noah to save a remnant of humankind from imminent divine destruction; calling Abraham to sacrifice his only son to prove his commitment to God; commissioning Moses from the Burning Bush and there revealing the ultimate divine name (I am who am); thundering forth with the Law on Sinai. Whereas God often spoke through "angels" in the Torah, prophets like Samuel, Nathan, Elijah, and Elisha became the principal intermediaries through the long histories of the Judges and of Israel's monarchy.

The Hebrew scriptures speak in colorful and moving terms of the means by which God connected with his prophets, as in Elijah's terrifying experience of unfolding discovery that God was not in the whirlwind nor in the earthquake nor in the fire, but in the "still small voice" (1 Kings 19:9–18). Although God occasionally spoke "directly" to Israel's leaders, the biblical record of that kind of more intimate contact focuses on revelation through prophets, particularly as manifest in the works attributed to specific individuals. For the great prophets Isaiah, Jeremiah, and Ezekiel (as well as the so-called minor figures such as Amos and Hosea), fear-filled encounters with God continued in the tradition of the earlier prophets, but with the additional impact of their committing the message to writing. Expressions that commonly preface the "text" of a revelation to the prophets include "Thus says the Lord" and "The word of the Lord came to me . . ." Here the God who revealed himself still delivered a sometimes incisive critique of the behavior of leaders and their people, but now increasingly the message emphasized divine forbearance and mercy. In the Wisdom literature (among the Writings of the Hebrew scriptures), the biblical authors hear the divine voice in yet another key and pass it along as the advice of a kindly paternal teacher.

New Testament and subsequent early Christian authors reoriented the fundamental understanding of revelation. Now God revealed himself directly in the "living Word" of Jesus Christ. Their task was less focused on describing how God had spoken to *them* as such, and more on articulating how Jesus embodied the divine communication and how the Old Testament texts had been foreshadowing this culmination of God's self-disclosure from the start. Now the mediating presence through whom God spoke to the inspired New Testament authors was the Holy Spirit, also adumbrated in the ancient scriptures but now fulfilling an expanded role in the divine dispensation.

From the Islamic perspective, prophets have played a more explicit, more prominent, and more consistent role in mediating the divine message since day one of their sacred history. Whereas Christians have typically regarded the major figures in pre-Israelite history rather as "patriarchs" than prophets, Muslims believe that the prophetic line began with Adam himself, continued through Seth to Noah, Abraham, Isaac, Ismāʿīl (Ishmael), Jacob, Joseph, Moses, and Aaron. Among other Old Testament figures, two of the kings of Israel, David and Solomon, rank as major prophets; Jonah and Job play notable roles as well, while Lot and Ezra are minor figures mentioned in many lists of prophets. In addition, Hūd, Sālih, and Shuʿayb are generally identified as uniquely "Arabian" prophets, since they were sent to tribes of (or near) the Arabian Peninsula—ʿĀd, Thamūd, and Midian.

Prophets fulfill two principal functions in the Islamic tradition. First, they deliver a revealed message to whomever God sends them. Most of the prophets go to a specific regional population, but a few go forth on a universal mission. All of the divine emissaries are known by the Arabic term *nabī*, but those to whom God gives a sacred text addressed to all peoples are known by the more specific term *rasūl*, "messenger." The latter category includes Moses (who brought the Torah), David (gifted with the *zabūr*, Psalms), Jesus (whose message was embodied in the *injīl*, or Gospel), and Muhammad (who recited the Qur'ān). The Qur'ān makes it clear in several texts (e.g., 2:136, 29:46) that Muslims are to consider all of the prophets equal in their exalted status, all delivering essentially the same message. God saw fit to continue this long line of revelatory initiatives, including those of the various universal Messengers, because human beings have so often declined to accept the divine disclosure. Secondly, the tradition describes the overall role of prophets as that of bringing their peoples "from darkness into light." Early theological thinkers in both Christian and Islamic traditions were heirs to that mission, sorting out contentious claims that arose very early in their histories.

## Early Movements and Theological Themes

Formal and systematic theological disciplines evolved over a period of several centuries in both Christian and Islamic contexts. But Christian and Muslims thinkers began early on in their histories to struggle with a host of important theological questions. Before looking at several major systematic theologians and schools of thought, it will be helpful to describe how some of the pristine theological problems took shape.

Early Christian apologists and church fathers addressed the increasingly apparent problem of divergent views about the nature of revelation and how one knows the truth, as well as the multiplicity of interest groups claiming authenticity and primacy as Christians. Questions concerning the articulation of distinctively Christian concepts of God (Christology and Trinitarian themes) and the nature of the church (ecclesiology) are among the most important formative issues. (Chapter 8 will address the critical question of *gnosis,* or authentic knowledge, as a major ingredient in the spiritual life.)

Christian scholars wanted to demonstrate that Jesus represented both a sacred continuity with the old dispensation and a departure from it, at least in the sense that his coming fulfilled all prophecies and expectations of a promised Messiah. The apostolic fathers generated a whole new lexicon, describing Christ as the Name, the Hope, the Divine Blood, the One Teacher, the New Man, the New Leaven, God's mouthpiece, the Head of the Body, the Bishop of believers. His Cross was the "Father's planting" whose branches are the faithful, the "derrick" that lifts the stones of the New Temple into place (Ignatius of Antioch). Christ was the Messenger, the Royal Son, the Ransom, the Incorrupt, the Healer, Wisdom and Light (Epistle of Barnabas, c. 135). Irenaeus called Christ and the Spirit the "two hands of God" at Creation, and Clement of Alexandria (d. 215) affirmed the equality of Son and Spirit to the Father.

Tertullian was the first to speak of "person" in relation to "trinity," insisting on both divine and human "natures" in Christ, with the Son "emanating" from the Father as a beam from the Sun. His was a type of "Spirit-Christology," in which the Word (*logos*) in the form of the Spirit assumes humanity; it is thus the Spirit who performs miracles while Jesus' humanity undergoes suffering. In a prime example of "Logos-Christology," Origen addressed the question of the incarnation directly by explaining that the Logos entered a woman's womb, while Christ's "human" soul had, like all souls, preexisted from all eternity and was the mediator between his humanity and divinity. Whereas the human soul undergoes suffering, the Logos does not. Though Origen's Christology was far from the final formulation adopted by the early ecumenical councils, it was he who introduced the Greek concepts of nature (*physis*), personality (*hypostasis*), substance (*ousia*), being of the same substance (*homoousios*), and the divine-human (*theanthropos*).[2]

During the fourth and fifth centuries, subsequent church fathers fur-

ther honed the language of Christology and Trinity, and officially acceptable formulations emerged piecemeal as the councils addressed one after
another the unacceptable or "heretical" formulations. Nicaea (325) condemned Arianism's assertions that the Logos (Christ) is the "first Creature"
(i.e., not divine), and that the Spirit in turn is the first creation of the Logos;
it affirmed that Son and Spirit were "of the same substance" (*homoousios*) with the Father. Constantinople I (381) condemned Apollinarianism's
opposite claims that while Christ had a human body and soul, his human
"spirit" was supplanted by the Logos: Jesus was fully divine, but not fully
human and experienced no "moral development." The Council of Ephesus
(431) condemned in its eight "canons" the claims of Nestorius (d. 451)
that there were two separate *persons* in Christ, who was united to the
Father only through his will and not "substantially." Finally (for present
purposes), the Council of Chalcedon (451) condemned the "Monophysite"
views of Eutyches (d. 454), who denied the coexistence of separate divine
and human natures in Christ. As we shall see shortly, early Muslim scholars dealt with analogous though perhaps less terminologically complex
problems concerning the divine, uncreated nature of the word of God.[3]

Much welcome recent scholarship has begun to provide a picture of
Islamic religious thought that is far richer and more nuanced than that suggested by the popular tidy dichotomy between orthopraxy (right action)
and orthodoxy (right opinion/belief). Editions and translations of works
of dozens of major Muslim theological authors, as well as more detailed
and better integrated histories of Islamic thought, reveal an intellectual
climate in which "theologians" play a critical role in the greater academy.
Some of the more adventurous philosophers and theologians have indeed
starred in major adversarial dramas through the centuries. New research
has, however, begun to put those roles in sharper perspective, especially by
clarifying the biases of highly partisan sources hitherto so largely responsible for our understanding of the story.[4]

One can suggest a rough analogy with the origins of Christian systematic theological thinking in the adaptation of Islamic tradition to the non-
Semitic contexts of newly conquered territories. Prior to the late eighth
or early ninth century, the principal theologically significant issues that
arose within the greater Muslim fold were rooted in divergences about the
makeup of community and related questions of authority and governance.
Chapter 2 described one of the first significant sources of division, the
conflict between 'Ali and the segment of his early supporters who disapproved of 'Ali's choice of mediation to resolve the standoff at the battle
of Siffin in 656. Beneath the obvious political significance of the "seces-

sion" of the Kharijites was the seed of an important theological/creedal concept, namely, criteria for claim to the title "Authentic Muslim." The Kharijites insisted that appeal to the Qur'ān must take precedence over all other options for deliberation and adjudication. Here lies the seed of later Muslim thinking about the nature of faith community, or "ummatology," for the Kharijites defined the true Muslim as one who is free of major sin. 'Ali thus became the prime exemplar for the unfaithful Muslim in that the dissenters accused him of giving human judgment priority over divine. In their preference for "charismatic community" over a "charismatic leader" ('Ali), the Kharijites effectively gave voice to what would become an important theological and heresiographical theme. Their distinction between "people of paradise" and the "people of hellfire" soon began to morph into a more complex ummatology in which the Kharijites seceded from the authentic community.[5]

In both Christian and Islamic traditions, all theological statements have political implications, and all political positions have theological implications. The ascendancy of the Umayyad clan as the first of many dynastic regimes through the history of Islamdom precipitated important questions that would become hallmarks of Islamic political theology. The Umayyads claimed to rule by direct divine authority, arguing that God's perfect and inscrutable control over human acts (*qadar*) rendered them impervious to human critique when they appeared to err ethically and/or religiously in their decisions. Umayyad attempts to elude criticism by an implicitly theological stance inspired opposition among various elements of Muslim society, who responded that God's predetermination of events, perfect as it was, nevertheless did not insulate malefactors from responsibility for their reprehensible deeds. Many scholars credit Ghaylān ad-Dimashqī (d. 720) with the first important articulation of an anti-predeterminist position, for his open refutation of claims of two Umayyad caliphs. Hasan al-Basrī (d. 728) further argued on Qur'ānic grounds that attempts to take cover under the shelter of divine predestination was futile, because they fly in the face of divine justice and undermine human moral responsibility. Later proponents continued to interpret the views of Ghaylān and Hasan until about the mid-ninth century, but by then the tide had turned decidedly in favor of a heavier emphasis on divine predetermination of events.[6] This theological turn represented in part a reaction to the Mu'tazilī "theology from below," which some believed attenuated God's power to the point that God was in effect subject to human strictures.

Further developments in thinking about "faith and works" emerged from concerns raised by various people now identified loosely as the postponers (murji'a) because of their views on whether human beings have the right to pronounce on the religious and ethical status of others. God alone, they argued, enjoys that prerogative, removing judgment as to who is a "true" Muslim from any human authority. Better described as disparate proponents of a theological theme rather than as a well-defined group or school of thought, the murji'a (or Murji'ites) raised important questions about the relationships among islām (basic surrender to God), īmān (more detailed assent in faith), and ihsān (putting islām and īmān into action). Key issues that would thereafter be taken up in detail by major theological schools included, for example, whether faith necessarily manifested itself in specific acts or was limited to a form of assent in the heart; whether one human being had the right to judge the quality of another person's faith; and whether faith was "quantifiable" and could be said to increase and/or decrease, or is a "fixed" quality defined as a type of knowledge of God.[7]

Questions of the limits of human freedom and ethical responsibility, and the judgment to which human beings are subject, naturally lead to further issues about Muslim eschatological beliefs. In basic theological terms, the Christian and Islamic traditions nowhere intersect more clearly than in their conceptions of the "four last things"—death, judgment, heaven, and hell. Early Jewish-Christian thought was informed by the distinctively Pharisaic belief (denied by the rival Sadducees) in resurrection and afterlife. From the earliest texts of the Qur'ān on, Muslim tradition likewise underscored human accountability under divine judgment in the next life. Conceptions of reward (the "garden," al-janna) and punishment (the "fire," jahannam, nār) developed soon thereafter.

A related shared notion is that of the resurrection of the body, at least as a general concept. The two larger traditions differ, however, with respect to specific imagery used to describe the immediate experience of life after death, the topography of the unseen world, and the specific function of hell. For example, the Muslim experience of judgment effectively begins in the tomb itself, with the interrogation of the angels Munkar and Nakīr. Imagery of the passageway between worlds is somewhat analogous, with Jesus' references to a "narrow" path paralleled by the Muslim concept of the perilous bridge (sirāt) spanning hellfire, into which unbelievers inevitably fall. But the notion of an intermediate state between realms, the separation (barzakh) or intermediate realm in which the soul sleeps prior to resurrection, is uniquely Islamic but functions at least partly in a way that is analogous to the generally discarded Christian concept of limbo.

Both traditions generally agree that reward in heaven is eternal, but many Muslim theologians (including, for example, Ibn Ḥazm and other traditionalists) insist that though hell will exist forever, some believers will experience needed purgation there but eventually win release to paradise. In other words, hell does double duty in Islamic thought and encompasses functions similar to those of the Christian purgatory.[8]

## MAJOR THEOLOGIANS AND THEOLOGICAL SCHOOLS

One can identify a number of major theological schools in the long history of Christian systematic theology. Here I will outline two Latin European schools whose influence shaped much of medieval and later thought—the Augustinian and Thomistic traditions—and I also mention one important and intriguing example of an alternative theological voice, that of Joachim of Fiore. I will conclude the consideration of the Christian side of the equation with an acknowledgment of the distinctive contributions of the so-called Eastern churches to the development of both uniquely Middle Eastern theologies and the foundations of Orthodox Christianities.

### Latin Theological Traditions

Augustine (354–430) was arguably the most influential of the Latin fathers of the church, not least of all because of the methodological foundations his thought provided for a number of later theologians, schools, and religious orders—and even for the thought of several major Reformers, including Luther and Calvin. Among the crucial formative influences on Augustine's thought were two movements eventually deemed heretical, namely, Donatism and Pelagianism. Theologically the Donatists shared with the Kharijites (by analogy) the view that only nonsinners were truly worthy of membership in the community of authentic believers. Holiness must be manifest in love-inspired observable actions, but Augustine countered that membership in the church depended on faith rather than on works alone.[9]

A Briton named Pelagius (c. 400) was arguing meanwhile, in a fine example of "theology from below," that human beings have no need of the extraordinary aid of divine "grace" and are inherently capable of responding to God's commands. He did not deny altogether that grace might be an additional boost, but insisted that human beings have access to adequate guidance from the gift of reason. Pelagius also denied that Adam's original sin was a genetic flaw plaguing all humankind and, in effect, dooming all to an ineluctable condition of sinfulness. Against Pelagius, Augustine countered that grace is necessary and available but cannot be earned.[10]

Here are some of the foundational themes in Augustine's theology. God the creator is the one eternal perfectly transcendent being who brought forth the universe from nothing. Augustine believed that true knowledge is possible and that all knowledge derives from the light of God, which suffuses creation and which is thereby available to the human intellect. Human beings can, alas, go wrong, because they have an innate tendency toward narcissism and are capable of breaking their original relationship with God, and indeed are so inclined because the will was corrupted through original sin. In their unredeemed state, human beings are incapable of choosing good. They require saving grace to be able to distinguish and choose between good and evil, and God makes that grace available through the sacramental life of the church. It is especially on this point that Augustine's thought has been subject to widely divergent interpretations. Some, like Luther and Calvin, have argued that Augustine's theology of grace implies divine predestination of human actions, because grace is irresistible. Salvation through grace within the context of membership in the church is thus ultimately, some would say, purely a matter of divine predilection independent of human works or merit. Like other major figures whose thought exemplifies "theology from above," however, Augustine was more concerned with clarifying who God is—that is, omnipotent and omniscient—than with defending human prerogatives.[11]

Augustinian themes perdured through late antiquity in the thought of such figures as Benedict of Nursia (d. 550), his successor leaders of the Benedictine order and later Fathers like (Benedictine) Gregory the Great. Isidore of Seville (d. 636), Bede (d. 735), and the great Carolingian theologian Alcuin kept knowledge of Augustine's texts alive through late antiquity. Among Augustine's most important medieval disciples, Anselm of Canterbury, is best known for his "ontological argument"—if one defines God as the reality than which humans can conceive of nothing greater, then human beings can know only that such a reality exists. His dictum *credo ut intelligam,* "I believe that I might understand," rearticulated Augustine's insistence that reason can operate properly only when building on faith. In other words, reason can support what one has already accepted in faith. Through the twelfth century, Abelard and Peter Lombard drew extensively on Augustine's thought, and Hugh of St. Victor's contemporaries dubbed him a second Augustine.[12]

During the thirteenth century, as I will describe shortly, proponents of Augustine's thought engaged in debate with the alternative views of Thomas Aquinas and his disciples. But yet another important Augustinian thread runs through the thought of the greatest of the thirteenth-century

Franciscan theologians, Bonaventure. He was familiar with Aristotelian thought as it was being introduced into Europe—that is, largely in the form of Latin Averroism (through translations of the works of Ibn Rushd)—but did not find the system as persuasive as did his contemporary Thomas Aquinas. Bonaventure leaned toward a more "mystical," less rationalistic epistemology. I will describe Bonaventure's work further in chapter 8; for the present, it will be useful to mention an intriguing anti-Augustinian development that occurred within Franciscanism.

Gerard of Borgo San Donnino (d. 1260) was a proponent of the so-called Spiritual Franciscan style and adapted the ecclesiology and apocalyptic worldview of Joachim of Fiore (d. 1202) as its theoretical underpinning. Joachim divided all of sacred history into three oddly overlapping stages using a Trinitarian model. The age of the Father encompasses the Old Testament period from Adam to John the Baptist; that of the Son the time from King Uzziah through forty-two generations to the birth of Christ; and that of the Spirit, commencing at the time of Saint Benedict and lasting twenty-one generations up to 1260, which was still in the future for Joachim. Whereas Augustine's interpretation of history regarded the "thousand-year reign" of Christ as ongoing, Joachim projected that critical period yet further into the future, thus necessitating a renewed sense of the imminence of the apocalypse.[13]

Through the fourteenth century, early Reformer John Wycliffe espoused a version of predestination that he attributed to Augustine. Known to his disciples as "John of Augustine," Wycliffe's interpretation of the theology of grace, divine predilection, and the nature of temporal authority in the face of divine control over events set the stage for the later Reformers. Former Augustinian monk Martin Luther further reasserted Augustine's principles concerning human depravity, need of grace, and the insufficiency of works in service of the Protestant Reformation. More importantly, perhaps, John Calvin made even more of a centerpiece of human moral incapacity, the priority of divine grace, and a muscular interpretation of God's control of events that has become the hallmark, accurately or not, of Calvinist tradition.

Roman Catholic theologians would subsequently argue vociferously that the Reformers were taking unacceptable liberties with Augustine to arrive at their conclusions. Contentious interpretations of Augustine again commanded the theological spotlight during the seventeenth-century Jansenist controversy. Cornelius Jansen (d. 1638) proposed his doctrine of irresistible grace and determinism in a work titled *Augustinus*. His theological positions led to a nearly two-century struggle in which the Jesuits took the lead, arguing for a more faithful, less distorted, interpretation of Augustine's theology of grace.[14]

Thomistic theology, developments of the thought of Thomas Aquinas (d: 1274), forms a second major stream in the history of Christian systematic argument. Thomas is perhaps best known for his global theological synthesis, the *Summa Theologiae,* founded on his interpretation of Aristotelian logic. He structured his magnum opus upon the classical two-part metaphor of "going forth" from and "return" to God, a construction well known to his Muslim contemporaries, such as Jalāl ad-Dīn Rūmī. In the first of three parts, Thomas discusses the nature of God and his creation; part 2 (itself in two large divisions) deals with God as the ultimate goal of humanity and the process of return to its origin; and the never-completed part 3 is dedicated to Christology, sacramental theology, and eschatology.

Thomas structures his treatment of the scores of topics in each area according to a classic Scholastic or dialectical pattern. He begins by asking a question, responding with likely rebuttals that often take the part of a devil's advocate, and concludes with his own corrective to those counterarguments. An important aspect of Thomas's work in this context is that many of his *quaestiones* (or articles) include considerable input from Jewish and Islamic authorities, especially Maimonides, Ghazālī, Ibn Sīnā, and Ibn Rushd. If the Augustinian tradition cedes priority to belief over understanding (*credo ut intelligam*), the Thomistic motto is *intelligo ut credam,* "I seek understanding in service of my faith."[15]

In Duns Scotus (d. 1308) we find a blend of classic Augustinian-Franciscan thought with Aristotelian-Thomistic themes, and a prime Christian example of what is sometimes called "theological voluntarism," focusing on God's supreme will (*voluntas*). Like Thomas, Duns Scotus argued that reason and revelation were not incompatible, but whereas Thomas ceded priority to reason or intellect in both God and human beings, Duns Scotus argued that love and will won the day. Though the difference may seem too subtle to have any practical consequences, it had a very important impact on theological ethics. If immutable divine reason is the foundation of natural law (see chapter 7), human beings can rely on reason to interpret God's will and the extent of human moral responsibility. But if natural law rests on mutable divine love and will, human beings can no longer depend on reason to guide them reliably in responding to God's designs for them. In other words, if God's decisions as to what is morally forbidden or required are based on the divine free choice, rather than on inherent qualities that reason can discern, human beings cannot be too comfortable in their ethical choices. God could in theory decree, for example, that murder is not evil, even though reason condemns it. Hence, the term "voluntarism" betokens an emphasis on God's complete and perfect freedom untrammeled by the strictures of frail reason.[16] As we shall see shortly, a similar form of "theology from above" is evident in the thought of Ibn Hazm and the Hanbalī school.

## Orthodox Christian Theological Traditions

While the medieval western Mediterranean and European theological schools were unfolding, other major developments in classical Christian theologies continued their already long history farther to the east. Two expansive developments of critical importance for any Islamic-Christian theological comparison were those of the Syriac and Arabic Middle East, and of the Greek-based traditions that grew into the various major Orthodox churches. These ecclesial communities include the Greek, Russian, Armenian, Serbian, Coptic, Ethiopian, Ukrainian, and other "national" churches not affiliated with Roman Catholicism that arose and flourished in the eastern Mediterranean and spread initially across much of eastern Europe. Their neighbors among the so-called oriental churches include various institutions that have always considered themselves Catholic and are known technically as Uniat churches (i.e., in union with Rome) and divided into the Alexandrian, Antiochene, and Byzantine "rites." I will not include these explicitly in this brief overview, though their theologies share many important common features with their Orthodox counterparts.

Numbering in the dozens, the Orthodox churches have fostered a rich and colorful variety of theological styles and traditions. As the introduction and previous chapters have suggested, a host of patristic theologians have filled considerable libraries with their writings in Greek and Syriac. Historians of Orthodox theological traditions often date their beginnings to the First Ecumenical Council of Nicaea, in 325. A dozen or more of the most influential Greek Fathers (such as the celebrated Cappadocians) lived and worked during the fourth and fifth centuries in and around the homelands of the gradually expanding Byzantine Empire. Major Syriac Fathers, such as Ephraem (c. 306–73) and Narsai (d. c. 503), lived in parts of what are now Syria and Iraq.

Like all Christian theological traditions, Orthodox theologies have turned around the doctrine of the Incarnate Word, the mystery of divine immanence, in the context of the notion of the triune Godhead or Trinity. There have, however, been important differences. According to one reading of history, the "official" split between Latin and Orthodox communions occurred in 1054, after protracted disputes over Western insertion of the phrase "and [from] the Son" (*filioque*) into the Nicene Creed in 589. Whereas the Latin church held that the Holy Spirit "proceeded" from both the Father and the Son, Orthodox tradition rejected that formulation on the grounds that it seemed to subordinate the Spirit to the Son. Increasingly politicized and bound up with the Roman claim to papal primacy, the complex dispute reached a tipping point in the eleventh century and is only now being addressed again by Western and Eastern authorities.

Four other themes that distinguish Orthodox traditions from Latin theologies are matters of emphasis rather than exclusiveness. One significant difference of perspective is that Orthodox Christology gives somewhat more attention to Christ the Logos and Creator of All (*Pantokrator*) featured in John's writings than to the more historical Jesus of the Synoptic Gospels. In addition, Orthodox tradition emphasizes a kind of human transcendence as a compliment to divine immanence—God uplifts humanity by descending to its level. A distinctive conception of divinization (*theosis*) sees the transfiguration of Christ (Mark 9:27, Luke 9, and Matthew 17) as the paradigm of the theological principle that God became human so that humanity might become divine. In Christ, human nature is brought to perfection, so that each human being is enabled to mirror the very energies of God.

Thirdly, Orthodox theologians generally think of theology as the most perfect form of prayer, a blend of intellectual striving and a more affective experiential illumination. Finally, Orthodox theological traditions, like their Western and Islamic counterparts, acknowledge the importance of apprehending evidence of divine initiative and presence in the wonders of creation. One can articulate and describe this apprehension in the symbolic language of "kataphatic" (Greek *kata-phasis,* "speaking out, affirming") theology. But since no theological language, however sophisticated, can fully grasp the reality of God, *kata-phasis* needs the counterbalance and clarification of a theology that emphasizes what God is *not*. As part 4 will discuss further, Latin theological traditions exhibit important mystical sensibilities. Orthodox theologies, however, have placed somewhat more integral emphasis on the importance of apophatic (or negative) theology. The Greek term *apo-phasis,* "unsaying," implies that human beings cannot fully express the intimate experience of divinity and must ultimately be content with the state of "unknowing."[17]

## Islamic Theological Traditions

Within the greater Islamic tradition there has also been considerable theological variety. Several of the theological themes described above were attributed to groups, such as the Qadarīya and Jahmīya, but the proponents of those positions represented inchoate movements rather than cohesive "schools" of theology with significant ongoing impact. Here I will discuss the Muʿtazilī and Hanbalī, or traditionalist, schools, which rose to prominence especially during their period of antagonism in the ninth and tenth centuries; major developments in Ashʿarī and Māturīdī theological method as they sought to mediate the rationalist-traditionalist debate during the tenth and eleventh centuries; and key themes in Shiʿi systematic theology.

During the early ninth century, caliphs of the Abbasid dynasty fostered lively intellectual exchange in the "House of Wisdom" in Baghdad. Participants from the various faith and cultural traditions debated matters of science and religion, and texts of Hellenistic philosophy entered the intellectual milieu thanks to translations from Greek into Syriac and finally into Arabic. Among the more successful schools of thought to emerge from the interchange were the Muʿtazila, whose fully developed method offers a prime example of Muslim "theology from below." The name means "those who hold themselves aloof" (from politics, presumably), but that meaning was clearly no longer applicable by the early ninth century, when the caliph declared Muʿtazilī thought the "official" theological system of the realm. He found their views politically advantageous because of their implications for caliphal authority. God not only bestowed the faculty of reason on humankind and fully expected people to use it in search of the divine truth, but was in effect himself subject to the laws and strictures of reason. Furthermore, since (as they argued) the Qurʾān was not the eternal, uncreated word of God but created in time, it was clearly subject to human interpretation and authority.

Within such a system, the caliph could claim considerable latitude in obeying and enacting scriptural sanctions. During the reigns of caliphs Hārūn ar-Rashīd (r. 786–802) and al-Maʾmūn (r. 813–33), the Muʿtazila enjoyed a season of high influence at court and were even charged with enforcing a kind of "orthodoxy." Through inquisitorial methods (the *mihna*), they used a litmus test to sort out the theologically compliant from dissenters. Those who refused to affirm the earthly, created nature of the Qurʾān were punished with imprisonment, and worse. By the mid-ninth century, however, the Muʿtazila suffered a dramatic reversal when the caliph Mutawakkil (r. 847–61) espoused a more traditionalist theology while withdrawing official support from the rationalists.

As a "school" the Muʿtazila nevertheless retained considerable momentum, and their thought continued to evolve as a coherent system especially during the tenth and eleventh centuries. Perhaps the single most influential systematic work was 'Abd al-Jabbār's (d. c. 1025) massive twenty-volume synthesis unabashedly titled *The Definitive Work* (literally, *The Work That Renders All Others Redundant*). Major themes in Mu'tazilī theology centered on the so-called five principles and their signature position on God's attributes. Abū 'l-Hudhayl (d. 841) is given credit for formulating the equivalent of a Mu'tazilī creedal formulation. Its five elements are, first, the oneness of God; second, that God will inevitably and predictably do what is just (the opposite of "voluntarism"); third, the concept of promise and threat, according to which an unrepentant serious sinner will assuredly suffer eternal punishment in hell; fourth, that the Muslim who sins enjoys a state between belief and unbelief and is therefore neither automatically condemned to hell nor accorded uncontested membership in the community of authentic Muslims; and finally, the active ethical mandate of "commanding the good and forbidding the evil."

On the critical subject of God's attributes, the Mu'tazila contributed a great deal to the often contentious debate. Their views flow from the first principle: since God is simply and irreducibly one, his "essential" attributes (power, knowledge, existence) are identical with God's being. But since God also acts in time, his speaking, hearing, seeing, and willing are separate from God's essence and subject to change. Hence, the Mu'tazila held that the speech of God in the Qur'ān is created—a position roughly analogous to the christological view of Arius and others who held that Jesus was not divine. The Mu'tazila dealt with obvious logical problems, such as the apparent need to think of knowledge and power, for example, as independent realities, by translating these and other terms from nouns into gerunds such as "knowing" and "exercising power." On this point, as well as their general tendency to constrain God's freedom by holding him answerable to the canons of reason, the Mu'tazila fell afoul of their staunchest opponents, Ibn Hanbal and the traditionalist theologians.[18]

Of all the citizens of Baghdad (and elsewhere in Iraq) caught in the Mu'tazila's inquisition, perhaps none was a more influential or redoubtable foe than Ahmad ibn Hanbal (d. 855). Sprung from prison by the caliph Mutawakkil, Ibn Hanbal lost no time redressing the theological injustices perpetrated by his Mu'tazilī foes and their royal patrons. Instead of starting from a fundamental conviction of the centrality of reason, Ibn Hanbal began with the undiminished transcendent unity of God. Where the rationalist systematicians in effect tried to remake God in the image of his reason-imbued creature, Ibn Hanbal went out of his way to release God of all earthly shackles. God's omnipotence and omniscience are without limit, so that, at least in theory, God need not act justly but is free to appear capricious and despotic.

What is at stake theologically for Ibn Hanbal, however, is not arguing what human beings are *not,* but what God *is.* Revelation as embodied in the uncreated sacred text of the Qur'ān took precedence over the use of reason. Ironically, perhaps, Ibn Hanbal's rejection of the Muʿtazilī reading of scriptural references to God's "face," "hands," and "sitting" on the throne as purely metaphorical left his interpretation of God open to anthropomorphism. Two thinkers, living over two and a half centuries apart and at opposite ends of the Mediterranean, made enduring contributions to the articulation of traditionalist theology. Ibn Hazm (d. 1064) of Cordova (Spain) penned a "creed," as did so many of his theological forebears, but also elaborated a distinctive systematic theology. Like earlier traditionalist thinkers, Ibn Hazm emphasizes God's sky-blue freedom and power and the insufficiency of reason in the quest for truth. As little scope as he might seem to leave for human moral initiative, he nevertheless gives a central place to human intention (*niyya*) and describes the process of belief in intimately personal terms.[19] Finally, arguably the most celebrated theologian in the Hanbalī tradition is the brilliant Damascene scholar Ibn Taymīya (d. 1328), a prolific author and polemicist whose thought the early modern Wahhābī movement would claim as its theoretical foundation.[20]

Discussion of God's attributes, God's relationship to his creation, and the interface between faith and reason occupied an increasingly central position in the views of Ashʿarī and Māturīdī. Abū 'l-Hasan al-Ashʿarī (d. 935) was the eponymous founder of one of the most influential schools of Islamic theology. Educated in the Muʿtazila tradition, Ashʿarī describes a crisis of conscience and intellectual conviction that led him to seek a more satisfying integration of faith and reason. He and his later defenders insisted that Ashʿarī's goal was to preserve the traditionalists' affirmation of divine transcendence without entirely abandoning the Muʿtazilī acknowledgment of the critical role of rational inquiry and the need to soften traditionalist anthropomorphism (i.e., the willingness to refrain from inquiry into the specific nature of God's face, hands, and other implied somatic characteristics). Nonetheless, the traditionalist Hanbalī school remained at odds with Ashʿarī's successors well into later medieval times. For Ashʿarī, reason was no longer the virtually freewheeling tool of the systematic theologian. Now rational method played second fiddle to the concept of scholarly consensus as the prime criterion of doctrinal authenticity, but Ashʿarī continued to engage the theoretical questions of the systematic theologians and to articulate the fundamental creedal elements in the formal language of *kalām.*

As a systematic theologian, Ash'arī incorporates themes and problems formulated during the earliest generations of Muslim thinkers (such as those mentioned above) into his own theoretical framework. He founds his synthesis on the conviction that the Qur'ān and Muhammad's entire message represent at root a comprehensive and rational—albeit not systematically packaged—religious worldview. Unlike his successors, he does not construct a philosophically founded argument for the existence of God, but he does present an analytical approach to statements about the nature of God and his attributes. An axiom for which Ash'arī is perhaps most famous is his insistence that while Muslims do not simply accept characteristics such as face, hands, and sitting on the throne anthropomorphically, neither do they reduce the Qur'ān's language to mere metaphor. Instead, one must confront the mystery of the revelation's mode of communication "without asking how" (bī-lā kayf) the statements are true. Ash'arī's theological progeny include a number of Islam's most gifted and influential thinkers.[21]

A central Asian contemporary of Ash'arī's named Abū Mansūr al-Māturīdī (d. 944) lived near the city of Samarqand in present-day Uzbekistan. Like Ash'arī, Māturīdī contended with the Mu'tazila, but his theological method differed from that of Ash'arī in several important ways. Whereas Ash'arī remained substantially influenced by Hanbalī traditionalism, Māturīdī leaned toward the more reason-friendly method of the Hanafī law school. On the other hand, while Ash'arī used the technical language of the Mu'tazila, Māturīdī fashioned a different set of terms. He agreed with the Mu'tazila that reason played an essential role in human access to knowledge of God, and left open the possibility of metaphorical interpretations of certain Qur'ānic "anthropomorphisms." With respect to both God's attributes and control of human actions, Māturīdī parted company with both the Mu'tazila and Ash'arī.[22]

Accounts of classical Muslim theological schools have once privileged Ash'arī thought as the central plot of the most widely accepted narrative. Though Māturīdī's thought has been far less studied and is only now achieving fuller appreciation as a distinctive theological method, it is becoming clearer that the central Asian school certainly equals the Ash'arīya in importance and was at its peak influential over an arguably broader expanse of Islamdom. Ash'arī and his major followers were mostly linked to the Shāfi'ī legal school (some to the Mālikī), whereas Māturīdī and his successors were allied to the Hanafī school, which over many centuries extended its sway over a vast swath of Islamdom from the eastern Mediterranean through central and southern Asia.[23]

Finally, Shi'i theology has made important and distinctive contributions to the history of Islamic thought. One of the more curious chapters in the story of the Mu'tazila is their intimate relationship with the majority branch of the Shi'a, the Twelvers. During the late ninth and early tenth centuries, Shi'i thinkers incorporated fundamental Mu'tazilī principles as they refined their distinctive theology of history centered on explaining the role and ongoing spiritual authority and teaching of the Hidden Imam. Two of the most influential Shi'i thinkers were Hasan ibn Mūsā an-Nawbakhtī (d. c. 912–22) and Shaykh al-Mufīd (d. 1032), both Iraqi. From a notable Shi'i family, Nawbakhtī and his uncle began a school of thought that integrated Mu'tazilī thought with an evolving theology of the imamate. Nawbakhtī elaborated on the Twelver Shi'i theology of history, fleshing out the distinctive doctrine of the "occultation" of the twelfth imam (the lesser, from 873 to 940, and the greater, after the death of the fourth official representative, or *wakīl*). Shaykh al-Mufīd continued the tradition but distanced himself somewhat from the Mu'tazilī insistence on the sole sufficiency of reason and disagreed with their positions on the certain punishment of unrepentant sinners (there's always hope) and their materialistic view of human beings. Finally, Mufīd set Iraqi Shi'i theology apart from the more traditionalist views of the "School of Qumm" (Iran).[24]

. . .

Several major themes stand out. First, though Christians and Muslims alike have long cherished the abstract notion of the "unity of all believers," the histories of both communities reveal at least as much evidence of pluralism as of uniformity. When it suits their purposes, members of both great traditions are generally pleased to note the immense size, global scope, and relative rates of growth of Christianity and Islam. At the same time, many are quick to point out that only those who conform to a list of essential beliefs and practices qualify as authentic Christians or Muslims, evidently choosing to ignore how such litmus tests decimate the rolls of true believers. Both early communities faced the challenge of making the new faith adaptable to new languages and cultures as they expanded. Both dealt likewise with early divergent views on key attributes of the word of God, whether of the Qur'ān's "uncreated" status or of Jesus' divinity.

As the earlier sections of this chapter have suggested, the notion of correct belief has meant a host of different things, not only to Muslims as distinct from Christians, but to divergent factions within both of the two great traditions. On a fairly basic level, the histories of both traditions are rife with examples of censorship. Book burnings have not been confined to works by "others," though both Muslim and Christian authorities have often enough consigned to the flames works of Jews and others already considered beyond the pale. Influential newly condemned or forbidden writings by authors widely accepted as Muslim or Christian have also drawn enthusiastic throngs of nonreaders to public squares as those writings went up in smoke. But Muslim and Christian specialists and religious authorities have also devised more sophisticated and nuanced methods of theological critique that go beyond more general heresiography into sharply honed polemics.

Second, sifting through the many explicitly theological formulations articulated by dozens of great thinkers and schools of thought in both traditions reveals a host of similarities and differences both in method and in content. Methodological analogies include most of all varying emphases on reason as the foundation of "theologies from below," and on God's transcendent prerogatives in "theologies from above." Both traditions share certain bedrock beliefs concerning God's communication with humanity: human beings are unable to discern ultimate truths on their own; God has been active in human history and constantly provides reminders of his prior messages; people have habitually rejected divine initiative; divine disclosure is a process; and there is an end to formal revelation marked by the lives of Jesus and Muhammad.

Major theological questions explored by both traditions have to do with relationships between faith and action, and between sinfulness and membership in community, and the implications of these issues for human accountability and political power (themes to be further discussed in parts 3 and 4). Muslim and Christian thinkers have contended among themselves over the relationships between inward faith and outward action. Although variations exist in both traditions, especially considering the entire spectrum of Protestant and Catholic Christians, certain doctrines were more firmly established in particular schools or denominations. In the Christian tradition, however, these diverging views on the nature of God and human responsibility have led in part to long-lasting and formally distinct denominations, with distinctive theologies and ways of worship. Though the various Islamic theological schools differ as to specific views, those divergent formulations have not led to quite the proliferation of structural and formal sectarian differentiation one finds in the history of Christendom.

Eschatological themes include a number of major theological convergences: there is broad overlap in the imagery of death, judgment, resurrection of the body, and final accountability. But there is significant variation in specific details, including the Islamic concept of a "sleep" in a separation zone (*barzakh*) before resurrection. Unlike the Christian notion of hell, Islam's infernal realm is not necessarily a permanent abode of those destined to experience it but does double duty as a state of purgation.

Finally, large thematic differences include Christianity's solution to the problem of divine immanence in the form of the incarnation, and of the need for salvation via Jesus' redemptive suffering and death—both of which Muslim tradition regards as an altogether unacceptable negation of divine transcendent unity. By contrast, Islamic thought features Jesus as one among many prophets, a mere mortal who nonetheless did not suffer death in any form, and who enjoys no intercessory prerogatives.[25] Whereas for Christians the Word became human, for Muslims the Word became a book, the former as "transmitted" by the Virgin Mary, the latter through the "unlettered" Muhammad. Though in Muslim tradition, Jesus' mother, Mary, conceived virginally, she is nothing like the intercessor to whom many Christians look for aid.

# PART III

# Institutional Dimensions

*The Structures of Theologically Grounded Community*

Both Christian and Islamic traditions have developed extensive institutional manifestations of their respective belief systems. An investigation of these institutional dimensions encompasses historical studies above all, including research into the documentary sources of both traditions. These include, for example, historical chronicles and archives on individual institutions (such as cathedrals, monasteries, mosques, and schools) and on community leaders most responsible for their foundation and maintenance. But in order to appreciate how the visible structures we so readily associate with religious traditions have evolved and functioned historically, we need some understanding of their nonmaterial infrastructures—the invisible, conceptual underpinnings of the brick and mortar. That, in turn, takes us back to scriptural roots and to the earliest conceptions of the nature of religious community, law, and authority. In this context, systematic theology too has its place, particularly as Christian and Muslim thinkers work out the relationships between religious and worldly power and authority.

Chapter 5 explores these underpinnings by asking questions about the conceptual foundations of the structures of authority, and the shape of authority within community. How does divine authority translate into human terms and manifest itself on a human scale? What metaphors are behind religious models of authority and the differentiation of earthly offices in reflecting the divine order of things? How do these metaphors and models take shape in functioning institutions that interpret sacred law and implement divine justice on earth? Both large faith communities have developed their "theologies of power," articulating however indirectly the prerogatives to be exercised by those elevated to the status of God's chosen representatives. These theological views in effect select and describe the relevant attributes of God (power, justice, mercy) to be emulated by those elected to exercise stewardship on earth.

Moving from theory to implementation, chapter 6 explores institutions in action, beginning with a look at some of the practical implications of the complex interface between theology and politics. Here and throughout the chapter, the historical disciplines (including, at the end, art history) carry the freight. Systematic, and, to a lesser extent, mystical theology, make cameo appearances in the sections on intentional communities and educational traditions. Even as more concrete manifestations of religious community take center stage, however, theological questions and presuppositions lurk in the wings. How and to what degree ought people of faith to succumb to the urge to invest in, build upon, and advertise on a grand scale their conviction that they are heirs to an empire of the spirit? How do the trappings of worldly influence express heavenly aspiration? And at what point do manifestations of material wealth give the lie to claims of privileging the soul of service over the body of earthly dominance? Finally, a brief consideration of how religious concerns have influenced the development of architecture in both traditions raises similar questions: for example, what visual metaphors, if any, can offer clues to the theological resonances of monuments to Christian and Islamic community?

# CHAPTER 5

# Beneath the Brick and Mortar

Religious institutions have taken a wide variety of forms in the histories of Christianity and Islam. Here I will focus on the origins of underlying invisible structures of authority, the further articulation of religious law, and the evolution of Christian and Muslim theologies of power.

## FOUNDATIONS OF THE STRUCTURES OF AUTHORITY

Initial institutional developments in both traditions took the form of a division of labor, identification of levels and grades of authority, and eventually formal structures of governance and the implementation of community canons of behavior—what one might loosely call religious law. Early Christians, for example, identified the roles of apostles, teachers, prophets, presbyters, deacons, and bishops. Even during Muhammad's lifetime, the fledgling Muslim community acknowledged honorific levels among the Companions. Though they did not delineate quite the kinds of role differentiation that arose within early Christianity, Muslim community leaders among the Companions were often singled out for expertise in one or another aspect of Islamic teaching. Recall, for example, that Hudhayfa ibn al-Yamān was the Prophet's choice as the community expert on hypocrisy and was entrusted especially with preserving traditions on that very important theme. In general, the Companions identified as closest to the Prophet in various ways came to embody the highest levels of authority and credibility. Clan and family associations accounted for an additional criterion of influence and potential leadership responsibility. By the time Muhammad died (632), the growing Muslim polity in Medina had developed definite, though somewhat informal and not always easy to identify, structures of authority.

Though it may seem too obvious to mention, particular religious institutions themselves have their own complex histories, and most evolved gradually over many centuries. Within the early Christian communities, the roles of presbyter (elder/priest), deacon, and bishop, for example, looked very different from the church offices with which most Christians today would be familiar. By the same token, the roles of both the Muslim leaders closest to Muhammad and the various specialists in particular aspects of the faith's patrimony soon took on very different, more complex dimensions as the Muslim community expanded into new cultural, social, ethnic, and religious settings in the central Middle East after Muhammad's death.

More importantly, as constituent parts of the larger units that have morphed into the world's Christianities and Islams, religious institutions frequently take on lives of their own. As often as not, these organizational structures evolve into foci of authority whose fundamental internal dynamic is geared to perpetuating the institution. Those entrusted with administering these institutions historically have tended to invest much of their organizational capital in preserving the tradition from change. Leaders once chosen for their ability to communicate the living teachings of a foundational figure to an increasingly diverse community have often come to regard themselves as the custodians of an immutable core tradition. Some Christians have called that core the "deposit of faith," while Muslims identify it generically as *shari'a,* "divinely revealed law." In fact, though, religious law and jurisprudence strictly so called (*fiqh* and *usūl al-fiqh*) comprise a set of specific disciplines that are part of, but not coextensive with, the larger reality of Sharia. As Bernard Weiss observes, "The Shari'a is, first and foremost, the totality of divine 'categorizations of human acts' (*al-ahkām fī 'l-af'āl, al-ahkām al-'amalīya*)."[1] As chapter 2 suggested, both traditions have made crucial distinctions between matters of teaching, on the one hand, and community discipline, on the other. Against the backdrop of these prefatory remarks, this chapter will describe a few of the more significant internal institutions within the two traditions. We begin with a brief sociology of religious authority and the legal structures to which the various specialists were attached.

## INVISIBLE STRUCTURES: THE SOCIOLOGY
## OF RELIGIOUS AUTHORITY

No other major religious traditions have spread over larger geographical expanses or in greater numbers than have Christianity and Islam. Global presence on such a vast scale naturally suggests some driving force, some specific discernible level of intention and evidence of organization. The dissemination of faith communities across multiple ethnic, cultural, national, and linguistic boundaries doesn't simply happen. Chapter 2 described some of the dynamics of the growth of Islam and Christianity as global faiths in terms of the missionary impulse that has characterized the histories of both traditions. In this section, I explore the main outlines of the key organizational structures that Christians and Muslims have evolved in the complex process of going global. Within both faith traditions, some components have developed largely vertical structures of authority while others have tended toward more horizontal organization. Even in this broad characterization, one sees evidence of underlying theological nuances, for in the history of religions on the whole, sources often describe earthly organizations as mirror reflections or microcosmic versions of some otherworldly dispensation.

### Authority and Administration in Christian Communities

Members of virtually all Christian denominations conceive of themselves as belonging to localized or regional organizations, but the size and complexity of those organizations vary widely. Largest of all Christian churches globally is Roman Catholicism, which is also arguably the most institutionally and administratively complicated. Its authority structure is most clearly vertical, with a hierarchical administration that begins at top with the papacy. Tradition has it that the first pope was Saint Peter, and that there has been an unbroken chain of "apostolic succession" from him down to the present supreme pontiff. A number of other church offices date back to very early times, including those of deacon, presbyter (or elder), and bishop—the latter administering a diocese (from the Greek *di-oikein*, "to keep house"). With the growth in the size and number of these episcopal jurisdictions (from the Greek *episkopos*, "overseer"), regional administrators known as archbishops came into being. An archdiocese might encompass several dioceses, each with its own bishop, and in the lead diocese the archbishop often has the assistance of one or more coadjutor bishops.

Dioceses are composed of parishes, each of which, ideally, has an ordained priest as its pastor. Bishops (in the United States, at least) can promote pastors or other priests with special duties within a diocese to the honorific rank of monsignor, which until later in the twentieth century consisted of two further ranks known as right reverend and very reverend (but this distinction is no longer used). Within many dioceses, parishes are grouped into regional clusters called deaneries, but pastors are ultimately responsible to the bishop of the place, also known as the "ordinary." Since at least medieval times, some bishops and archbishops have been chosen for elevation to the honorific rank of cardinal. Cardinals are further differentiated functionally into three "orders," with six cardinal-bishops residing in Rome and administering small dioceses adjoining the pope's diocese (Rome itself); cardinal-priests, who exercise "titular" authority over churches in Rome in addition to their function as bishops and archbishops of their "home" dioceses; and cardinal-deacons, who officiate as deacons during papal liturgies. In antiquity, the pope could appoint even laymen as cardinals, but now only ordained priests are elevated to that rank.[2] As a group, they form the college of cardinals, which has been responsible for selecting a pope from its ranks since about the twelfth century. The most important move in that direction occurred in 1059, when a decree of the Lateran Synod restricted authority for papal elections to bishops and cardinals; further refinement limited the vote to cardinals within the next generation or so.[3]

Various other church groups have largely vertical hierarchies, including the Anglican and (outside of England) Episcopalian tradition, and several of the Orthodox communions, but second only to Roman Catholicism in the strict verticality of its administration is the Church of Jesus Christ of Latter-day Saints, or Mormons.[4] In general, vertical flow of authority, whatever the specific church in question, goes hand in hand with the expectation that a certain percentage of income from local and regional levels will be shared with the central administrations as well.

The Church of Latter-day Saints presents a particularly interesting example. Mormon Church hierarchical structure begins with the president, also known as a prophet, revelator, and seer, who heads a presidential council, the First Presidency, comprised of the president and two counselors. Successors to a first president and his counselors are chosen from the Quorum of the Twelve Apostles, which has its own president. In addition the Council of Seventy oversees the church's mission organization. Presiding bishops, a three-man financial committee, oversee regional units called stakes (comparable to dioceses in other churches). Smaller local units (similar to parishes) are known as wards. All Mormon males over the age of twelve are eligible for ordination to the bi-level priesthood. Ranks within the lower level Aaronic priesthood are deacon, teacher, priest, and bishop; and within the Melchizedek priesthood are the ranks of elder, high priest, patriarch, (member of the) Seventy, and apostle. Throughout Mormon history, the various ranks and roles have undergone some internal modification, but the highly vertical structure has been a constant.[5]

Some communities blend strong hierarchical elements with horizontal governance. Most churches in the Anglican Communion acknowledge the leadership of the archbishop of Canterbury, under whom the bishops of local and regional dioceses serve. Parish clergy in turn are answerable to their bishop. The far-flung Orthodox communion has had a very complex history. Fourteen "autocephalous" (self-governing) and seven "autonomous" churches constitute the larger Orthodox family. The patriarchates of Constantinople, Alexandria, Antioch, and Jerusalem are the most ancient of the autocephalous churches, while the remaining ten have historically taken the form of "national" churches (such as the Russian, Serbian, and Bulgarian). Bishops administer eparchies (the Orthodox analogue to dioceses). Regional administrators in these groups are sometimes known as metropolitans. Priests, archdeacons, and deacons serve Orthodox parishes.[6] A host of other "Eastern" churches include two Nestorian and four "non-Chalcedonian" Orthodox groups (the Armenian Orthodox, Coptic, Ethiopian, and Syrian).[7] Some Lutheran, Presbyterian, and Methodist organizations similarly emphasize the union of groups of churches (or subdenominations) within their denominations, with varying levels of authority vested in bishops or governing bodies and relative autonomy allowed to individual local churches.[8]

Still other churches, particularly the so-called nonliturgical denominations, are almost entirely horizontal in structure. "Congregational" or "democratic" models of church polity govern a wide variety of groups. Baptist communities, for example, typically identify themselves as conventions (such as the Southern or American Baptist) that are administered by presidents and advisory councils. Local churches, however, enjoy considerable autonomy. Groups affiliated with the United Churches of Christ are also major examples of congregationalism. Some smaller churches may list local leaders as "bishops," but their authority is typically limited to a single community, and they function in reality like senior pastors in larger Protestant churches.[9]

A distinctive feature of Christian traditions concerning the mechanisms by which individuals are empowered with specific authority roles is the sacramental character of ministry or "orders." Many Christian denominations, with the notable exception of Roman Catholicism and some Orthodox communions, today regard only baptism and the Lord's Supper (aka the Eucharist or Holy Communion) as sacraments. But prior to the Reformation, "ordination" to the offices of deacon, presbyter/priest, and bishop had become widespread in Christendom. During the first several centuries, bishops were elected officials who appointed subordinate ministers. They were considered "first" among presbyters, who were likewise chosen with the participation of the faithful and consecrated by bishops. Tertullian (d. 228) was the first to refer to those of clerical rank collectively as an *ordo*, and Origen (d. 254) further refined the concept with a clear distinction among the various orders (bishop, priest, deacon) and between clerics and the laity.

Peter Damian (d. 1072) was the first to claim that seven orders (parallel to the Seven Gifts of the Holy Spirit) comprised the hierarchy, with bishops and presbyters together constituting the first order, followed by archdeacons, deacons, subdeacons, and the various minor orders (porter, lector, acolyte, and exorcist). By the end of the eleventh century, formal acknowledgment of "holy order" as one in an integrated system of seven "sacraments" was widely accepted. A century and a half later, Alexander of Hales (d. 1245) had begun a tradition of identifying the sacrament of orders explicitly with the authority to celebrate the Holy Eucharist and to forgive sins in the sacrament of reconciliation. Finally, as Reformers like Martin Luther had begun arguing for a "priesthood of the faithful" led by those commissioned to preach, the Council of Trent (1545–63) responded by shoring up Catholic hierarchical structures. It formally defined the role of bishops as superior to that of priests, in that bishops can confer the sacraments of ordination and confirmation, while priests are commissioned to teach, baptize, and offer the sacred liturgy.[10]

## Muslim Structures of Authority and Governance

Shi'i Islam presents the clearest analogy to the largely vertical authority structure evident in the history of Roman Catholic Christianity. To be more specific, the most obvious example of complex hierarchical governance is that of the majority Shi'i "denomination," commonly known as Twelvers or Imamis. Twelver hierarchical structure, like that of Roman Catholicism, evolved gradually over many centuries into its present elaborate pyramidal model. At the apex stands the Prophet Muhammad and the spiritual descendants, the "People of the House," known as the Twelve

Imams. Especially since the Iranian Revolution of 1979, the preeminent representative of the twelfth or "Hidden Imam" has been the chief lawgiver (*faqīh*). Two leading *ayatollahs* (from *āya* [sign] and Allāh, hence "sign of God") have thus far filled that position, Ruhollah Khomeini and his successor, ʿAli Khamenei. A step lower in rank are a cluster (seven in times past, according to some scholars, but up to twelve in the era of Iran's Islamic Revolution) of the most prominent "Grand Ayatollahs," with the distinctive honorific title "Sources of Imitation" (*marājīʿ at-taqlīd*). Shiʿi faithful of both Iran and Iraq, whose majority populations are Twelvers, are expected to attach themselves to one or other of these authorities for guidance in matters of faith and ethics.

Several score other religious scholars enjoy the title of ayatollah and are loosely divided into two ranks, grand and lesser. On the next lower rungs are two levels of scholars with the title "Proof of Islam" (*hujjatolislam*). Shiʿi religious scholars (*ʿulamāʾ*) achieve the various degrees of distinction on the basis of their perceived acumen in the sources of the tradition and advance by a form of popular acclaim and on the strength of their respective constituencies. In contemporary Iran and Iraq, some members of the religious establishment claim the title *sayyid* and wear a black turban symbolizing their descent from the Prophet Muhammad. Occupying the most basic rank of religious officialdom are the *mullahs* who staff the mosques and serve their local communities pastorally. In both Iran and Iraq, religious scholars receive a more or less standardized curriculum of "seminary" education and must sit for various kinds of accrediting examinations. With various high-ranking *madrasas* ("places of study," institutions of higher learning) capable of attracting a large complement of well-known teachers, the Iranian city of Qumm is generally recognized as the center of Shiʿi formal religious education.[11]

The vast majority of the world's local and regional Muslim communities, known generically as Sunni, have been linked together as a global communion largely by a sense of horizontal affinity as servants of the one God. If one can draw a loose structural analogy between Shiʿi Islam and Roman Catholicism, one might also suggest a very general organizational parallel between Protestant Christianity and Sunni Islam. The principal point of comparison in this context would be the relative lack of vertical authority mechanisms and the emphasis on the responsibility of each believer to seek out appropriate sources of guidance and interpretation. Sunni Muslims in traditional societies are still accustomed to acknowledging the expertise of specially educated individuals (the *ʿulamāʾ*) in exegesis of the Qurʾān and jurisprudence. As in predominantly Shiʿi contexts, Sunni institutions of religious learning occupy prominent positions in major cities, and some enjoy notoriety through a reputation for ideological or historical priority. Students still come from all over the globe specifically to study at Al-Azhar in Cairo, at various institutions in Mecca and Medina, and at major madrasas in South Asia. Individual Sunni teachers, often known by the honorific title *shaykh* (elder) or *imām* (but not in the Shiʻi sense), sometimes achieve a high level of celebrity and authority and attract large followings; but they are not part of a formal overarching hierarchical structure. Faculties of theology exist in virtually every country with a significant population of Muslims, with new programs developing in the United States for the training of religious scholars and military chaplains, for example.

An important general feature of the overall Sunni approach to religious authority has to do with the way in which Muslims identify an individual as an expert in interpreting the tradition legally. Not all individuals who claim followers and issue legal advisories called *fatwās* have received formal education in the recognized institutions of religious learning. Usāma bin Lādin is a case in point. His followers have called him their shaykh, and a number of early interviews filmed him in front of bookshelves stocked with learned tomes in exegesis, Hadith, and law. Bin Lādin's actual credentials, however, are hailed almost exclusively by his private coterie of disciples.

Individuals who pursue a formal course of study in Islamic law (*fiqh*) earn the title *faqīh*, "one who has a deep understanding" of the sacred sources. Such scholars (*ʻulamāʼ*) have traditionally been formed in small group study sessions centered around a teaching shaykh noted for expertise in the various subdisciplines of religious studies: Qurʼān, exegesis, Hadith, Sharia in general, positive law (*fiqh*), and jurisprudence or principles of law (*usūl al-fiqh*). After successfully completing a course of study with a particular shaykh-specialist, students earn a license (*ijāza*) or permission to practice or teach others in the subject. A largely honorific title conferred on major religious scholars since about the tenth century, *Shaykh al-Islām* recognized noteworthy knowledge and authority and in some historical contexts denoted a leading legal specialist or chief *muftī*.[12] I will develop the theme of educational institutions further in chapter 6.

## PRACTICAL INSTITUTIONS: LAW AND THE IMPLEMENTATION OF AUTHORITY

For Muslims as well as for Christians, God is the ultimate and only lawgiver and the sole arbiter of justice.[13] In both traditions, however, vexing questions have long exercised religious authorities. Areas of special inquiry include precisely what injunctions constitute divine law, the extent of a given injunction's applicability, whether or not a given injunction may no longer be in force if the conditions that originally prompted it are judged to have lapsed, what sanctions attach to a given injunction, and how authorities are required to enforce those sanctions. Here I will begin with a brief overview of the histories of religious law as it has evolved in both traditions, and a look at some key principles of jurisprudence.

## Christian Canon Law

Christian authors began working out the practicalities regulating matters of internal church discipline as early as the Pauline Letters of the New Testament. Through most of the patristic period, major theologians discussed solutions to various specific problems by deducing them, in effect, from principles they discerned in the sacred scriptures. Early quasi-systematic summaries of such principles were called "Church Orders." Among the first were the *Didache* (fuller title, *Teaching of the Lord through the Twelve Apostles,* c. 100), with its instructions on the sacraments and the roles of prophets, bishops, and deacons; the *Didascalia Apostolorum* (*Teaching of the Apostles,* c. 250), focusing on a wide variety of states of life within the church, from married laypeople on up to the bishop's duties, and emphasizing that Jewish ritual stipulations are no longer in force for Christians; the mid- to later fourth-century *Apostolic Constitutions,* which compiled segments of the two earlier works, along with eighty-five "canons" ascribed to the apostles; and a work mistakenly attributed to Hippolytus of Rome (d. c. 235) but likely from the very early sixth century.[14]

In the Theodosian Code (c. 435), Emperor Theodosius II ordered a collection of earlier legal "constitutions" since Constantine, including a lengthy section dedicated to religious matters. But arguably the first attempt at a definitive systematic work was a collection of canons promulgated by the early church councils and attributed to Dionysius Exiguus of Rome (d. c. 550). In addition to republishing some material from the works just mentioned, the collection added canons from a number of synods, and papal documents, to its compilation of legislation from major ecumenical councils such as Nicaea, Constantinople, and Chalcedon. Dionysius's volume retained its importance through late antiquity on up to early Carolingian times (i.e., the ninth century). Roughly contemporary with Dionysius's work was Justinian's Code (534), which, though not church law as such, was a landmark in the legal systematization in the Eastern

Church with important implications for the limitation of papal authority vis-à-vis the emperor. During the subsequent half-millennium or so, various other compilations appeared across Europe, adding canons from later councils, as well as papal documents.

Canon law came of age as a theological subdiscipline with Gratian's (d. c. 1179) *Systematization of Diverse Canons* (*Concordia Discordantium Canonum*), also known as the Decree of Gratian (*Decretum Gratiani*, c. 1140). Gratian undertook his seminal work after encountering Justinian's Code of "civil" law and concluding that the church needed a systematic counterpart. Three further compilations of papal "decretals" based on the proceedings of various church councils were promulgated by popes Gregory IX (1234), Boniface VIII (1298), and John XXII (1317). For three and a half centuries, Gratian's compilation (supplemented by the three papal collections) remained the definitive text. Together these sources inspired a tradition of commentaries that were themselves gradually standardized in the form of *Ordinary Glosses* (*Glossa Ordinaria*), encyclopedic hypertexts with Gratian at the center of each page and surrounded by the accretions of layer on layer of decretals. The result was analogous to the Talmud's arrangement of rabbinic commentaries (*Gemara*) around the central text of the Mishnah. As we shall see, similar commentarial traditions attended the history of Islamic religious law.

Gratian's Decree and the papal additions formed the core of the first truly comprehensive *Body of Canon Law* (*Corpus Juris Canonici*) of 1500. With the full emergence of the Protestant Reformation, dissenting churches largely repudiated canon law's claims to central papal authority. And as early modern states emerged on the basis of civil law, canon law receded in importance across Europe. Orthodox and Anglican traditions, however, continued to rely on the sources and mechanisms of canon law, which they adapted to resolve their distinctive questions of internal discipline.[15] The *Corpus* remained the bedrock of Catholic legislation for another four hundred years, until Pope Pius X (d. 1914) responded to the need for a clearer systematization of the law. The result was the 1917 *Code of Canon Law* (*Codex Juris Canonici*). Its five major sections organized material on (1) general norms, (2) persons (especially clergy and hierarchy), (3) things (ritual, authority, and church finances), (4) process (the roles of church tribunals tasked with adjudicating marriage, applying disciplinary sanctions, and investigating causes for canonization of saints), and (5) penal law. Sections 2–4 followed the traditional divisions of ancient Roman law.

Pope John XXIII (d. 1963) called for another revision of the *Code* as he revealed that he would convene the Second Vatican Council, and twenty years later the new *Code* appeared. In an important revision the 1983 *Code* replaced the old organizational categories of Roman law with a more explicitly theological orientation. The emphasis shifted to the church as "people of God," nurtured by the "word of God" as manifested in the "sacraments." Matters of material wealth, canonical punishments, and due process were relegated to separate sections. In practice, a wide range of canonical cases have been, and continue to be, prosecuted. Individuals or groups persistently at odds with the disciplinary policies of an archbishop, such as in the management of church finances or in unauthorized forms of ministry, might be threatened with "interdict" (i.e., they might be ordered to cease and desist), and even excommunicated if they fail to comply. In the legal proceedings, defendants have a right to a canon lawyer to assist in their defense.

Canon law in current practice rarely, if ever, intrudes into the workings of ordinary civil or criminal law. Through most of its history, canon law has included mechanisms that take into consideration mitigating circumstances, and the notion of *sensus fidelium* (general understanding of believers) has consistently acknowledged that not all provisions of canon law will be "accepted" by the community and cannot be enforced in practice. Today, a number of Roman universities (as well as the Catholic University of America) grant doctorates and licentiates in canon law (JCD, Juris Canonici Doctor, or JCL, Juris Canonici Licentiatus), degrees held typically by clergy, some of whom teach, sit on local diocesan tribunals, or act as advocates for individuals involved in ecclesiastical legal cases. Some canon lawyers become bishops, archbishops, or cardinals and are responsible for the higher tribunals and sacred congregations that oversee "matters of faith and morals" in the Vatican. Among the Protestant and other non-Catholic denominations, legal codes as such have played a lesser role, although many churches have promulgated rules of order and polity, such as the Anglican Church's Lambeth Quadrilateral (1888).

## Muslim Sharia and Fiqh

Islamic religious law likewise has evolved through a complex history. As in the case of Christianity, the sacred scripture did not take the form of a legal handbook, and it was left to the early generations of Muslims to work out the details of the relationship between revealed text and the daily workings of religious community. During Muhammad's lifetime, problematical lacunae could be more or less instantly filled by the Prophet's ad hoc responses and clarifications of Qur'ānic issues. Not long after his death, what had begun as a rather informal process of preservation of Muhammad's utterances in the living memory of Muslims, evolved into a more formal development. To prevent the loss of Prophetic tradition, scholars went in search of Hadith across the world. Collecting massive numbers of them, they sifted through the material, attempting to sort out the authentic from the spurious. By the end of the ninth century, Muhammad's words and deeds had been institutionalized into a number of written collections, six of which have been considered especially authoritative. These collections of Hadith came to form the second major source upon which scholars would base their advisories and rulings on the shape of Muslim life.

From about the late seventh century, the community as a whole began elaborating various interpretative principles and procedures. Schools of legal methodology came into being, each with its own peculiar emphasis on one or another aspect of juristic thinking. As the initially all-Arab Muslim community came into contact with an ever wider range of ethnic groups and cultural settings, the need to be able to address new problems grew. Since each culture and ethnic group the Muslims met already had its own legal and religious history, the Muslims had to find ways to put their stamp on the conquered territory without destroying what they found there. They thus had to learn how to incorporate the customary law of the place, extending the umbrella of their own system so as to allow the conquered peoples some latitude of practice.

As one might expect, a city like Medina, whose people considered themselves custodians of the original legacy of Muhammad, would naturally tend toward a more cautious and conservative approach. Meanwhile in territories such as Syria and Iraq the conquering Muslim armies had been posted as a matter of policy away from the major existing cities, in newly founded garrison towns. Eventually such sites grew into cities of importance in their own right. In Iraq, for example, there were Basra and Kufa; across Egypt and North Africa there was Fustat near present-day Cairo and Qayrawan in Tunisia. Located as they were in areas more culturally and ethnically diverse than the Arabian Peninsula, these cities frequently fostered more innovative and flexible approaches to religious issues.

All Muslims agree on the primacy of the Qur'ān as the source of revealed truth, and on the importance of the Hadith as the principal source of information about the example of the Prophet—the Sunna. According to an idealized scenario, Muslim scholars deduced the Sunna from the Hadith. In theory, at least, all that one could know, or needed to know, about the Prophet's example one could find in the collected sayings. In actuality, notions of the Prophet's exemplary behavior preceded the full elaboration of the Hadith, so that the content of the Hadith literature expanded to fill out the growing content of the Sunna. In other words, individual Hadiths came into being to "document" what the community had agreed was sanctioned by the Prophet. A Hadith in which Muhammad is reported to have said "My community will not agree on an error" eventually came to be the standard of veracity as applied to the Sunna. It followed naturally that the community, striving in good faith to live out the Sunna of the Prophet, embodied a living Sunna that already presupposed an interpretation of Muhammad's example. In simple terms, the community strove to live as Muhammad surely would "if he were here now." But while the Hadith has always been traditionally considered the "second" root of law, consensus has in effect supplanted it to the extent that consensus concerning the content of the Hadith preexists much of the actual Hadith literature.[16]

Consensus (*ijmāʿ*), traditionally considered the third source of religious law, after Qurʾān and Hadith, turns out to have been an engine powering the growth of Hadith. Beyond that role, consensus functioned further as a tool in extending the applicability of the revealed law and was restricted to consensus among religious scholars. If a question arose upon which neither Qurʾān nor Hadith made any specific statement, one could seek the solution in the actual practice of the community. The idea is roughly analogous to the classical Roman Catholic notion of *sensus fidelium*, the "conviction of the faithful." It involves a grassroots elaboration of how religious persons acting in good faith live out their commitments.

Suppose now that an issue arose upon which neither Qurʾān nor Hadith nor actual practice could shed definitive light. What then? In the earliest days of the Islamic expansion, the religious judges (*qādī*) appointed to oversee the ordinary affairs of communities in newly conquered territory were accorded considerable latitude in the exercise of individual judgment (*raʾy*). Many scholars were concerned that the practice was too fluid and easy prey to the unbridled use of personal opinion. As a result, the more informal process of *raʾy* was gradually forged into the more rigorous and tightly controlled tool of reasoning called analogy (*qiyās*), similar to what lawyers today call argument from precedent. In the introduction, I offered a concrete example of how the process works.

By the end of the ninth century, about the time the major authoritative written collections of Hadith had come into being, a number of distinctive schools of jurisprudence had formed. Most faded into insignificance by the around the twelfth century, but four Sunni schools remain authoritative today. Each traces its origins back to an eponymous ancestor—a "founding figure" in the broadest sense of the term. Abū Ḥanīfa (d. 767 C.E.) lived and worked in the Iraqi town of Kufa. His school or *madhhab,* the Hanafī, developed a somewhat greater tolerance for the use of analogy than the other schools. Today the Hanafī is the dominant school in Turkey, central Asia, India, and Pakistan. At the other end of the spectrum stands the school named after Ibn Hanbal (d. 855). A major figure in the religious and intellectual life of ninth-century Baghdad, Ibn Hanbal debated with the Mu'tazila over what he considered their unconscionable elevation of speculative reason to a position effectively above divine revelation. The harder the Mu'tazila pushed, the harder Ibn Hanbal pushed back, so that the two sides grew further and further apart. As chapter 4 described in greater detail, when the Mu'tazila fell out of favor at the caliphal court, the new caliph released Ibn Hanbal from prison. Over the next century or so, the more conservative and traditional approach of Ibn Hanbal became the order of the day in Baghdad and its environs. Direct Hanbalī influence in our time is largely limited to the Arabian Peninsula, where it has virtually no competition from other *madhhabs.*

Between the Hanafī and Hanbalī schools, methodologically speaking, stand the Shāfi'ī, named after Shāfi'ī (d. c. 819), and the Mālikī, founded by Mālik ibn Anas (d. 795). The former functions largely in Southeast Asia and parts of Egypt and East Africa, and the latter mostly in North and West Africa. On the whole, Islamic jurisprudence seeks to strike a balance between individual and community, both in terms of needs, rights, and responsibilities, and in terms of legislative authority. Shi'i legal scholars also developed at least two major law schools, of which one currently dominates the scene in Iran. That school, called the Mujtahidī, emphasizes the requirement for every Muslim to subscribe to the teaching of a particular living *mujtahid,* a legal scholar authorized to exercise independent legal investigation, called *ijtihād.* To promote the notion of fixity, Sunni legal tradition has long claimed that the "door of *ijtihād*" swung closed around 900 C.E. Historical evidence suggests a very different picture, with independent investigation remaining alive and well. Shi'i traditions of jurisprudence have more frankly acknowledged the reality of ongoing elaboration and reinterpretation.[17]

Many observers of Islam assume that the term "Sharia law" implies a monolithic, inflexible, intolerant system geared entirely to infringing on rights and punishing severely any and all infractions of religiously sanctioned policy. A widespread misconception is that Sharia law is inextricably entwined, perhaps even simply synonymous, with theocratic regimes in which authorities make no distinction whatsoever between religious and secular, or civil, affairs. Islamic law is in reality a multifaceted, sophisticated complex of disciplines that has over many centuries incorporated a variety of principles of adaptability that acknowledge mitigating circumstances and presuppose the primacy of intention in all forms of behavior. In fact, all human acts conceived in legal terms are labeled according to a spectrum of five "normative" (or "impositional," *taklīfī*) and two "non-normative" (or "postulative," *waḍ'ī*) categories. The normative spectrum runs from required to recommended to neutral to disapproved to forbidden; the non-normative are a pair of opposed qualities: acts are either valid or invalid, on the one hand, and either modified by extenuating circumstances or not. The latter non-normative categories relate on the whole to required actions. Of the five normative categories, only the first and last are strictly legal, that is, "prohibited" at one extreme and "required" at the other.[18]

In addition to these built-in elements of flexibility, there are several other important principles of adaptability. Two of these principles are in a way refinements of the notion of analogical reasoning (*qiyās*). One of the broader and more capacious adaptive concepts involves "seeking the good" (*istiḥsān*). The relatively conservative Shāfi'ī school tended to reject its use (though it was the school's eponym who coined the notion), for fear that its elasticity might open a loophole and thus give rise to scholars arriving at more arbitrary conclusions lacking methodological rigor. On the other hand, the Hanafī school embraced *istiḥsān*, answering Shāfi'ī objections by further clarifying methodological implications and referring to it as covert analogical reasoning (*qiyās khafī*). By giving the concept a specific role in the process of legal reasoning, the Hanafī scholars sought to define its applicability more narrowly.

Secondly, the concept of seeking the common good or broader public interest (*istislāḥ* or *maslaha*) represents yet a further restriction of the applicability of *istiḥsān*. It effectively redefined "seeking the good" as a general concept in relation to the more concrete goal of "seeking the public interest." For some scholars, this too was a problematical concept in that the common good might in some instances seem to compete with the plain sense of the Qur'ān and the Sunna. Suppose, for example, that non-Muslim enemies were to take Muslim prisoners and use them as human shields as they advanced in attack. The prohibition against killing innocent fellow Muslims might have to be set aside in the interest of the safety of a much greater number of Muslims. The concept appears more commonly in scholarly discourse in the eleventh century, when, for example, Ghazālī (a Shāfi'ī in law) defines "common good" as referring to the preservation of religion, life, rationality, progeny, and material possessions but restricts its application to questions whose outcomes will affect the entire community, and not merely individuals. Some more cautious jurists, however, such as the thirteenth-fourteenth century Hanbalī theologian Ibn Taymīya, argue that one must assume concern for common welfare as inherent in the revealed law. One simply needs to know how to read it, and need not trot out more conceptual machinery.[19]

Thirdly, the concept of istihsāb [al-ḥāl] (literally, "presumption of a condition's perdurance" or "joining the present with the past") was developed by al-Āmidī (d. 1233), who began as a Hanbalī and switched to the Shāfiʿī school. In short, the principle asserts that, for example, a person who has entered a state of ritual purity intending to perform his daily liturgical prayer may proceed with the prayer on the assumption that, absent any clear indicators to the contrary, his state of ritual purity remains inviolate at the moment he proposes to begin the prayer. The same principle applies in much more consequential matters as well, such as marriage and property rights, injecting the benefit of the doubt. In other words, should some uncertainty occur as to whether the previous state (marriage to a particular person or ownership of a particular item) is still in force, the presumption is that the former condition does indeed persist. Some religious scholars disagree fundamentally, however; the majority of Hanafī jurists tend to reject the principle, arguing that any doubt cast on the perdurance of a prior state requires a fresh reconsideration of the case.[20]

Another adaptive concept developed by two later medieval Hanbalī theorists, Ibn Taymīya and Ibn Qayyim al-Jawzīya (d. 1350), emerged as a way of describing the necessary compatibility between the governance of those exercising civil power, and divinely ordained fiqh. Known as siyāsa sharʿīya (rule by Sharia standards), the principle aimed at reconciling apparent (or in some cases real) contradiction between established positive religious law, fiqh, and the decisions taken by a given ruler, whether imam, sultan, amir, or wali (guardian). Ibn Taymīya argued that, presuming good faith on the part of a ruler, any such perceived discrepancies were exactly that, the result of inaccurate perception based on faulty reading of the law.

One effect of Ibn Taymīya's interpretation was to promote a more prominent level of participation in civil matters by the religious scholars, the ʿulamāʾ. In other words, he envisioned a balance of power between civil and religious authorities. His views suggest that by the late thirteenth/early fourteenth centuries, the authority of civil rulers had shifted significantly from the concept of a more unitary authority of the earlier caliphs (with the caliph even exercising discretion over questions of fiqh) to a de facto differentiation of roles and status of civil and religious authorities. Ibn Taymīya's interpretation, with its presumption of accord between a ruler's decisions and established *fiqh,* was in effect a desire to reunify what had once been a seamless mantle of authority over all spheres of Muslim life. He sought, in part, to nullify the need for works on political theory (*siyāsat nāma*) and a genre of literature sometimes called "mirrors for princes" (*nasīhat al-mulūk*). Works of this ilk had emerged since the eleventh century in at least tacit acknowledgment that civil rule sometimes led to decisions on the part of a ruler that might suggest incompatibility with the conclusions of religious jurisprudents.[21] In practice, the breach between *fiqh* and the canons of civil governance continued to widen, with the Ottoman dynasty's elaboration of administrative (or dynastic) law known as Qānūn standing as perhaps the most complete monument to the divide.

With the passage of centuries and changes in the social, cultural, and political contexts of Islamic life across the globe, Muslim jurisprudents had to take two other sets of adaptive conditions into account. Local and regional (pre-Islamic) custom, or customary law (*'āda,* or *'urf*), representing practices long enshrined in a given context, often made it necessary to make accommodations between *fiqh* and the de facto accepted behavior in the new context into which Islamic religious law had been "imported." In some instances, "customary" law may actually be a matter of *siyāsa,* civil administrative usage or principles surviving from prior to the arrival of Islam in a given area. Even today, it is not unheard-of for a regional population of Muslims to adhere to non-Qur'ānic practices, especially with regard to ancient social structures and customs, such as honoring strongly matriarchal family systems. In recent times, however, there have been concerted efforts on the part of reform-minded movements to "purify" Islamic practice of remnants of pre-Islamic custom.[22]

## THEOLOGIES OF POWER

All things considered, it is not such a stretch to suggest that all politics has theological implications and that all theologies have political implications, since both politics and theology are at heart about the nature and exercise of power and authority.

### Christian Political Theologies

Christian authors began elaborating basic principles of various theologies of the church, or ecclesiology, by the later second century. Early Fathers, such as Clement of Alexandria and Hippolytus (d. 235), explored ways in which the church on earth mirrored the heavenly archetype, and developed metaphors such as body of Christ, spouse of Christ, and ship. Origen was the first to refer to the church as the "City of God on earth," a state within a state whose laws are consonant with established "civil" law. In the long run, however, the ecclesial "state" will overcome the secular state by the power of the Logos at work within it. Cyprian of Carthage (d. 258) pursued that line of argument in the second version of his *On the Unity of the Church*. He argued that bishops are answerable to God alone, and that not even the pope exercises higher juridical authority, only primacy of honor.

A consistent theme among the Fathers is that "there is no salvation outside of the church," but Augustine was arguably the first to elaborate a global systematic ecclesiology in his *City of God (De Civitate Dei)*. Dramatic events precipitated his reflection on the relationships between earthly and heavenly power and authority. In 410, the Visigoths invaded Rome, with disastrous consequences, and many blamed the Christian rulers for the failure of the city's defense. Since Constantine, Christianity had indeed become inextricably identified with secular rule. Augustine accordingly set out to distinguish between civil and religious spheres, and between pagan and Christian worldviews. He described a conflict between the heavenly and earthly cities, identifying Christianity with the former. Regardless of the fortunes of the earthly realm, believers could have full confidence that the heavenly realm would survive and ultimately provide safe haven. Here on earth, members of both "cities" live together, and not all members of the church can presume to be counted citizens of the heavenly city, for not all are assured of salvation.[23]

Augustine's work was enormously influential, but other voices through late antiquity and into the Middle Ages argued both sides of the church-state question. The theme of the "two swords" enunciated by Bernard of Clairvaux (d. 1153) and others acknowledged the existence of distinct spheres of authority but also elicited a variety of views on their relative shares of power. Gratian's work on canon law affirmed the supremacy of papal authority to which princely rulers must submit in spiritual matters while exercising temporal power independently. Popes like Hadrian IV (d. 1159) insisted on the authority to crown emperors and kings who would do the pope homage. Theologians like John of Salisbury (d. 1180) began preferring the term "church militant" to the previously more common "pilgrim church." Pope Innocent III (d. 1216) defended the papacy's "fullness of power" and right of feudal overlordship, and even the duty to intervene in secular matters where civil rulers failed morally. He claimed the right for popes to examine candidates for imperial office and be the final authority in actually appointing the emperor. Gregory IX (d. 1241) further sought to erode secular authority, at least indirectly, by organizing the Inquisition in 1232 and twice excommunicating Emperor Frederick II.[24]

Eminent Scholastic theologians, however, began to enunciate moderating views, suggesting clearer limits on the reach of the papal arm, even as the papacy confronted stiffer challenges from temporal rulers arising from new conceptions of authority rooted in human community. Thomas Aquinas sought to promote a balance of religious and secular power, while William of Ockham (d. 1347) later preferred to subordinate papal power to princely rule. By the dawn of the age of Protestant reform movements, papal authority yielded increasingly to lay control over regional Catholic communities. Protestant leaders Luther and Calvin led a frontal assault on papal and episcopal authority as devoid of scriptural foundation. Ironically, though Calvin insisted on the separation of church and state, he became in effect the head of a theocratic state, as did his contemporary Ulrich Zwingli. Meanwhile, in England, separation from papal authority similarly resulted in a "state church," with John Knox and the Congregationalists dissenting and forming their own church systems. Influential Catholic Reformation figures, such as Robert Bellarmine, SJ (d. 1621), and Francisco Suarez (d. 1617), argued that papal authority was limited to spiritual matters. Finally, the Enlightenment era emergence of secular national states such as France and the United States saw a shift to natural human rights and the role of conscience as the foundations of authority. And the Second Vatican Council called for a combined effort of church and civil authority to protect human rights and dignity.[25]

## Muslims and Political Theory

From very early on, Muslim authors have addressed complicated questions of the varieties of power and authority in the administration of Muslim community. Even if during the Prophet's lifetime political entity (*dawla*) and religion (*dīn*) were virtually indistinguishable, the expansion of Muslim rule beyond the Arabian Peninsula forced Muslim administrators to confront new complexities in very different social and cultural settings. Political theorists analyzed the relationships between civil and religious authority in a variety of literary genres. One approach, embodied in the genre "mirrors for princes," features direct advice for those on the seat of power.[26] For present purposes, works that address more explicitly the qualifications, prerogatives, and responsibilities of leaders are more germane to our theological frame of reference. The pristine ideal of the caliph as the "shadow of God on earth" and "commander of the faithful" presupposed from the start that the ruler was an individual of unimpeachable moral character, acting after the example of the Prophet. (One could say the same for the role of imam, whether in the distinctively Shi'i sense or in the more generic meaning of "leader" of the Muslim community.)

Factionalism within the Islamic community emerged during the earliest generations of Muslims, with questions about religious, ethical, or genealogical deficiency that critics discerned in candidates or claimants to rule. Sunni, Shi'i, Khāriji, and other contending ideologies all proposed their distinctive criteria for legitimacy in guidance of the Muslim community. Some even argued that an authentic Hadith said that the caliphate as such would be supplanted by mere kingship after the last of the Rightly Guided Caliphs ('Ali). Indeed many pious critics of the Umayyad and Abbasid dynasties argued that their claims to religious legitimacy were empty precisely to the degree that their motives and methods had been corrupted by lust for temporal power. During the eighth and ninth centuries, as the schools of Islamic law were taking shape, jurists argued about the desired qualities of a caliph or imam and the degree to which a given ruler enjoyed a divine mandate.

A major turning point came in 1055, when the Saljuqid Turks reduced the caliph in Baghdad to a mere figurehead. After suffering a de facto dramatic erosion of control for two centuries, the caliph's authority now officially shrunk to merely spiritual leadership, while real political power devolved to the new institution of the sultanate. As I indicated briefly in the introduction, the subject of the imamate (in the general sense) had become a virtually required topic in the earliest treatises of systematic theology. By the early eleventh century, political pragmatism was clearly edging out concerns over theological legitimation in works by such major figures as the Ash'ari theologian Bāqillāni (d. 1013) and Māwardi (d. 1058), a Shāfi'i jurist best known for his work on the principles of political authority (sultāniya). Through the twelfth and thirteenth centuries, marked by continued disintegration of the Abbasid empire, theologically concerned theorists still felt the need to address the relationships between the offices of caliph and sultan. Most upheld the ideal of parallel administrations of spiritual and temporal power, even in the face of clear evidence that the former lacked genuine authority.

After the Mongol sack of Baghdad in 1258 relegated the role of the caliph to little more than a nostalgic ceremonial figure, major late thirteenth-/early fourteenth-century theorists sought to deal theologically with the undeniable realities of the situation. Jurist Ibn Jamā'a (d. 1333) ceded true authority to the conquerors, and Ibn Taymīya went so far as to argue that the caliphate was no longer an essential ingredient in Muslim belief.[27] Though subsequent dynasties, such as the Mamluk and later Ottoman, continued to maintain the fiction of a spiritual ruler, the ideal of the caliph's universal authority would never again be a serious issue.

. . .

Working out and naming precisely the relationships between the two worlds of faith—this and the next, the seen and the unseen, the earthly and the heavenly—have been among the most important theological challenges facing Christians and Muslims alike since the very beginning. If God is both King and Lawgiver, as both traditions affirm in many ways, it follows that both realms comprise his kingdom governed by his law. Drawing the visible lines of community using an invisible divine template has proven an enormous challenge and elusive goal in both traditions.

In the scriptures of the two traditions one finds various metaphors from which Christian and Muslim thinkers have taken their cues as to how God must surely envision human beings enacting the divine mandate on earth. A biblical image of human beings as stewards of creation yielded eventually to imagery of a people under royal authority that was in turn subject to the corrective of prophetic critique. The basic metaphor in the Qur'ān portrays the prophets, beginning with Adam, as God's caliphs. Though the caliphate originally embodied a unitary vertical model of authority for Sunni Muslims, its universal reach began to shrink dramatically as early as the ninth century. With other models of de facto governance supplanting the caliphate, Sunni Islam increasingly looked more like Protestant Christianity. By contrast, Shi'i communities retained more distinctly vertical structures of authority, roughly analogous to those of Roman Catholicism.

Both great communities have experimented continuously with various models by which to inform mundane governance with celestial principles, and with varying degrees of success. Alas, with enormous power and wealth at stake, an immeasurable abyss inevitably opens between heavenly blueprint and earthly realization. On the whole, the histories of both traditions are marked by partial solutions and renewed attempts at adaptation, but precious few "official" admissions that previous models had in fact failed. As they have worked out the nature and limitation of the exercise of authority, both traditions have witnessed development of diverse schools of thought. Sunni Muslims generally believe that the "door" of new legal interpretation closed in 900 C.E., and many Protestant Christians also believe that inspired authority ended with the apostles. Shiʻi tradition, on the other hand, historically left that door open more or less indefinitely, while Catholic tradition accords ongoing authority to the Magisterium, or teaching office of the church. In other words, there have been de facto developments in systems and structures of authority—occasional reforms and revisions of codes of canon law, for example, and the disappearance of a host of early Sunni Sharia *madhhabs* (legal methodologies), leaving in the end only the four currently functioning schools. Nevertheless, in both traditions the dominant tendency has been to deny that such changes have significantly altered the core of their teaching.

In practical terms, the community's reception of "official" formulations—*sensus fidelium* for Catholics, for example, and *consensus* for many Muslims—has often become a decisive factor in shaping issues that have not been clearly and definitively delineated by scripture or positive law. Actual practice, however, is a fluid measure and always exists in tension with canons of internal discipline and belief that have developed in both great traditions. In general, "legal" standards have played a more overt role in Muslim than in Christian communities. On the other hand, while the papacy has maintained at least symbolic central spiritual authority for about half the world's Christians, the caliphate never recovered a parallel role after medieval times. Both traditions have historically struggled with the relationships between secular and religious power, as exemplified in the rise of "defenders of the faith" and "militants" in both histories.

We move now from a consideration of the exercise of power from within the traditions to the various outward forms power and authority have taken. Chapter 6 will explore further how both traditions have fostered institutional developments in hopes of at least some pale imitation of an eternally established archetype.

# Institutions in Action

Against the backdrop of internal structural and theoretical developments, the present chapter explores outward expressions of divinely sanctioned authority and power. After a look at the institutional connections between theology and politics, I will discuss religiously sponsored education and intentional religious communities. Theological implications of the architecture of religious institutions will conclude the chapter.

## THEOLOGY AND POLITICS

In the histories of both Christianity and Islam, the relationships among theology and politics, spiritual and temporal authority, faith community and civil spheres, have been enormously complex and varied. Many people today—Christian and Muslim alike—take it for granted that Christianity has generally maintained a distinction between heavenly and earthly dispensations, while Islam has always been hardwired to join the two inextricably. "Give to God the things that are God's and to Caesar the things that are Caesar's," Jesus says in all three Synoptic Gospels (Matthew 22:21; Mark 12:17; Luke 20:25). Many Christians have interpreted the text as a mandate for separation of church and state, though the history of Christianity is replete with examples that the dichotomy has rarely, if ever, been surgically precise.

Ask almost any Muslim about the scope of the Islamic faith, and he or she will likely respond that Islam is a complete way of life, not merely a religious creed and set of rituals divorced from more mundane concerns. Some Muslims continue to believe, despite overwhelming historical data to the contrary, that the ideal of a global *umma* under the leadership of a "commander of the faithful" known as a caliph (*khalīfa*) enjoyed a long and glorious reign and is destined to return the world to a unitary rule. The real story, however, is very different on both sides.

## Christian Community and the Exercise of Power

In many of its historical embodiments, Christendom has often been dominated by rulers, whether royal or ecclesiastical, whose ideal church was a heavily armed fortress, a juggernaut before which all resistance was futile. One theme in early Christian history describes the church as a beleaguered minority movement that suffered horrific persecutions under Roman rule well into the third century. Refusing to accede to imperial demands that they worship at the altar of Caesar, many Christians paid the price of martyrdom. Because the Christians held themselves aloof from the regime, many emperors regarded them as a political threat to be exterminated.

Their status changed markedly, it seems, after Constantine (d. 337) battled his way to the top of the Roman Empire, but even before his formal conversion and baptism very near the end of his life. His so-called Edict of Milan (promulgated jointly with Emperor Licinius in 313) declared the churches legal entities under Roman law, thereby granting them official toleration along with all other religious groups. Constantine, still unbaptized, convened and presided over the Council of Nicaea (325) to settle the christological debates precipitated by the Arians, who denied the full divinity of Jesus. He decided in favor of Christians in various other ways as well prior to his conversion and is still known as the "thirteenth apostle" in some Orthodox churches. Constantine became the sole Roman emperor in 324, but it was Theodosius I (r. 379–95), the last ruler of both East and West, who proclaimed Nicene Christianity the creed of the realm in 380.[1]

After the de facto split between the Eastern and Western segments of the Roman Empire, conditions of rule began to deteriorate in the West. Constantine's centralization of effective Roman rule in Constantinople had the unintended consequence of leaving the popes, the bishops of Rome, enough independence to begin consolidating greater temporal power. The so-called barbarian invasions through the fifth century hastened the official demise of the Roman Empire in 476, further leaving church authorities to fend for themselves. Pope Leo I "the Great" (d. 461) rose to the challenge, defending Rome against the threat of Attila (d. c. 453) and the Huns. One of Leo's most important successors, Gregory I (d. 604), continued the papal role of political leader, fending off the invading Lombards. He held at arm's length the attempts of the Western emperor to regain control, as well as the patriarch of Constantinople's moves to extend his reach westward, and ended the Byzantine exarchate of Ravenna. Still, Western Christianity's fortunes continued to decline and suffered well into the tenth century.[2]

During late antiquity, through the so-called Dark Ages of the church, and into early medieval times, papal claims on temporal as well as spiritual power waxed and waned. From his newly founded capital in Aachen (western Germany), Charlemagne (d. 814) secured papal approval to revive the Holy Roman Empire with his coronation as its emperor in 800. The new temporal ruler lost no time attempting to erode the pope's spiritual authority by establishing a level of administration called "metropolitan" jurisdictions by which he could easily control the bishops in his realm, thus circumventing papal oversight at the diocesan level. He weighed in doctrinally by calling the Synods of Frankfurt and Aachen, but on the political side Charlemagne failed to overcome the centrifugal tendencies of the tribal powers. After the emperor's death, his heirs split the realm among themselves, thereby setting the stage for the rise of the feudal system that would successfully ward off attempts at centralized rule for generations to come.

In the wake of the Carolingian regime's disintegration, strong popes again assumed a major share of temporal and spiritual power. Both Leo IV (d. 855) and Nicholas I (d. 867) raised significant armed forces and claimed precedence over secular powers. They and their Roman successors also widened the breach with their Eastern counterparts, the patriarchs of Constantinople, by insisting on Roman primacy. For their part the patriarchs reaffirmed the doctrine known as Caesaropapism, ceding authority over the five eastern patriarchates to the Byzantine emperor. By 1054, the divide between Eastern and Western Christendom had become virtually unbridgeable, and less than a quarter-century later the victory of migrating Turkish forces in eastern Anatolia over a Byzantine army at the battle of Manzikert (1071) would usher in the era of the Crusades.[3]

Meanwhile, in the heart of Europe, a mid-tenth-century monastic reform led by the abbots of Cluny presaged the end of the Dark Ages. The Ottonian rulers revived the Holy Roman Empire in 962, the emperor once again claiming the right to appoint bishops and thus gain control over the considerable wealth of church institutions. A crisis over this problem of "lay investiture" came to a head in 1077 when Pope Gregory VII confronted Ottonian emperor Henry IV, leading to a partial settlement promulgated in the Concordat of

Worms in 1122. By then, the church was firmly committed to launching what would become the First Crusade. Commissioned in 1096 by Pope Urban II (d. 1099), the Crusaders wrested control of Palestine from the Cairo-based Muslim Fatimid dynasty (969–1171) and proclaimed the Latin Kingdom of Jerusalem (1099–1189).

Urban began the tradition of promising Crusaders that their liberating the Holy Land from infidel rule would win them forgiveness of sin and a heavenly reward. Urban, a former abbot of Cluny, encouraged the Crusaders to think of themselves as a holy fraternity, setting the stage for the rise of such lay orders as the Knights Templar. Monastic leaders such as Bernard of Clairvaux (d. 1153) continued to function as prominent advocates of subsequent Crusades. But when the Fourth Crusade (1202–4) deteriorated into a slaughter of Eastern Christians by Western Crusaders, and the sack of Constantinople, support for the Crusading ethos began to wane dramatically.[4]

In the heart of Europe, yet another incarnation of the Holy Roman Empire gradually expanded from Germany and northern Italy to encompass much of France and Portugal. By the time of the Fourth Lateran Council (1215), church leadership was turning its drive for comprehensive power against the enemies within—sectarian Christian movements such as the Bogomils, Cathari, Albigensians, and Waldensians, which were now condemned as heretical—and against the Jews of central Europe. New religious orders, especially the Dominicans, played a major role in these efforts. This new kind of Crusade arose side by side with the drive by Iberian kings against Muslim rule in Spain, known as the Reconquest. Through the thirteenth and fourteenth centuries, the balance of power continued as a tug-of-war between papal/episcopal contenders and claimants to royal authority. Along with the emergence of new religious orders, the development of the university added an important new institutional dimension and a new arena in which the struggle for religious authority would play out.

Contention over temporal and spiritual power moved into a new phase as early Christian reformers John Wycliffe and John Hus directed trenchant critiques at what they regarded as papal misappropriation of authority. As the Protestant Reformation came on full force in the early sixteenth century with Luther's Ninety-five Theses (1517), the clash of factional armies led by religious authorities soon pitted Catholics against Protestants. Meanwhile, the Catholic kings of western Europe took advantage of the increasing prospects of global exploration to combine the quest for projecting their power abroad with the express desire of winning souls for Christ. Virtually every major expedition to the New World to the west or the ancient civilizations to the east sailed with the pope's blessing and boarded cohorts of missionary chaplains to deliver the message of salvation to the vanquished who wisely opted not to resist subjugation.[5]

## Islam and the Theopolitical Connection

Many Muslims through the centuries have treasured a notion of the ideal Umma as a perfect amalgam of religious and civil authority, and many Christians have historically resisted the threat of domination that such a notion presented. However real that threat may have been at various times, the scenario of a unitary religio-political Muslim rule presupposes several conditions that one looks for in vain in the history of Islamic political regimes. First, the caliphate of nostalgia is supposed to have been a truly global centralized rule in which the commander of the faithful exacted the fealty of Muslims everywhere. In fact, at no time during the history of the caliphate did it extend simultaneously across the full expanse of territories in which Islam would eventually become a dominant presence or majority faith community. I have given a general outline of these developments previously, but the breadth and complexity of the subject is such that some details of the large picture bear repeating here.

At its broadest extent, the caliphate, by any account a vast and extraordinary project, stretched from Spain to northwestern India. However, no truly centralized rule was established firmly in Iberia, and within half a century after the Abbasid dynasty had founded its new capital of Baghdad in 762, the fabric of the caliphate began to unravel from the edges. By the early ninth century, restive provinces broke off as practically independent amirates; by the mid-tenth century, a Shi'i faction had become the power behind the throne in Baghdad; and a century later, the Saljuqid Turks had virtually neutered the caliphate by establishing the sultanate as the de facto parallel institution with all the real power. Around the same time, rival caliphates were well established in Spain and Egypt. In other words, the political map of Islamdom quickly took on the look of a patchwork quilt, and the notion of a resurrected global Muslim rule is in reality a dream that has never come true as people who fantasize about it might imagine. By the time the Ottoman dynasty incorporated the great middle swath of what had been the Byzantine Empire, even that great power included only part of North Africa and went no farther east than Iraq. In addition, the kind of caliphate whose resurrection radical/puritanic/extremist groups (such as the Taliban and Al-Qa'ida) envision is in reality not the extended dominion represented for several generations by the Umayyad and Abbasid dynasties. These groups look back instead to the pristine days of the Prophet and his four immediate successors, the Rightly Guided Caliphs. They typically regard the subsequent dynastic regimes with their pretensions to royalty as betrayals of the Prophetic age. The problem here is that the Rightly Guided Caliphs ruled a much reduced realm even at its greatest extent.[6]

Second, the ideal of the caliphate assumes the seamless integration—indeed, the simple identity—of political and religious institutions. The historical reality is that the majority of the many political regimes under Islamic auspices across the globe over more than a millennium actually represent a wide variety of blends and interrelationships of political and religious institutions. Take early modern Iran, for example. In 1500, Shi'i Islam was proclaimed the "state" creed by the ascendant Safavid dynasty. For most of the subsequent five hundred years, the royal establishment and the religious establishment remained institutionally and functionally distinct. Religious officialdom played, on the whole, the role of a loyal opposition for the most part, and at no time did religious scholars mount a serious campaign to exercise actual political rule. Not until the Iranian Islamic Revolution in 1979 did Khomeini's radical reinterpretation of Iranian Shi'i traditions of political theology call for direct religious establishment control over political institutions.[7]

## MONKS AND SUFIS, MASTERS AND SHAYKHS

In both the Christian and Islamic traditions, two seminal forms of living institutions have made essential contributions to the growth of the faith communities and to their success in adapting to new social and cultural contexts. First, organizations that gave shape to the desire for intentional communities within the larger society of believers have taken the form of Christian monastic foundations and Muslim Sufi "brotherhoods." Second, the rise of institutions of higher learning in Europe and the development of advanced curricula of religious studies and law in the madrasas in the Middle East have more in common than might at first be apparent.[8]

### Christian Intentional Religious Communities

During the early Christian centuries, concerns about hostilities directed at the minority community of believers as well as a sense of the transience of earthly life prompted a quest for a more dedicated practice of the faith. By the third century, leaders such as Egyptians Antony (d. 356) and Pachomius (d. 347) began to promote withdrawal to a life of ascetical discipline and manual labor. Combat against Satan and the forces of evil required one's full attention, and the harsh solitude of the desert seemed the ideal setting. Whereas Antony favored the eremitical (or anchoritic) life of complete solitude under a shared superior, Pachomius structured his organization as a community whose members engaged more actively with each other in all aspects of the daily order (cenobitic life).

Some scholars suggest that the monastic alternative became popular as the age of Roman persecutions, and hence of martyrdom, came to an end.[9] By the later fourth century, various major church fathers founded, or were members of, monastic communities both anchoritic and cenobitic. Cappadocian Father Basil of Caesarea (d. 379, in eastern Anatolia) formulated one of the earliest "rules," setting the pattern for virtually all later Orthodox monastic foundations. In his cenobitic model, monks pursued an active life of service to the needy, prayer, and study under the absolute authority of an abbot. European foundations began with Martin of Tours (d. 397), and John Cassian's (d. 435) *Institutions* and *Conferences* became seminal works of monastic theology.

Jerome led a monastery in Bethlehem; farther west, in North Africa, Augustine reoriented the purpose of monastic formation toward service to the larger church. Over a century later, Benedict of Nursia's (d. 550) *Rule* set the pattern for the nearly absolute authority of the abbot in cenobitic communities throughout medieval Latin monasticism. Throughout late antiquity and through the Dark Ages, Benedictine and Augustinian foundations were by far the most numerous in western Europe.[10]

Beginning in the tenth century, new monastic and other mendicant orders were in the vanguard as the church entered a new institutional era. Reforms at Cluny reestablished classic Benedictine rule and monastic practice (910), setting the stage for variations on the Benedictine regime in the highly cloistered Carthusian (1084) and Cistercian (1098) orders, both of which generated hundreds of monasteries during the twelfth and thirteenth centuries. During the early eleventh century, orders of "canons" (so called because of their abbeys' relationships to major cathedrals) also rose to prominence. Most influential were the Victorines, of the abbey of St. Victor (1113), best known for their contributions to scholarship and mystical literature. But it was above all the new orders of the early thirteenth century, the Franciscans and Dominicans, that fostered the most noteworthy institutional developments in the church. Like virtually all earlier monastic or mendicant organizations, the great medieval orders required celibacy; but "third order" affiliates facilitated a close association between devout married laypersons and the orders proper, with their "first order" priests and brothers and "second order" nuns.

Among the growing number of new organizations, emphasis on several matters of mission, discipline, and organization varied. In addition to obvious differences between anchoritic and cenobitic foundations, orders differed with respect to engagement with the outside world, attitudes toward material wealth and resources, the relative blend of members considered clerics (that is, ordained priests and deacons) and laypersons (that is, religious "brothers" and "sisters"), structures of accountability among members and their superiors, the role of manual labor, and the administrative relationships among monasteries following a given rule (e.g., Benedictine, Augustinian). But in the context of theological themes, nothing in the history of monasticism figures more prominently than the contribution of the "active" orders to the emergence of the universities. I will return to that topic after a look at the evolution of Islamic intentional communities in the form of Sufi "brotherhoods."[11]

The early sixteenth century saw the emergence of a new generation of intentional communities more explicitly focused on active ministry outside the confines of the order, and less emphasis on the shared daily order of prayer and work pursued by the classic monastic and mendicant institutions. One of the largest and most influential of these communities was the Society of Jesus, also known as the Jesuits, founded in 1540 by a spirited Basque named Ignatius of Loyola. The Jesuit constitution and spirituality became models for many later nonmonastic active orders of both men and women. Two important new communities included the Franciscan order called the Capuchins, founded in 1520 by Matteo da Bascio, and the Ursuline teaching order of religious women, founded in 1535 by Angela Merici.[12]

## Muslim Intentional Communities and the Sufi Brotherhoods

One of the most intriguing—and often controversial—institutional developments in Islamic history is the growth and spread of intentional communities associated with the complex phenomenon known as Sufism. Some scholars have speculated that the term derived from the word for "wool" (sūf) and referred to the rough garments worn by early ascetics. Whatever its origin, traditional sources have identified individuals from among the first two generations of Muslims, the Companions and Followers, as remarkable for their piety, devotion, and closeness to the Prophet.

Muhammad's father-in-law and eventual successor (Caliph) Abū Bakr (d. 634) was known as The Authentic One (Siddīq) for his truthfulness, and as the Friend of the Cave because he was Muhammad's sole companion in a cave where they took refuge from the pursuing Quraysh warriors during the Hijra from Mecca to Medina. Abū 'd-Dardā' (d. 652) and Abū Dharr (d. 653), both known for their asceticism and simplicity of life as modeled by the Prophet, were among the first of the "Helpers" (Ansār) of Medina who came to Muhammad's aid after the Hijra. Later Sufis looked back to these and other early exemplars of a life of prayer and discipline.

During subsequent generations, other men and women who gained reputations for holiness and wisdom attracted circles of spiritual seekers who would meet for sessions of prayer and guidance in their humble residences (zāwiyas, "corners"). As followers increased in numbers and came greater distances to visit their shaykhs and shaykhas (female shaykhs), larger venues and facilities became necessary. Small circles gradually grew into more complex, semiformal organizations, with specific tasks assigned to individual members. At the death of a spiritual guide, a successor (sometimes hand-picked) kept the group going, and the tomb of the deceased leader often became the focal point of the organization.

According to traditional sources, diverse spiritual pedagogies and orientations began to develop in the spirit of the various foundational figures centered in different geographical areas and cities. The Iraqi cities of Basra and Baghdad, for example, and the northeastern province of Persia, Khurasan, became renowned for their own paragons of the spiritual life. For several generations these groups continued to thrive in their places of origin, while new ones arose in other areas of the central Middle East.

By the later tenth and early eleventh centuries, more formal, complex, and extensive organizations appeared in Persia and elsewhere under the aegis of charismatic figures like Ibn Khafīf (d. 982) and his own grand-student Kāzarūnī (d. 1033). As numbers of followers burgeoned (Ibn Khafīf's are said to have exceeded one thousand), differentiation of tasks within the organizations increased, and facilities capable of housing and sustaining many seekers developed. Known variously as ribāt, khānqāh, or zāwiya, these institutions came to encompass residential areas for teachers and disciples, kitchens (often with a social outreach component), prayer and ritual spaces, and funerary chambers enclosing the mortal remains of founders and/or past leaders.

Intentional communities increasingly developed their own individual identities based on the teachings of their foundational figures. Signature traditions naturally included forms and methods of prayer and community discipline. Members came to refer to such traditions as the way (*tarīqa*) of the original teacher. But the various organizations also developed distinctive systems of religious formation and administration.

At the heart of each *tarīqa* was the role of relationship of individual seekers to their spiritual guides or shaykhs. Methods of pedagogy grew increasingly complex and sophisticated, as did criteria and rituals of formal initiation into full membership. By the mid-thirteenth century a variety of Sufi *tarīqas,* each with its version of a rule, training regime, and authority structure, had begun to appear across the Middle East and central Asia.

Institutions of over a dozen major Sufi brotherhoods became highly visible fixtures in many cities, from North Africa through the Arab Middle East, from Turkey through the Caucasus to Persia and into central Asia, and across South and Southeast Asia. Among the largest and most influential were the Shādhilīya, founded by Abū 'l-Hasan ash-Shādhilī (d. 1258) and important especially across North Africa and Egypt; the Mevlevi (Arabic, Mawlawīya), named after its inspiration, Jalāl ad-Dīn Rūmī (d. 1273), whose honorific title was Mawlānā (Our Master), founded in central Anatolia and then spreading through the central Middle East; the Naqshbandīya, named after Bahā' ad-Dīn Naqshband (d. 1389), a major presence in the Balkans through Turkey and Persia/Iran and into Afghanistan and India; the Chishtīya, traced traditionally to Muʿīn ad-Dīn Chishtī (d. 1236) and of critical importance throughout the Indian subcontinent; and the Qādirīya, named after ʿAbd al-Qādir al-Jīlānī (d. 1166), arguably the most widespread of the brotherhoods, with branches everywhere from Morocco to Malaysia, including major segments of sub-Saharan Africa.

As confraternities proliferated, so did the association of Sufi organizations with the new institution of the madrasa, which spread rapidly from the mid-eleventh century on. Larger orders generated multiple subfoundations often far from their ancestral origins, with the later foundations enjoying varying degrees of independence financially as well as in their ways of engaging the outside world. As I will describe further in chapters 8 and 9, an extensive literature of mystical theology and spiritual formation, as well as the development of Arabic and Persian mystical poetry, became hallmarks of Sufism especially from the thirteenth through the fifteenth century.[13]

## Christian Universities

Since the earliest days of Christianity, New Testament authors had recognized the role and office of teacher. Much of early Christian education occurred informally in homes and smaller local venues. There were, however, exceptions, such as the second- to third-century catechetical school of Alexandria. One of the first developments in institutional education was the evolution of the cathedral school, beginning (arguably) at York around 700. Originally dedicated largely to seminary training, many such institutions eventually took in lay students and included facilities for boarders. During Merovingian and Carolingian times (eighth–ninth centuries), the palace school functioned mostly to train courtiers, while a tradition of monastic schools in the Benedictine tradition continued to provide more explicitly religious curricula. By the late tenth century, the typically small-scale cathedral schools were no longer able to accommodate increasing demand for ecclesiastical education.

As cathedral schools developed in the larger cities and expanded in size and complexity, new educational needs called for new structures, including the accreditation of graduates in a variety of advanced specializations. Thus began the era of the European universities, with Bologna first to confer degrees (around 1088). Major schools followed during the subsequent 150 years or so, beginning with Paris and Oxford (1160 and 1167), and important foundations in Spain, France, and Italy into the mid-thirteenth century. In many of the early universities, the students and their families enjoyed astonishing control over the institution and its faculty, but that would eventually change dramatically. By the later thirteenth century, papal decrees had conferred a remarkable degree of autonomy and academic freedom on the universities and allowed masters both internal authority and mobility to move between and among institutions. At the same time, a high percentage of church officials were taking degrees from the great universities.

"Secondary" schools had not yet been established as a phase in formal education. Beginning university students were often the age of today's high school freshmen, and in some settings, church law granted scholars the highly protected status of cleric. University curricula in many areas followed the ancient Roman division of the seven liberal arts into the *trivium* (grammar, rhetoric, logic) and *quadrivium* (arithmetic, geometry, astronomy, music). But it was Scholastic philosophy and theology as taught by renowned masters that had the greatest impact on Christian life as such. Colorful and controversial dialectician Peter Abelard was among the first to elevate philosophy to a high profile. Meanwhile, Aristotelian and Neoplatonic thought had begun to infiltrate European circles through Latin translations of the works of Ibn Rushd (aka Averroes, d. 1198). Masters like Aquinas and Bonaventure solidified the reputation of Paris as a center of Scholastic theology, although pursuing very different styles.

Credentials of an advanced education became increasingly important for churchmen of all kinds through the Middle Ages and into early modern times. Public disputation was a regular and demanding exercise, and the acquisition of "master's" status was a long, arduous process of over ten years. It was widely believed that degrees in theology were among the most difficult to win. During the years when Ignatius of Loyola was in the process of organizing what would become the Society of Jesus (mid-sixteenth century), for example, the first seven core members were all students seeking the master of arts degree at the University of Paris. One of the major goals in the early history of the Society of Jesus was the establishment of schools throughout Europe, and institutions of both secondary and higher education became a hallmark of the order thereafter.

Education, especially at higher levels, was largely available only to males throughout the Middle Ages and well into modern times, though even in earlier days, daughters of privilege (such as Charlemagne's two girls) had access to formal schooling. Since students at many of the cathedral schools and early universities had the legal status of clerics, accepting women was unthinkable for more reasons than one. Women were to be formed educationally, if at all, as befitted future wives and mothers. Some religious authorities argued, however, that education in morals was essential for women and men alike. Girls ought, therefore, learn to read and write, argued Dominican encyclopedist Vincent of Beauvais (d. 1264), for example; and girls who entered orders of religious women often studied Latin, the better to participate in the liturgical life of the church.[14]

## Madrasas and Muslim Higher Religious Education

In recent years, the term *madrasa* has unfortunately been disconnected not only from its simple root meaning of "place of study," but from the rich history and tradition of institutions of higher learning that it represents. Widespread misuse of the term has identified it exclusively with small schools, mostly in South Asia, whose mission is to indoctrinate the youngest children in a "jihadist" ideology. Historically, Muslim children with access to traditional primary curricula received solid grounding in literacy, grammar, arithmetic, and the basics of Muslim faith and practice.

Very early on, instruction occurred in homes, but the institution of the *kuttāb* soon became the standard institutional structure for the tutelage of the young. As the section above on the various roles in the religious authority structure suggested, ancient Islamic tradition placed high value on knowledge (*'ilm*) and thus accorded religious scholars (*'ulamā'*) a place of honor in society. Obtaining a license (*ijāza*) was an often lengthy and demanding process, and the responsibilities of one credentialed to teach others were considerable. For some four centuries after the death of Muhammad, the circle/shaykh (in the sense of teacher rather than Sufi spiritual guide) system of advanced learning was the standard among Sunni Muslims. Such circles at first typically convened in mosques, but educational venues for advanced instruction grew more specialized. Some of the earliest mosque complexes came into being with the addition of a residential facility (*khān*) for students living at a distance. Students focused on memorizing the Qur'ān and studying (and often memorizing) Hadith, Arabic philology, exegesis, and law.

Patrons of education, especially certain government ministers, funded lectureships in major city mosques, providing room and board as well as salaries for the teachers. By the early eleventh century, mosque-hostel complexes had become common across the Middle East, with often extensive libraries an integral part of the best-endowed among them. On the shelves of the most important libraries students had access to works not only in the traditional disciplines, but in the "imported" sciences as well—philosophy, logic, math, astronomy, medicine, music, and belles lettres.

In Shi'i circles, other intriguing developments marked the growth of institutions of higher learning. Twelver Shi'i education traditions included a special focus on the writings and sayings of the imams, and on exegetical studies geared to extracting the ways in which the sacred text illuminated the Shi'i interpretation of Islamic history. Second in size among Shi'i communities, the Ismā'īlīs (sometimes called the Seveners) placed greater emphasis on the role of itinerant *dā'īs* ("those who invite," i.e., missionaries) in communicating to seekers basic religious disciplines and the intricacies of distinctively Shi'i emphasis on the priority of the inward (*bātin*) meaning over the outward (*zāhir*). By the mid-eleventh century, Shi'i influence and political power had manifested itself in the Fatimid dynasty with its newly founded city of Cairo; and in the Buyid dynasty, which became effectively the power behind the enthroned Abbasid caliph in Baghdad (c. 945–1055).[15]

By the time the Saljuqid Turks swept across Persia from central Asia and took control of Baghdad in 1055, the madrasa typically consisted of a mosque with attached residential facility, and the curriculum offered a wide range of subjects, including law. Under Saljuqid patronage, the shape and function of the madrasa as an institution of higher learning underwent significant change. Whereas the founder of the earlier mosque-based institution exercised only limited control over the makeup and orientation of the foundation, the person who endowed a madrasa-centered institution enjoyed full legal control and could thus stipulate virtually all the particularities of staffing and student body. The new form of madrasa expanded the prominence of instruction in the legal methods of the four Sunni law schools. Individual madrasas were often dedicated to one of those *madhhabs,* but by the thirteenth century some patrons chose to include facilities and funding for two, three, or even all four schools in their deeds of endowment. In addition, part of the Saljuqid rulers' motivation in founding madrasas across the realm was to counteract the influence of Shiʿi groups.

Some madrasas anchored expansive complexes that housed public libraries, soup kitchens, medical facilities, funerary structures for the founder and his family, and Sufi residences, as well as facilities dedicated to instruction in Hadith. Formal disputation became the standard measure of a student's proficiency, presuming solid grounding in all the positions of major jurists, facility in dialectical argument, and skill in debating. One could obtain a license after four years, typically, after presenting a written synthesis of the shaykh's course of instruction.

A full complement of faculty in a major madrasa included specialists— shaykhs (or *ustādhs,* "masters" or "chair holders") of Hadith, of Qurʾān studies and recitation, and of jurisprudence (*fiqh*). Hierarchical structures of authority varied, depending on the size and wealth of an endowment, but a professor (*mudarris*) might enjoy the services of the equivalent of assistant professors (*nāʾib mudarris*), and together they would form the rough equivalent of an academic department. Especially renowned professors might receive the title "leader" (*raʾīs*), and some of those might have "associates" (*nāʾib raʾīs*). As for students, they could specialize serially in various disciplines, holding a license in one while pursuing licensure in another—perhaps akin to a "double major," except that they could obtain their diplomas from various madrasas, migrating to the homes of professors best known in a given field. Professors also often enjoyed the services of teaching and research assistants, all of this funded in full (including all faculty upkeep as well as student tuition, room, and board) by the founding endowment. All in all, the medieval system of advanced education that Muslim patrons and rulers had in place across North Africa, the Middle East, central Asia, and South Asia was remarkable, to say the least.[16]

## VISIBLE STRUCTURES: ARCHITECTURE, COMMUNITY, AND RELIGIOUS ECONOMY

Institutional developments, of course, require space. That means brick and mortar, and that takes money.[17] In addition, visible expressions of the institutional life of major religious communities typically merit particular attention to the aesthetic and symbolic dimensions that transform a building into a work of monumental art.

## Cathedrals, Monasteries, and the Spatial Arts

Christianity's earliest liturgical venues were not purpose-built structures, but "house churches" in the homes of believers blessed with more ample dwellings. During more than two centuries of official persecution, Christians often felt compelled to hide their religious activities from the eyes of Roman authorities. Systems of subterranean tombs called catacombs, constructed for burial by Jews and pagans as well, sometimes doubled as places of worship. Official Roman policy, however, did not always dictate such covert strategies for survival. The exceptionally large, elaborate house-church in the Syrian garrison town of Dura-Europos is evidence that Christians in some contexts could safely express their faith somewhat more publicly.[18]

After Christianity became the official creed of the Roman Empire, its new legal status allowed the faith to spread, and fairly rapid growth called for the creation of new public worship facilities. The first major model of church architecture was the imperial audience hall called the basilica, where the *basileus* (king, ruler) held court. Known to Latin Christians as the *aula ecclesiae* (hall of assembly), it was a hypostyle structure (post and lintel) with a main aisle with clerestory (elevated roof the width of the main aisle) flanked by two side aisles with lower vaulting, with an apse located at the eastern end of the main aisle. The relatively simple structure facilitated a processional ritual in which petitioners and courtiers marched ceremonially to be received by the ruler enthroned in the apse. Christians adapted the form liturgically, situating the altar in the apse and using the side aisles for circumambulatory processions on certain occasions.[19]

With Christendom's expansion across the greater Mediterranean basin, artists created a variety of functional and decorative styles for principal ritual needs. In addition to spaces for the Eucharistic liturgy, separate facilities for baptismal rituals became more common, often taking the form of an annex to the basilical hall. Early Christian Byzantine emperors innovated especially influential architectural variations based on the use of increasingly ambitious domes. Justinian's spectacular Hagia Sophia arranged a vast processional space, not under a modest hypostyle central nave (as in the traditional basilica) but under a massive central dome over a hundred feet in diameter and nearly eighteen stories high, with two axial half-domes. While Eastern churches further exploited the structural and design advantages of the dome, Western architects in Romanesque style expanded on the aisled basilica by heightening the nave vaulting, adding the transept (forming a Latin cross), and extending the apsidal end.

During subsequent centuries, architects developed the distinctive features of Gothic style by raising the roof still further, increasing interior light by thinning buttressed walls and expanding window area dramatically, and enriching iconographic content through both elaborate stained glass and exterior and interior sculptural programs. Churches were traditionally oriented along west-east axes, so that the sun arose over the altar apse and set over western rose windows and portal sculptures with Last Judgment or resurrection themes.

As early monastic orders spread their regional foundations across Europe and attracted greater numbers, they required larger and more specialized facilities. By the tenth century, monastery architecture included not only residential spaces and facilities for apostolic outreach, but often monumental church architecture as well. During the eleventh and twelfth centuries, institutions of higher religious learning began as cathedral schools, but as universities developed into freestanding institutions, architectural design followed suit.[20]

Funding for increasingly monumental institutional architectural creations demanded increasingly wealthy sources. A far cry from the humble house-church, cathedral and monastery depended on either royal or high ecclesiastical (episcopal, if not papal) patronage. Holy Roman emperors and bishops alike demonstrated their power and authority by bankrolling massive projects, many of which spanned the lifetimes of more than a few patrons. In some cases, it was donations from countless much less well-heeled patrons that kept projects going during lean times. Art historians have produced important studies of architectural patronage, occasionally foregrounding or at least giving significant attention to the religious motivations behind patronage. One key to the "theological" dimensions of religious architecture—both in general and in relation to this narrower topic of funding and motivation—lies in the dominant visual metaphors embodied in the edifices, from house of the people to the house of God, from quiet refuge for prayer to bulwark of global salvation, from earthly fortress to image of the heavenly Jerusalem.[21]

## Mosques, Madrasas, and Sufi Complexes in Islamic Architecture

During the fledgling Muslim community's Meccan period(c. 610–22), the institutional dimensions of Muslim worship practice were apparently somewhat fluid. Muhammad and others prayed at the ancient ritual site at the center of the city, the Ka'ba, and it is possible (though not certain) that the earliest Muslims may also have prayed facing Jerusalem. The young community does not seem to have made use of a proprietary ritual space until about two years into the Medinan period (i.e., 624), probably after Muhammad received the divine instruction (Q 2:144) that he was to reorient Muslim liturgical prayer from Jerusalem toward Mecca. A small building in Medina called the "mosque of the two prayer-directions" (masjid al-qiblatayn) today marks the spot identified with this important reorientation—one that evidently signaled a formal breach with the local Jewish communities. The first quasi-formal distinct architectural setting for ritual prayer (masjid, "place of prostration") was set up in Muhammad's own house in Medina, its qibla (ritual orientation) facing Mecca's Ka'ba. When Muhammad and his supporters marched on Mecca in 630, the Prophet rededicated the Ka'ba by cleansing it of its idols and declaring it the symbolic center of Islamic monotheism.[22]

After Muhammad's death, Muslim forces began to introduce Islam into surrounding areas, establishing garrison cities at Basra and Kufa in Iraq, at Fustat (near present-day Cairo), at Qayrawan (in present-day Tunisia), and in other newly conquered territories. Early mosques in areas of expansion assumed the form of the hypostyle basilical hall, with the apse adapted into what would become the prime symbol of the orientation to Mecca, the mihrāb (prayer niche). Architects gradually added visual embellishments, such as a small dome over the niche and later a similar dome at the opposite end of the central aisle (or nave) topped by a clerestory. Though the prayer hall was the principal covered space of the early mosques, an uncovered courtyard of equal or greater size surrounded by a covered portico became a standard compositional element in the ritual space. In time, another functional/symbolic element became a regular feature of mosque architecture—the minaret, a galleried tower from which the muezzin intoned the call to prayer (adhān) five times daily.

Between the tenth and fifteenth centuries, Muslim architects from Spain to Indonesia adapted various construction and decorative materials, compositional elements, and design plus aesthetic considerations. The long-term result was the evolution of half a dozen major architectural styles, characteristic of Spain and North Africa (hypostyle prayer hall with clerestory over a central nave, square single-stage minarets), Syria and Egypt (hypostyle halls early on, later more prominent monumental domed prayer halls in stone and marble, multistaged and shaped elaborately carved minarets), Turkey (central domed prayer halls in gray granite, multidomed courtyard porticoes, slender cylindrical conical-topped minarets with up to three balconies), Iran and central Asia (domed prayer halls, arcade-enclosed courtyards with *iwān*-facade side halls, baked brick structures with elaborate tile decoration, cylindrical single-balcony minarets), and India and Southeast Asia (forms similar to those in Iran, but of marble and sandstone building materials, multicolored decorative mosaics).

In addition to mosques, a variety of other architectural forms and functions became the focus of considerable creativity. By the mid-eleventh century the institutions of higher learning known as madrasas came into their own as architecturally significant works, whether as freestanding structures or as integral components in larger mosque complexes. Classic design, whatever the dominant regional style, included a central courtyard with residential and instructional facilities built into surrounding covered structures. Major freestanding madrasas also often incorporated a prayer hall and sometimes the mausoleum of the patron or founder and his or her family.

Funerary structures also became an important focus of architectural creativity, despite Muhammad's warnings against the temptation to aggrandize any mere mortal's final resting place. Finally, many of the larger Sufi brotherhoods eventually developed distinctive forms of residential/ritual complexes as symbols of their prominence and influence. The wealthier brotherhoods sometimes designed and built extensive and architecturally distinctive foundations, often with the financial assistance of royal patrons seeking spiritual merit. Tomb shrines have been particularly important in the histories and legacies of many Sufi orders, and major institutions have developed around a founder's grave.[23]

Muslims, like Christians, have had to develop mechanisms for funding these and other types of monumental building projects. The single most important device has been the *waqf* (pious endowment), by which a donor can stipulate in a legally binding document that his or her bequest be used for a particular project in perpetuity, or as long as the funds last. Scores of these dedicated trusts now centuries-old remain in force across the Middle East and South Asia, for example, administered by descendants of the original donor or by government officials entrusted with their oversight. Though most such *waqfs* have historically been funded by royal or princely patrons, many others have derived from middle-class sources, whether individuals or pious organizations. Grantors have historically left instructions in *waqf* documents, indicating in considerable detail such considerations as the salaries and duties of resident faculty and students in madrasas and the upkeep of structures such as the Dome of the Rock in Jerusalem, whose *waqf* the king of Jordan currently administers.[24]

. . .

There is considerable evidence that both Christian and Islamic traditions wrestled with a variety of solutions to the knotty theological problem of translating divine power and authority into human terms. Theological ideals have never morphed smoothly into earthly institutional manifestations, nor have political vicissitudes always left scope for more than a token nod to religious mandates. From very early in their histories, both traditions struggled to find the right balance between religious and secular institutions. Both traditions have experienced seasons in which spiritual and temporal rule converged, as well as those in which civil and religious authority comprised virtually separate, if overlapping, spheres. Stated ideals in any given period notwithstanding, historical realities have rarely if ever mirrored the theoretical archetypes in precise detail.

Earliest Christians and Muslims alike met to worship in small gatherings in domestic structures and did not develop much larger and more elaborate purpose-built churches and mosques for several generations. As for intentional communities, they coalesced in both traditions around personalities who embodied ideal qualities and leadership abilities, and one can see various parallels in the internal division of labor in administration and formation of members. Both traditions have historically valued education, but one could argue that explicit formation in the way of the foundational figure began to assume institutional forms earlier in Islamic history (e.g., in the study of Hadith and elaboration of religious law) than it did in Christian history. Religious educational systems, both Christian and Islamic, became more complex and specialized as the purpose and accessibility of education shifted. Outward institutions, both those of higher learning and the intentional communities dedicated ostensibly to spiritual development, have played an important role in the spread of both traditions as well as in reform movements and in the survival of the faith during lean times in various parts of the world.

Though both traditions have at times aspired to some form of unified global dominion in faith, neither has achieved that goal. Compromise, it seems, has finally triumphed in practice, except in the case of unbending extremist movements that have periodically gripped portions of the planet in the names of "true" Christianity or Islam. One important area in which spheres of authority, spiritual and temporal, have invariably intersected is the matter of funding. In both traditions, the fundamental value of spiritual poverty has often contended with the need to produce increasingly visible statements of dominance and power, a need that has in turn often resulted in a Faustian bargain with the moneyed and influential.

Finally, attempts to communicate and interpret theological elements in religious architecture deserve special attention, for they represent an aspect of visual metaphor and symbolism not discussed here as yet. Architecture projects religious institutions and theological values symbolically, not only to members of a faith community but to outsiders as well. Noted historians of architecture in both traditions have searched for possible links between fundamental theological themes and the ways in which Christians and Muslims have elaborated their distinctive spatial arts. Erwin Panofsky's classic work *Gothic Architecture and Scholasticism* and Otto von Simpson's *Gothic Cathedral* explored *thematic* intersections between the regnant European intellectual and artistic cultures of the twelfth and thirteenth centuries.[25] The parallels they identified between visual and textual metaphors opened doors and windows to a more integrated understanding of medieval humanities and worldviews.

A generation or two later, Charles Radding and William Clark moved beyond the earlier scholarly focus on theological *content* by comparing overarching *methodologies* required in constructing the enormous synthetic systems. Instead, they underscored similarities in ways of thinking that were hallmarks of both monumental religious architecture and the conceptual edifices erected by Scholastic theologians and philosophers. They argued that two major factors brought architects and academics together: the simultaneous evolution of their respective disciplines, and the high-level cognitive processes that allowed both builders and thinkers to "impose order on materials, to shape several variables into a whole, and to take account of potential differences in viewpoint." As Radding and Clark note, "These skills matter whether it is space, sound, or doctrine that is being manipulated."[26]

A small coterie of Muslim scholars has likewise sought an integrated explanation for the distinctive features of Islamic spatial arts. Some have argued that the simple, perfect concentration of thought and spiritual commitment required by Islam's uncompromising monotheism (*tawhīd*) has manifested itself spatially in architectural forms both expressive of and conducive to that very habit of mind and soul. The problem with this ultimately reductive approach in general is that it yields absolute priority to creedal content and implicitly limits the role of the concrete realities of form and function to the direct, if abstract, expression of doctrine. Here a major difference between classic Christian and Islamic religious spatial arts is that while Christian sacred architecture does incorporate explicit theological "content" through elaborate iconographic programs in sculpture, mosaic, and stained glass, Islamic religious spaces express their message through much less direct devices of overall layout and aniconic decorative form whose symbolic valences are tantalizingly elusive. Epigraphy in the form of sacred texts (Qur'ān and Hadith) or foundational/historical inscriptions provides the nearest evidence available as to indicators of possible theological programs in Islamic buildings. Beyond such texts, however, designers and builders have, unfortunately, left meager specific evidence of their religious intent.[27]

# PART IV

# Ethical and Spiritual Dimensions

*Mapping Outward and Inward Journeys of Faith*

As always, recourse to scripture and exegesis, as well as to other early sources of tradition, leads the list for investigations into Christianity and Islam's ethical and spiritual dimensions. Also in the forefront of essential theological disciplines in this context are the study of religious law and the related institutions discussed in chapters 5 and 6. To this list we add a subdiscipline only briefly referenced in prior chapters, namely, the study of paradigmatic lives and "sacred biography," of the sort enshrined in shorter, anecdotal forms in Islam's Hadith literature and on a larger scale in the hagiographies of both faith communities.

Drawing on disciplines related to scripture and law, chapter 7 investigates sources, methods, and social values in theological ethics. Here I will emphasize principles over practice, with some reference to specific suggestions the two faith traditions offer for implementing fundamental values.

Chapter 8, on sources and models of spirituality, likewise opens with reflections on spiritual themes in the Bible and the Qur'ān, and follows up on chapter 7's discussion of mimetic ethics, but from a different angle—that of Jesus and Muhammad as paradigms of the inner life. Moving beyond the two exemplary founding figures, I will introduce yet another large body of theologically themed literature—hagiography—before reprising the role of narrative theology in spiritual guidance.

Finally, chapter 9's exploration of theological themes in devotion and prayer reaches back into the disciplines of systematic thinking discussed earlier, bringing to the fore an important segment of such thinking, namely, mystical theology. Examples of personal prayer from both traditions illustrate vividly key features of the individual's relationship to God and central theological aspects of the divine-human connection. I conclude the chapter with a brief survey of classic themes in Christian and Muslim works on mystical theology.

# CHAPTER 7

# Sources, Methods, and Social Values in Theological Ethics

In chapters 5 and 6, I discussed major institutional aspects of the development of religious law systems; here we turn to larger implications of those systems. We begin with the scriptural foundations of both traditions of ethics, survey the history of theoretical developments in the discipline of theological ethics, and conclude with a nod in the direction of the scores of problems and themes that Muslim and Christian ethicists have addressed over the centuries.

## SCRIPTURE AND ETHICS

Sacred texts often include at least general guidelines for the kind of comportment expected of believers. Some, including the Bible and the Qur'ān, provide fairly detailed and specific requirements about both ritual propriety and social relationships. These sacred texts are not treatises of theological ethics, or even manuals of behavior, but Christians and Muslims have long mined them for their ethical ore. The more obvious veins to be tapped are the occasional texts that appear to lay out explicitly how to resolve certain types of problems that arise in communities of believers. Such codified texts, relatively abundant in earlier books of the Old Testament, are much rarer in the New Testament and Qur'ān. Some exegetes have produced commentaries geared to legal concerns, but Christian and Muslim authors have also generated ethical treatises and handbooks of religiously appropriate action.

Theological ethics needs to be distinguished clearly from other varieties of ethical thinking. At the heart of moral philosophy, for example, the use of rational principles undergirds the elaboration of ethical guidelines. A well-informed conscience, in concert with rational inquiry, identifies actions as either good or evil on the basis of certain characteristics inherent in the actions. Depending on the methodological orientation of the chosen philosophical system, critical characteristics can include, for example, the relationship of a proposed action to the common good, its potential effect on certain individual rights, or its implications for conflicting claims over political or economic power.

Natural law theory, by comparison, is a blend of theological and philosophical ethical thinking, in that it presupposes that the fundamental orientation of all rational beings is innately consistent with most divinely revealed canons of behavior at the heart of major religious traditions. This specifically does not include, for example, religious prescriptions concerning ritual practices unique to a given religious community. According to natural law theory, the Creator has imbued all human beings of sound mind with the capacity to discern these core values, even if the ethical code to which they subscribe formally remains flawed and incomplete. All human beings, therefore, instinctively know that murder is evil, and that awareness is consistent with the prohibition one finds in the ethical codes of major faiths.

By contrast, theological ethics, also known to some Christians as moral theology, argues that merely understanding instinctively or rationally that one ought to do or avoid actions perceived to be inherently good or evil is inadequate. Motive is of the essence here. Murder may be perceived to be essentially evil, but the larger truth of the matter is that it is evil because God forbids it. Believers therefore seek to motivate their actions according to their faith tradition's commands and prohibitions.

One could argue that many religiously based ethical codes embody a blend of rational objectivism and theistic subjectivism, in the sense that although human beings are capable of divining the moral valence of most options for action, God's supremacy and pure freedom may place many events beyond human ken. Here the theme of "theodicy" (from the Greek *theou dikē,* "God's justice") comes into play. Both Christian and Islamic ethical traditions have developed a considerable literature over the question of how and why a good, just deity seems so often to allow innocent people to come to great harm.[1]

For Christians and Muslims alike, the bedrock of religiously acceptable behavior is to be found in sacred scripture.

## Christian Scripture and Ethics

Christian interpreters of scripture often underscore the difference between "gospel" values and what they see as the pervasive "legal" orientation of the Hebrew scriptures. Even if Christians have not always agreed with the classic Lutheran dichotomy between law and gospel, there is no doubt that distinguishing between Old and New Testament ethics has been an important theme. Some general background on the foundational principles of biblical ethics will be helpful here. If "Thou shalt's" and "Thou shalt not's" are relatively rare in the New Testament, large sections of the Hebrew Bible are dedicated to the equivalent of early ethico-legal codes (see, e.g., Leviticus). But at the heart of Old Testament ethics is the divine-human covenant relationship with an ever-faithful God, whose steadfast love has embraced the people of Israel from its very foundation. Even before Israel came to be as a people, God initiated a covenant with Noah (Genesis 9:1–17, the basis for the "seven Noachic laws" on which rabbinic authorities constructed a scripture-based "natural law" governing the whole human race), and then with Abraham, who would be the father of a chosen people (Genesis 15:1–21).

Finally, God's covenant with Israel embodied in the law revealed through Moses at Sinai formally sealed God's relationship with a people uniquely his own (Exodus 19:1–24:18). Throughout the Old Testament one sees, arguably, a progressive refinement of the principles of religious ethics. The five books of the Torah tell the primal history of the people and its patriarchs, centered on the giving of the Law. Then the Historical Books provide in generally chronological order countless concrete examples of how the leaders of Israel, from the first judges through the last kings, measured up—or not—against the standard of the Law. The historians, generally identified as the Deuteronomist school, do not mince words, and a surprising number of leaders fall woefully short of the divine benchmark. Not even David and Solomon escape withering critique. In the Prophets and the Wisdom literature, the biblical authors emphasize the interior demands of a "law written on the heart," a spiritual code that, while not dispensing with the act-oriented Law of the Torah, puts still more stringent demands on the believer, recalling the covenant core of the ethical life.[2]

Christian ethics is in a way a hybrid development. On the one hand, Christians believe the ethics of the New Testament further develop and refine the moral principles of the Old Testament. On the other, Christian tradition interprets the teaching of Jesus as moving definitively beyond the Law-centered moral system of the Hebrew scriptures. Jesus and his early followers were Jewish by birth and education, and Jesus himself was in many important ways theologically in agreement with the Pharisees, though the Gospels might lead one to assume that they were at ideological daggers drawn. The Pharisees of Jesus' day taught, for example, the resurrection of the dead and God's Fatherhood of each individual. They based their teachings on the Prophets as well as the Torah and already had a long tradition of "oral Torah."

By contrast, the Sadducees denied any notion of resurrected afterlife and rejected any authoritative teaching beside the written Torah. In several Gospel texts, Jesus responds to a Pharisaic criticism by using the exegetical principles of one of the last great "pairs of teachers," Hillel (d. 10 c.e.; as in the example, cited in chapter 1, of Jesus' disciples plucking and eating grain on the Sabbath). A classic anecdote about the divergence of ethical views between the Pharisee Hillel and his more conservative nemesis Shammai (d. 30 c.e.) sums up their views on law and ethics. One day, a potential convert asked Shammai to recite the whole law while standing on one foot. After Shammai sent him away summarily, he posed the same challenge to Hillel. Hillel raised a foot and said: "You shall love the Lord your God with your whole soul, mind and heart, and your neighbor as yourself" (Deuteronomy 6:5; Leviticus 19:18). Putting his foot down, Hillel concluded: "Everything else is commentary. Go and study." Jesus was evidently of one mind with Hillel on matters of this kind (Babylonian Talmud, Shabbat 31a).

A fundamental (if polemical) principle in New Testament ethics is that the Christian's personal relationship to God makes moral demands more stringent than any requirement that can be enshrined in a code of law. Mercy and love require far more of the Christian than mere adherence to the Law as the Pharisees interpret it. "Unless your righteousness exceeds that of the scribes and Pharisees, you will never enter the kingdom of heaven" (Matthew 5:20). In some texts, Jesus reminds his listeners that the Law teaches, for example, that they must not kill or commit adultery, that they may divorce a wife and avenge an eye for an eye and a tooth for a tooth, and that they must love their neighbor. He then proceeds to forbid even anger, lustful thoughts, divorce except in cases of infidelity, vengeful behavior of any kind, and enjoins love of one's enemies (Matthew 5:21–48). Underlying ethical principles emphasize the equality before God of all individuals regardless of gender or social station and the universal human right to service, respect, and love. Each of the Synoptic Gospels has its own ethical focus. Matthew underscores the advance of Jesus' teaching beyond the Law; Mark highlights the centrality of willingness to serve Jesus through enduring the suffering he endures; and Luke, the Gentile, emphasizes the universality of salvation along with the ready availability of divine mercy and forgiveness.

Major New Testament ethical themes build upon these pervasive principles. Particularly in the Pauline Letters and the book of Revelation, Jesus' teaching appears in the larger sociopolitical context in which the young Christian community finds itself. Christians must look beyond their inner circles to engage the world at large, not merely as missionaries but as citizens of a more inclusive human community. Within that expanding orbit of relationships, Christians must face the challenges and pressures of material success and temptations to selfishness and hedonism. Throughout the New Testament, the ideals of generosity and service to those in need are essential not only for building up the edifice of the community of believers, but for establishing the church's many interfaces with the wider world. Within the church, the scripture emphasizes the need for integration of essential ethical values with the wellsprings of individual and communal prayer.[3]

## Muslim Sacred Sources and Ethics

Several texts in the Qur'ān offer summaries of ethical values that identify the true believer. In general, the Muslim scripture juxtaposes prevailing values of the pre-Islamic era, the "age of ignorance" (al-jāhilīya), with the new moral orientation demanded by the revelation delivered through Muhammad's preaching. To understand this concept of ethical development, some background on the socioethical context in which Muhammad lived and Islam arose will be useful. Tribalism was a major social factor in the sixth-century Arabian Peninsula.

Three kinds of conditions shaped the basic features of social ethics: intratribal relations, intertribal relations, and the gradual rise of individualism. First, within each of dozens of tribal groups, fierce loyalty was the primary bond. Those who violated that bond were ostracized, as Muhammad himself was disowned by many in his own tribe, the Quraysh, who felt threatened by his preaching. Had he not retained the essential support of his clan, the Banu Hāshim, his message might never have been heard as it has. Tribes are not permanent social entities: they wax and wane, disappear entirely, or are absorbed through pacts in larger confederations. Blood feud was the principal deterrent in intertribal relations, but a refugee from one tribe could seek sanctuary for a limited time with another.

By Muhammad's time, however, Arabian society was witnessing a transition in trading centers like Mecca, from nomadic life to a more urbanized economy. With private financial support, individual families could survive with less encompassing tribal protection, and the sense of "immortality" formerly associated with belonging to the tribe was gradually displaced by the hoarding of wealth. To this overall situation the Qur'ān responded that wealth is merely on loan, not owned by individuals. Possessions cannot immortalize one, and people are called to stewardship of God's gifts. A sense of equality and shared humanity, the scripture enjoined, must replace the class-oriented society fostered by hoarding wealth.[4]

Secondly, pre-Islamic personal ethics were similarly dominated by ancient tribal concepts and values. Here the regnant notions of time and immortality, as well as of fundamental sources of ethical criteria, are at the heart of the matter. For pre-Islamic Arabs, human life was a purely this-worldly affair, with a reputation for extravagance in generosity the only hope of surviving one's own death. Time, or impersonal fate (dahr), predetermined one's gender, prospects for happiness, hopes for sustenance, and length of days. Given the limited options available for personal freedom, a measure of hedonism became an important ingredient in individual ethical choices.

Personal choices, meanwhile, must conform to ancestral custom (sunna), regardless of the objective quality of a given deed. To this state of affairs, the Qur'ān insisted that the divine will must replace uncritical acceptance of tribal custom. As ethical norms, hope of reward and fear of punishment in the hereafter must supplant the quest for honor and avoidance of shame here. In place of hedonistic pursuits, the Muslim bears in mind moral responsibility in view of ultimate accountability at judgment.

Finally, the ethical person is not the most extravagantly generous, but the most God-fearing. In short, the Qur'ān transformed the three dominant pre-Islamic virtues into faith-grounded values. Courage is thus no longer purposeless and undisciplined bravado, but fortitude "in the way of God." Generosity develops from sheer prodigality to spending "in the way of God" for those most in need, and loyalty was shifted from the tribe to God as a response to the divinely initiated covenant.[5]

The overall result of the transformation is that jahl (stubborn adherence to a sense of arrogant self-sufficiency), with its emphasis on honor, rivalry, and capricious behavior, gives way to islām, "surrender to the supreme authority of God." One text of the Qur'ān (90:12–19) characterizes the ethical conversion as the "Steep Ascent," with a heavy emphasis on social responsibility. The final lines are reminiscent of Jesus' parable of the Sheep and Goats (Matthew 25:31–45):

What will convey to you what the Steep Ascent is?
It means freeing a slave,
and feeding in time of hunger
an orphan of your extended family,
or a poor person on hard times [lit., "in the dust"],
and to be among people of faith who encourage each other to patience
and urge each other to deeds of compassion.
Such as these will have a place on the right,
while those who reject our signs will find themselves on the left,
around whom there will be a wall of fire.

Texts of the Qur'ān consistently require Muslims to share their resources with the needy (e.g., 51:19, 76:8–9, 3:134). Such sharing is an essential ingredient of the ethical life, and I will return to this central focus of Muslim ethics later in this chapter.

Three large elements comprise the fundamental principles of Qur'ānic ethics in aid of the Steep Ascent: the fundamental *criterion* of Islamic theological ethics, the underlying *motive* for seeking ethical conversion, and a set of *conditions* under which a believer must negotiate the delicate balance between divine initiative and human responsibility. First, the Qur'ān distinguishes between those who "believe and do good works" and those who refuse to acknowledge the Giver as the source of all good, and insist that they themselves are self-sufficient and the masters of all they claim as their own. It juxtaposes *islām*, founded on gratitude (*shukr*), to rebellion by worshiping other than God (*shirk*—note the pun on the inverted consonants *sh, k,* and *r*).

Second, the only worthy *motive* for the ethical life is awe in God's presence, not as if cowering before a capricious despot but out of the conviction that all one's actions will bear fruit in kind. God's mercy precedes all else and is manifest in countless revelatory signs (on the horizons, in the sacred text, and in oneself), and all who reject that mercy have already condemned themselves. Awe before God is therefore not impersonal, nor is it mere enlightened self-interest, but the refusal to regard oneself as pure and unaccountable, the result of a right relationship between creature and Creator. In a sense this healthy fear of God is the beginning of faith, which is in turn the bedrock of moral conduct.

Finally, the Qur'ān describes five *conditions* of the human ethical dilemma, reasons why human beings remain accountable for their deeds even as God owns ultimate freedom and power over all human affairs. First, in search of earthly collaboration in stewardship of creation, God offered the sacred "trust" to heaven and earth, but they both declined out of fear. When

God offered the trust to humankind, they gladly accepted (33:72). The angels warned that if God made Adam his vice-gerent, humankind would bungle the responsibility by shedding blood and sowing injustice, but God reassured them (2:29). All would work out, for God had summoned forth all the unborn children of Adam and asked them "Am I not your Lord?" on that day of covenant, and they had affirmed God's sovereignty with one voice (7:172).

Second, the Qur'ān underscores human freedom of choice with the word "perhaps"—God shows his "signs" so that "perhaps" they will understand, be aware, give thanks, and act accordingly. Human beings are not coerced, for every "perhaps" implies a "perhaps not."

Third, the sacred text consistently describes God as guiding and leading astray "whom he will," but the emphasis is not on the divine caprice, but on God's perfect and complete power over all things. These expressions often occur in the context of metaphors of the "kingdom" and divine "permission" and are therefore more about what God is than what human beings are not. "God does not change a people's estate until they change the thoughts of their own hearts" (13:11), says the Qur'ān. Many scholars have made a distinction between God's overarching will, which by definition occurs no matter how human beings might fight and reject it, and the specific divine commands (mashī'a), which human beings may choose not to enact.

Fourth, the Qur'ān continually calls human beings to seek forgiveness in view of final accountability. But one who acts under coercion is not responsible for his or her deeds and need not ask forgiveness—unless God is a callous despot, which he is not. Forgiveness implies the need to accept one's ethical responsibility and is part and parcel of arriving at receptivity to God's mercy and rejection of the pervasive and destructive moral climate of jahl.

Finally, surrounding all these conditions of human ethical responsibility is the inevitable drift of history, so evident throughout the Qur'ān, toward impending judgment and the end of time. Without some measure of human freedom of choice, however limited in relation to divine omnipotence, accountability is a cruel hoax, and that is clearly not an ingredient in divine mercy. Taking all these often subtle features of Qur'ānic ethics into consideration, it seems clear that even if divine foreordainment of all events remains a dominant theme in Islamic theology, one cannot deny the essential role of human moral accountability.[6]

## Ethics and the Hadith Literature

As earlier chapters have suggested from various perspectives, the "sayings" of Muhammad, the Hadith, represent a unique source—not sacred scripture as such, but still articulating divinely originated teaching. Almost by definition, virtually the whole corpus of Hadith literature is oriented toward religiously motivated behavior, for it enshrines the sayings and deeds of Muhammad. As the primary record of the Prophet's *sunna* (exemplary conduct), the Hadith literature catalogues a full range of ethical and ritual cases. Here the emphasis is on the ideal, paradigmatic nature of a divinely guided charismatic model. Anecdotes featuring the Prophet's responses to a host of questions function at least implicitly in Muslim tradition as the standard of religiously acceptable conduct. Most Muslims presuppose that "sound" Hadiths represent behavioral guidelines: They do not of themselves demand further discussion or debate, except to the degree that Muslims, in whatever historical period, have had to translate certain blatant anachronisms into terms that made sense in their particular historical and cultural contexts.

In several of the major Hadith collections, such as that of Muslim, separate sections are dedicated to the more clearly theological dimensions of desirable attitudes and behavior. For example, just after his lengthy section on the virtues of the Companions (described in chapter 1), Muslim places a substantial section heavily slanted toward recommendations on social ethics. The beautiful "Book of Piety, Relationships, and Good Comportment" offers abundant concrete instruction on dealings with everyone from one's parents to complete strangers in the marketplace. A bit later, after chapters on matters controlled by divine destiny, knowledge, and supplication, Muslim inserts another brief but theologically relevant section, "The Book of Repentance," describing the appropriate response when one has failed ethically.[7]

Chapter 2 described some of the more explicitly theological or creedal themes in the Hadith. An enormous variety of topics comprise the substance of the mimetic Hadith ethic as well, from expressions of appropriate attitude or spiritual orientation to the modeling of specific virtues to recommended rituals and social interactions to criminal sanctions and examples of just the right ways to perform them. As extended sections on excellent qualities or virtues (*fadā'il*) indicate, Muhammad embodied faith, generosity, sagacity, truthfulness, patience, courage, compassion, humility, and simplicity of life, among a host of other lofty attributes that he shared with previous prophets. His Companions modeled similar virtues, perhaps to a slightly less stellar degree, but one of the signal qualities that tradition discerns in the greatest of the earliest generation of Muslims is the intimacy of their personal relationships with Muhammad. Many of the major Hadith collections include at least brief summaries of the distinctive exemplary qualities of several dozen individuals, including prominently the Prophet's wives, also known as the Mothers of the Faithful.

Muslims find in the Hadith emphasis on the importance of continual remembrance of God, repentance, and asking forgiveness, and an attitude of compassion ("softening the heart") that plays out in deeds to alleviate the suffering of others in every kind of action, from providing food or drink or clothing to funding the construction of a mosque to following a funeral procession or praying at graveside. Ritual correctness is essential in daily prayer, fasting during Ramadan, pilgrimage rites, and slaughtering animals for food.

There is extensive exemplary material on ethical propriety in more mundane matters, including mercantile exchange, inheritance, dowries and questions of marriage and divorce, proper dress for both men and women, personal hygiene and sexual conduct, criminal proceedings and penalties, conduct of warfare, and the duties and prerogatives of civil administrators such as rulers and judges. Though many Muslims over the centuries have considered following the Prophetic example to be a relatively simple matter of imitation, it is in fact rather complex because of the variety of specific cases in which one can find apparently contradictory Hadiths on a given topic. Here is where careful scholarship steps in to offer guidance as to which of the possible traditions one might choose to emulate represents the soundest evidence. I will return to a reconsideration of Muslim mimetic ethics later, in the context of themes in social ethics.

## THEOLOGICAL ETHICS: THEORETICAL DEVELOPMENTS AND METHOD

Christian and Muslim moralists, whether philosophical or theological in basic methodology, have written a variety of works on ethical themes. Here I will outline the history of some of the major concepts, and early theorists and works in both traditions.

### Christian Moral Theology

Though the biblical text stands at the foundation of all Christian ethics, Roman Catholic, Protestant, and Orthodox Christian elaborations of the principles of scripture-based ethics have incorporated the sacred sources in varying ways. Not until the second millennium did Christian authors elaborate a specific theological subdiscipline of ethics. Postbiblical authors began to address ethical issues rather obliquely, arguably beginning with the *Didache* (*Teaching [of the Apostles]*) and its "two ways" of life and death, and the *Shepherd of Hermas* with its "twelve mandates" on various aspects of Christian virtue based on faith. *Hermas* was perhaps the earliest document to argue for the necessity of ritual forgiveness of sins at least once after an individual has been baptized a Christian.

Early fathers of the church, such as Tertullian and Clement of Alexandria, argued that God's will is the pivotal criterion of ethical behavior. Among the earliest systematic developments of theological ethical themes are works by Ambrose and Augustine. Ambrose based his work on Cicero, while Augustine's *Confessions* and *City of God* taught that charity or Christian love is the wellspring of all other religious virtues.

Catholic moral theology blossomed into a distinct subdiscipline of the sacred sciences when Thomas Aquinas devoted a large segment of his grand synthesis, *The Summa of Theology*, to the subject. He opens the "second part" of the work with a discussion of happiness as the ultimate goal of humankind, thus situating himself in the tradition of Aristotelian ethics, but with a very different analysis of means to the end. Thomas divides human actions into involuntary and voluntary, inward and outward, all capable of good or ill. In that context, he analyzes human proclivities, or "passions," and the more enduring characteristics or "habits" of the soul, with particular attention to virtue and vice. Thomas roots his discussion of sin in the concept of original sin, with its pernicious influence through the ages. He explains sin as a violation of the divine law but goes on to insist that the heart of the matter remains dependent on human volition. In that context he comes round to describing the eternal law as the standard against which one must assess the moral valence of all actions. At this juncture, Thomas introduces the element of divinely bestowed grace as the prime impetus to good action.

Against the backdrop of these general principles, Thomas moves into a more detailed discussion of moral theology in light of more concrete characteristics and implications of the various virtues and vices, beginning with the "theological virtues": faith, hope, and love. He expands on this by exploring the specific results of the "four cardinal virtues": prudence, justice, fortitude, and temperance. His analysis culminates in an exploration of the relationship between virtue enacted and the requirements of the various "states of life" to which believing Christians might devote themselves. In a manner reminiscent of the master work of earlier Muslim theologian Abū Hāmid al-Ghazālī (to whom I will return shortly), Thomas associates the life of advanced virtue with lofty spiritual (even perhaps mystical) attainment.

Later Scholastic authors produced systematic works devoted to moral theology, collating key texts from scripture, patristic writings, and early church councils. Their sourcebooks in turn paved the way for early modern manuals, which categorized ethical deeds and moral problems in the form of cases, complete with pastorally oriented solutions to each problem. Works using this "casuistic" method were particularly useful in the Roman Catholic tradition, with its growing emphasis on the need for seeking forgiveness regularly through the sacrament of penance, or confession of sins to a priest.

Orthodox theologians placed still greater emphasis on spiritual transformation as the foundation of ethical life, with God-likeness the ultimate goal. A hallmark of Orthodox moral theology is the inseparable bond between morality and spirituality, emphasizing the need for inner purification as a condition for outward lawfulness. From patristic times through the Middle Ages, Orthodox ethicists exhibited variously the influence of three classical Greek traditions: the Aristotelian, the Neoplatonic, and the Stoic. During the seventeenth century Piotr Moghila (d. 1646) employed principles of Scholastic thought as a tool with which to argue against Roman Catholic theological ethics. Three schools of thought developed during the nineteenth century: the heavily philosophical Athenian, the scripture-based christocentric Constantinopolitan, and the monastically inspired and mystically oriented Thessalonian school.[8]

From the early sixteenth century on, Protestant theological ethics emphasized gospel freedom, as distinct from the Catholic preference for ethical merit. Faith takes precedence over action, and divine grace is the single most powerful force in the transformation of human action. A focus on the divine freedom is consistent with that theme's prominence in the views of many classical Muslim theologians, while a general tendency to avoid philosophical debate over ethical fine points distinguishes much Protestant ethics from traditional Scholastic approaches. Among the Reformers, Calvin modified Luther's emphasis on God's transforming love by according a greater role to divine and human will as active ingredients in moral choice.

Perhaps the most important single development in Protestant theological ethics occurred during the Enlightenment, under the influence of Friedrich Schleiermacher (d. 1834). He emphasized God's active role in shaping history at the macro level and human experience at the micro. Along with subsequent "liberal" Protestant theologians, he shifted the ethical spotlight from the individual's need to be reconciled with God to the broader demands of the "Social Gospel."[9] There have been many important developments in contemporary Protestant ethical thinking, but this brief overview of an enormous subject must suffice for now.[10]

## Muslim Theorists, Ethical Behavior, and the Science of Character

Early seventh-century Arabs referred to ancestral exemplary values with the term *sunna*, and the Muslim tradition soon effectively restricted the word's meaning to the most important *sunna* of all, the behavior of the Prophet. Another important early ethical term, *adab*, encompassed laudable behavior and hereditary custom or habit. *Adab* soon came to connote civility, courtesy, and refinement as well and eventually broadened to mean culture in general, especially as embodied in refined literature and in what we now call the Humanities as a field of intellectual and creative endeavor.

Some Muslim authors, however, retained the term's original essentially ethical connotations but shifted its focus to spiritual comportment. Pastoral theologians, such as Ghazālī, and major Sufi theorists understood a fundamental feature of the individual's relationship to God in terms of positive or negative *adab* (*ḥusn al-adab, sū' al-adab*).[11] I will return to these developments shortly.

I now revisit a large issue of systematic theology first raised in chapter 4, but of sufficient importance in this new context to bear restating briefly. A critical theological ingredient in Muslim ethical theory is the question of the degree to which God controls human affairs. All Muslims believe that God is omnipotent, but there are various ways of explaining how that ultimate power manifests itself and how human beings remain morally culpable and accountable. Debates about ethical power (*qadar*) were among the earliest to shape truly theological discourse. On the one hand, the "rationalist," Mu'tazila systematic theologians argued that God had equipped human beings with both sufficient ability to discern good from evil and the freedom to choose.

More traditionalist thinkers, however, such as Ahmad ibn Hanbal, insisted that Mu'tazila ethical theory effectively deprived the deity of omnipotence and omniscience in the interest of shoring up human responsibility—a fool's bargain at best, and heretical at worst, they thought. Attempting to strike something of a compromise, Ash'arī and his students elaborated on the concept of acquisition (*kasb, iktisāb*) whereby God created from eternity all possible human actions, and individual human beings then in effect "appropriate" acts by choosing from among the virtually infinite possibilities.

Ash'arīte theory's accommodation preserved God's role as primary agent, leaving to human beings a much reduced function of secondary agency and limited freedom of choice (*ikhtiyār*). Earlier thinkers had first crafted the concept of acquisition in the context of epistemological discussions about how human beings acquire knowledge. The concept was first applied specifically to ethical discourse by Dirār ibn ʿAmr (d. 815), who wanted to preserve some human agency, but still subordinate it to divine initiative and power. Later theorists refined the discourse, especially with a view to making clear that human beings are agents only in an analogous sense, and that God alone is the creator of all things, including everything any human being does.

The Muʿtazila rejected the implications for human ethical freedom and argued that human agents actually have the power not only to acquire but to create their own acts. It was the attribution of "creative" power to human beings that spurred the Ashʿarite school to resurrect the older, more restrictive notion of acquisition, based on the theological principle of radically diminished or contingent human power that nonetheless preserves the ability to act. The underlying freedom and responsibility, however, remained largely a device whereby the human agent remained answerable to the law while in no way diluting or infringing on the divine omnipotence. In other words, the human being functions virtually as a vessel in which God's acts are played out. From the human perspective, the critical feature of such ethical discourse is the need to avoid any sense of entitlement in relation to God's will and power.

In addition to the almost diametrically opposed traditionalist (especially of Ibn Hanbal and Ibn Hazm) and rationalist/Muʿtazilite schools of ethical thinking, and the Ashʿarite attempt at a mediating response, another major but little acknowledged approach is that of the Māturīdī theologians. Māturīdī himself and his disciples and like-minded thinkers took a subtly different approach to the concept of *iktisāb*. God's power produces the metaphysical basis of an action, while human power influences the ultimate ethical quality of an act. In other words, the Māturīdī view accords slightly more moral agency to the human being, defining "acquisition" as the process whereby the individual does not merely appropriate a ready-made act, complete with moral characteristics, but actually imposes the ethical value on the act being appropriated—a significant nod in the direction of human choice. God's creative role, therefore, stops just short of complete ethical qualification of an act, leaving that up to the human being. This theological debate, with the Ashʿarite position arguably emerging as the regnant view, was largely driven by the overwhelming conviction that the ultimate function of theology is to defend God's divine transcendent unity from the slightest hint of compromise.[12]

Islamic philosophical ethics naturally shares some features of rationalist theological ethics but is grounded in Aristotelian or Platonic concepts rather than in scriptural images of God, his names, and attributes. Ahmad ibn Muhammad Miskawayh (d. 1030) stands out for his enduring influence in the history of Sunni ethical thinking. His virtue-centered ethics suggests tantalizing comparisons with the work of later medieval Christian ethical systems. In his *Refinement of Character* (*Tahdhīb al-akhlāq*), Miskawayh develops six major themes based on his analysis of the soul and its faculties: ethical principles, character and what many Christians would call conscience formation, the many aspects of the good, justice, friendship and love, and the health of the soul.

Miskawayh argues that the soul's kingly rational faculty (brain), its beastly concupiscence (heart), and its leonine irascibility (liver) must ultimately strive, respectively, for the pivotal virtues of knowledge leading to wisdom, temperance leading to liberality, and magnanimity whose perfect expression is courage. Together these three virtues culminate in a fourth— justice. Strikingly similar to the Christian cardinal virtues, the four find their highest purpose in the formation of character, which manifests itself in social responsibility driven by specific active virtuous qualities deriving from each of the four principal virtues. Wisdom generates intelligence, alacrity of apprehension, and clarity; temperance engenders modesty, good disposition, and piety; liberality begets altruism, charity, and generosity; from courage come composure, self-possession, and steadfastness. Finally, justice expresses itself in friendship and harmony. Christians will recognize many of these qualities in the Pauline catalogues of the fruits and gifts of the Holy Spirit (Galatians 5:22): love, joy, patience, peace, kindness, goodness, faithfulness, gentleness, and self-control.

In Miskawayh's system, the virtues hold the middle ground between extremes on both sides, the vices. Thus, for example, wisdom is the mean between imprudence and stupidity. Miskawayh assumes that the highest purpose of the ethical life is not the refinement of character as a solitary exercise, but the full engagement of the moral person in society.[13]

Other major Muslim religious scholars have taken a different approach, placing greater emphasis on spiritual (including in some cases ascetical) refinement. Important developments in theologically informed ethics occurred in Sufi-oriented modifications of the philosophical concept of *akhlāq*, "behavioral disposition or character." Ghazālī, whom I mentioned above in connection with Thomas Aquinas's ethicospiritual system, was a leading figure in appropriating elements of philosophical ethics and adapting them to more "personalist" theological purposes. He was thoroughly familiar with major works in the *akhlāq* tradition, including, for example, that of Miskawayh.

To the degree that Ghazālī assessed works of this kind as fully consistent with the Qur'ān and Sunna, he incorporated their methods in the ethical sections of his masterwork, *The Revitalization of the Religious Disciplines* (*Ihyā' 'ulūm ad-dīn*), as well as in smaller treatises, such as his Persian *Alchemy of Happiness* (*Kīmīyā-yi sa'ādat*), which covers many of the same themes as the *Revitalization*. At the heart of Ghazālī's personalist ethic is the individual spiritual seeker's struggle (*jihād*) to "polish the mirror of the heart," ridding it of the corrosion of narcissism and self-will so that it reflects the light that God casts within the core of each person's being.

Ghazālī's *Revitalization* is one of the great synthetic works of the ethical and spiritual life from a Muslim perspective. Like Thomas Aquinas, Ghazālī believes that human beings are made for felicity. The eleventh-century Muslim also builds his ethical treatise on a discussion of the optimal way of performing a host of often mundane deeds and proceeds to analyze in great detail "acts that lead to perdition," before building to a grand and lofty treatment of "acts that assure salvation." This last section, like that pertaining to Thomas's theological ethics, is virtually an essay on the path to spiritual perfection. Beginning with repentance, the journey leads through patience and gratitude, fear and hope, and poverty and asceticism. Acknowledging the unity of God, one proceeds to perfect trust, love and desire for God, purity of intention and sincerity. Achieving the states of mindfulness of God, self-examination, and meditation, the ascent culminates in a rich contemplation of death and the hereafter.[14]

## FUNDAMENTAL THEMES IN CHRISTIAN AND ISLAMIC SOCIAL ETHICS

Against this more theoretical backdrop, two overarching themes in social ethics can emerge in higher relief. Both Christian and Islamic ethical traditions enshrine a host of important personal and social ethical concerns. Among the larger-scale issues, both traditions have attended in varying degrees to matters of race, ethnicity, and gender; the environment and stewardship of creation; social justice, economic equity, slavery, and human rights; war and peace.[15] On a more personal or individual level, Christian and Muslim authors, especially in more recent times, have addressed thorny questions of biomedical and broader health-care ethics as well as of sexual morality.[16] The breadth and depth of possible topics is far too vast and complex to be described adequately in a survey such as this. Here I will sample two specific thematic aspects of social ethics common to the two great traditions. First, Muslims and Christians share the fundamental conviction that their founding figures, Muhammad and Jesus, respectively, embodied the loftiest moral standards in their personal lives. Second, both traditions expect their adherents to engage the wider world on the basis of their ethical conviction.

### Mimetic Ethics: The Importance of Imitating the Founder

Jesus and Muhammad represent for their respective traditions the ultimate in moral example. Earlier chapters have hinted at various aspects of the two foundational figures' pivotal role in inspiring and molding the believer's behavior and motivation. Chapter 8's consideration of Christian and Muslim hagiographical traditions will again address the relationship between admirability and imitability in the context of the individual's personal spiritual journey. The "average" person may be capable only of distant admiration, and perhaps intense gratitude, for the most exalted qualities of a paradigmatic figure. Here I will consider ethical mimesis in terms of three paradigmatic categories—the founder's actions, values, and experience—each with a different set of possibilities for admirability and imitability.

While it is difficult to characterize in a single term the whole of Jesus' exemplary legacy, several possibilities stand out. His obedience to the will of his Father, for example, suggests a goal to which the individual believer can aspire in a humble way, knowing that only Jesus was capable of perfection in this respect. On the other hand, Jesus directs his followers to "be perfect even as your heavenly Father is perfect" and tells a rich young man that if he "would be perfect," he must give his wealth to the poor and follow Jesus (Matthew 5:48, 19:16–30). A brief survey of Jesus' christological titles sheds helpful light on the subject. His "messianic" identity draws on both royal and priestly traditions, each suggesting a very different function, and here the "royal" theme predominates. Three overlapping roles—those of prophet, healer, and teacher—relate more directly to the lives of early Christians.

As a moral teacher, Jesus spoke often of his deepest values. Much of the ethical language of the New Testament is couched in the form of parables and recommendation of key virtues. Some parables exemplify central values of social justice and compassion while implicitly criticizing the hypocrisy of some individuals who represent the religious establishment. The story of the Good Samaritan, for example, tells of a Jewish traveler who was savagely beaten, robbed, and left for dead. A priest and a Levite (temple official) passed by the suffering man without a second glance. Then a Samaritan, a member of a religiously and socially marginal group in the time of Jesus, stopped to assist the man. He ministered to the man, transported him to an inn, and paid in advance for his care before going on his way. Jesus then asks his listeners which of the travelers was the man's true neighbor (Luke 10:25–37).

Parables of the Kingdom in Matthew 13 describe imaginatively the goal of human life and the kinds of behavior expected of those who will make the grade. Later in Matthew's gospel (25:31–46) we find a more explicit set of criteria that will separate the acceptable from those who fall short at judgment. Here the criteria are components of social ethics: giving food to the hungry and drink to the thirsty, welcoming the stranger, clothing the naked, and ministering to the sick and imprisoned. Perhaps the best-known summary of lofty religious virtue is the Beatitudes as reported by Luke and Matthew in the context of Jesus' Sermon on the Mount (Matthew 5:1–7:29; or on the Plain, as in Luke 6:20–49). "Blessed are" the poor in spirit, for theirs is the kingdom; those who mourn, for they will be comforted; the meek, who will inherit the earth; those who hunger and thirst for justice, and will be satisfied; the merciful, who will receive mercy; the pure in heart, who will see God; the peacemakers, who are children of God; those persecuted in pursuit of justice, who will come into the kingdom. In addition, both versions of the Sermon go on to outline (Matthew gives considerably more detail than Luke) a variety of key ethical considerations.

Jesus prominently refers to himself as "Light of the World" and enjoins his followers to be "light and salt" (John 8:12; Matthew 5:13–16). Finally, at the heart of Jesus' ethical teaching is the law of love: you will love the Lord your God with all your heart and your neighbor as yourself (Mark 12:28–34; Matthew 22:34–40; cf. John 13:34–35, adding the "new commandment": to love one another as Jesus has loved believers).

Jesus did not merely talk a good ethical game. He lived as he spoke. In the category of imitability, the New Testament abounds with narratives that showcase the core social values that Jesus models for Christians. Over and over, Jesus responds with compassion to the needs of the poor and the sick, embraces the socially and religiously marginalized, denounces the hypocrisy and arrogance of the mighty, and publicly subverts those who claim religious privilege to exempt themselves from fundamental ethical demands.[17]

When Christians seek to epitomize the ethical values Jesus exemplified, they generally gravitate to the conviction that he embodied the love of God on earth. In this connection one of the most striking ethical metaphors is Paul's development of the image of the church as the body of Christ, implying that believers are to be the very hands, eyes, ears, and feet carrying on God's work on earth (1 Corinthians 12:27–30, Romans 12:4–8, and many other texts).[18]

Muslim tradition, for its part, sums up in a single term virtually the whole of Muhammad's exemplary role, namely, Sunna, or Prophetic patterning. Neither the Qur'ān itself nor early exegetes use the term to refer to Muhammad as a behavioral example, but by the mid-ninth century some religious scholars had begun to associate the term *sunna* with the Qur'ānic verse "In the Messenger of God you have a superb model [*uswah*]" (33:21).

A debate arose early over the relationship between the exemplary deeds of Muhammad as enshrined in the Hadith and the need to interpret difficult passages of the Qur'ān. The central question was whether a Hadith text, understood as articulating a *sunna* (deed of the Prophet), had the authority to abrogate a scriptural injunction. At issue here was the concern that subsequent generations of Muslims might, not always with the purest of intentions, put forth "new *sunnas*" by "discovering" Hadiths, in an attempt to skew interpretation of the Qur'ān.[19]

In any case, over the centuries, the broad majority of Muslims have come to associate the Sunna with exemplary Prophetic conduct, so that the Hadith function virtually as an encyclopedic repository of proper ethical and religious behavior. Though Muhammad was altogether human in every respect, he bears in effect a mantle of moral and spiritual impeccability. As an imitable standard, many of the Prophet's more mundane actions are relatively easy for an individual Muslim to reproduce—especially those relating to specific actions in ritual performance (how to say a certain prayer) or ordinary daily life (dietary and hygienic discipline). More demanding, but still imitable, are Muhammad's exemplary attitudes and inner values, including compassion, evenhandedness, and steadfastness in the face of injustice. Some qualities, however, are well out of reach. Distinctively Prophetic prerogatives, such as Muhammad's intimate relationship with God as exemplified in his night journey and ascension, represent the purely unattainable. Only a handful of bold mystics, such as Bāyazīd al-Bistāmī (d. 873), have presumed to pattern their own spiritual odysseys on that of Muhammad.

Islamic tradition has distilled telling interpretations of Muhammad's paradigmatic roles in the various names by which Muslims have known him. In many instances these are appellations bestowed on him by God in the Qur'ān, while Muhammad himself or members of his family or his Companions gave him others. Some are creedal in the sense that they articulate aspects of Muhammad's place in the history of prophetic revelation or his relationship to God: for example, Messenger (*Rasūl*), Seal of Prophecy (*Khatm an-nubūwwa*), Chosen (Mustafā), Unlettered (*Ummī*), and God's Interlocutor (*Kalīm Allāh*). These attributes are clearly beyond the capabilities of ordinary believers and celebrate the uniqueness of Muhammad, even among the prophetic brotherhood.

Other titles are more broadly functional, describing the Prophet's multiple leadership roles, such as Your Guardian (*Hāris ʿalaykum*), Giver of Light (*Munīr*), and Help in Affliction (*Ghawth*). Still others are more properly devotional, in the sense that they describe attitudes toward Muhammad (e.g., Most Praised, *Ahmad*), or spiritual qualities to which one might aspire, however faintly (e.g., Leader of Those Who Fear God, *Imām al-muttaqīn*).

These are all arguably theological titles, but there are also many that suggest more attainable aspects of Muhammad's character, referring to more imitable ethical qualities. Muhammad was virtuous (*sālih*), truthful (*sādiq*), inspiring confidence (*musaddaq*), perfect authenticity (*sidq*), devout (*barr*), one who lived the religious law fully (*muqīm as-sunna*), compassionate (*ra'ūf*), the spirit of equity (*rūh al-qist*), one who shows forth good deeds (*dalīl al-khayrāt*), and guarantor of the rightness of action (*musahhih*). Above all, as Servant of God (ʿAbd Allāh), Muhammad modeled the apex of all human ethical aspiration—and capacity—doing all things in light of his fundamental relationship to God.

In the celebrated Hadith of Gabriel discussed earlier in another context, the angel visits Muhammad and asks him about his understanding of the three foundations of the religion. Muhammad replies that they are the outward ("surrender," *islām*), the inward ("faith," *īmān*), and the embodiment of both outward and inward ("doing the good/beautiful," *ihsān*). The last is the ultimate ethical principle: acting in all things as though you see God, in full knowledge that even if you do not see God, God sees you. For Muslims, Muhammad models *ihsān* more perfectly than any human being but sets a genuinely imitable example in doing so.[20]

*Faith and Social Responsibility*

Both Christian and Islamic traditions have emphasized in various ways the duty of all believers to become morally engaged in stewardship of creation. It is not enough merely to be a bemused spectator or even mildly curious bystander, particularly when the forces of entropy seem to be gaining a foothold in one's moral universe. Here is a brief look at how the two traditions have formulated the mandate to become ethically involved.

"Am I my brother's keeper?" Cain asked God when the Creator inquired as to the whereabouts of the just-murdered Abel (Genesis 4:9). Both the Christian and Islamic traditions have, in their distinctive ways, answered that question in the affirmative. For Muslims and Christians alike, divinely mandated responsibility for their fellow human beings and for their earthly home covers a broad spectrum, from stewardship for creation to upholding the dignity and God-originated rights of each person, from establishing just social and religious institutions to seeking a religiously ideal world in which all people espouse the same system of beliefs.

Here limited space allows only a suggestion as to overarching attitudes toward the degree to which believers are called to engage their wider world in specifically religious ways. An important theme in the Gospels is Jesus' insistence that believers are not to hide their values, but to "let [their] light shine" so that people "will see [their] good works and give glory" to God (Matthew 5:14–16). An important underlying principle is the Christian version of the "golden rule" (Matthew 7:12), but beyond that, Jesus continually calls for active care for others.

Over and over, Jesus' actions on behalf of people suffering a variety of maladies, both physical and spiritual, combine healing with forgiveness (e.g., Matthew 2:1–12; Luke 5:17–26), and he expects of his followers a broad willingness to forgive. Though ordinary Christians cannot imitate Jesus' often spectacular healing and restorative powers, they can emulate his model of forgiveness. Among the essential criteria at final judgment will be the degree to which disciples responded to the needs of the stranger, the sick, the naked, the hungry and thirsty, and the imprisoned (Matthew 25:31–46). Followers are to go abroad and "make disciples of all nations" (Matthew 28:16–20; Mark 16:15–18).

Since very early in Islamic history, Muslims have confronted three kinds of overarching ethical questions: what constitutes legitimate religious authority, how that authority regulates the behavior of members of the community of believers, and to what degree individuals bear responsibility for influencing the behavior of their fellow believers. Various Qur'ānic texts establish the principle of social engagement in establishing shared values. Frequently cited verses include, for example, "You are to be a community that invites to the good, commands right and forbidding wrong" (3:104); and "You are the best of human communities, [in that you] command right and forbid wrong" (3:110).[21]

Issues of social justice stood at the core of the community's evolving value system. A number of Qur'ānic texts, including the following, offer a concrete sense of the importance of social justice in the tradition:

Give to kin, the poor and the traveler what they need; that is best for those who seek the face of God, and they will indeed fare well. What you give in the hope of profiting at the expense of people will gain you nothing in God's sight; what you give in the form of alms [zakāt] as you seek the face of God—that will produce abundant return. (30:38–39)

Speaking to people who praise God in good times and complain when their wealth and prosperity fade, the Qur'ān says: "Indeed you [all] pay no heed to the orphan, you have no deep concern for feeding the poor, you devour ravenously the inheritance that comes your way, and you love wealth above all else" (89:15–20). The underlying ethical principle is the unstinting thirst for social justice, even to the extent of having to bear witness against oneself or one's family. These and other texts are redolent of the moral indignation of many of the Old Testament prophets. "For what God requires of you transcends wealth and poverty. You must not pursue your own selfishness in subverting the right. God knows well what you are doing when bias and prejudice guide your actions" (4:135–37).

The Hadith literature abounds in recommendations of kindness, justice, and fair treatment of others. Most collections of the traditions include large chapters on general behavior (adab), assembling scores of injunctions about proper demeanor in interpersonal relationships in general, with special emphasis on honoring one's parents and kinsfolk.

One entertaining extended narrative sets the question of the broad efficacy of kindness toward others in an unusual context. Three travelers once took refuge in a cave from a sudden storm. Just as they entered the cave, a landslide dropped a boulder at the opening, blocking their exit. The terrified trio agreed to reflect on the good deeds they had done for God's sake, and prayed accordingly for deliverance. The first told the Lord how he used to see to the needs of his elderly parents, preparing their food daily and attending them through the night. Suddenly the boulder budged enough to admit a shaft of light. Then up spoke the second, recalling how he had fought off inappropriate feelings for his own beautiful daughter and eventually sent her off with funds to keep her safe. At that, the boulder slid still farther to the side, but not quite enough. In earnest entreaty, the third man narrated how one of his former workers failed to show up for his pay. He had taken that laborer's wage and bought a goat, who later gave birth to a kid. After a few years, his investment had multiplied into a small herd, when suddenly, out of nowhere, the missing worker reappeared to collect his wages. The employer gave the worker the whole flock because it was the result of his delayed payday. In response, God liberated the three by nudging the boulder one last time.[22]

Another touching Hadith has the Prophet say: "Once there was a man who loaned money to people, and who used to say to his assistant, 'When you encounter a person going through hard times, go easy on him, and perhaps God will go easy on us.' And [Muhammad went on] when he came to meet God, God went easy on him."[23] And as for the importance of intent in ethical motivation, in another lovely Hadith, God's Messenger quotes God as saying: "When a servant of mine takes a notion to do good, but does not do it, I record it as a good deed for him; but if he does it, I record from ten to seven hundred good deeds to his credit. And if he considers doing evil but does not do it, I do not record it against him; but if he does the evil deed, I record him [as responsible for] one evil deed."[24]

Finally, Islamic social ethics sometimes requires the individual to step forward more boldly. Someone once asked Muhammad about the most important form of *jihād,* and he replied that it was "to speak a word of truth in the presence of a tyrant."[25]

. . .

Both traditions root the demands of an ethical life in the divine qualities of justice and mercy, and the divinely ordained integrity of communities of faith in their scriptures. In addition, both emphasize the roles of their foundational figures as moral exemplars. Here, however, there is a significant difference: Jesus represents the highest values of a divine being who nevertheless shares in human nature and thus models imitable values realistically through his incarnation. Muhammad, by contrast, is an entirely human paradigm whose intimacy with God and direct access to revelation nonetheless positions him as the loftiest interpreter of God's will for humankind.

Both traditions have in the course of their long histories developed complex ethical theories based on philosophical and theological principles. While their theoretical methods do not always coincide in detail, they intersect significantly in their emphasis on religiously motivated virtue and the importance of acting in view of longer-term goals and ultimate accountability before God. Virtue plays a significant role in both traditions, but the scriptural roots of virtue ethics differ. The Qur'ān juxtaposes the values of the "age of ignorance" with the new moral orientation as revealed through the Prophet Muhammad, thus completely transforming the fundamental moral virtues of the culture. On the other hand, Christian ethics incorporates moral principles of the Old Testament as reinterpreted by Jesus: beyond the Law-centered system of the Torah, Jesus stressed that a Christian's personal relationship with God made still more stringent moral demands. Both scriptural traditions emphasize social responsibility.

Both Muslim and Christian traditions of religious ethical theory span a broad theological spectrum. From the idealist perspective, theology begins with incontrovertible assumptions about the nature of God and the divine attributes most directly associated with action in creation. "Theology from above" argues that if all power, freedom, and knowledge belong to God alone, it follows that human action is under enormous constraints and has no part in determining the ethical valuation of any given act. Murder is evil, for example, purely because God forbids it, and God could, in theory, have decreed just the opposite. This "theistic subjectivism," also sometimes called "voluntarism," since God's choices rule the day, appears to banish reason from the moral calculus. It turns, nonetheless, on its own inner logic, a reasoning designed to maintain God's unquestioned supremacy.

For the broad majority of "traditionalist" Muslims and Christians, the living example of the foundational figure softens the hard edge of theistic subjectivism by injecting a decidedly human element. Muhammad and Jesus model a grace-filled way of responding to the demands of a God whose mercy ultimately outweighs his wrath, demonstrating concretely what is morally acceptable conduct. For Christians, however, the crux of the matter is Christ's condescension to taking on the experience of suffering humanity.

From the "realist" perspective, by contrast, rationalist ethics elaborates a "theology from below." Instead of beginning with God's prerogatives, it elaborates the implications of the conviction that God's greatest gift to humankind is the use of reason. Since rationality implies a measure of human independence in arriving at truth, "rational objectivism" asserts that murder is evil not because God forbids it, but because any reasonable being can discern that it is inherently and objectively evil. And since God is reasonable, God forbids murder.

Finally, a "personalist" approach combines elements of traditionalist and realist ethics. Here a central criterion is the nexus between possible ethical options and the individual's personal relationship to God, as mediated or interpreted by a guide or leader divinely invested with unique insight. In classical Sufism such a guide is the shaykh, to whom the aspirant submits in obedience; in Shi'i tradition, the living ethical standard is embodied in the imam or his representatives; and in various Christian denominations, being overcome by the Spirit personalizes and interiorizes moral guidance.

We now consider various aspects of the spiritual quest, the inward journey that mirrors the outer journey governed by religious ethics.

# CHAPTER 8

# Sources and Models in Traditions of Spirituality

Behind the often intimidating public facades of their institutional manifes-tations, Christians and Muslims have cultivated less imposing, more invit-ing private gardens of inspiration, repose, and refreshment. A wide range of literary genres in both traditions maps out a variety of paths to deeper insight through personal reflection, discipline, and devotion. Neither the Bible nor the Qur'ān was intended to be read as a manual of spirituality, but over the centuries Muslim and Christian spiritual guides have elaborated on their scriptures' allusions to the most important aspects of the divine-human relationship. After a look at some of those key scriptural images and texts, I will explore briefly how Jesus and Muhammad have functioned as primary exemplars for spiritual seekers. In addition, Christian and Muslim traditions of hagiography supply examples of faith and personal commit-ment embodied in the life stories of men and women singled out as the most successful in following the lead of the founding figures. Finally, I suggest several examples of narrative theology whose themes further develop those of scripture and hagiography in service of spirituality.

## SCRIPTURE AND SPIRITUALITY

The Bible and the Qur'ān have functioned over many centuries as treasur-ies of spiritual wisdom to countless millions of Christians and Muslims. Preachers, exegetes, and spiritual authors in both traditions have tutored members in sifting their scriptures for the most evocative texts. A critical ingredient in this reading is the process, virtually automatic for well-schooled believers, of translating texts not necessarily intended as spiritual aids into sources of personal inspiration. Often enough, this complex process of appropriation involves symbolic or metaphorical interpretation. So, for example, Christians might read a text that originally referred to the Law revealed to the ancient Israelites as applicable to themselves in a very different context. Muslims can see as illuminating their own daily struggle a text originally related to a problem encountered by Muhammad and his community in early seventh-century Arabia. Below are a few of the numerous examples of how the foundational texts have supplied ongoing soul sustenance for the faithful of the respective traditions.

### Christian Spiritual Reading of Scripture

Christians generally look to both Old and New Testaments to tap into the spiritual wellsprings of their various denominational traditions. Most Christians will affirm that they accept the Old Testament as revealed to them, but the message they take from it is very different from what their Jewish brothers and sisters find there. Paradigmatic images come to the fore as they filter the text of the Hebrew Bible wearing their uniquely Christian lenses. For example, a text of Deuteronomy distills a core dynamic of the divine-human relationship in a way that readily appeals to many Christians. God says:

> I call heaven and earth to witness against you this day, that I have set before you life and death, blessing and curse; therefore choose life, that you and your descendants may live, loving the Lord your God, obeying his voice, and cleaving to him; for that means life to you and length of days, that you may dwell in the land which the Lord swore to your fathers, to Abraham, to Isaac, and to Jacob, to give them. (Deuteronomy 30:15–20)

Christian readers typically have no trouble understanding "the land" metaphorically as a reference to reward in the next life rather than a piece of earthly real estate. Texts describing Israel's survival of countless trials during the Exodus translate readily into images of God's guidance through life and deliverance from all manner of enslavement into spiritual freedom.

For many Christians, the Psalms (known to Muslims as the *zabūr,* revealed by God to David) are a crucial source of Old Testament insight. Many "liturgical" churches incorporate psalmody into their worship and paraliturgical services (e.g., Divine Office or Liturgy of the Hours). A common method incorporates psalm readings as antiphonal recitation or song, interspersed with refrains. Preachers of virtually all Christian churches cite the Psalms in sermons, often drawing out their christological implications. In the Roman Catholic tradition, for example, the lectionary pairs a psalm reading with the day's gospel reading largely on the basis of christological resonance. Christian authors, beginning in the New Testament and including many from Augustine to Luther, have read the Psalms as referring to Christ. Through the centuries, countless Christians have also used the Psalms in personal devotion and spiritual reading.[1]

Perhaps most important of all are texts from the Prophetic and Wisdom books, with their often intensely personal language of spiritual challenge and guidance. In the "call" of Jeremiah (Jeremiah 1:4–10), for example, the prophet hears God say: "Before I formed you in the womb I knew you, and before you were born I consecrated you; I appointed you as a prophet to the nations. . . . See, I have set you this day over nations and over kingdoms, to pluck up and to break down, to destroy and to overthrow, to build and to plant." With a spiritualized interpretation of the concepts of divine law and chosen people, many Christians hear God talking to them as Jeremiah reports God saying: "I will put my law within them, and I will write it upon their hearts; I will be their God and they will be my people" (Jeremiah 31:33). Similarly, texts like Ezekiel 36:25–26 spiritualize and personalize the concept of divine law:

> I will sprinkle clean water upon you, and you shall be clean from all your uncleannesses, and from all your idols I will cleanse you. A new heart I will give you, and a new spirit I will put within you; and I will take out of your flesh the heart of stone and give you a heart of flesh.

Wisdom texts like the books of Job, Ecclesiastes, and Proverbs speak to many Christians about the reality of suffering, and survival with the assurance of ultimate redemption. A major theme in Job, for example, is the dilemma of good people suffering the effects of evil and holding fast to the conviction that their good God is still in control and has not forsaken them. The story of Job (Ayyūb) is also important in Islamic traditions of prophetology, and for very similar reasons.[2] Chapter 7 raised the problem of theodicy in an ethical context. Here it is a question of how believers can endure in hope and faith even as their world seems to collapse around them.

## Muslim Spiritual Reading of Scripture

Muslims draw extensively on the Qur'ān for personal inspiration in their daily struggles to remain faithful to the tradition they have received. By far the most often cited (and recited) text is sura 1, "The Opening," which is very similar in tone to the Christian Lord's Prayer:

> In the Name of God, the Compassionate and Merciful:
> Praise to God, Lord of the Universe.
> The Compassionate, the Merciful,
> Master of the Day of Judgement.
> You alone do we serve; from you alone do we seek aid.
> Lead us along the Straight Path,
> the path of those who experience the shower of your grace,
> not of those who have merited your anger
> or of those who have gone astray. (1:1–7)

Here, as in all but one of the Qur'ān's suras, the text opens by invoking God with the two most often used divine names, Merciful and Compassionate (*ar-rahmān, ar-rahīm*). Muslims are keenly aware of God as perfectly transcending all other realities, and yet being also intimately accessible, indeed "closer than the jugular vein" (50:16). God's awe-inspiring majesty (*jalāl*) is paired with his attractive beauty (*jamāl*), and most Muslims seek to balance a sense of healthy fear in God's presence with confidence that God is ever-forgiving and attentive to those who seek his "face" with a sincere heart. As the Qur'ān says, "To God belong the east and west, and wherever you turn, there is the face of God" (2:115); "All things pass away, save His face" (28:88); and "Everything on earth perishes; but the face of your Lord remains, majestic and most revered" (55:26–27). This imagery recalls chapter 4's discussion of God's seemingly anthropomorphic attributes.

Another seminal scriptural text, to which I referred in passing earlier, is the "Verse of Light":

> God is the Light of the Heavens and the Earth. His light is analogous to a niche in which there is a lamp, and within the lamp a glass. It is as though the glass were a glittering star lit from a sacred olive tree neither of east nor west, whose oil would fairly radiate even though no fire touched it. Light upon light, and God guides to his light whom he will. (Q 24:35)

Here is an image of God's pervasive revelatory presence, combined with an allusion to a tree on fire but not consumed, not unlike the Burning Bush of Exodus. Divine guidance is available to all who seek it, so long as one remembers that access to the Light is, like all things, ultimately God's doing. Since the Light is all-suffusing, guidance to the Light does not require a directional trajectory, but an openness to perceive the signs (*āyāt*) of God in all things. Though the final sentence appears to hint that God's preferences can be arbitrary, even capricious, the individual's fundamental orientation remains up to the person. As the Qur'ān explains elsewhere, "God is the guardian of those who believe; He brings them forth from darkness into his light. Those who choose arrogantly not to believe will be led from light into darkness, there to be denizens of the fire forever" (2:257). On the positive side, God says: "I am truly near: I answer the prayer of the petitioner who invokes me. Therefore let them respond to me and have faith in me, that they might receive guidance" (2:186). Another text clarifies the situation further:

> I will turn away from my signs those who walk proudly on earth. Though they see every sign, they will put no credence in them. Though they may see the way of uprightness, they will not set out upon it. Should they see the way of the misguided, that they will claim as theirs; for they denied and refused to attend to our signs. (Q 7:146)

Muslims read or listen to recitations of the Qur'ān in a host of devotional settings. From quiet reflection at home to large gatherings convened on the thirty nights of Ramadan (one-thirtieth of the text recited per night), the Qur'ān is the constant thread in Islamic piety and devotion. Preachers typically choose for their Friday sermons thematically apposite texts, but unlike many Christian churches, Muslim practice does not arrange the Qur'ān thematically according to a revolving liturgical calendar.

A uniquely Islamic genre with profound implications for Muslim spirituality is the Sacred Hadith (Ahādīth Qudsīya), extrascriptural texts in which God speaks in the first person, as reported by Muhammad. These "words of God" differ from the text of the Qur'ān as follows: Sacred Hadiths are mediated by the Prophet explicitly (i.e., "Muhammad said that God said . . ."); they are not acceptable for use in liturgical prayer (salāt); they are not considered inimitable (i'jāz), as are scriptural texts; and one need not be in a state of ritual purity when repeating them. These Ahādīth Qudsīya characteristically emphasize God's immanence and accessibility. Many of the sayings are short but poignant in their simplicity: "Heaven and earth cannot contain Me, but there is room for Me in the heart of the believer"; "I was a hidden treasure and I wished to be known; so I created the world"; "The Heart of the believer is between the two fingers of the Merciful"; and "I am in the midst of those whose hearts are broken for My sake." In one of the most famous sacred traditions, transmitted in several slightly different versions, God describes how supererogatory devotion establishes the most intimate bond between servant and Lord:

> My servant continues to come near to me by piety beyond what is required, so that I love him; and I show my love by becoming the eye with which my servant sees, the ear by which he hears, the hand with which he grasps. And if my ser-

vant approaches a hand's breadth, I go toward him an arm's length; and if he approaches an arm's length, I go forward the space of outstretched arms; and if he comes toward me walking, I go toward him running. And if my servant should bring to me sins the size of the earth itself, my forgiveness will be more than equal to them.[3]

Dozens of other Sacred Hadiths testify to the conviction that for all his unimaginable majesty, God remains intimately accessible to the humblest faithful Muslim.

### JESUS AND MUHAMMAD, PRIME EXEMPLARS OF THE LIFE OF FAITH

In addition to the numerous scriptural texts that provide general and specific guidelines for the life of committed faith, both Islamic and Christian traditions center on the ways in which their respective foundational figures model that commitment. Both traditions have produced extensive literatures on the importance of imitation, albeit in an attenuated form, of the paradigmatic figures. Since Jesus and Muhammad represent, each in distinctive ways, the ultimate in human response to the divine initiative, no other person can expect to emulate them perfectly. Muslims and Christians nonetheless strive to incorporate the example of their spiritual models to the extent that they are humanly imitable. In addition to their function as ethical exemplars (as discussed in chapter 7), Jesus and Muhammad also lead by example on the spiritual path.

### Jesus, Spiritual Model for Christians

Countless texts from the New Testament prompt Christians to reflect on central characteristics of their relationships with God. In this context, Jesus models spiritual perfection, while the apostles and others close to Jesus supply helpful images of the struggle to remain faithful to God's call. Even though the four Gospels provide documentary access to only about 10 percent of Jesus' life—the three years of his "public ministry"—Christians distill numerous specific canons of behavior from that relatively limited documentation. Responding to the query "What would Jesus do?" in a given situation provides ethical guidance to many Christians.[4] Jesus' ways of dealing with a host of individuals and groups offer one of the most important paradigmatic patterns. He did not hold himself aloof from the poor, the socially and religiously marginal or outcast (such as women, lepers, and Samaritans and other non-Jews), or even members of the religious establishment (such as the scribes and Pharisees) with whom the Gospels often portray Jesus in conflict of various kinds. Christians often single out Jesus' attitude toward the exercise of earthly power as diametrically opposed to Muhammad's openness to taking up the reins of authority. Justice ultimately means sharing with all who are in need the riches bestowed on the most fortunate.

In this context, the question is not so much "What would Jesus do?" as it is "What can Christians learn from Jesus about their relationships with God the Father?" In all of his personal relationships, Jesus models for Christians the ideal of selfless love blended perfectly with openness and responsiveness to the will of God the Father.

There is perhaps no clearer summary of Jesus' teaching on the highest spiritual values than the so-called Beatitudes. Jesus proclaims "blessed" the spiritually poor, those who mourn, the meek, those who hunger and thirst for justice, the merciful, the pure of heart, the peacemakers, and those persecuted for the sake of justice (Matthew 5:1–12; Luke 6:17–26). Indeed, the entire Sermon on the Mount (Matthew 5:1–7:29) is an epitome of brief sayings, in which Matthew has gathered the core of Jesus' spiritual teaching to his followers. Here the teacher offers his interpretations of everything, from the commandments in general (prohibition of killing and adultery in particular) to specific practices such as prayer, fasting, and almsgiving to the believer's fundamental orientation of complete confidence in God.

For many Christians, however, it is the overall pattern of Jesus' life, suffering, and death that takes center stage. One model, that of Greek spiritual author John Climacus (d. 649), sees the thirty years of Jesus' private life as a template for thirty successive stages in the development of the monk from aspirancy (the initial stage of training, sometimes called the novitiate) to spiritual perfection. Others focus more on the three years traditionally associated with Jesus' public ministry, with its inexorable trajectory toward suffering and death in Jerusalem. For Athanasius (as well as Gregory of Nyssa and Gregory Nazianzen), for example, the core of Jesus' spiritual meaning is the stark reality that God chose to become human.[5] Here Athanasius takes his cue from the Pauline christological hymn:

> Have this mind among yourselves, which is yours in Christ Jesus, who, though he was in the form of God, did not count equality with God a thing to be grasped, but emptied himself, taking the form of a servant, being born in the likeness of humankind. And being found in human form he emptied himself and became obedient unto death, even death on a cross. (Philippians 2:5–10)

One study of patristic soteriology discerns four christological "models" in the early fathers. Christ the "Illuminator" features prominently in the Apostolic Fathers. As "Victor," Christ's sacrifice counters the power of the devil. In the thought of Irenaeus and Athanasius, Christ "recapitulates," or sums up in himself, all things and thus restores fallen humanity. Finally, Christ the "Victim" depicts the Son as sacrifice to the Father.[6]

Still other models use the whole life story of Jesus as a representation of various stages in the progress of the soul toward union with Christ. Laying out the life of Jesus as a map for a journey of "four weeks," Ignatius Loyola's *Spiritual Exercises* envisions a spiritual transformation that leads from repentance through illuminative insight to union with Christ.[7]

Finally, Jesus modeled the ideal way to pray. When the apostles asked Jesus for instructions on how to address God, he taught them to avoid public display in the conviction that only God's awareness matters. "When you pray," he told them, say:

> Our Father in heaven, may your name be sanctified, may your kingdom come and your will be done on earth as it is in heaven. Give us today our daily bread and forgive us our misdeeds as we forgive those who have mistreated us; and lead us not into temptation, but deliver us from evil. (Matthew 6:9; Luke 11:2–4)[8]

## Muhammad, Spiritual Model for Muslims

For Muslims, information about Muhammad as prime exemplar, and about the Companions, comes not so much from the Qur'ān as from the Hadith. Those traditions provide specific (though often disparate) guidelines on virtually every facet of daily life. Muhammad's actions—in everything from where to place one's hands during ritual prayer to what foods are acceptable to modesty in clothing to comportment at funerals—comprise a canon of behavioral norms. More importantly, the Prophet models for Muslims the highest ethical and spiritual aspirations, so that he represents the best in human relationships, honesty, kindness, fatherly care, spousal responsibility, and the pursuit of justice.

Muhammad's entire life sets a paradigmatic pattern of experiences and responses to God's initiatives toward the Prophet. Three symbolic journeys constitute the single most important pattern in this context: the Hijra, the Hajj, and the Isrā'/Mi'rāj. Though Muslims generally understand the three journeys primarily as historical events, actual moments in the Prophet's life, they also think of them as symbolic markers. For example, the *hijra,* or "emigration," from Mecca to Medina in 622 marked the historic transition of the young Muslim minority from a time of relative persecution under the Quraysh to a time of dominance and rule in Medina.

Many of the earliest Companions, as mentioned in chapter 1, were accorded a particularly high rank in the community because they were *muhājirūn*, "those who made the *hijra*" with Muhammad. Countless other Muslims over the centuries have considered "making Hijra" an ongoing duty for themselves. In this sense, the Hijra means not simply retracing Muhammad's steps from Mecca to Medina, but obeying God's command to all believers that they set out from the security of home in confidence that God will guide them to a new home, as God once did for Muhammad.

Muhammad also made a *hajj*, or "(major) pilgrimage," from Medina to visit the Ka'ba in Mecca in 630. Muslims are enjoined to make a pilgrimage at least once in their lives, during the formal Hajj season (the eighth through thirteenth days of the twelfth lunar month). In Mecca they symbolically retrace the steps of the Prophet's paradigmatic pilgrimage: they circumambulate the Ka'ba, with the Black Stone ensconced in one of its corners, and visit the Mount of Mercy in the plain outside Mecca to commemorate the farewell sermon Muhammad preached there as he concluded his own final pilgrimage in 632. They also seek to share in Muhammad's experience of symbolic unity and connection with Abraham and his son Ishmael, whom God had commissioned to reestablish the Ka'ba as a spiritual focal point. In that connection, pilgrims run symbolically (or walk rapidly) between the two small hills Safā' and Marwa, recalling Hagar's frantic search for water for herself and her infant son Ishmael (Ismā'īl).

Finally, Muhammad's third symbolic experience of travel was the combination of the night journey (*isrā*') from Mecca to Jerusalem and the ascension (*mi'rāj*), in which Gabriel led the Prophet from the Dome of the Rock through the heavens to the very throne of God. Most Muslims read the narratives of this complex experience as a record of an actual physical journey. Whether one interprets the journey literally or spiritually (as some Muslim sources have done over the centuries), the important point here is that the journey is paradigmatic. That is not to say that Muslims believe they are called to imitate Muhammad's remarkable experience (indeed, most believe that would be simply impossible); it is rather an acknowledgment that this journey is an indication of Muhammad's uniquely privileged relationship with God.[9]

Just as Jesus was the prime source for the Christian's prayer, the best Muslim prayer is any that Muhammad first pronounced. Even the angels took their cue from the Prophet as the best of those who call on and praise

God. A favorite prayer of Muhammad's was a plea for divine forgiveness that he recommended for pilgrims on their way to Mecca:

> O God, indeed you know and see where I stand and hear what I say. You know me inside and out; nothing of me is hidden from you. And I am the lowly, needy one who seeks your aid and sanctuary, aware of my sinfulness in shame and confusion. I make my request of you as one who is poor; as a humbled sinner I make my plea; fearful in my blindness I call out to you, head bowed before you, eyes pouring out tears to you, body grown thin for you, face in the dust at your feet. O God, as I cry out to you, do not disappoint me; but be kind and compassionate to me, you who are beyond any that can be petitioned, most generous of any that give, most merciful of those who show mercy [a reference to Q 12:92]. Praise to God, Lord of the universe. Amen.[10]

## EXEMPLARY FAITH: TRADITIONS OF HAGIOGRAPHY

Stories of religiously exemplary figures have played important roles in the lives of many Christians and Muslims. In both traditions, however, one finds varying degrees of theological legitimacy and importance attributed to saints and Friends of God. I will explore several of those questions shortly, after a look at the phenomenon of religious exemplary persons and the historical development of Christian and Muslim hagiographical literatures.

### Acknowledging Exemplary Piety

Many hundreds, perhaps thousands, of exemplary figures in the histories of both Islam and Christianity have been acknowledged as Friends of God or saints, but that acknowledgment occurs in very different ways in the two faith communities. Virtually all Christian denominations recognize as paragons of piety a group of figures most closely associated with Jesus— the apostles, New Testament authors, and others among the early disciples who are regarded as especially important in the spread of the church. Some churches also acknowledge important church fathers as saints. Major denominations, such as Methodists, Baptists, and many Evangelicals, do not go so far as to recognize any individuals as saints formally; and some Christians do not single out individuals beyond major biblical figures as models of piety or virtue at all. Other churches, however, notably the Roman Catholic and Orthodox, have developed elaborate institutional procedures to elevate individuals to the catalogue of saints.

In Roman Catholicism, for example, the process begins with an acknowledgment that some deceased individual is so noteworthy for his or her probity of life, piety, and impact on the life of the church as to merit a special investigation. Most such "causes" develop many years, even centuries, after the person's death. Some individuals, however, such as Mother Teresa and Pope John Paul II, acquire such a devoted following in life that a call for canonization can begin almost immediately. People initially identified as candidates for canonization have sometimes been called "Venerable," but the formal process begins with an investigation initiated by the bishop where the individual lived and forwarded to the Sacred Congregation of Rites. It is the task of this panel or "tribunal," composed of a notary, three judges, and a "defender of the faith" also known as a "devil's advocate," to ferret out weaknesses in the case as it unfolds. The tribunal reviews anecdotal and material evidence submitted, and assuming that the devil's advocate fails to discredit the initial evidence, the cause moves from the "ordinary process" phase to that of the "apostolic process."

At this stage, the Sacred Congregation weighs evidence supporting claims to two "miracles," breaches of the natural order unexplainable by ordinary scientific means. Once two such events are authenticated, the individual is "beatified," that is, declared "Blessed." Some individuals remain at this level for many years, but a cause may proceed to a further investigation of two additional miracles, after which the pope can declare the final canonization of a "Saint." A primary difference between Blesseds and Saints is that whereas the former may be "venerated" (that is, revered but not worshipped) locally or regionally where he or she lived (or in institutions he or she founded or belonged to), the latter may be venerated by the universal church. Though he was canonized only in 2009, the famous Damien the Leper (d. 1889) of Molokai was celebrated by generations of Catholics on May 10, his feast day, even as a Blessed. Veneration falls far short of worship and refers only to specific recognition of a unique relation to God and the communion of believers, along with limited access to intercessory aid.[11]

Within the global Islamic tradition, acknowledgment of exemplary piety and special relationships with God occurs in a much less structured fashion. Hundreds of millions of Muslims today recognize Friends of God, both men and women, as models of intimacy with God and symbols of hope and assistance. One could argue that roughly the same percentage of Muslims as of Christians—at least half—consider exemplars of piety spiritually significant. On the other hand, many Muslims will insist that Islamic teaching explicitly rules out the existence of any distinct category of exemplary individuals, for mediation between God and humanity is unnecessary. Resistance to the notion of elevating mere mortals to a special status is, in general, born of an abundance of caution lest any human being begin to trespass on divine (or prophetic) prerogatives. Identifying remarkable people as Friends of God differs from Christian canonization in two principal ways: first, Muslims have sometimes been recognized as Friends while still alive; and second, the process is largely one of popular acclaim, from the ground up rather than from the top down. Finally, local and regional communities of Muslims across the globe continue to identify individuals as new Friends of God. Like their Christian counterparts, many Muslim Friends are associated with particular sites and special days on the calendar.[12]

### Christian Hagiographic Themes and Literature

A brief visit to the Library of Congress BX section in a good theological library will reveal thousands of volumes in English and various European languages. Though Muslim religious literatures do not use a precise equivalent to the term "hagiography" (from the Greek *hagiē graphē*, "writings about holy persons"), it is analogously useful to describe such narratives in both traditions.

Hagiographic themes began to appear in Christian literature as early as the New Testament itself. Most notably, the Letter to the Hebrews assembles a group from the Old Testament on the basis of their exemplary faith. Along with more obvious figures such as Abraham and Moses, the list includes Abel, Enoch, Noah, Sarah, Isaac, Jacob, Joseph, those who crossed the Red Sea, various biblical judges, and King David. The Letter to the Hebrews sums up the paradigmatic qualities of this "cloud of witnesses," noting how they suffered torture, imprisonment, brutal executions, all manner of hardship, "wandering over deserts and mountains, and in dens and caves of the earth." These paragons of faith encourage believers to "lay aside every weight, and sin which clings so closely," to "run with perseverance" the race set before them, "looking to Jesus as the pioneer and perfecter of our faith" (Hebrews 11).[13]

Early Christian authors began producing works on saintly individuals during the patristic period, first in the form of martyrologies—accounts of the suffering and death of those who chose to follow Christ in the ultimate commitment. Luke's brief account of Saint Stephen's execution in Acts 7:54–60 may have planted the seed of the genre. The *Martyrdom of Polycarp* (d. 155) is apparently the earliest and among the most famous of the martyrological texts, along with the *Passion of Perpetua and Felicity* (c. 203).[14] Christian hagiography arguably flowered as a literary tradition during the fourth century with the *Life* of Antony, dubiously attributed to

Saint Athanasius. Antony (d. 356) was an Egyptian hermit credited with founding the first community of anchorites, monks who lived a solitary life within a communal structure. Eusebius of Caesarea (d. 340) is thought to have compiled the earliest collection of primary source material, including brief martyrologies or "passion" accounts of saints' suffering and deaths, and devotional texts attributed to various holy persons, but that collection is no longer extant.[15] Early *Vitae* of holy persons were typically polemical in intent, designed to set the central figure forth as a paragon of ortho-dox faith in contrast to a specific heresy. Paulinus of Nola (355–431), for example, composed a *Life* of Ambrose of Milan (c. 339–97) to demonstrate that Ambrose was God's chosen champion against the Arian heresy.[16]

Major developments in hagiographic literature occurred during and after the thirteenth century. Among the most influential works were *Lives* of mendicant founders, especially Francis of Assisi (d. 1226). Franciscan friar Thomas of Celano (d. 1260) produced two major *Lives* of Francis, as well as a narrative of Saint Clare of Assisi (d. 1253). Franciscan theologian Bonaventure also wrote a more highly symbolic *Greater Life* (*Legenda Major*) of Saint Francis, a text whose scenes were soon incorporated visu-ally into the frescoes and windows of the Basilica of St. Francis in Assisi. The *Golden Legend* (*Legenda Aurea*, c. 1260–75) was a major medieval hagiographical compendium.

Lives of important saints enjoyed seasons of popularity through the later Middle Ages, but Christian hagiography did not emerge as a distinct theological discipline until the Jesuit Bollandists, led by John van Bolland (d. 1665), introduced the critical study of the literature with the publication of the multivolume *Deeds of the Saints* (*Acta Sanctorum*). In more recent times, *Lives* of the saints have functioned as a staple in the meditative read-ing of many Christians, as well as in pedagogy and preaching.[17]

## Muslim Hagiographic Traditions

Muslim literary acknowledgment of the importance of paradigmatic fig-ures took its cue from the earliest biography of Muhammad. Ibn Ishāq's (d. 767) pioneering work was revised substantially by Ibn Hishām (d. 833), both authors relying heavily on Hadith and other traditional reports as well as poetry dating to the Prophet's time. The work begins with a geneal-ogy tracing the last Prophet back to Adam, much as Luke's gospel does with Jesus' lineage.[18] This classic biography offers a rare commentary on the nature of Muhammad's night journey and ascension. Acknowledging the patchwork nature of the surviving accounts, the author calls the story "a searching test and a matter of God's power and authority wherein is a lesson for the intelligent; and guidance and mercy and strengthening to those who believe." After observing that one might interpret the events as a spiritual, rather than a clearly physical, experience, the author continues: "It was certainly an act of God by which He took him by night in what way He pleased, to show him His signs which He willed him to see so that he witnessed His mighty sovereignty and power by which He does what He wills to do."[19]

An early postprophetic genre influential in the development of Muslim hagiography was the biographical dictionary (discussed earlier in a different context), devised as an aid to Hadith scholars in assessing the authenticity of prophetic traditions. From the eighth century on, such reference works provided basic data about thousands of individual transmitters. Any Hadith transmitted by individuals known to be less than truthful was to that degree judged less than perfectly authentic. By around the late tenth century, works dedicated to recounting the lives and teachings of Muslims known for their piety and learning were becoming more common. Muslim hagiographic sources often use terms like "tales of the Prophets/ [God's] Friends" (qisas al-anbiyā'/awliyā') and the "literature of amazing feats" (adab al-manāqib) to describe works of the genre. Hagiographical anthologies such as Sulamī's (d. 1021) Generations of the Sufis, Abū Nu'aym al-Isfahānī's (d. 1038) multivolume Ornament of the Friends of God, and Farīd ad-Dīn 'Attār's (d. 1221) Remembrances of God's Friends enjoyed immense popularity in the Arabic- and Persian-reading regions of the Middle East. Hagiographical anthologies remained an important religious genre through the Middle Period, with Jāmī's (d. 1492) Persian Warm Breezes of Intimacy gaining perhaps the widest readership of any work of the kind.

In addition to the anthology, life stories of major individual paragons of devotion began to appear during the eleventh century. Leading religious figures, including many mystics and Sufi leaders,[20] merited their own hagiographic works. Muslim hagiographical traditions have generated an expansive literature in some two dozen major languages, but only a relative handful of publications in European languages have yet made their way to the stacks of libraries. Publishing houses in the Middle East and South Asia continue to produce a wide range of hagiographical materials, from new original-language editions of classic works mentioned above to regional vernacular accounts of Friends of God newly acknowledged as well as of spiritual giants of the past.[21]

## A Shared Narrative Theme: Marvels and Miracles

An important theme about which both Christian and Muslim theologians have written important texts is the realm of supernatural deeds attributed to exemplars of holiness. Scriptural foundations for belief in the miraculous are apparent in both Christian and Islamic traditions. Many Old Testament narratives describe divine interventions in the natural order, both unmediated and through the instrumental agency of a prophetic figure. Noah and the flood are among the crucial early themes. More importantly, God instructs Moses to raise his arms so that the sea will reveal dry ground for the fleeing Israelites, and to strike a rock to provide water for his thirsty people (Exodus 17:1–7; Numbers 20:2–13).

Early fathers of the church, such as Ambrose of Milan, use these and other marvels worked through Moses and other patriarchs to demonstrate divine presence and power over all creation. Prophets like Elijah and Elisha effect marvels of miraculous provision of food, healing, and even raising from the dead (1 Kings 18:16–44, 19:5–7; 2 Kings 4–5). Miracles are an integral part of many narratives about Jesus in the New Testament, and in the Acts of the Apostles especially, Jesus' successors wield similar powers for healing as well as other breaches of the natural order.

In the Qur'ān, such wonders are proportionately fewer and characteristically worked through and on behalf of a prophet rejected by the unbelieving people to whom God has sent him. According to ancient Muslim tradition, Muhammad's only miracle was the Qur'ān itself; but accounts of other marvels attributed to the Prophet, as well as some worked in the presence of (and possibly through) his Companions, appear as early as the Hadith literature. Muslim tradition distinguishes three types of supernatural "custom-shattering" events: the sign (āya) worked directly by God alone; the miracle (mu'jiza) worked through a prophet; and the marvel (karāma) effected through a nonprophetic figure.

Miracles and marvels might appear to be quite similar externally, since both involve an interruption in the natural order. The crucial theological distinction here has to do with the function rather than the apparent nature of the action. God brings about "apologetical" miracles as proof of the authenticity of the prophet's divine mission. Friends of God also enjoy occasional access to marvelous powers, primarily for the purpose of confirming the individual's own spiritual conviction, though marvels often also have a profound effect on others.[22]

The important point here is that supernatural events play significant roles in both Christian and Muslim hagiographic traditions. Featuring either prophets or saints, narratives of the extraordinary point to a spiritual dimension that transcends both the admirable and the imitable, suggesting a distinctly higher level of spiritual attainment in the exemplary figures who are the focus of so much wonderful literature in both traditions. Before considering more explicitly theological aspects, we conclude this chapter with another look at the role of narrative as a communicative device.

## NARRATIVE THEOLOGY REVISITED

Dante's *Divine Comedy* is perhaps the best known Christian allegorical poem, but it is one of many medieval allegorical works with important theological themes. Like so many of these works, Dante's centers on the theme of "journey." Here I will offer a brief comparison between another medieval European work, the anonymous fourteenth-century Middle English poem entitled *The Pearl,* and a masterwork of Persian Muslim mystical poetry, 'Attār's (d. 1221) *Conference of the Birds.* According to noted anthropologists Victor and Edith Turner, pilgrimage is "extroverted mysticism, just as mysticism is introverted pilgrimage. . . . The pilgrim physically traverses a mystical way; the mystic sets forth on an interior pilgrimage."[23] Here are two examples of how poets from two traditions have given expression to this major theme.

At the outset of *The Pearl,* our narrator, a jeweler, tells of his deep distress after losing the Pearl of Great Price as he was fashioning a suitable setting for it. He falls asleep and dreams of a magical garden in which he strolls along a lovely river on whose other shore he thinks paradise awaits him. Seeking to ford the stream, the dreamer spies a young woman and believes that she is the lost Pearl. From the far bank she welcomes him to the wondrous realm, and the two begin an extended conversation. Though he still suspects that she is his Pearl, she assures him that his pearl is actually a rose that has withered as all living things must. When the dreamer asks how he can cross the stream, she replies that he can do so only by surrendering to God's will and mercy. He inquires further about who she is, and she explains that she is the queen of the eternal Lamb (from the book of Revelation).

Our inquisitive traveler asks if the maiden has therefore supplanted Mary as heaven's queen, but she reminds him of the parable of the Vineyard with its teaching that all members of Christ's body are equal. When the dreamer insists that God must surely treat individuals differently as each person merits, she retorts that Christ died to redeem all equally. The lady proceeds to teach the dreamer the basics of salvation from sin as available to all who accept the grace of repentance, explaining that she received the Pearl of Great Price only after being baptized in the blood of the Lamb. He must, she counsels, be willing to risk everything to purchase the Pearl.

At length, the dreamer inquires about the nature of heavenly Jerusalem, and she explains that it is the city of God. Though he may not go to the city now, God will allow him a glimpse of it as a rare gift. As they stroll on opposite banks of the river toward the city, the dreamer sees Jerusalem just as the book of Revelation described it, complete with a host of its inhabitants in solemn procession. Unable to control himself any longer, the dreamer dives into the stream and tries to swim across. At that moment, alas, he finds himself awakened and realizes that he can recover the Pearl and return to the city only by a life of surrendering to the divine will.[24]

An equally marvelous tale of spiritual realization by the Persian poet Farīd ad-Dīn 'Attār, entitled *The Conference of the Birds,* admirably illustrates the concept of mystical pilgrimage from an Islamic perspective. Once upon a time, all the birds of the world assembled to discuss their place in creation. They decide that they, no less than the other animal kingdoms, ought to have a king. In their quest for the feathered monarch, however, they would need an experienced guide. Fortunately one of the birds, the crested hoopoe, had served the prophet Solomon as his ambassador to the queen of Sheba and volunteers his services. In his inaugural address he announces that the birds indeed already have a king who dwells in a mysterious and mountainous land many days distant. Already experienced in the demands of life in the Unseen World, the hoopoe warns that the journey will be arduous.

One after another the birds stand up to express their misgivings and offer excuses for staying at home. To each in turn the hoopoe responds with a further elaboration of the importance of the journey and the magnificent prospect of meeting the king, the Simurgh. We are but the king's shadow on earth, he explains; and though none of us is truly fit to gaze on the king's beauty directly, "by his abounding grace he has given us a mirror to reflect himself, and this mirror is the heart. Look into your heart and there you will see his image."

A grueling trek through seven perilous valleys separates the birds from their goal: quest, love, understanding, detachment, acknowledgment of God's unity, bewilderment, and, at last, poverty and death to self. Many give up along the way, and by the end survivors numbered only thirty birds (*si* = "thirty," *murgh* = "bird" in Persian). After the bedraggled flock wait for what seems an eternity at the door of the king's palace, a chamberlain emerges to advise them to turn back, for they could never hope to endure the king's glorious presence. The birds insist on their steadfast desire. Finally, the servant opens the door and ushers them in. As he vanishes from their sight he draws a hundred veils from a vast mirror. With that "the sun of majesty sent forth its rays, and in the reflection of each other's faces these thirty birds of the outer world contemplate the face of the Simurgh of the inner world." Their pilgrimage does not end there, however, for the additional stories of the death of the martyr-mystic Hallāj and the king's sacrifice of his own beloved suggest that their journey in God is just beginning.[25]

. . .

All of the theological dimensions of both traditions are fundamentally rooted in and drawn from their scriptures. Biblical and Qur'ānic spiritualities skim off the rich cream of imagery and narrative accounts that reveal critical aspects of the divine-human relationship. Both scriptures supply abundant, though not always detailed, intimations of divine transcendence and immanence, God's mercy and justice, and the range of spiritual options available to believers. Postscriptural resources in both faith traditions pick up and develop those cues from the sacred texts.

As in matters ethical, the concrete example of the foundational figures, Jesus and Muhammad, offers spiritual seekers specific values and canons of behavior. While both traditions emphasize the importance of emulating the spiritual example of their foundational figures, a far greater percentage of Christians than of Muslims speak of striving toward spiritual union with the exemplar. Ordinary folk need more accessible models, and both Christian and Islamic traditions have developed ample resources in response to that need. Stories of saints and Friends of God cloak profound spiritual values in more readily appealing garb. For roughly half the world's Christians (mostly Catholics and Orthodox communities), and a similar proportion of the world's Muslims, exemplars of faith and piety play important roles in the spiritual quest. For the other half on either side, resort to such paradigmatic figures also raises theological questions that pose nettlesome problems. Topping that list are miraculous deeds, accessibility to divine blessing, the function of holy places often associated with saintly relics, and the availability of intercession.

A major difference in the elevation of human exemplars in the two traditions is that whereas Friends of God are acknowledged largely by popular acclaim, saints achieve their status through a more structured process of inquiry and validation. Both traditions continue to add saints and Friends of God, though on the Christian side, by contrast, a greater percentage of saints have lived and been canonized in early modern and more recent times than in earlier centuries. In either case, paradigmatic figures enjoy a privileged relationship to God and set the bar dauntingly high. In the final analysis, therefore, members of both traditions must, at least implicitly, weigh the qualities of their spiritual models on the scales of imitability and admirability: ordinary folk can reenact concrete examples and embody paradigmatic values to a limited degree and acknowledge that the loftier spiritual estate of the exemplars ultimately remains an unattainable ideal.

Finally, in addition to the vast resources of their hagiographical literatures, both great faith traditions have benefited from the talents of countless authors who have penned works of narrative theology. Like hagiographical works, these spiritual classics highlight the attributes of God and his human paragons of soul virtue that are most engaging to sincere believers, and appeal to their imagination and sense of wonder. Unlike hagiography, this type of literature is generally populated by more fictional characters and leans avowedly toward allegory.

Chapter 9 picks up where these stories end, shifting the focus from spiritual example set by others to the ways Christian and Islamic traditions provide resources designed to facilitate personal engagement in the everyday lives of people of faith. There I will also discuss explicitly how various forms of pastoral and mystical theology have given further theoretical shape to the great spiritual motifs.

# CHAPTER 9

# Themes in Prayer
# and Mystical Theology

Both the Christian and Islamic traditions have historically expanded upon the foundational sources and models of spiritual inspiration in a variety of ways. I begin here with personal prayer and the individual believer's relationship to God, providing samples of striking outpourings penned by some of the most celebrated spiritual poets of both traditions. After developing several theological aspects of the divine-human connection, I will provide an overview of both traditions' literatures of the rarified reaches of mystical theology.

## PERSONAL PRAYER AND THE INDIVIDUAL'S
## RELATIONSHIP TO GOD

Traditions of personal prayer in both Christian and Islamic traditions afford essential but often overlooked theological insights. Extensive bodies of devotional literature in dozens of major languages put troves of spiritual riches at the disposal of anyone who wishes to sample the more private dimensions of the lives of countless believers. Images of God are a critical ingredient in this context, since they provide valuable insight into the affective temperament and intent of the one who prays. It may be tempting to presume that since Christianity centers on the incarnation, and Islamic doctrine denies any such divine-human intimacy, images of God's immanence would be more characteristic of Christian prayer, and those of transcendence a hallmark of Muslim prayer. As it turns out, images of both transcendence and immanence permeate devotional prayer in both traditions.[1]

Prayer that has nourished the inner lives of Christians and Muslims over the centuries has generally served three theological purposes: praise, supplication, and intercession. Praise is naturally directed primarily to God, his attributes, and deeds. In an attenuated form, encomia (statements of exaltation) sometimes also laud the divinely inspired qualities of human beings. For Christians, such secondary praise prayers honor (but do not worship) God's power worked through figures from Mary on down to lesser saints. In Muslim tradition, a genre called na't ("description, attribute," hence "exalted qualities") features primarily the Prophet Muhammad, and secondarily members of the Prophet's family and early community as well as countless Friends of God. Christians and Muslims alike offer prayers of supplication, or petition, to ask God's aid in countless circumstances from direst disaster to the more predicable frustrations of daily life.

Intercessory prayer, however, raises more complex questions. In its most basic form intercession implies a communal dimension of prayer based on the conviction that one human being's prayers for another are good and useful. Virtually all Christians presume at least minimal efficacy in "praying for" others, especially in times of loss, illness, and death. Catholics and some other Christians take a large step beyond that, petitioning Mary and the saints for aid. They believe this is perfectly acceptable, and indeed recommended, in two ways: directly, in that the paragons of intimacy with God may draw on a God-given reservoir of spiritual efficacy by which to assist the faithful; and indirectly, in that Mary and the saints can function as go-betweens capable of interceding with God from their positions of privileged access.[2]

For Muslims, the first type of intercessory prayer is perfectly acceptable, and in fact required. It has nevertheless become commonplace for Muslims to insist that because no human being stands between the individual and God, Muslims neither need nor benefit from intercession (shafā'a, from a root meaning "to make the odd even"). Ancient tradition nevertheless recommends that Muslims utter as a basic form of intercessory prayer every time they mention the name of Muhammad, "May God bless him and give him peace." In other words, ordinary human beings are expected to offer their prayers even for the Prophet himself. They are expected, traditionally, to append to every mention of the name of a Companion the phrase "God to be merciful to him." When Muslims visit the sick or attend funerals, they pray for the recovery of the one suffering or for God's mercy and forgiveness for the deceased. All of these simple invocations are in fact forms of intercessory prayer. Since constituents of Friends of God typically describe their patrons as providing intercessory services, many Muslims would argue that cultivation of Friends of God is a form of "innovation" at best, downright heretical at worst. In addition, widely accepted Muslim tradition has it that Muhammad enjoys the prerogative of a more exalted power of intercession. Some find this unacceptable, arguing that the Qur'ān does not countenance such a thing. Many others say that the text "Who is it that can intercede with Him, except by His permission?" (2:255) would not have hinted at the possibility of divine permission had it not actually been granted—at least to the Prophet.

Even so, the vast majority of Muslims across the globe have in fact recognized as uniquely privileged the prophets, culminating with Muhammad, and those closest to the Prophet (i.e., the Companions and/or members of his family). Hundreds of millions of others expand the prospects for intercessory help to include Friends of God. In sum, the key theological distinction generally operative within (and between) the two traditions has to do not with intercession in general, but with the extent of its applicability.

Christian tradition teaches that the ultimate spiritual goal is to "take on" the spirit of Christ (Galatians 2:20). For many, however, intercession, with its promise of assistance from outside, presents a more attainable condition. Christian teaching has insisted from the beginning on the essential mediatory role of Jesus and has developed a rich array of theological imagery that features Mary and the saints in intercessory roles.[3] This brief hymn of Hildegard of Bingen (1098–1179) is a fine example of a prayer that celebrates Mary's intercessory prerogatives:

> O mediating branch
> your physical reality
> has conquered death
> and your womb
> has enlightened all creation
> with the lovely bloom
> sprung from the sweetest perfection
> of your virginity.[4]

Many (non-Protestant) Christians believe that Mary and the saints enjoy mediatorial prerogatives at the service of believers who petition them. Most Protestant Christians, however, do not consider Mary a prime mediator and regard saintly intercession unnecessary and irrelevant. Many Muslims, particularly reform-minded people, express the same reservations about Friends of God, though not necessarily about Muhammad. On the other hand, Christians in the hundreds of millions (especially among the many

Protestant denominations) reject with equal vigor any such role, beyond that attributed to Jesus Christ.

## EXAMPLES OF PRAYER IN THE TWO TRADITIONS

In addition to the wide variety of theological functions and themes they express, prayers have taken diverse forms and occurred in many ritual and devotional settings. Here I will offer samples of prayer, first from individuals known for their advanced attainments in the spiritual life, and then from the treasuries of supplication recommended to the generality of believers in both traditions.

Some of the most widely appreciated works of the greatest Christian theologians are not their multivolume tomes of theological analysis, but small jewels of devotional prayer. Thomas Aquinas's two often-performed Latin poems have become staples of classic hymnography. His "Panis Angelicus" (Angelic Bread) and "O Sacrum Convivium" (O Holy Banquet) are lovely examples of Eucharistic hymns performed both in the context of the liturgy and in concerts of devotional music. The first prayer of praise goes as follows:

> Angelic bread becomes the bread of humankind.
> How wondrous that Heavenly bread
> Puts an end to all imagined realities,
> As the Lord nourishes the poorest,
> Humblest servant, the poorest,
> Humblest of servants.

In "O Sacrum Convivium," Thomas addresses the theme of God's willingness to become the very food of believers, in other words with a more explicitly christological focus:

> O Holy Banquet in which Christ is received,
> Reviving the memory of his Passion,
> Filling the soul with grace and granting us
> A pledge of future glory.[5]

Both brief poems are still often performed in splendid musical settings, whether of simply elegant Gregorian chant or Renaissance polyphonic motets.

Noted Christian poets over the centuries have penned even more arresting imagery describing the divine-human relationship in the form of prayers. John Donne (1575–1631) wrote a number of amazing sonnets, none perhaps more astonishing in tone than "Batter My Heart":

Batter my heart, three-person'd God, for you
As yet but knock, breathe, shine, and seek to mend;
That I may rise and stand, o'erthrow me, and bend
Your force to break, blow, burn, and make me new.
I, like an usurp'd town to'another due,
Labor to'admit you, but oh, to no end;
Reason, your viceroy in me, me should defend,
But is captiv'd, and proves weak or untrue.
Yet dearly'I love you, and would be lov'd fain,
But am betroth'd unto your enemy;
Divorce me,'untie or break that knot again,
Take me to you, imprison me, for I,
Except you'enthrall me, never shall be free,
Nor ever chaste, except you ravish me.[6]

The poet begs God to lay siege to his inmost being, beginning with military imagery, proceeding through metaphors of alienation and imprisonment, and ending with thinly veiled sexual allusion. Donne is part of the tradition of the "metaphysical poets," and they in turn part of a still greater tradition of religious longing for intimacy with God. Donne's contemporary George Herbert (1593–1633) authored many equally striking prayers, such as "Bitter-Sweet":

Ah, my dear angry Lord,
Save thou dost love, yet strike;
Cast down, yet help afford;
Sure I will do the like.

I will complain, yet praise;
I will bewail, approve;
And all my sour-sweet days
I will lament and love.[7]

Herbert expresses with stark simplicity the paradox at the heart of any human claim to a relationship with the deity, the sense of desperate need melded with impossibility.

More recently, the English Jesuit poet Gerard Manley Hopkins' (1844–99) "As Kingfishers Catch Fire, Dragonflies Draw Flame" reflects on the signs in nature with a distinctly christological twist:

As kingfishers catch fire, dragonflies dráw fláme;
    As tumbled over rim in roundy wells
    Stones ring; like each tucked string tells, each hung bell's
Bow swung finds tongue to fling out broad its name;
Each mortal thing does one thing and the same:

Deals out that being indoors each one dwells;
   Selves—goes itself; *myself* it speaks and spells,
Crying Whát I do is me: for that I came.
Í say móre: the just man justices;
   Kéeps gráce: thát keeps all his goings graces;
Acts in God's eye what in God's eye he is—
   Chríst. For Christ plays in ten thousand places,
Lovely in limbs, and lovely in eyes not his
   To the Father through the features of men's faces.[8]

With the obvious exception of this christological theme, many great
Muslim poets in over a dozen languages have spoken of God in ways that
few Christians would find alien in sentiment. Sanā'ī (d. 1131) was a Persian-
writing mystical poet whose most important work is a lengthy didactic
poem called *The Garden of Ultimate Reality*. It begins, as do virtually
all works of its kind, with a lovely invocation to the God of all creation.
Sanā'ī emphasizes the divine transcendence and grandeur, adding a note of
supplication at the end of a song of praise:

O you who nourish the soul and ornament the visible world,
And you who grant wisdom and are indulgent with those who lack it;
Creator and sustainer of space and of time,
Custodian and provider of dweller and dwelling;
All is of your making, dwelling and dweller,
All is within your compass, time and space.
Fire and air, water and earth,
All are mysteriously within the scope of your power.
All that is between your Throne and this earth
Are but a fraction of your handiwork;
Inspirited intelligence acts as your swift herald,
Every living tongue that moves in every mouth
Has but one purpose: to give you praise.
Your sublime and exalted names
Evidence your beneficence and grace and kindness.
Every one of them outstrips throne and globe and dominion;
They are a thousand plus one and a hundred less one.
But to those who are outside the spiritual sanctuary,
The names are veiled.
O Lord, in your largesse and mercy
Allow this heart and soul a glimpse of your name![9]

Thirteenth-century Egyptian mystic Ibn al-Fārid (d. 1235) addressed
an ode to the divine presence as the Ka'ba of perfect beauty whose tone is
warmer and more intimate. Here only the mention of Mecca's iconic shrine
clearly marks the poem as Islamic:

O Kaʿba of Splendor, toward your beauty the hearts of those intent on you
make pilgrimage and cry, "Twice at your pleasure!" [a ritual phrase often
repeated by pilgrims]

Lightning blazing through mountain passes has brought us the finest of
gifts: your flashing smile,

revealing to my eye that my heart was your neighbor; and I longed for the
full vision of your loveliness.

But for you I would not have sought guidance in lightning, and my heart
would not have saddened and wept at birdsong from forest depths.

Still, the lightning guided me, and birds on their branches of wood sang me
past need of tunes from lute of wood.

For so long I have wanted you to look my way, and how much blood have I
shed between desire and fulfillment!

They called me fearless before I came to love you; but I have set bravery
aside and no longer hold myself in safety.

My endurance has fled from me and I am led captive; my former sadness
gone, new grief has come to my aid.

Will you not turn from your aversion, from your preference for tyranny
over kindness, from cruelty will you not turn?

Greatest of all gifts would be your slaking the thirst of one at the point of
death that he might revive.

It is not my longing for one beside you that has wasted me: out of affection
for you alone have I perished.

The beauty of your face has quickened me and left me dead, for I am
barred even from kissing its veil.[10]

Everyone who journeys toward God's splendor is on pilgrimage. God's
smile flashes as lightning through mountain passes en route, enticing the
wayfarer to yearn for the full vision of God. What else could lure someone
out of a safe haven onto a perilous road? the poet wonders. The last line
here alludes to the veil (kiswa) over the Kaʿba; as the poet continues, he
laments the loss of his youth and friends. His longing for the Kaʿba has
made chaos of his life. At length God rewards Ibn al-Fārid's long suffering, lifting the veil from the Kaʿba and showing the seeker his face. This
Muslim mystical poet thus expresses an experience remarkably similar to
those of Donne and Herbert.

Prayers penned by literary luminaries in the mystical firmament do not
tell the whole story in either tradition. Examples of heartfelt outpourings
of more ordinary folk, as well as more formal expressions of piety recommended for times when words fail, also abound in Christian and Islamic
sources. In the latter category, few authors have been more attentive to the
daily needs of devout Muslims than Ghazālī. Citing a favorite prayer of the
Prophet, he advises:

So when you go out to the mosque, say: "O God, make a light in my heart and a light in my tongue. Make a light in my ear; and make a light in my eye; make a light in back of me and a light in front of me; make a light above me. O God give me light." . . . If you go out of the house for a need, say: "In the name of God, My Lord, I take refuge with You that I should not wrong nor be wronged, or that I should not be foolish nor be fooled . . ." [On looking in the mirror, say:] "Praise be to God, Who has given moderation and uprightness to my person and has given nobility and beauty to the form of my face, and to Him Who has made me one of the Muslims."[11]

And from a collection of Shi'i prayers comes this lovely supplication:

O God, carry us in the ships of Thy deliverance, give us to enjoy the pleasure of whispered prayer to Thee, make us drink at the pools of Thy love, let us taste the sweetness of Thy affection and nearness, allow us to struggle in Thee, preoccupy us with obeying Thee, and purify our intentions in devoting works to Thee, for we exist through Thee and belong to Thee, and we have no one to mediate with Thee but Thee![12]

Although millions of Muslims repudiate all forms of music, particularly in ritual religious contexts, it is safe to say that far more, in societies from Morocco to Malaysia, treasure devotional songs of the *na't* tradition as expressions of reverence and deep affection for Muhammad and countless Friends of God.[13]

## THEOLOGICAL ASPECTS OF THE DIVINE-HUMAN CONNECTION

Before exploring the lofty realms of Islamic and Christian mystical theologies, it will be helpful here to describe briefly several additional distinctive theological themes running through the literatures of the two traditions. Islamic and Christian sources converge in their understandings of some core features of the human dilemma but diverge as to the specific remedies available. Both emphasize the fundamental and, at least theoretically, unbridgeable gap between Creator and creature, divine and human realities; and both have articulated theological mechanisms by which to explain that God nevertheless maintains a firm bond with all creatures, and with human beings in particular. Both speak in various ways of salvation, deliverance, or redemption from the reality that at the heart of the human condition is a centrifugal tendency that threatens to separate the individual permanently from his or her source.

In addition to the theme of "miracle and marvel," mentioned earlier in the context of hagiographic narrative, several major theological themes inhabit the spiritual dimension of both traditions. All of them contribute to Christian and Muslim ways of imagining the unimaginable, describing the indescribable—the divine-human connection. As chapter 8 indicated, Christians and Muslims alike over the centuries have looked to extraordinary individuals, whether prophets or saints, not only as models of the human relationship to the Creator, but as essential links to the divine. There has, however, been considerable disagreement, within both traditions, about the extent and nature of this linkage.

Both Christian and Muslim traditions have generated extensive spiritual literatures that emphasize various modalities by which human beings have more or less unmediated experience of their individual relationships with God. But here, too, one finds enormous diversity within the two great families of traditions. Christians often speak the language of "sacramentality," the system of signs and symbols by which they embody their spiritual connections in ritual. Not all Christians, however, agree on the number or role of the various sacraments. Roman Catholics number seven sacraments, while most Protestant churches acknowledge only baptism and the Lord's Supper.

Muslims engage in a variety of specific rituals (known generically as the Five Pillars) but do not regard them as "sacramental" in the Christian sense of the term. Nevertheless, many Muslims consider their ritual participation as spiritually efficacious in itself, assuming the requisite intention and "presence of the heart." Some commentators suggest a rough parallel between the sacramentality of the Eucharist or Lord's Supper and the Muslim spiritual experience of Qur'ān recitation: both involve the reception of the word of God on one's tongue.[14] Both Christian and Muslim traditions emphasize the need for continual repentance and asking God's forgiveness, but here again there are many approaches. For Catholics, the sacrament of reconciliation involves a kind of priestly mediation, along with the conviction that it is God who forgives. Other Christians, as well as most Muslims, emphasize unmediated forgiveness without specific related ritualization.

## TRADITIONS OF MYSTICAL THEOLOGY

"Mysticism" is famously hard to define, but for practical purposes, I will offer a simple working definition of the term: a complex blend of religious practices, disciplines, experience, literary works, and institutions that facilitate the individual seeker's intentional journey toward a more intimate relationship to the ultimate reality, however his or her religious tradition describes that reality. The journey involves a sometimes dramatic, but more typically drawn out and disciplined, transformation from ascetical purgation through illumination to unification. Mystical theologies, for their part, explore the scriptural bases and creedal implications of this spiritual development, in light of theological concepts of God and the limits of the divine-human relationship.

First, one needs to address the question of whether mysticism and theology are mutually exclusive categories. Many theorists have suggested that theology, God-talk, is after all largely discursive, whereas mysticism is about experiencing the ineffable. If mysticism is heavily experiential and personal, and theology more analytical, how can the two overlap? Both Christian and Islamic traditions have implicitly resolved the apparent paradox: theology and mysticism can indeed come together, since both are ultimately about expressing the ineffable and knowing the unknowable. In the following sections I will take spiritual knowledge as my point of departure.

## Christian Mystical Theology

Christian writers began exploring the complex theme of "knowledge of God" as early as the late first/early second century. Many of the early theologians were responding to the emergence of "gnostic" groups, characterized by an elitist focus on the centrality of esoteric, arcane knowledge. Apostolic fathers Clement of Rome, Ignatius of Antioch, and Justin Martyr identified authentic *gnosis* as the product of contemplation of Jesus Christ as revealed in scripture and as the very incarnation of true *gnosis*. Irenaeus of Lyons built on that understanding by identifying *gnosis* as the essence of the relationship of Father to Son and Son to Holy Spirit. Clement of Alexandria expanded further by suggesting that Hellenistic philosophy could serve as a propaideutic to Christian knowledge; Christian love (*agape*) leads to *gnosis* and that in turn reinforces love. Tapping the wellsprings of Hellenistic philology and Platonic cosmology, Origen in turn refined the function of *gnosis:* by facilitating the discovery of the cosmos as revelatory, *gnosis* becomes a preparation for a deeper understanding of scriptural revelation. Origen was arguably the first to develop the concept of *gnosis* into a "Logos mysticism," in which a spirit divinized through contemplation enjoys oneness (*henosis*) with God that transcends the communion (*koinonia*) enjoyed by believers generally.[15]

During the fourth and fifth centuries, the emergence of diverse forms of monasticism introduced new variations. Antony, founder of anchoritism (heremitical life), emphasized solitude and identified asceticism with true *gnosis,* available only to those totally dedicated to a life of introspective discernment. More open (cenobitic) intentional communities, with Pachomius in the lead, associated *gnosis* with *agape* and a more active apostolic life. Meanwhile, leading Greek and Latin Fathers elaborated the foundations of mystical theology in the context of their cenobitic monastic foundations.[16] Learning together in community, monks dedicated themselves to an "ethical *gnosis*"—knowledge of God, source of all good, manifested itself in moral action. For these Fathers, mysticism was oriented toward the integration of the individual into the greater church rather than to the solitary salvation of the individual ascetic. Augustinian monasticism, for example, became reoriented toward seminary formation of clergy and future church administrators (Augustine himself was bishop of Hippo in North Africa).

Early monastic movements found a major achievement in the ecclesial spirituality of Benedict's seminal *Rule,* a "Western" development of Basil's "Eastern" monastic ideal. Around the same time, early mystical theology emerged in writings attributed to one Pseudo-Dionysius the Areopagite (c. 500). His grand cosmic synthesis envisions the universe as a system of hierarchies animated by a circular dynamic in which all things continually return to God whose ongoing love is in turn continually manifest in new creation. Pseudo-Dionysius developed concepts introduced earlier by authors like Evagrius of Pontus (346–99), who taught that repentance for sin spiritualizes created matter. More importantly, Pseudo-Dionysius integrated various critical concepts into the lexicon of mystical theology, especially that of unknowing (*agnosia*). Authentic knowledge of God leads, paradoxically, to unification (*henosis*), which in turn culminates in divinization (*theosis*) and the "obliteration" of distinction between knower and Known (*extasis*).[17]

Knowledge-oriented mysticism, however, did not disappear with Pseudo-Dionysius's emphasis on metaphysical union. Gregory I (the Great, d. 604) extolled the confluence of action and contemplation, setting the agenda for "Western" monasticism and mysticism. Following in Gregory's footsteps, Bede the Venerable (d. 735), Boniface (d. 754), and others expanded European monastic emphasis on the intimate relationship between contemplation and theology. John Scotus Eriugena (d. 877) underscored the role of *intellectus* as the apex of the journey of return to God. He also introduced into theological parlance the distinction between affirmation and negation, the theological analogue to kataphatic and apophatic mysticism. Meanwhile, Eastern Fathers such as John Climacus (d. 649), Maximus the Confessor (d. 662), and Simeon the New Theologian (d. 1022) further developed the Dionysian emphasis on divinization as the heart of mystical experience.

During the eleventh and twelfth centuries, European monastic establishments underwent dramatic changes, particularly in response to need for reform. Many cenobitic monasteries had grown affluent and lax in religious observance. In response, reformers like Romuald (d. 1027) and Peter the Venerable (d. 1156) thoroughly revamped the disciplines of earlier orders. Founders such as Bruno of Camaldoli (d. 1101; Carthusians) and Bernard of Clairvaux (d. 1153; Cistercians) established new foundations around solitude and separation from the outer world. Two more influential new orders arose during the thirteenth century. Francis of Assisi (d. 1226) and Dominic Guzman (d. 1221) brought forth organizations very different from each other, but similar in that both oriented themselves toward active apostolates—the Franciscans to conversion of Muslims, and the Dominicans to preaching and pastoral work.

Several major systematic theologians within these two orders addressed themes essential to mystical discourse. Both Dominican Thomas Aquinas and Franciscan Bonaventure anchored their monumental works in philosophy, especially epistemology. While Thomas tends toward a knowledge-based mystical theology expressed in hard-core Scholastic terms, Bonaventure takes more direct account of the relational and affective dimensions of advanced spiritual experience. Thomas addresses the subject of divine-human relationship, its possibilities and limitations, in the form of questions and detailed answers. A large section of the first part of his *Summa Theologiae* deals with "knowledge of spiritual realities." Thomas was developing the dialectical method of earlier Scholastics, such as Anselm, Abelard, and Alexander of Hales.

Bonaventure, on the other hand, approached the enormous and complex topic in a narrative mode, especially in his masterpiece *The Soul's Journey to God (Itinerarium Mentis in Deum)*. With its overarching structure of journey away from and return to God (*exitus/reditus*) the work developed themes earlier elaborated by theologians of the school of St. Victor, Hugh (d. 1141) and Richard (d. 1173). In contrast to the Scholastic thinkers of the universities, Hugh and Richard regarded philosophy and psychology as stages on the way to the human appropriation of aspects of divine perfection, rather than merely speculative sciences. Contemplation is at the heart of the spiritual journey, beginning with reflection and meditation on creation and the soul. In Bonaventure's view, the journey begins in the sensible world and proceeds through the psychological and metaphysical before approaching the presence of God. Through the progression from purgative to illuminative to unitive experience, the seeker arrives at the first of seven degrees of contemplation, which in turn yields peace, truth, and love.

Important developments in medieval mystical literature also include the works of many poets and theorists who elucidated a wide variety of mystical metaphors. Hildegard of Bingen, an accomplished poet and musician mentioned above, emphasized the need to overcome one's vices—modeling Christ's victory over forces of evil—to approach the gift of visionary contemplation. Another influential woman, Hadewijch (mid-thirteenth century), expanded on the theme of "bridal mysticism," with its already ancient roots in the biblical Song of Songs and the exegesis of early fathers such as Origen. Love urges the soul beyond self-preoccupation to turn back to God, culminating in union with God's simple essence. A generation or two later, the celebrated Dominican Meister Eckhart (d. 1327) further developed Hadewijch's "mysticism of essence" by giving it a Thomistic twist: the individual contacts God through the soul's intellectual faculty. Eckhart's preeminent Dominican disciple, John Tauler (d. 1361), reemphasized the ethical dimensions of the mystical experience, at the heart of which is the cultivation of virtue on the way to abandonment to the divine will. Union with God in turn increases charity and the capacity to endure a life of sacrifice.

Scores of other major mystical authors populated Christian history over the subsequent half-millennium, including important figures in the Greek and Russian Orthodox traditions. Gregory Palamas (1296–1359) developed the controversial "hesychastic" ("quietist") spirituality of Simeon the New Theologian, with its emphasis on attaining a vision of divine light through ascetical discipline. Gregory's insistence on the possibility of experiencing God in himself, rather than merely in the effects of his creative activity, remained a hallmark of Orthodox mystical theology until the seventeenth century. Russian monastic reformer Nil Sorsky (1433–1508) refined the mystical theologies of Macarius (c. 300–390) and his chief disciple, Evagrius of Pontus. Nil insisted on a critical reading of earlier sources of spiritual teaching and emphasized the need to purify one's heart by banishing all conceptual images of God that might distract one from true intimacy in prayer.[18]

Few later mystics were more influential than the sixteenth-century Spaniards Teresa of Avila (d. 1582) and John of the Cross (d. 1591). Teresa is noted for elaborating the intervening states of prayer between discursive meditation and ecstasy, and for offering a more systematic analysis of the process of "mystical marriage" in her *Interior Castle*. John, perhaps best known as a poet, authored *The Dark Night of the Soul* and *The Ascent of Mount Carmel,* focusing on the central role of intense purification in the ultimate union with God. John and Teresa joined forces to found the Order of Discalced Carmelites, dedicated to integrating action and contemplation.[19]

## Islamic Mystical Theology

As always, the story begins with the Qur'ān and Hadith, which shelter countless images and tonalities that caught the attention of the earliest "mystical" exegetes. Key texts include references to God's beauty and allusions to divine immanence and accessibility, as well as to Muhammad's night journey and ascension (Q 17:1 and 53:1–18). Muslim spiritual traditions have long credited the Prophet and various Companions with unique affinities for intimate knowledge of God. Other early Muslims recognized as exemplars of the spiritual life include such intriguing figures as Hasan of Basra (d. 728), noted especially for his stringent asceticism. Rābi'a (d. c. 801), also from Basra in southern Iraq, is traditionally recognized as the first true "mystic" because she moved beyond ascetical fear to love of God.

Major ninth-century mystics include the enigmatic Dhū 'n-Nūn of Egypt (d. 860), noted for shocking friends and critics alike with his edgy, idiosyncratic characterizations of the spiritual life. Bāyazīd al-Bistāmī (d. 874, from eastern Persia) is traditionally identified as the first of the "intoxicated" mystics, while his younger contemporary Junayd of Baghdad (d. 910) became known for his more "sober" approach. The dichotomy of intoxication and sobriety roughly parallels the more scholarly distinction between kataphatic and apophatic mystical theologies. Bāyazīd fell afoul of religious authorities for his intemperate utterances apparently in reference to his personal relationship to God. Reported to have declared "Glory be to me! How exalted is my state," the extroverted mystic explained that he was not arrogating divine prerogatives to himself but simply could not prevent himself from giving voice to his loss of personal identity in his relationship to God. Invaded completely by the divine presence, there was no longer a "Bāyazīd" left to speak of—no self, no self to control.

The more theologically cautious Junayd, on the other hand, argued that one not only could but *must* refrain from speaking injudiciously of one's more elevated experience of God. He spoke of the human condition prior to ecstatic experience as "first sobriety," and the state to which the individual returned inevitably as "second sobriety." Any attempt to wrap the intermediate, and necessarily transient, state of intoxication in conventional language was sheer folly, at best. From a theological perspective, these early mystics began to fashion a new vocabulary designed to articulate the ineffable. They spoke of doing battle against the ego-soul (*jihād an-nafs*), and testing and repentance (*balā', tawba*), as critical moments on the way to intimate, experiential knowledge of God (*ma'rifa*). In the presence of God, one might experience, paradoxically, both expansiveness (*bast*) and constriction (*qabd*); passing away, or extinction (*fanā'*), of the self and survival (*baqā'*); all were part of the ultimate experience of ecstasy, expressed by a root that connotes simultaneously finding, being found, and existing (*wajd*).

Sahl at-Tustarī (d. 896) was arguably the first to articulate an integrated mystical theology. At its center stands the Prophet Muhammad, whose pivotal role Sahl situates in the context of creation and the primary symbolism of divine light. Sahl traces the beginnings of the divine-human relationship to the day of covenant, when God asked all yet-uncreated souls in the form of particles of light if they affirmed God as their sovereign, and all responded in the affirmative. At that timeless moment, the "light of Muhammad" as a "cosmic and corporate prototype" of humankind became manifest as a transparent column of divine light (Q 24:35). In this form, Muhammad preexisted even Adam, so that the human race actually descends as intelligent specks of light from the Prophet's primal light. Still, paradoxically, the prophetic prototypes existed in embryonic form in Adam. Sahl thus positions Muhammad as the matrix of divine-human union, his heart the spring of illuminative revelation. Though Sahl was a pioneer in this respect, his theology was already highly polished and imaginative.[20]

Some of the earliest intentional proponents of an inward dimension of Islamic spiritual wisdom found that their approach was not always welcomed by critics, who regarded them as taking refuge in idiosyncratic notions at odds with mainstream orthopraxy and obedience to the revealed law. Surely the most celebrated example was Hallāj (d. 922) of Baghdad. Famed as the first martyr-mystic, he was executed, ostensibly for the temerity of his apparent claim to perfect oneness with God, "I am the Truth." In response to the critique of Sufi mysticism as antinomian and potentially heretical, various elaborations of Islamic mystical theology emerged in the form of compendia of Sufi life and spirituality. Most of the dozen or so major handbooks that appeared in Arabic and Persian between around 950 and 1200 treat the core topic of experiential knowledge of God in chapters explicitly devoted to the subject.

Authors of several of the first manuals of mystical theology analyzed the complex elements of spiritual experience and developed psycho-spiritual typologies designed to help seekers discern shape and direction in an often bewildering journey. These typologies were not meant to function as checklists of stages through which the wayfarer must pass (as if to measure oneself against an elusive norm), but more generally as maps of the diverse kinds of terrain in which journeyers in the interior life might find themselves. These authors speak of two large categories of experience, stations (*maqāmāt*) and states (*aḥwāl*). Stations they describe as persistent conditions that involve some degree of effort on the part of the seeker. States, by contrast, are more transitory conditions bestowed as pure gift quite apart from any human effort. The various authors differ in the experiences they list under these two large categories (what one calls a station, another might rank as a state), in the numbers of stations and states they reckon, and in the order in which they list items in the respective categories.

One example of such a psycho-spiritual typology is that of Sarrāj's (d. 988) *Book of Light Flashes*. He lists the following seven stations: repentance, abstinence or spiritual reticence, renunciation, poverty, patience, trust in God, and satisfaction or acceptance of God's dispensation. He follows these with ten states: proximity to God, love, fear, hope, longing, joy or intimacy, tranquillity, contemplation, and certainty. Sarrāj then fashions a third large category, place (*makān*), to describe a still more advanced level of experience that transcends both station and state. Other authors list as many as forty steps along each of the two main phases of the inward path. In virtually every instance, however, an overriding concern of these mystical theologies is the centrality of constant attentiveness and spiritual discernment known as the "science of hearts" (*'ilm al-qulūb*). Seekers cannot simply take complacent refuge in a station or state as though it marked some achievement to be proud of. One must be ever vigilant, ready to repent, for example, even of repentance itself, the better to ward off spiritual torpor.[21]

Two of the most important theorists of the spiritual life were Abū Ḥāmid al-Ghazālī and Ibn 'Arabī. Abū Ḥāmid al-Ghazālī, discussed earlier in the context of religious ethics, produced one of the most influential and perhaps also the most systematic treatment of the spiritual quest. He organized his multivolume *Revitalization of the Religious Disciplines* into four large sections consisting of ten "books" each. Structuring the whole work along the lines of a juridical treatise, he begins with the fundamentals required of those just embarking on the journey: external comportment in relation to God. Section 2 treats external obligations in relation to other

people. After ending the second section with a book on the Prophet as ultimate human exemplar, Ghazālī moves from action to virtue and addresses
the more difficult task of inward disposition required for the reformation
of character. Finally, drawing on such earlier masters as Muhāsibī and Abū
Tālib of Mecca, he leads the traveler up the steep slope to the pinnacle of
mystical experience, ecstatic love of God. Ghazālī's work integrates mystical theology into the larger framework of pastoral theology, embracing the
spiritual needs of the broadest possible spectrum of Muslim faithful.

Iberian-born Ibn 'Arabī (d. 1240) practiced his art on a still broader
stage. His formidable *Meccan Revelations* presumes considerable spiritual
and intellectual attainment, leading the seeker on a mind-boggling journey
of cosmic dimensions. Divine self-disclosure is a central theme, a timeless
revelatory process that permeates all things, from the tiniest particle to
the whole of creation. He thus envisions the individual seeker as at once
a miniscule sojourner in an unimaginably vast landscape and a privileged
recipient of the ultimate reality. Ibn 'Arabī, as perhaps no other Muslim
theological figure (some prefer to call his work "theosophy"), emphasizes
the centrality of the "imaginal" dimension in the seeker's discovery of the
greatest truths of divine disclosure. The imaginal realm is, however, a far
cry from the merely "imaginary," for it is indeed an actual dimension of
human/cosmic consciousness. Though love is an essential ingredient in Ibn
'Arabī's mystical theology, knowledge is clearly the centerpiece.[22]

Ibn 'Arabī makes extensive use of the metaphor of journey, but here
again he puts his distinctively complex spin on the theme. He discerns six-
teen journeys in the Qur'ān. God begins by taking the primordial journey
from the utter transcendence and inaccessibility of sublimity downward to
his throne. From there God dispatches creation on its journey from nonbe-
ing into being and sends down the Qur'ān. Adam he sends on the journey
of calamity from paradise to earth. Noah embarks on the journey of safety,
and Moses on the journey of divine appointment to meet God—Moses'
chief attribute is that he conversed with God.

In Ibn 'Arabi's view, and that of other important mystics before and
since, every spiritual journey is one of three types in relation to God. There
are journeys away from, toward, and in God. The first occurs when God
banishes a fallen angel, when shame drives a sinner away, or when God
sends a prophet or messenger into the world. Second, though all beings
travel toward God, not all reach their goal. Unrepentant sinners experience
the frustration of endless wandering; those who have obeyed but remain
imperfect in their acknowledgment of the absolute unity and sovereignty
of God arrive in the divine presence but are veiled from the divine vision;

and the elect find the ultimate goal. Of those who journey in God, some (known as philosophers) falter along the way because they rely on the rational faculty; the elect, saints, and prophets make easy progress.[23]

In addition to the early manuals and treatises on spirituality, dozens of other Sufi authors articulated both explicitly and implicitly a host of important theological perspectives in other genres, both prose and poetry. Perhaps the most influential and widely read of Islam's mystics have been the great poets. Writing in Arabic, Persian, and a dozen other major Middle Eastern and South Asian languages, the mystical poets treated the themes of spiritual sojourning in less systematic and more allusive ways than the authors of treatises. Often acclaimed as the greatest of the Arabic lyric bards, Ibn al-Fārid of Cairo, from whom I quoted earlier in this chapter, fashioned allegories and metaphors of the soul's longing for the lost beloved (God) and the perilous search across desert wastes in hopes of reunion. Persian poets wrote extensively in both lyric and didactic genres, some noted also for a prose/poetry blend of "wisdom" literature.[24] In this context, the most striking "theological" contribution these poets have made to the Islamic tradition is the ingenious manner in which they transform metaphors of ordinary human experience into images of the divine-human relationship. In their tantalizing ambiguity lies their power to shatter relational stereotypes like so many mute idols. Sacralizing the mundane, the mystical poets lead their readers into a hall of mirrors in which one loses track of any distinction between divine transcendence and immanence.[25]

Beneath the highly structured psycho-spiritual typologies of the manuals and the myriad untamed images of the poets lie the same fundamental theological concerns one finds in the creeds and treatises of systematic theology: the transcendent unity of God, revelation through prophetic messengers, resurrection, accountability before God at judgment, and reward or punishment in eternity. Indeed, virtually all of the early theorists and the great poets of subsequent centuries gladly acknowledged their adherence to both specific schools of religious law and related systematic theological orientations. Muhāsibī was known as a *mutakallim* (systematic theologian) who engaged Mu'tazilī thought and was a Shāfi'ī in law; Kalābādhī was a Hanafī in law and Māturīdī in theology; Hujwīrī a Hanbalī in law and traditionalist in theology; Qushayrī and Ghazālī Shāfi'ī in law and Ash'arī in theology. Mystically inclined authors, whether poets or theorists, nevertheless ultimately consider theological speculation about as useful as a ladder after one has arrived at the roof.[26]

. . .

Christian and Islamic traditions of spirituality include some of the loveliest prayers that have ever graced the human voice. They exemplify a full range of forms, themes, and affective intensity. Beneath these songs and cries of the spirit lies the conviction that God somehow apprehends, receives, and responds to such outpourings. Both traditions cherish the hope that the aspirations of a sincere heart cannot be for naught. A story from Rūmī makes an important theological point about personal prayer. A devout man had spent many long vigils calling out "O Lord," and after many years of seeming to get no response, he was on the point of giving up. Aware of the situation, God sent an angel with a personal message, "Behind every 'O Lord' from you hide a thousand 'Here I Am's' from Me."[27] As the Christian tradition also affirms, if God were not already present in the believer's heart, no individual could even conceive of the need for supplication.

Points of theological divergence in the spiritual traditions surround questions of sacramentality and intercessory prayer. In Christian practice, a great deal of formal praying occurs in the context of rituals that many identify as sacraments. Muslims likewise attend to formal, generally standardized formulations in ritual contexts, such as the five daily prayers, pilgrimage, and special communal sessions during times of heightened attentiveness, such as the nights of Ramadan's fast. But those rituals do not carry the soteriological freight of Christian sacraments, and among Christians, Roman Catholic and Orthodox soteriologies involve ritual more than do most Protestant communities.

Most Christians believe that no person should hesitate to address his or her prayer directly to God, assuming an appropriate attitude of reverence. This conviction they share with Muslims. Christians typically, however, address prayers to Jesus, and for many Christians intercessory supplication addressed to Mary and countless saints is a staple of spiritual sustenance. Intercessory appeals play a much more limited role in Islamic practice, out of concern that such supplication presupposes human intermediaries between the individual believer and his or her Creator. For most Christians, on the other hand, the essential mediatorial role of Christ also opens the possibility of lesser mediation by other spiritually lofty figures.

For hundreds of millions of believers in both traditions, blessed places associated with paragons of piety and devotion continue to play an important role. At the same time, large numbers of Christians and Muslims reject any explicit association of "holiness" with any earthly site, but even here one finds rejection hedged with some qualification. For example, only the most conservative Muslims would suggest that maintaining for purposes of pilgrimage visitation sites associated with the life of Muhammad presents a danger to the faith. Some fear that such visitation might lure unsophisticated believers into the trap of wanting to pray *to* rather than merely *for* the Prophet. At the other end of the spectrum, hundreds of millions of Muslims continue to make visitation to the tombs of a wide variety of Friends of God, leaving requests that the deceased person strengthen their case at the heavenly court as a result of his or her privileged proximity to God.

Among Christian traditions, one finds an equal diversity and breadth of attitudes toward the sites associated with sanctity. Large numbers of devout pilgrims visit the Holy Sepulcher in Jerusalem, the graves of the popes in St. Peter's Basilica in Rome, and the final resting places of countless saints, especially across Europe and the eastern Mediterranean. Pilgrims also gravitate to sites sanctified by stories of appearances of Christ or his mother, Mary, where they are said to have vouchsafed new revelations. Outside of Roman Catholicism and the Orthodox communions, however, many Christians generally reject pious symbolism and ritual attached with such sites, with their overtones of hierarchy and centralized authority.

Finally, a type of systematic thinking has taken the form of treatises in spirituality. While works of mystical and pastoral theology play less prominent roles than writings on ethics and creedal issues, they nonetheless represent an important development in both traditions. At the core of mystical and pastoral theologies is the conviction that scriptures and later repositories of Christian and Islamic wisdom contain essential images and insights into the human condition. It takes a special kind of reflection on the sources to foster a deeper sensitivity to both the innate resources and the weaknesses of the human soul, the better to suggest the surest path and the best remedies. As a result, this branch of theological literature in both traditions is extraordinarily rich in metaphors of inward pilgrimage and ultimate discovery. In both traditions, privileged knowledge and the paradox of "unknowing" play a central role, and authors affiliated with Catholic religious orders and the institutional developments in Sufism have produced the most important works of this genre. Treatises in both traditions generated their own distinctive methodologies, but Muslim authors arguably evolved consistently more complex psychological analyses of spiritual life and progress.

Against the broad background of these nine chapters on the similarities and differences in Christian and Islamic theological themes, an epilogue offers some suggestions about where the path of theological dialogue might lead.

# Epilogue

*Reflections on the Prospects for Christian-Muslim
Theological Dialogue*

Once upon a time an itinerant grammarian came to a body of water and enlisted the services of a boatman to ferry him across. As they made their way, the grammarian asked the boatman, "Do you know the science of grammar?" The humble boatman thought for a moment and admitted somewhat dejectedly that he did not. Issuing his definitive conclusion, the grammarian declared, "You've wasted half your life." Not much later, a storm began to blow up on the sea so that the small vessel was in peril of capsizing. The boatman asked the grammarian, "Do you know the science of swimming?" When the grammarian replied that he did not, the boatman said, "You've wasted your entire life."[1]

A decade into the new millennium, too much of our theological activity remains shockingly intramural. Instead of allowing it to propel us into the larger reality of global religiosity, Christians are still attempting to protect their theologies from the threat of contamination. If we continue to resist serious engagement with other theological traditions, and that of Islam in particular, our theology may prove as useful as grammar in a typhoon. But what would swimming look like in theological terms? In the words of Robert Neville, "One of the most important tasks of theology today is to develop strategies for determining how to enter into the meaning system of another tradition, not merely as a temporary member of that tradition, but in such a way as to see how they bear upon one another."[2]

Here we move beyond the prologue's four historical models of Christian-Muslim theological engagement by proposing a method (or a model for future experimentation) and reflecting on possible motives—from a Christian perspective—for pursuing the great project further.

## METHOD: WORLD THEOLOGY
## AS A MODEL FOR THE FUTURE

Unfortunately, none of the historical models has proven perennially useful, though, in fairness, those of Küng and Cragg have hardly been tried. All ultimately take their stand on grounds already acceptable only, or largely, to Christians. John's polemical model appeals to a scriptural authority Muslims cannot regard as definitive. Thomas's Scholastic model seeks a common ground in its appeal to reason, but on the whole the Islamic tradition has maintained a healthy skepticism about reason's vaunted and alleged objectivity. Küng's Christian-inclusivist model begins with formal systematic categories (definitive revelation, word of God, salvation) that, while shared to some extent with Muslim theological articulation, presuppose largely Christian doctrinal preoccupations, thus ultimately seeking to take Islam in by osmosis. And Cragg's more genuinely dialogical use of intertheology formulates its functional cross-references (Christ and the Qur'ān, Mary and Muhammad, incarnation and prophethood, etc.) from a frankly Christian perspective.

But what else is one to do? Would it not be disingenuous at best to suggest yet one more time that we strive for greater objectivity? Perhaps not. What we desperately need is a way to step momentarily outside of our theological structures, not to consign them to the Waring blender of relativism, but to see ourselves on an equal footing with all other believing human beings. This is not merely humanism masquerading as Christianity. I am not suggesting that Christians give up a single syllable of our most cherished beliefs, or even that we admit publicly that interaction among faith communities and cultural forces has always effected some change, however glacial, in doctrinal expression and will surely continue to do so. We need a mechanism for cooling our theologically fevered brows, for calming our fears of compromise or even assimilation, for dealing with the specter of threat and challenge that Islam particularly raises for so many Christians. We need a way to come together in an open field where at least for a time what matters is neither winning nor proving, nor even negotiating, but merely standing together in appreciation of our genuinely shared theological underpinnings and resolving to find ways to prevent our disagreements from causing a meltdown.[3]

Several creative thinkers have recently described such a mechanism under the name "world theology." One can profitably view it not as a sub-stitute for our divergent confessional theologies, but as a way of gaining greater perspective on the current human condition, and of losing at least a little of that sense of salvational superiority that inevitably dulls the edge of dialogue. In *Beyond the Masks of God,* Neville describes the threefold task of the theologian in this context. The elements are, first, scholarly responsibility in describing one's own tradition, including those aspects with which one can only disagree (e.g., support of slavery); second, the need to represent a tradition so defined that one can actively support it; and third, identifying one's role in effecting change in one's own tradition.[4]

World theology seeks, as the Scholastic model would like to have done, to establish criteria from outside a given theological tradition. Unlike the Scholastic model, the criteria it proposes are theological rather than philo-sophical. Unlike any of the earlier models, world theology neither defines Islam or any other tradition explicitly in terms of Christian doctrine nor attempts to measure it against the standard of Christian truth. Its basic assumption is that it is possible to discern a common underlying thread in all human religiosity without denying that all major religious traditions are indeed different. In *A World Theology: The Central Spiritual Reality of Humankind,* Ross Reat and Edmund Perry attempt to "construct a valid *theological theory* on the basis of factual information amassed by scholars of *religious studies.*" They define the desired result as "religious thought that is informed by the faiths of all humankind but dominated by no one of them."[5]

Reat and Perry's *World Theology* examines the varying ways adherents of five major religious traditions give symbolic expression to their experi-ence of the central spiritual reality or ultimate referent, which is character-ized by three essential qualities: undeniability, desirability, and elusiveness. The authors analyze four types of symbolic expression in each tradition. Intellectual symbolism uses evidence and argument to persuade the mind as to the being and importance of the tradition's ultimate referent. Moral symbolism seeks to move individuals to make choices consistent with the ultimate referent by laying out the consequences of various courses of behavior. Mythological symbolism employs images of the sublime and powerful, fostering awe by its appeal to the imagination. Finally, spiritual symbolism seeks to elicit commitment to the ultimate referent by showing how a relationship to that reality is essential to individual existence.

With respect to Islam the analysis proceeds as follows. Reat and Perry begin by reading the widespread popular and usually negative character-izations of Islam as exlcusivist, literalist, and predeterministic as "points of entry for our examination of Islam's ultimate referent under the headings of undeniability, desirability, and elusiveness."[6] As spiritual symbolism, Islam's exclusivism is an "appeal for personal consent to the inevitability of living with reference to an ultimate spiritual reality" that will brook no denial,[7] and an assertion of Islam's inclusiveness of all humankind in the divine plan. As moral symbolism, the Qur'ān's insistent condemnation of all misguided vanity and aimless wandering similarly underscores God's undeniability: God alone is the arbiter of morality, while rational ethics represents little more than an "indeterminate groping toward the good, doomed ultimately to falter short of its goal."[8] The Qur'ān's frequent creation and eschatological imagery emphasizes God's undeniability as sovereign master in narrative and heavily didactic mythological symbolism. Cosmological imagery in the scripture, along with the doctrines of the inimitability of the Qur'ān and the unlettered character of the Prophet, and the possibility of achieving a kind of unshakable certitude, all constitute intellectual symbolism of God's undeniability.

While many outsiders regard a perceived propensity to literalism among Muslims as a largely negative attribute, Reat and Perry interpret that perceived quality as a result of the Islamic sense of God's desirability. The Qur'ān's imagery of the deity is unabashedly anthropomorphic; but Islamic theology has from the start both repudiated any tendency to think that God is at all like human beings, and condemned all attempts to reduce the scriptural imagery to mere metaphor. Given that curious combination, it seems clear that Islamic literalism is neither simply naive nor to be taken as a literal truth claim. "Evocative depiction" of God and of the eschaton expresses mythologically "the desirability of the ultimately real by attempting to devalue the material reality that is so immediately appealing to the thoughtless."[9] That very mythological symbolism in turn underscores the spiritual symbolism of the desirability of meeting, being with, and being accepted by God, the Beloved of so much splendid mystical poetry and the goal of life's journey as symbolized in the Ka'ba in Mecca. In its refusal to accord to human reason the power to arrive unaided at the ultimate truth, and in its consequent insistence that human beings wait entirely on God's good pleasure, mainstream Islamic thought reinforces intellectually the concept of infinite possibility as an aspect of the divine desirability. From the perspective of moral symbolism, Islam underscores the importance of desire to conform to God's will, rather than fear of punishment or hope of reward, as the only worthy ethical motivation.

Finally, Reat and Perry reorient a third prevailing stereotype of Muslims in a positive direction. What so many non-Muslims regard as simplistic fatalism, Reat and Perry interpret as a positive clue to Muslims' sense of the ultimate reality as elusive. Theologians have elaborated some of the most amazing intellectual symbolism for affirming God's sky-blue freedom and absolute control, even at the risk of portraying a virtually despotic deity. Their statements are about who God is rather than about what human beings are not. In other words, "the Islamic doctrine of predetermination expresses the elusiveness of Allah as radical inaccessibility to human striving alone."[10] God is elusive not out of spite or coquettishness, but because elusiveness follows logically from absolute freedom. As a corollary, the moral symbolism of elusiveness is that no human being can guarantee salvation by mere good behavior. Islam's mystical tradition expresses perhaps most effectively the spiritual aspect of the divine elusiveness in the poetry of unrequited love (such as the poem of Ibn al-Fārid cited in chapter 9). But however frustrating the incomparably unworthy one's quest for the incomparably lovely, the seeker must never forsake the discipline of striving. Finally, Reat and Perry discern mythological expressions of the divine elusiveness in the very absence of explicit iconography of the deity, and in the paucity of expressly metaphorical descriptions of God in the Qur'ān.

Reat and Perry have made a worthwhile beginning toward what Neville considers the task of theology in our time: "to develop interpretants that allow us to see how the symbols, concepts, gestures, and other meaningful signs of religious practice do indeed represent divinity in some important respect or fail to do so." Later in his book Neville observes: "Theology has unassailable vigor insofar as it positively comprehends without perversion the experiences relevant to its subject, and at the same time is able to make a case for its claims within the world of reference of anyone interested in the truth."[11]

## MOTIVES: FIVE PROOFS FOR THE NEED FOR THEOLOGICAL DIALOGUE

A key question for Christians and Muslims alike is simply "Why engage in theological dialogue at all?" Here I will suggest a range of motives, beyond the need for polemical dominance or theological chest-pounding. My five "proofs" for the need for theological dialogue are the following: the argument from practical necessity, the argument from authority, the argument from intellectual integrity, the argument from beauty, and the neglected, or humble, argument.

First, the argument from practical necessity. Muslims live right down the street, they have kids in the local school, they pay taxes, they vote, and as they become more politically savvy, they lobby. Sooner or later, even theologians will have to begin doing the theological equivalent of what citizens and other folks will have begun to do in their everyday lives, namely, account for the ever-more imposing and undeniable fact of Islam in our world. From a purely pastoral point of view, we will need a theologically coherent way of explaining to the folks in the pew the relationship of Christians to their increasingly visible non-Christian neighbors, an explanation that affirms our common humanity in every possible way.

For those not persuaded by practical considerations, there is the argument from authority. Here is a Muslim story of Abraham and the Zoroastrian that illustrates the mandate from the highest authority. Abraham, the paragon of hospitality, used to put off eating breakfast each morning until some hungry traveler should wander by and accept his invitation. One day a very old man became Abraham's guest. As they were preparing to eat, Abraham said a blessing, but he noticed the old man's lips mouthed a different prayer—that of a fire-worshipper. Abraham immediately rescinded his invitation and drove the man away, saying, "I will not share my food with one who prays thus," for, to borrow from Nietzsche, thus spoke Zarathustra. God looked down with some irritation and chided the patriarch: I have given this man life and sustenance for a hundred years; could you not be hospitable to him for one hour? Abraham ran after the old Zoroastrian and brought him back home.[12]

Bringing the argument back home, the Christian cannot fail to notice that Jesus talked to the Samaritan woman (John 4:7–38). The scene does not work well as a model, since Jesus is clearly the teacher and dominant in the conversation. His "Hegelian" method, however, bears further investigation, with its obvious allusion to Thesis (Jerusalem), Antithesis (Gerizim), and Synthesis (Spirit and Truth).[13] The problem with the argument from authority is that down the road from Jacob's well we find that while Vatican II says some form of dialogue is desirable, it stops far short of even suggesting genuinely theological encounter. The Vatican Council's failure even to pronounce the name of Muhammad says volumes. On the other hand, the Council's statement that "the Church rejects nothing that is true and holy" in other religious traditions strongly suggests a kind of theological cross-reference centered on the notion of holiness.[14] Jesus spoke of worshipping neither in Jerusalem nor on Gerizim, but in spirit and truth; if the latter merely raises the specter of absolutist claims all over again, the former at least leaves open the possibility of further mutual Christian-Muslim appreciation of what our respective traditions regard as theory and practice of sanctity.

The argument from intellectual integrity urges that one might take up the challenge of encountering Islam "because it's there." In its degraded form, the argument from idle curiosity, this motive easily allows one to slide back into the polemical mode and thus foster competition. At the very least, the argument goes, there is no need to worry about being somehow tainted by the contact in any case. One need only recall Paul's observation about food offered to idols, namely, that one can eat it with impunity because it has in effect been offered to nothing and is therefore, at the very least, undefiling (1 Corinthians 8:1–6). Recalling Thomas and the Scholastic model, it is essential that we must at a minimum account for this huge mass of people and their beliefs as intellectual ideas. Whether one agrees with them or not, one cannot simply dismiss them as intellectual inferiors.

When we come to the aesthetic argument, we are getting closer to the heart and humanity of the matter: so much beauty of insight and expression in both traditions cries out for the engagement of theological dialogue. Some of the most deeply consoling experiences of my forty-year encounter with the sources of Islamic tradition have turned on the apprehension of stunning beauty in verbal and visual expression, as well as in thought and feeling. Countless Hadith, for example, express exquisite spiritual insight with arresting simplicity. Some of the most glorious and moving intimations of divinity both in itself and in relation to humanity have come from the tongues and pens of Muslim religious scholars and theologians. Theology has become for most of us a science of words, of texts, of ideas. There is, in addition, a parallel universe, that of the visual arts, with its silent articulation of profoundest truth in both the Christian and the Islamic traditions. The aesthetic argument finally comes down to this, but unlike the other arguments it presupposes an inaugural experience: once one has had a taste of the beauty and charm of the Islamic theological tradition, one can hardly imagine not engaging it further.

Finally, the American philosopher Charles Sanders Peirce had a favorite proof for the existence of God that he called the "neglected" and, alternatively, the "humble" argument. I borrow his argument and adapt it to the notion of an unassailable reason for engaging Islamic religious thought seriously and open-mindedly. According to Peirce's argument, if God exists and in divine benevolence willed religion to be a supreme good, and therefore one that could be proven so, then "one would expect that there would be some Argument for His reality that should be obvious to all minds . . . that should earnestly strive to find the truth of the matter; and further, that this Argument should present its conclusion, not as a proposition of metaphysical theology, but in a form directly applicable to the conduct of life." It takes a "certain agreeable occupation of mind," which Peirce calls Pure Play. Whether of aesthetic contemplation or distant castle-building, or of considering some wonder of the universe, it begins with Musement: "Impression soon passes into attentive observation, observation into musing, musing into a lively give and take of communion between self and self. If one's observations and reflections are allowed to specialize themselves too much, the Play will be converted into scientific study; and that cannot be pursued in odd half hours." It works like this. Some cloudless night, walk out into an open field. Lie down on your back and gaze upward into the velvet stellar infinity and know God is.[15]

In relation to the boatman and the grammarian, the neglected argument is the one that is most capable of proving beyond doubt that there comes a time for swimming. In relation to the need for a serious theological encounter with the Islamic tradition, the neglected argument says simply and finally: It is time. The neglected argument urges us beyond our convenient categories and comfortable ways of thinking, as illustrated in this story. Once upon a time, a mystic sat down with a grammarian. Said the grammarian, "Words can be only one of three things: nouns, verbs, or particles." In mock astonishment the mystic tore his garment and exclaimed, "Twenty years of my life, twenty years of striving and searching have been in vain. I labored all these years in hopes of there being a word outside of these, but you have destroyed my hope." In fact, the mystic had already found that much-sought word, and he was only trying to goad the smug grammarian.[16]

The neglected argument lives in the actual experience and example of individuals some of us have had the privilege of knowing, and I now introduce you to one such person. Among my prize possessions is a signed copy of *Freedom and Fulfillment* by a noted scholar of Islamic theology, the late Richard J. McCarthy, SJ. For all his professional accomplishment and stature, Richard was a comfortable old shoe of a Jesuit, who in his work and his person embodied the neglected argument in his own discovery of Islam's importance for Christians. Richard knew the science of grammar and had the deepest appreciation for the Arabic language. Muslim listeners used to swell the otherwise Christian audiences where he preached in Baghdad, because they had heard he spoke splendid Arabic, a tongue whose sonorities Arabs prize almost as highly as its substance. Richard dedicated most of his adult life to the study and interpretation of several major Islamic theologians, laboring painstakingly over critical editions and translations. During most of the 1950s and 1960s he served on the faculty, and as president, of the Jesuit-run Al-Hikma University in Baghdad. Exiled with his brother Jesuits from Iraq by the Baath Party in 1968, Richard joined the faculty of Oxford University, where he had earned his doctorate in 1951. When ill health forced him to retire from that work, he joined the Jesuit community at LaFarge House in Cambridge, Massachusetts. There, just down the hall from me, he continued his work of translating Arabic theological texts. There, too, he discovered *The Muppet Show*, which he watched without fail every Friday evening. Next to Miss Piggy, his favorite characters were Statler and Waldorf. Richard clearly saw a playful reflection of himself in the two craggy geezers who kibitzed acerbically from their private balcony.

Richard would howl at the very idea of mentioning his name in the same sentence with mysticism. But for all his grammatical proficiency and precision, he also knew that "other word." It was this openness to a dimension beyond the syntactical that allowed Richard to engage in Musement, and that in turn led to his lifelong fascination with a Muslim theologian and mystic named Abū Hāmid al-Ghazālī. Both men spent significant parts of their adult lives working in Baghdad. The crowning work of Ghazālī's life was a four-volume compendium entitled *The Revitalization of the Religious Disciplines,* and it was Richard's hope that he might one day produce a complete translation of it. Although he did not live to finish that, Dick did have the pleasure of seeing in print, in *Freedom and Fulfillment,* his translation of several of Ghazālī's shorter works. Toward the end of the introduction to that volume, Richard had this to say about Ghazālī's magnum opus, the *Ihyā':*

> To sum it all up, I have . . . found, and I believe others can find, in the words and example of Ghazālī a true *ihyā'* [quickening, revivification, bringing back to life, causing to live]—an *ihyā'* from the dark, dead coldness of atheism, or, more accurately, 'without-Godness'; an *ihyā'* from enervating, debilitating, and crippling sinfulness; an *ihyā'* from lifeless and spiritless intellectualism; an *ihyā'* from the tepidity and listlessness and uncaring of social and moral mediocrity.[17]

Few people would have thought to characterize Richard McCarthy as theologically "liberal." Even so, the last words he ever published sum up admirably how he embodied the neglected argument, the humble argument for the necessity and possibility of bold theological dialogue. "Someday," he wrote, "be it close or distant, I hope to sit down with Ghazālī in a quiet corner of heaven. We shall have many things to talk about, if indeed in heaven one can be 'distracted' from the Vision of God. I shall want to thank him—him and so many others of his coreligionists."[18] When Richard set out across the sea of Islamic theology, a region still but faintly sketched on Christian thought-faring charts, he expected to reach the far shore eventually. But the journey was riskier than he had imagined. Somewhere out in the deep, amid rising swells, he took swimming lessons from Ghazālī, the mystical boatman. Now the two are doing a leisurely backstroke together in the ocean of infinite mercy some people call God. "C'mon in!" they call out. "The water's fine."

# Notes

ABD     *The Anchor Bible Dictionary.* Edited by Daniel Noel Friedman. 6 vols.
New York: Doubleday, 1992.

EEC     *Encyclopedia of the Early Church.* Edited by Angelo Di Berardino,
Adrian Walford, and W. H. C. Frend. 2 vols. Oxford: Oxford University
Press, 1992.

EI²     *The Encyclopedia of Islam.* Edited by C. E. Bosworth et al. 12 vols. 2nd
ed. Leiden: Brill, 1986–.

EQ     *The Encyclopedia of the Qur'ān.* Edited by Jane Dammen McAuliffe.
6 vols. Leiden: Brill, 2001–2006.

ER     *The Encyclopedia of Religion.* Edited by Mircea Eliade et al. 16 vols.
New York: Macmillan, 1987.

ICMR     *Islam and Muslim-Christian Relations.* Annual publication. Leiden: Brill.

JAOS     *Journal of the American Oriental Society.*

NCE     *New Catholic Encyclopedia.* Edited by Berard Marthaler et al. 15 vols.
2nd ed. Detroit: Thomson/Gale, 2003.

ODCC     *The Oxford Dictionary of the Christian Church.* Edited by F. L. Cross
and E. A. Livingstone. Oxford: Oxford University Press, 2005.

PROLOGUE

1. John Moorhead, "The Earliest Christian Theological Response to Islam,"
*Religion* 11 (1981): 265–74; quoting from p. 266.

2. Daniel J. Sahas, *John of Damascus on Islam: The Heresy of the Ishmaelites*
(Leiden: Brill, 1972), xiii.

3. For comparison of John and Aquinas, see Deno John Geanakoplos, *Byzantine East and Latin West: Two Worlds of Christendom in Middle Ages and Renaissance* (New York: Harper, 1966), 22–25.

4. Translation in John W. Voorhis, "John of Damascus on the Moslem Heresy," *Muslim World* 24 (1934): 391–98; see also Paul Khoury, "Jean Damascene et l'Islam," *Proche Orient Chrétien* 7 (1957): 44–63; 8 (1958): 313–39. Outline of document's contents in Sahas, *John of Damascus,* 94–95.

5. Sahas, *John of Damascus,* 95.

6. Above sections summarized from Sahas, *John of Damascus,* 99–122.

7. Sahas, *John of Damascus,* 128–29. See also on these matters Sahas, "The Seventh Century in Byzantine-Muslim Relations: Characteristics and Forces," *ICMR* 2:1 (1991): 3–22. Further excellent studies concerning Middle Eastern Christian theologies in late antiquity and early medieval centuries include, e.g., Hugh Goddard, A *History of Middle Eastern Theologies* (New York: RoutledgeCurzon, 2003); Sidney H. Griffith, "Islam and the *Summa Theologiae Arabica,*" *Jerusalem Studies in Arabic and Islam* 13 (1990): 225–64; idem, "The View of Islam from the Monasteries of Palestine in the Early Abbasid Period: Theodore Abu Qurrah and the *Summa Theologiae Arabica,*" *ICMR* 7:1 (1996): 9-28; idem, "Greek into Arabic: Life and Letters in the Monasteries of Palestine in the Ninth Century," *Byzantion* 106 (1986): 117-38; idem, "The Monk in the Emir's *Majlis:* Reflections on a Popular Genre of Christian Literary Apologetics in Arabic in the Early Islamic Period," in *The Majlis: Interreligious Encounters in Medieval Islam,* ed. Hava Lazarus Yafeh et al., Studies in Arabic Language and Literature 4 (Wiesbaden: Harrassowitz, 1999), 13–65; idem, "Disputing with Islam in Syriac: The Case of the Monk of Bêt Hãlê and a Muslim Emir," *Hugoye: Journal of Syriac Studies* 3:1 (2000): http.//Syrcom.cua.edu/Hugoye/Vol3No1/HV3N1/Griffith.html; idem, *The Beginnings of Christian Theology in Arabic: Muslim-Christian Encounters in the Early Islamic Period* (Aldershot, UK: Ashgate Variorum, 2003); idem, *The Church in the Shadow of the Mosque: Christians and Muslims in the World of Islam* (Princeton, NJ: Princeton University Press, 2008); idem, "Faith and Reason in Christian Kalām: Theodore Abū Qurrah on Discerning the True Religion," in *Christian Arabic Apologetics during the Abbasid Period (750–1258),* ed. Samir Khalil Samir and Jørgen Nielsen (Leiden: E. J. Brill, 1994), 1–43; David Thomas, "The Doctrine of the Trinity in the Early Abbasid Era," in *Islamic Interpretations of Christianity,* ed. Lloyd Ridgeon (New York: St. Martin's, 2000), 78–98.

8. See, e.g., A. Pegis, ed. and trans., *On the Truth of the Catholic Faith* (New York: Doubleday, 1955), 1:73–74. See also Thomas Aquinas, "Reasons for the Faith against Muslim Objections," trans. Joseph Kenny, OP, *Islamochristiana* 22 (1996): 31–52; and Gabriel S. Reynolds, "Saint Thomas' Islamic Challenges: Reflections on the Antiochene Questions," *ICMR* 12:2 (April 2001): 161–89.

9. See James Kritzeck, *Peter the Venerable and Islam* (Princeton, NJ: Princeton University Press, 1964). For more of Peter's texts, see Reinhold Glei, ed. and trans., *Petrus Venerabilis: Schriften zum Islam* (Altenberge: Corpus Islamo-Christianum, 1985); Dominique Iogna-Prat, *Order and Exclusion: Cluny and Christendom Face Heresy, Judaism, and Islam (1000–1150),* trans. Graham R. Edwards (Ithaca, NY: Cornell University Press, 2002).

10. James Waltz, "Muhammad and the Muslims in Thomas Aquinas," *Muslim World* 56:2 (1976): 81–95.

11. J. M. Casciaro, *El dialogo teologico de Santo Tomas con musulmanes y judios: El tema de la profecia y la revelacion* (Madrid: Instituto Francisco Suarez, 1969).

12. See, e.g., J. Hoeberichts, *Francis and Islam* (Quincy, IL: Franciscan, 1997); Gwenolé Jeusset, *Saint François et le sultan* (Paris: Albin Michel, 2006); John Tolan, *Saint Francis and the Sultan: The Curious History of a Christian-Muslim Encounter* (Oxford: Oxford University Press, 2009); Paul Moses, *The Saint and the Sultan: The Crusades, Islam, and Francis of Assisi's Mission of Peace* (New York: Doubleday, 2009); Farid Munir, "Sultan al-Malik Muhammad al-Kamil and Saint Francis: Interreligious Dialogue and the Meeting at Damietta," *Journal of Islamic Law and Culture* 10:3 (2008): 307–17.

13. A sample of research available on this general topic: George C. Anawati and S. de Beaurecueil, "Une preuve de l'existence de Dieu chez Ghazali et s. Thomas d'Aquin," *Mélanges d'Institut des Études Orientales* (1956): 207–14; A. Ascher et al., *The Mutual Effects of the Islamic and Judeo-Christian Worlds* (Brooklyn: Brooklyn College Press, 1979); David Burrell, CSC, *Knowing the Unknowable God: Ibn Sina, Maimonides, Aquinas* (Notre Dame: Notre Dame University Press, 1986); D. Burrell and B. McGinn, eds., *God and Creation: An Ecumenical Symposium* (Notre Dame: Notre Dame University Press, 1990); J. G. Flynn, "St. Thomas Aquinas' Use of the Arab Philosophers on the Nature of God," *Al-Mushir* 16 (1974): 278–86; idem, "St. Thomas and Averroes on the Knowledge of God," *Abr Nahrain* 18 (1978–79): 19–32; idem, "St. Thomas and Averroes on the Nature and Attributes of God," *Abr Nahrain* 15 (1974–75): 39–49; idem, "St. Thomas and Avicenna on the Nature of God," *Abr Nahrain* 14 (1973–74): 53–65; Louis Gardet, "La connaissance que Thomas d'Aquin put avoir du monde islamique," in *Aquinas and the Problems of His Time,* ed. G. Verbeke and D. Verhelst (Leuven: Leuven University Press, 1976), 139–49; idem, *Regards chrétiens sur l'Islam* (Paris: Desclee de Brouwer, 1986), esp. 115–62, on Thomas and the Muslims; idem, "Deux grands maitres: Al-Bīrūnī et Albert Le Grand; Essai de typologie comparative," *Islamochristiana* 1 (1975): 25–40. Also Salvador Gomez Nogales, "Los arabes en la vida y en la doctrina de Sto. Tomas," in *Tomasso d'Aquino nel suo settimo centenario* (Naples: Edizione Domenicane Italiane, 1975), 1:334–40; idem, "Santo Tomas y los arabes: Bibliografia," *Miscelanea Comillas* 63 (1975): 205–50; Alfred Guillaume, "Christian and Muslim Theology as Represented by Al-Shahrastani and St. Thomas Aquinas," *Bulletin of the Schools of Oriental and African Studies* 13:3 (1950): 551–80; J. Lohmann, "Saint Thomas et les Arabes," *Rev. Philos. Louvain* 74, 4th ser., no. 21 (1976): 30–44; and another eight articles in *Tomasso d'Aquino nel suo settimo centenario,* 1:261–360; Muammer İskenderoğlu, *Fakhr-al-Dīn al-Rāzī and Thomas Aquinas on the Question of the Eternity of the World* (Leiden: Brill, 2002).

14. Hans Küng, "Christianity and World Religions: Dialogue with Islam," in *Toward a Universal Theology of Religion,* ed. Leonard Swidler (Maryknoll, NY: Orbis, 1987), 194.

15. Hans Küng, *Christianity and the World's Religions: Paths of Dialogue with Islam, Hinduism, and Buddhism* (Garden City, NY: Doubleday, 1986), 3–132.

16. Ibid., 28.

17. Hans Küng, *Islam: Past, Present, and Future* (Oxford: Oneworld, 2007), xxvi.

18. Paul Knitter, "Hans Küng's Theological Rubicon," in Swidler, *Universal Theology of Religion,* 224–30.

19. K. Cragg, *The Christ and the Faiths* (Philadelphia: Westminster, 1986), 10.

20. Ibid., 29–47.

21. K. Cragg, "Legacies and Hopes in Muslim/Christian Theology," *Islamochristiana* 3 (1977): 1–10; example from pp. 2–3.

22. Cragg, "Legacies," 4. Cragg has continued his remarkable scholarly publishing career of over half a century, which includes *The Qur'an and the West* (Washington, DC: Georgetown University Press, 2005).


INTRODUCTION

1. Rex Mason, "Chapter 1: The Old Testament/Hebrew Bible," in *The Biblical World,* ed. John Barton (London and New York: Routledge, 2002), 1:6.

2. See Adele Reinbartz, "Chapter 2: The Apocrypha," in Barton, *Biblical World,* 1:15–27, on the discussion of these Second Temple Jewish writings and the different views on their authority held by Catholics and Protestants. See also J. C. Turro, "2. History of Old Testament Canon," under "Canon, Biblical," *NCE* 3:22–27. The Orthodox canon also includes two additional books of Maccabees; see, e.g., http://www.bible-researcher.com/canon2.html.

3. See, e.g., John Goldingay, *Models for Interpretation of Scripture* (Grand Rapids, MI: Eerdmans, 1995).

4. Regina A. Biosclair, "Historical Criticism," in *An Introductory Dictionary of Theology and Religious Studies,* ed. Orlanddo Espín and James B. Nickoloff (Collegeville, MN: Liturgical, 2007), 566–67. William R. Telford, "Modern Biblical Interpretation," in Barton, *Biblical World,* 2:427–47, provides a clear overview of biblical criticism.

5. Gerhard von Rad, *Old Testament Theology: The Theology of Israel's Historical Traditions,* 2 vols. (New York: Harper and Row, 1962).

6. See W. J. Burghardt and J. W. O'Malley, "Historical Theology," *NCE* 6:868–71.

7. Dated from 4 B.C.E. according to a corrected version of the calendar.

8. See Justo L. González, *A History of Christian Thought,* rev. ed. (Nashville: Abingdon, 1987), 1:61–96. Regarding Clement, technically the monepiscopacy of Rome was not established until 150 C.E. or later. Here and throughout this volume I have frequently relied on Jaroslav Pelikan, *The Christian Tradition: A History of the Development of Doctrine,* vol. 1, *The Emergence of the Catholic Tradition (100–600)* (Chicago: University of Chicago Press, 1975); vol. 3, *The Growth of Medieval Theology (600–1300)* (Chicago: University of Chicago Press, 1980); vol. 4, *Reformation of Church and Dogma (1300–1700)* (Chicago: University of Chicago Press, 1985); and vol. 5, *Christian Doctrine and Modern Culture (since 1700)* (Chicago: University of Chicago Press, 1991).

9. González, *History of Christian Thought,* 1:101–9 (Justin); 1:171–85 (Tertullian).

10. Ibid., 1:186–227, 303–25.

11. See F. Dvornik, "Councils, General (Ecumenical), History of," *NCE* 4: 298–303.

12. See Willemien Otten, "Carolingian Theology," in *The Medieval Theologians*, ed. G. R. Evans (Oxford: Blackwell, 2001), 76–80; and González, *History of Christian Thought*, 1:119–23.

13. Otten, *Medieval Theologians*, 94–155.

14. Ibid., 187–220.

15. Ibid., 250–65, 334–54.

16. González, *History of Christian Thought*, vol. 3, esp. chaps. 2–7, offers a concise description of Reformation thinkers,.

17. See, e.g., Christopher Bellitto, *The General Councils: A History of the Twenty-One Church Councils from Nicaea to Vatican II* (Mahwah, NJ: Paulist, 2002).

18. See E. L. Lampe and P. Soergel, "Counter Reformation," *NCE* 4:308–14.

19. See, e.g., Scott Hendrix, *Recultivating the Vineyard: The Reformation Agendas of Christianization* (Louisville, KY: Westminster John Knox, 2004).

20. See J. F. Broderick, "4. The Modern Period (1789–1958)," under "Papacy," *NCE* 10:845–49.

21. See J. M. Gres-Gayer, "Jansenism," *NCE* 7:715–20.

22. González, *History of Christian Thought*, 3:300–317.

23. See Martin Forward, *Inter-Religious Dialogue: A Short Introduction* (Oxford: Oneworld, 2001).

24. See David F. Ford, ed., *The Modern Theologians: An Introduction to Christian Theology in the Twentieth Century*, 2nd ed. (Cambridge, MA: Blackwell, 1997).

25. Jack A. Bonsor, *Athens and Jerusalem: The Role of Philosophy in Theology* (New York: Paulist, 1993), 22–35, describes the "Hellenistic reception of Christian faith" succinctly.

26. See, e.g., Pope John Paul II and John P. Beal, *Theotokos—Woman, Mother, Disciple: A Catechesis on Mary, Mother of God* (Boston: Pauline Books, 1999); Christopher Veniamin, ed., *Mary the Mother of God: Sermons by Saint Gregory Palamas* (South Canaan, PA: Mount Tabor, 2004); Saint Cyril, Patriarch of Alexandria, *Against Those Who Are Unwilling to Confess That the Holy Virgin Is Theotokos* (Rollinsford, NH: Orthodox Research Institute, 2004).

27. C. Vogel et. al., "Canon Law, History of," *NCE* 3:37–58, esp. 46–49.

28. See Claude Gilliot, "Traditional Disciplines of Qur'ānic Studies," *EQ* 5:318–39, for a survey of Muslim scholarship on study of the sacred text.

29. See, e.g., John Burton, *The Collection of the Qur'an* (Cambridge: Cambridge University Press, 1979).

30. See further Angelika Neuwirth, "Sūra(s)," *EQ* 5:166–77, on the classification of the chapters; and Gerhardt Böwering, "Chronology and the Qur'an," *EQ* 1:316–35.

31. See Angelika Neuwirth, "Verse(s)," *EQ* 5:419–29, on further aspects of the "gradual self-theologization of Qur'anic discourse."

32. See further R. Marston Speight, "The Function of Hadith as Commentary on the Qur'an, as Seen in the Six Authoritative Collections," in *Approaches to the History of the Interpretation of the Qur'an*, ed. Andrew Rippin (Oxford: Clarendon, 1988), 63–81; G. H. A. Juynboll, "Hadīth and the Qur'ān," *EQ* 2:376–97.

33. For more detail, see Claude Gilliot, "Exegesis of the Qur'ān: Classical and Medieval," *EQ* 2:99–124; Rotraud Wielandt, "Exegesis of the Qur'ān: Early Modern and Contemporary," *EQ* 2:124–42.

34. See John Burton, *An Introduction to the Hadith* (Edinburgh: Edinburgh University Press, 1994), esp. 92–105, "The Theological Dimension of the Hadith."

35. On the tripartite division of the subdisciplines (biography, prosopography, and chronography), see Chase Robinson, *Islamic Historiography* (New York: Cambridge University Press, 2003), 55–79.

36. Ibn Hishām, *The Life of Muhammad: A Translation of Ibn Ishāq's "Sīrat Rasūl Allah,"* trans. A. Guillaume (Oxford: Oxford University Press, 1955), 181–82.

37. R. Steven Humphreys, "Qur'anic Myth and Narrative Structure in Early Islamic Historiography," in *Tradition and Innovation in Late Antiquity*, ed. F. M. Clover and R. S. Humphreys (Madison: University of Wisconsin, 1989), 271–90, citing 278. See also, e.g., the book of Judges, chapter 2.

38. Ya'qūbī (d. 897) wrote the *Book of the Lands,* Tabarī (d. 923) the *History of Prophets and Kings,* Mas'ūdī (d. 956) the *Meadows of Gold,* and Bīrūnī (d. c. 1050) the *Chronology of Ancient Peoples.*

39. Persian and Turkish authors likewise composed in this genre for centuries to come. Rashid ad-Din's early fourteenth-century *Universal History* (*Jāmi' at-Tawārīkh*), Hāfiz-i Abrū's early fifteenth-century *Compendium of History* (*Majma' at-Tawārīkh*), and Sayyid Luqmān's late sixteenth-century Turkish *Cream of Histories* (*Zubdat at-Tawārīkh*) all include important episodes from the lives of prophets and saints. In these universal histories, the emphasis shifts from edification to education and entertainment for the already well-educated. The Ottoman Turkish work *Rosary of Historical Reports* (*Subhat al-Akhbār*), for example, does in abbreviated fashion what the universal histories do at length: it traces in a genealogical mode the lineages of the sultans all the way back to the beginning of creation via the prophets. A "theology of history" is at work here, similar to the one that carefully traced Muhammad's lineage back to Adam in the first great biography of the Prophet. In this case, the historian also positions the sultans over a line of mostly Persian heroes and mostly Arab rulers. The genre has potential for expressing at least an implied theory of political legitimacy; the positioning of members of a royal line, such as the Ottoman sultans, as successors to the prophets makes a powerful claim to religious as well as temporal authority.

40. See W. M. Thackston, trans., *The Tales of the Prophets of al-Kisā'ī* (Boston: Twayne, 1978); William Brinner, trans., *Lives of the Prophets as Recounted by . . . Tha'labī* (Leiden: Brill, 2002).

41. For an overview, see, e.g., Marshall Hodgson, *The Venture of Islam* (Chicago: University of Chicago Press, 1974), 1:315–58, esp. tables on pp. 319 and 338, showing major jurists and outlining the process of generating a legal decision, respectively.

42. On the overlap between theology and law, especially in more recent times, see David L. Johnston, "An Epistemological and Hermeneutical Turn in Twentieth-Century *Usūl al-Fiqh*," *Islamic Law and Society* 2:11 (2004): 233–82.

43. See, e.g., Al-Māturīdī, *Kitāb al-Tawhīd,* ed. and intro. Fathalla Kholeif (Beirut: Dār al-Mashriq, 1970); Ulrich Rudolph, *Al-Māturīdī und die sunnitische Theologie in Samarkand* (Leiden: Brill, 1996); Richard McCarthy, SJ, ed.

and trans., *The Theology of Al-Ashʿarī* (Beirut: Imprimerie Catholique, 1953); Al-Bāqillānī, *Kitāb al-Tamhīd,* ed. Richard McCarthy, SJ (Beirut: Al-Maktabat ash-Sharqīya, 1957); Al-Juwaynī, *A Guide to Conclusive Proofs for the Principles of Belief,* trans. Paul E. Walker (Reading, UK: Garnet, 2000).

44. See, e.g., ʿAbdʾ al-Qahir al-Baghdadi, *Moslem Schism and Sects,* pt. 2, trans. A. S. Halkin (Tel-Aviv, 1935); al-Shahrastani, *Muslim Sects and Divisions,* trans. A. K. Kazi and J. G. Flynn (London and Boston: Kegan Paul International, 1984).

45. Theorists of the period includ Abū Nasr as-Sarrāj (d. 988), Abū Tālib al-Makkī (d. 996), Kalābādhī (d. c. 990), Qushayrī (d. 1072), and Hujwīrī (d. 1072). See Michael Sells, *Early Islamic Mysticism* (Mahwah, NJ: Paulist, 1996); John Renard, *Knowledge of God in Classical Sufism* (Mahwah, NJ: Paulist, 2004), for translations of primary texts.

46. See, e.g., Jawid Mojaddedi's translations of the first two "books" of Rūmī's mystical "epic," *The Masnavi* [or *Spiritual Couplets*] (Oxford: Oxford University Press, 2005 and 2007, with a third volume forthcoming); and translations of selections of lyric poetry by A. J. Arberry, R. A. Nicholson, and more recently Coleman Barks, such as *A Year With Rumi: Daily Readings* (San Francisco: HarperOne, 2006). For further analysis, see Fatemeh Keshavarz, *Reading Mystical Lyric: The Case of Jalal al-Din Rumi* (Columbia: University of South Carolina Press, 1998).

47. See, e.g., for an anthology of Persian work, David Fideler and Sabrineh Fideler, *Love's Alchemy: Poems from the Sufi Tradition* (Novato, CA: New World, 2006); for one of many available works on individual poets, see a selection from a great Punjabi poet: Jamal J. Elias, *Death before Dying: The Sufi Poems of Sultan Bahu* (Berkeley: University of California Press, 1998); for religious and literary analysis of a broad range of such poetry, see Annemarie Schimmel, *As Through a Veil: Mystical Poetry in Islam* (New York: Columbia University Press, 1982).

## 1. SACRED SOURCES AND COMMUNITY ORIGINS

1. In this section, unless otherwise noted, I have summarized information from the *Cambridge History of the Bible,* vol. 1, *From the Beginnings to Jerome,* ed. Peter Ackroyd and C. F. Evans; vol. 2, *The West from the Fathers to the Reformation,* ed. G. W. H. Lampe; vol. 3, *The West from the Reformation to the Present Day,* ed. S. L. Greenslade (Cambridge: Cambridge University Press, 1975); Henri de Lubac, *Medieval Exegesis,* vol. 1, trans. Mark Sebanc, and vol. 2, trans. E. M. Macieroweski (Grand Rapids, MI: Eerdmans; Edinburgh: T&T Clark, 1998–2000).

2. Cf. Michael P. Knowles, "Scripture, History, Messiah: Scriptural Fulfillment and the Fullness of Time in Matthew's Gospel," in *Hearing the Old Testament in the New Testament,* ed. Stanley E. Porter (Grand Rapids, MI: Eerdmans, 2006), 59–82.

3. On Pauline use of Jewish traditions, see Leonhard Goppelt, *Typos: The Typological Interpretation of the Old Testament in the New,* trans. Donald H. Madvig (Grand Rapids, MI: Eerdmans, 1982), 127–51; on Johannine use of Jewish tradition, see pp. 179–95.

4. See, e.g., Herbert W. Bateman, *Early Jewish Hermeneutics and Hebrews 1:5–13: The Impact of Early Jewish Exegesis on the Interpretation of a Significant*

*New Testament Passage* (New York: Peter Lang, 1997); for Donald Verseput's informative review, see http://findarticles.com/p/articles/mi_qa3803/is_199804/ai_n8786473.

5. Conflicting ideas on how circumcision should be recognized by Christians are summarized in Robert G. Hall, "Circumcision," *ABD* 1:1029–31.

6. See Willis A. Shotwell, *The Biblical Exegesis of Justin Martyr* (London: S.P.C.K., 1965).

7. For Irenaeus's explication of the relationship between Adam and Christ, see Justo L. González, *A History of Christian Thought,* rev. ed. (Nashville: Abingdon, 1987), 1:165–68.

8. For Tertullian's exegetical method, see J. W. Trigg, "Tertullian, Quintus Septimius Florens," *Dictionary of Biblical Interpretation* (Nashville: Abingdon, 1999), 2:536–37; for Clement's exegetical method, see 1:200–201. See also John L. Thompson, *Reading the Bible with the Dead: What You Can Learn from the History of Exegesis That You Can't Learn from Exegesis Alone* (Grand Rapids, MI: Eerdmans, 2007).

9. J. N. D. Kelly, *Early Christian Doctrines* (London: Adam & Charles Black, 1965), 73.

10. See L. F. Hartman and R. E. McNally, "Exegesis, Biblical," *NCE* 5:506–24, esp. 512–14 (McNally's account of the period "from the Patristic to the Medieval").

11. Ibid., 511–14.

12. See, e.g., Christopher A. Hall, *Reading Scripture with the Church Fathers* (Downers Grove, IL: InterVarsity, 1998); Sebastian Brock, *The Bible in Syriac Tradition* (Piscataway, NJ: Gorgias, 2006). See also A. K. M. Adam, Stephen E. Fowl, and Kevin J. Vanhoozer, *Reading Scripture with the Church: Toward a Hermeneutic for Theological Interpretation* (Grand Rapids, MI: Baker, 2006); and Ronald E. Heine, *Reading the Old Testament with the Ancient Church: Exploring the Formation of Early Christian Thought* (Grand Rapids, MI: Baker, 2006).

13. See, e.g., http://catholic-resources.org/ChurchDocs, with link to "Documents of the Pontifical Biblical Commission," for examples of Roman Catholic developments and problems in this connection.

14. On this topic in nonscriptural texts, see Khalil 'Athamina, "Biblical Quotations in Muslim Religious Literature: A Perspective of Dogma and Politics," *Shofar* 16 (1998): 84–103. On "tampering," see Etan Kohlberg and Mohammad Ali Amir-Moezzi, eds., *Revelation and Falsification: The Kitāb al-qirāʾāt of Ahmad b. Muhammad al-Sayyārī* (Leiden: Brill, 2008); Shari Lowin, "Revision and Alteration," *EQ* 4:449–51.

15. Further on this critical text, see Jane Dammen McAuliffe, "Text and Textuality: Q. 3:7 as a Point of Intersection," in *Literary Structures of Religious Meaning in the Qurʾān,* ed. Issa J. Boullata (Richmond, Surrey: Curzon, 2000), 56–76; idem, "Qurʾānic Hermeneutics: The Views of al-Tabarī and Ibn Kathīr," in *Approaches to the History of the Interpretation of the Qurʾān,* ed. A. Rippin (Oxford: Clarendon, 1988), 46–62.

16. 2 Peter 3:15–16 makes an intriguingly analogous comment: "Paul wrote to you according to the wisdom given him, speaking of this as he does in all his letters. There are some things in them hard to understand, which the ignorant and unstable twist to their own destruction, as they do the other scriptures."

17. For examples in translation, see Andrew Rippin's renderings of *tafsīr* on Sura 1 in *Windows on the House of Islam,* ed. John Renard (Berkeley: University of California, 1998), 29–34.

18. See, e.g., Marston Speight, "The Function of Hadith as Commentary on the Qur'ān as Seen in the Six Authoritative Collections," in Rippin, *Approaches,* 63–81.

19. See, e.g., Meir M. Bar-Asher, *Scripture and Exegesis in Early Imāmī Shiism* (Leiden: Brill, 1999).

20. Historical background summarized from Claude Gilliot, "Exegesis of the Qur'ān: Classical and Medieval," *EQ* 2:99–124; Rotraud Wielandt, "Exegesis of the Qur'ān: Early Modern and Contemporary," *EQ* 2:124–42.

21. See, e.g., Philip Jenkins, *The Next Christendom: The Coming of Global Christianity* (New York: Oxford University Press, 2002); idem, *The New Faces of Christianity: Believing the Bible in the Global South* (New York: Oxford University Press, 2006).

22. See Walter A. Elwell, *Encountering the New Testament: A Historical and Theological Survey* (Grand Rapids, MI: Baker Books, 1998), for an outline of the different approaches to the New Testament; and Joel B. Green and Max Turner, eds., *Jesus of Nazareth: Lord and Christ; Essays on the Historical Jesus and New Testament Christology* (Grand Rapids, MI: Eerdmans, 1994), on different New Testament Christologies.

23. See, e.g., Uri Rubin, *The Eye of the Beholder: The Life of Muhammad as Viewed by the Early Muslims—A Textual Analysis* (Princeton, NJ: Darwin, 1995).

24. See, e.g., Hava Lazarus-Yafeh, *Intertwined Worlds: Medieval Islam and Bible Criticism* (Princeton, NJ: Princeton University Press, 1992), 75–110, "The Prediction of Muhammad and Islam"; Jane Dammen MacAuliffe, "The Prediction and Prefiguration of Muhammad," in *Bible and Qur'an: Essays in Intertextuality,* ed. John C. Reeves (Leiden: Brill, 2004), 107–32; Abdu I. Ahad Dawud, *Muhammad in the Bible* (New Delhi: International Islamic Publishers, 1996); Kais Al Kalby, *Prophet Muhammad: The Last Messenger in the Bible* (Bakersfield, CA: American Muslim Cultural Association, 2005); Jamal Badawi, *Muhammad in the Bible* (Halifax, NS, Canada: International Islamic Publishing House, 1997); and for a broader sweep, Abdul Haq Vidyarthi, *Muhammad in World Scriptures: The Parsi, Hindu, and Buddhist Scriptures* (Kuala Lumpur: Islamic Book Trust, 2006). For an illustration and commentary on this scene, see Priscilla Soucek, "An Illustrated Manuscript of al-Bīrūnī's *Chronology of Ancient Nations,*" in *The Scholar and the Saint,* ed. P. J. Chelkowski (New York: New York University Press, 1975), 107–9.

25. See further, e.g., Uri Rubin, *Between Bible and Quran: The Children of Israel and the Islamic Self-Image* (Princeton, NJ: Darwin, 1999); John C. Reeves, ed., *Bible and Qur'an: Essays in Scriptural Intertextuality* (Leiden: Brill, 2004); M. S. Seale, "How the Qur'ān Interprets the Bible," in *Qur'ān and Bible: Studies in Interpretation and Dialogue* (London: Croom Helm, 1978), 71–77; David Thomas, "The Bible in Early Muslim Anti-Christian Polemic," *ICMR* 7:1 (1996): 29–38. On another aspect of the topic, see Neal Robinson, "Varieties of Pronouncement Stories in *Sahih Muslim:* A Gospel Genre in the Hadith Literature," *ICMR* 5:2 (1994): 123-46.

26. See Daniel J. Harrington, SJ, *The Church according to the New Testament: What the Wisdom and Witness of Early Christianity Teach Us Today* (Chicago: Sheed & Ward, 2001), 159–62.

27. See John F. O'Grady, *Disciples and Leaders: The Origins of Christian Ministry in the New Testament* (New York: Paulist, 1991).

28. John McKenzie, *Dictionary of the Bible* (Milwaukee: Bruce, 1965), "Deacon, Deaconess," 182.

29. See E. Glenn Hinson, *The Church Triumphant: A History of Christianity up to 1300* (Macon, GA: Mercer University Press, 1995), 26–27, 102–6.

30. See Mary Margaret Pazdan, "Mary, Mother of Jesus," *ABD* 4:584–86.

31. Ben Witherington, "Women: New Testament," *ABD* 6:957–60.

32. Peter Lampe, "Tryphaena and Tryphosa," *ABD* 6:669.

33. Ben Witherington, "Lydia," *ABD* 4:422–23.

34. Peter Lampe, "Junias," *ABD* 3:1127; Eldon Jay Epp, *Junia: The First Woman Apostle* (Minneapolis: Fortress, 2005).

35. Marshall Hodgson, *The Venture of Islam* (Chicago: University of Chicago Press, 1974), 1:214 n. 6, argues that the gloss "Associates" might more accurately capture the tone of the relationships of the various "Companions" to Muhammad, since "Companions" might suggest that these early community leaders were in relatively constant and deeply personal contact with the Prophet. See also Herbert Berg, ed., *Method and Theory in the Study of Islamic Origins* (Leiden: Brill, 2003).

36. See M. Muranyi, "Sahāba," *EI²* 8:827–29.

37. Muslim, *Sahīh Muslim* (Beirut: Dār Ibn Hazm, 1995), 4:1478–1566. See also Fred M. Donner, *Narratives of Islamic Origins: The Beginnings of Islamic Historical Writing* (Princeton, NJ: Darwin, 1998); see also Fu'ād Jabalī, *The Companions of the Prophet: A Study of Geographical Distribution and Political Alignments* (Leiden: Brill, 2003).

38. See, e.g., James A. Bill and John A. Williams, *Roman Catholics and Shi'i Muslims* (Chapel Hill: University of North Carolina Press, 2002), 47, 52–55.

39. Barbara F. Stowasser, *Women in the Qur'an, Traditions, and Interpretation* (New York: Oxford University Press, 1994), 82.

40. Further on women in the early Muslim community, see Barbara F. Stowasser, "Wives of the Prophet," *EQ* 5:506–21; Amina Wadud, *Qur'an and Woman: Rereading the Sacred Text from a Woman's Perspective* (New York: Oxford University Press, 1999); Asma Barlas, *"Believing Women" in Islam: Unreading Patriarchal Interpretations of the Qur'an* (Austin: University of Texas Press, 2002); Ghassan Ascha, "The 'Mothers of the Believers': Stereotypes of the Prophet Muhammad's Wives," in *Female Stereotypes in Religious Traditions,* ed. Ria Kloppenborg and Wouter J. Hanegraaff (Leiden: Brill, 1995), 89–107; on the Shi'ī tradition, see David Pinault, "Zaynab Bint 'Ali and the Place of the Women of the Households of the First Imams in Shi'ite Devotional Literature," in *Women in the Medieval Islamic World: Power, Patronage, and Piety,* ed. Gavin Hambly (New York: St. Martin's, 1998), 69–98; and on the larger picture, see Gavin Hambly, "Becoming Visible: Medieval Islamic Women in Historiography and History," in Hambly, *Women in the Medieval Islamic World,* 3–28.

41. See, e.g., 'Allāmah Sayyid Muhammad Husayn Tabataba'i, *Shi'ite Islam,*

trans. Seyyed Hossein Nasr (Albany: SUNY Press, 1977), 40 and passim, on the origins of the Sunni/Shiʻi divide.

42. For further detail on the work of the early theologians as well as on the concept of the messianic role of the imams, see Abdulaziz A. Sachedina, *Islamic Messianism: The Idea of the Mahdi in Twelver Shiʻism* (Albany: SUNY Press, 1981).

## 2. DEVELOPMENT AND SPREAD

1. About the early relations and conflict between "Jewish" Christians and "Gentile" Christians, see Jack T. Sanders, *Schismatics, Sectarians, Dissidents, Deviants: The First One Hundred Years of Jewish-Christian Relations* (Valley Forge, PA: Trinity International, 1993); also Francis Watson, *Paul, Judaism, and the Gentile: Beyond the New Perspective* (Grand Rapids, MI: Eerdmans, 2007).

2. See, e.g., Everett Ferguson, *Baptism in the Early Church: History, Theology, and Liturgy in the First Five Centuries* (Grand Rapids, MI: Eerdmans, 2009); major sources on early Christian identity include the Apology of Aristides (second cent.), as well as Justin Martyr and Irenaeus. See also H. Mueller, "Baptism (in the Bible)," *NCE* 2:56–60, for the theological meaning of baptism; J. A. Jungmann and K. Stasiak, eds., "Baptism, Sacrament of," *NCE* 2:60–67.

3. See Justo L. González, *A History of Christian Thought*, rev. ed. (Nashville: Abingdon, 1987), 1:126–37; James D. G. Dunn, *Unity and Diversity in the New Testament: An Inquiry into the Character of Earliest Christianity* (Philadelphia: Trinity International, 1990), 267–308.

4. Summarized from J. N. D. Kelly, *Early Christian Doctrine* (London: A. C. Black, 1977), 27–28, 92.

5. About the early councils and the formation of "orthodoxy," see Leo Donald Davis, *The First Seven Ecumenical Councils (325–787): Their History and Theology* (Collegeville, MN: Liturgical, 1990).

6. For a new interpretation of the origins of the Muslim community, see Fred M. Donner, *Muhammad and the Believers: At the Origins of Islam* (Cambridge, MA: Harvard, Belknap, 2010).

7. Summarized from Marshall Hodgson, *The Venture of Islam* (Chicago: University of Chicago Press, 1974), 1:212–17.

8. See, e.g., John Henderson, *The Construction of Orthodoxy and Heresy* (Albany: SUNY Press, 1998); Alexander Knysh, "'Orthodoxy' and 'Heresy' in Medieval Islam: An Essay in Reassessment," *The Muslim World* 83:1 (1993): 48–67; also J. Robson, "Bidʻa," *EI²* 1:1199.

9. Richard Bulliet, *The Case for Islamo-Christian Civilization* (New York: Columbia University Press, 2006).

10. E.g., Nicholas Thomas Wright, *What Saint Paul Really Said: Was Paul of Tarsus the Real Founder of Christianity?* (Grand Rapids, MI: Eerdmans, 1997); David Wenham, *Paul: Follower of Jesus or Founder of Christianity?* (Grand Rapids, MI: Eerdmans, 1995). For an intriguing Muslim perspective, see Gabriel S. Reynolds, *A Muslim Theologian in the Sectarian Milieu: ʻAbd al-Jabbâr and the "Critique of Christian Origins"* (Leiden: E. J. Brill, 2004); and idem, "A New Source for Church History? Eastern Christianity in ʻAbd al-Jabbâr's (415/1025) Confirmation," *Oriens Christianus* 86 (2002): 46–68.

11. Franklin H. Littell, *The Macmillan Atlas History of Christianity* (New York: Macmillan, 1976), 6.

12. Kenneth Scott Latourette, *A History of the Expansion of Christianity* (Grand Rapids, MI: Zondervan, 1970), vol. 1, esp. chaps. 3 and 4.

13. Ibid., chap. 5.

14. See Samuel Hugh Moffett, *A History of Christianity in Asia,* vol. 1, *Beginnings to 1500* (San Francisco: HarperCollins, 1992); Christoph Baumer, *The Church of the East: An Illustrated History of Assyrian Christianity* (New York: I. B. Tauris, 2006). See also Sidney Griffith, *The Church in the Shadow of the Mosque: Christians and Muslims in the World of Islam* (Princeton, NJ: Princeton University Press, 2007).

15. Adrian Hastings, ed., *A World History of Christianity* (Grand Rapids, MI: Eerdmans, 1999), 58–65. Nestorians were those who rejected the doctrine of the Council of Chalcedon. Discussion of Jesus Christ's "nature," and the question of how or whether Christians should understand Christ as both human and divine, are complex and highly nuanced. The term "Monophysite" has generally been applied to groups that disagreed with the Chalcedonian definition of Christ as "fully human and fully divine" and argued rather that Christ's humanity was absorbed by his divinity. I use the term throughout to refer to non-Chalcedonian Christologies, while avoiding the complexities introduced by the term "Miaphysite," which is sometimes used to refer to christological positions that held that Jesus was "fully human and fully divine," but with divinity and humanity cohering in a single "nature." In short, "Monophysite" and "Miaphysite" are two words of almost identical literal meaning that refer to two very different Christologies.

16. For the development of the church in the Middle Ages, see, e.g., Latourette, *History of the Expansion of Christianity,* vol. 2; F. Donald Logan, *A History of the Church in the Middle Ages* (London and New York: Routledge, 2002). For the Western and the Eastern churches' conflict, see Hans Küng, *Christianity: Essence, History, and Future* (New York: Continuum, 1995), chap. 3.

17. For a thorough study of the history of Christian expansion during and after the early modern period, see Latourette, *History of the Expansion of Christianity,* vols. 3–7.

18. See, e.g., Bulliet, *Case for Islamo-Christian Civilization; idem, Conversion to Islam in the Medieval Period: An Essay in Quantitative History* (Cambridge, MA: Harvard University Press, 1979); idem, "Conversion to Islam and the Emergence of a Muslim Society in Iran," in *Conversion to Islam,* ed. N. Levtzion (New York: Holmes & Meier, 1978); idem, "Conversion to Islam and the Spread of Innovation," *Fathom: The Source of Online Learning,* 2002, http://www.fathom.com/feature/2199/index.html. Michael Morony, "The Age of Conversions: A Reassessment," in *Conversion and Continuity,* ed. Michael Gervers and Ramzi Jibran Bikhazi (Rome: Pontifical Institute of Medieval Studies, 1990), surveys a number of writers who have discussed the subject (to 1990) and examines Richard Bulliet's numbers; Robert Schick, *The Christian Communities of Palestine from Byzantine to Islamic Rule* (Princeton, NJ: Darwin, 1996), examines the question from the record of archaeology and concludes his chapter on Muslims and conversion to Islam as follows: "The historical and archaeological evidence does seem to show that the total number of Muslims was still a small portion of the total by the

end of the Umayyad period roughly matching the conclusion reached by Bulliet" (158). The last chapter in Fred Donner, *Early Islamic Conquests* (Princeton, NJ: Princeton University Press, 1981), deals with conversion in the context of tribal migrations. See also Anton Minkov, *Conversion to Islam in the Balkans: Kisve Bahası Petitions and Ottoman Social Life, 1670–1730* (Leiden: Brill, 2004). On South Asian developments, see Richard Eaton, "Islamic History as Global History," in *Islamic and European Expansion,* ed. Michael Adas (Philadelphia: Temple University Press, 1993), also available in a collection of Eaton's essays: *Essays on Islam and Indian History* (Oxford: Oxford University Press, 2000); Eaton's *Rise of Islam and the Bengal Frontier, 1203–1760* (Berkeley: University of California Press, 1996) describes the predominantly nonviolent adoption of Islam in Bengal; see also idem, "Temple Desecration and Hindu-Muslim States," in *Beyond Turk and Hindu: Rethinking Religious Identities in Islamicate South Asia,* ed. David Gilmartin and Bruce B. Lawrence (Gainesville: University of Florida Press, 2000), 246–81, for a well-researched alternative narrative of Muslim conquest; and Devin DeWeese, *Islamization and Native Religion in the Golden Horde: Baba Tükles and Conversion to Islam in Historical and Epic Tradition* (College Station: Pennsylvania State University Press, 1994).

19. Summarized from Hodgson, *Venture of Islam;* Ira Lapidus, *A History of Islamic Societies* (New York: Cambridge University Press, 1990).

20. See John J. Collins, ed., *The Encyclopedia of Apocalypticism,* vol. 1, *The Origins of Apocalypticism in Judaism and Christianity* (New York: Continuum, 1991).

21. See Collins's work and also Stephen L. Cook, *The Apocalyptic Literature* (Nashville: Abingdon, 2003), esp. chaps. 7–9; Greg Carey, *Ultimate Things: An Introduction to Jewish and Christian Apocalyptic Literature* (St. Louis: Chalice, 2005).

22. Summarized from David Cook, *Studies in Muslim Apocalyptic* (Princeton, NJ: Darwin, 2002), 270–74; on the Hour, see, e.g., Qur'ān 18:21, 22:7, 6:31, 22:55, 7:187, 31:34, 34:3, 42:18, 54:1, 22:1.

23. See, e.g., A. J. Wensinck, *The Muslim Creed: Its Genesis and Historical Development* (Cambridge: Cambridge University Press, 1932), 25.

24. See, e.g., Muslim, *Sahīh* 4:1749–96; further on Hadith collections see Cook, *Studies in Muslim Apocalyptic,* 326–32.

25. Cook, *Studies in Muslim Apocalyptic,* 275–99. See further, e.g., Abbas Amanat, *Apocalyptic Islam and Iranian Shi'ism* (London: I. B. Tauris, 2009).

26. John O. Voll suggested the term "religio-cultural styles" in *Islam: Continuity and Change in the Modern World* (Boulder, CO: Westview, 1982), 29–31. I have borrowed some basic features of the four "styles" and recast them as "orientations to history and sources," while modifying other characteristics as well as the primary identifying features.

27. See Robert K. Whalen, "Dispensationism," *Encyclopedia of Millennialism and Millennial Movements,* ed. Richard A. Landes (New York: Routledge, 2000), 125–28; Christian groups that support Israel unconditionally typically subscribe to this ideology, popularized by Tim LaHaye and Jerry Jenkins's wildly popular "Left Behind" series of apocalyptic novels.

3. FROM STORY TO CREED

1. I am confining my examples here to the Gospels, but the book of Revelation provides another striking and very different genre of narrative, which I have mentioned at the end of chapter 2.

2. On the Synoptic Gospels, see, e.g., Bart D. Ehrman, *The New Testament: A Historical Introduction to the Early Christian Writings,* 3rd ed. (New York: Oxford University Press, 2003); John Riches, William R. Telford, and Christopher M. Tuckett, *The Synoptic Gospels* (Sheffield, England: Sheffield Academic, 2001); Robert H. Stein, *Studying the Synoptic Gospels: Origin and Interpretation* (Grand Rapids, MI: Baker Academic, 2001).

3. On this interpretation of Mattthew, see also Donald Senior, *The Gospel of Matthew* (Nashville: Abingdon, 1997).

4. See also Acts 2:24–36, 3:12–26, 10:34–43, 13:17–47. Paul's speech before the crowd at the Areopagus in Acts 17:22–31, as well as his later speeches in defense of himself before the civil authorities, 21:37–22:29, and chapters 25 and 26, are very different in tone and content. See also Angelo Di Berardino and Basil Studer, *The History of Theology,* vol. 1, *The Patristic Period* (Collegeville, MN: Liturgical, 1997), 34–42, on "narration."

5. See, e.g., Dennis McCarthy, SJ, *Treaty and Covenant: A Study in Form in the Ancient Oriental Documents and in the Old Testament* (Rome: Biblical Institute, 1978).

6. See, e.g., Bart D. Ehrman, *Lost Scriptures: Books That Did Not Make It into the New Testament* (New York: Oxford University Press, 2005); Elaine Pagels, *The Gnostic Gospels* (New York: Random House, 2004); idem, *Beyond Belief: The Secret Gospel of Thomas* (New York: Random House, 2004); M. Myer and Elaine Pagels, eds., *The Gnostic Gospels* (London: Folio, 2008); and an older compendium of a wide range of narrative apocryphal works: Edgar Hennecke and Wilhelm Schneemelcher, *New Testament Apocrypha,* 2 vols. (Philadelphia: Westminster, 1963).

7. For further detail, see, e.g., Mustansir Mir, "The Qur'ānic Story of Joseph: Plot, Themes, and Characters," *Muslim World* 76:1 (January 1986): 1–15; see also Anthony H. Johns, "Joseph in the Qur'ān: Dramatic Dialogue, Human Emotion, and Prophetic Wisdom," *Islamochristiana* 7 (1981): 29–51; M.S. Stern, "Muhammad and Joseph: A Study of Koranic Narrative," *Journal of Near Eastern Studies* 44:3 (July 1985): 193–204; Marilyn Waldman, "New Approaches to the 'Biblical' Materials in the Qur'ān," *Muslim World* 75:1 (January 1985): 1–16; Gary A. Rendsburg, "Literary Structures in the Qur'ānic and Biblical Stories of Joseph," *Muslim World* 78:2 (April 1988): 118–20; for a still more explicitly comparative approach, see M.A.S. Abdel Haleem, "The Story of Joseph in the Qur'ān and the Old Testament," *ICMR* 1:2 (1990): 171–91; John Macdonald, "Joseph in the Qur'ān," *Muslim World* 46:2 (1956): 113–31; and for a study of Moses from a similar comparative perspective, see Muhib O. Opeloye, "Confluence and Conflict in the Qur'ānic and Biblical Accounts of the Life of Prophet Musa," *Islamochristiana* 16 (1990): 25–41.

8. See Ismail Hamid, *Arabic and Islamic Literary Tradition* (Kuala Lumpur: Utusan Publications, 1982), 125, 150. There is also a famous Swahili epic dedicated to the story of Joseph, *Utenzi wa Yusupu,* on which see J. Knappert, *Four Swahili Epics* (Leiden: Drukkerij "Luctor et Emerigo," 1964), 9–58.

9. For some of the lengthier "short" narratives of prophets in the Qur'ān, see, e.g., Noah 11:25–49, 17:1–28; Hūd 11:50–60; Abraham 6:74–87, 21:51–70, 29:16–27; Lot 11:74–83; Shu'ayb 7:85–93, 11:84–95; Moses 2:47–61, 7:103–25, 7:148–58, 20:49–69, 20:80–98, 26:10–51, 40:23–46. For the prophets' stories and samples of exegetical elaborations on them, see Brannon M. Wheeler, *Prophets in the Quran: An Introduction to the Quran and Muslim Exegesis* (New York: Continuum, 2002).

10. Gregory of Nyssa, *The Life of Moses,* trans. Abraham Malherbe and Everett Ferguson (Mahwah, NJ: Paulist, 1978); see also Robert Slesinski, "The Doctrine of Virtue in St. Gregory of Nyssa's *The Life of Moses,*" in *Prayer and Spirituality in the Early Church,* ed. Pauline Allen, Raymond Canning, and Lawrence Cross, with B. Janell Caiger (Everton Park, Qld.: Australian Catholic University, 1998), 1:341–52.

11. Dante, *The Divine Comedy: Inferno, Purgatorio, Paradiso,* trans. John Ciardi (New York: Norton, 1977); H. C. Beeching, ed., *The Works of John Milton* (New York: Oxford University Press, 1938), 177–502.

12. *Sahīh Muslim,* 5 vols. (Beirut: Dār Ibn Hazm,1995), *Kitāb al-īmān* 1:62–63 (no. 49).

13. Story cited in Ghazali, *The Book of Fear and Hope,* trans. William McKane (Leiden: Brill, 1965), 64.

14. *Sahīh Muslim, Kitāb al-īmān* 1:168–69 (no. 374); for an account of the transformation of Hadith material on theological topics, see Tilman Nagel, *The History of Islamic Theology from Muhammad to the Present* (Princeton, NJ: Markus Wiener, 2000), 73–81.

15. *Sahīh Muslim, Kitāb al-Fadā'il* 4:1427–28 (no. 16).

16. Ibid., 4:1430–31 (nos. 26, 27).

17. Ibid., 4:1428 (no. 17).

18. Ibid., 4:1428–29 (nos. 20–23), cited by Suhrawardī; see John Renard, trans., *Knowledge of God in Classical Sufism* (Mahwah, NJ: Paulist, 2004), 333.

19. Cited by Suhrawardī in Renard, *Knowledge of God,* 333.

20. See, e.g., *Sahīh Muslim, Kitāb al-īmān,* 1:155–56 (no. 326); see also 1:154–55 (no. 322 and other variants in the same section).

21. See John Renard, *Seven Doors to Islam* (Berkeley: University of California Press, 1996), 231–35, for an overview of these works.

22. Summarized from Rumī, *The Masnavi: Book One,* trans. Jawid Mojaddedi (Oxford: Oxford University Press, 2004), 56–93.

23. See Liuwe H. Westra, *The Apostles' Creed: Origin, History, and Some Early Commentaries* (Turnhout, Belgium: Brepols, 2002). An older but complete introduction to the three Christian creeds is C. A. Swainson, *The Nicene and Apostles' Creeds* (London: J. Murray, 1875).

24. Text from Robert Broderick, ed., *The Catholic Encyclopedia,* rev. and updated ed. (Nashville: Thomas Nelson, 1987), 45.

25. See, e.g., Theodore W. Jennings, *Loyalty to God: The Apostles' Creed in Life and Liturgy* (Nashville: Abingdon, 1992).

26. The earlier "Nicene Creed" is a brief document deriving directly from the First Council of Nicaea (325) that includes four "anathemas" condemning the christological heresy known as Arianism. The "later" Nicene Creed is also dubbed the "Niceno-Constantinopolitan Creed," because its origins are generally traced to

Constantinople in the mid-fifth century. See the articles on "Creed," "Athanasian Creed," "Apostles' Creed," and "Nicene Creed" in F.L. Cross, ed., *ODCC* (London: Oxford University Press, 1958).

27. See, e.g., Sachiko Murata and William Chittick, *The Vision of Islam* (New York: Paragon, 1994), xxv-xxxiii.

28. My rendering of the Arabic text, with commentary from A.J. Wensinck, *The Muslim Creed: Its Genesis and Historical Development*, 2nd ed. (Cambridge: Cambridge University Press, 1979), 102–24; on the other earlier creeds, see pp. 124–276. See also W. Montgomery Watt, "'Akīda," *EI²* 1:332–36; and on the Jahmīya, see idem, "Djahmiyya," *EI²* 2:388; and excellent coverage of a wide range of creeds in idem, *Islamic Creeds: A Selection* (Edinburgh: Edinburgh University Press, 1994).

## 4. THE EMERGENCE OF THEOLOGICAL DISCIPLINES

1. Jean Daniélou, *Gospel Message and Hellenistic Culture,* trans. John Austin Baker (Philadelphia: Westminster, 1973).

2. See Brian O. McDermott, *Word Become Flesh: Dimensions of Christology* (Collegeville, MN: Liturgical, 1993); P. Smulders, *The Fathers on Christology: The Development of Christological Dogma from the Bible to the Great Councils* (De Pere, WI: St. Norbert Abbey, 1968).

3. Summarized from J.N.D. Kelly, *Early Christian Doctrines* (London: A.C. Black, 1977), passim. See also Edward Schillebeeckx, *Christ: The Experience of Jesus as Lord,* trans. John Bowden (New York: Crossroad, 1980). On the councils, see Leo Donald Davis, *The First Seven Ecumenical Councils (325–787): Their History and Theology* (Collegeville, MN: Liturgical, 1990).

4. See, e.g., Tim Winter, ed., *The Cambridge Companion to Classical Islamic Theology* (Cambridge: Cambridge University Press, 2008).

5. W. Montgomery Watt, *The Formative Period of Islamic Thought* (Oxford: Oneworld, 1998), 9–37. See also Patricia Crone, *God's Caliph: Religious Authority in the First Centuries of Islam* (Cambridge: Cambridge University Press, 1986).

6. Watt, *Formative Period of Islamic Thought,* 82–118. See also, e.g., Suleiman A. Mourad, *Early Islam between Myth and History: Al-Hasan al-Basrī (d. 110H/728 C.E.) and the Formation of His Legacy in Classical Islamic Scholarship* (Leiden: Brill, 2006).

7. Watt, *Formative Period of Islamic Thought,* 119–48. Further on early theological diversity, see Sarah Stroumsa, *Freethinkers of Medieval Islam: Ibn al-Rāwandī, Abū Bakr al-Rāzī, and Their Impact on Islamic Thought* (Leiden: Brill, 1999).

8. See, e.g., Thomas J. O'Shaughnessy, *Eschatological Themes in the Qur'ān* (Manila: Cardinal Bea Institute/Ateneo de Manila University, 1986); Marcia Hermansen, "Eschatology," in Winter, *Cambridge Companion,* 308–24; and William Chittick, "Eschatology," in *Islamic Spirituality: Foundations,* ed. Seyyed H. Nasr (New York: Crossroad, 1987), 378–409.

9. See James P. Keleher, *Saint Augustine's Notion of Schism in the Donatist Controversy* (Mundelein, IL: Saint Mary of the Lake Seminary, 1961).

10. See Augustine, *Four Anti-Pelagius Writings,* trans. John A. Mourant and

William J. Colling (Washington, DC: Catholic University of America Press, 1992); Dennis R. Creswell, *St. Augustine's Dilemma: Grace and Eternal Law in the Major Works of Augustine of Hippo* (New York: Peter Lang, 1997).

11. See, e.g., Mark Ellingson, *The Richness of Augustine: His Contextual and Pastoral Theology* (Louisville, KY: Westminster John Knox, 2005); Eugene Teselle, *Augustine the Theologian* (New York: Herder & Herder, 1970); R. J. Teske, "Augustine, St.," *NCE* 1:850–68.

12. Allan D. Fitzgerald, ed., *Augustine through the Ages: An Encyclopedia* (Grand Rapids, MI: Eerdmans, 1999), offers a comprehensive view of Augustine's influence on later theologians and thoughts.

13. See, e.g., Kenan Osborne, ed., *History of Franciscan Theology* (St. Bonaventure, NY: Franciscan Institute, 1994); idem, *The Franciscan Intellectual Tradition: Tracing Its Origins and Identifying Its Central Components* (St. Bonaventure, NY: Franciscan Institute, 2003).

14. See, e.g., Warren T. Smith, "Augustine of Hippo," *ER* 1:520–27; R. P. Russell, "Augustianism," *NCE* 1:875–82; see also relevant articles in Fitzgerald, *Augustine through the Ages.*

15. See, e.g., James Weisheipl, "Thomas Aquinas," *ER* 14:484–90; W. A. Wallace et al., "Thomas Aquinas, St.," and J. A. Weisheipl, "Thomism," *NCE* 14:13–28, 40–52; see also John Renard, "The Dominican and the Dervish: A Christian-Muslim Dialogue That Might Have Been—Between Thomas Aquinas (d. 1274) and Jalal ad-Din Rumi (d. 1273)," *Journal of Ecumenical Studies* 29:2 (Spring 1992): 189–201.

16. C. Balíc and T. B. Noone, "Duns Scotus, John," *NCE* 4:934–40; Thomas Williams ed., *The Cambridge Companion to Duns Scotus* (New York: Cambridge University Press, 2003); A. Vos et. al., *Duns Scotus on Divine Love: Texts and Commentary on Goodness and Freedom, God and Humans* (Aldershot, UK: Ashgate, 2003).

17. Summarized from John Meyendorff, *Byzantine Theology: Historical Trends and Doctrinal Themes,* 2nd ed. (New York: Fordham University Press, 1987); Jaroslav Pelikan, *The Christian Tradition: A History of the Development of Doctrine,* vol. 2, *The Spirit of Eastern Christendom (600–1700)* (Chicago: University of Chicago Press, 1977); articles on "Christ," "Theology," and various individual theologians in *The Oxford Dictionary of Byzantium,* ed. Alexander Kazhdan et al. (New York: Oxford University Press, 1991); articles on "Christology," "Heresy," "Theology," "Theiosis," "Trinity," and various individual theologians and churches [as in "Greek Orthodox Church"], in *Historical Dictionary of the Orthodox Church,* ed. Michael Prokurat et al. (Lanham, MD: Scarecrow, 1996); Norman Russell, *The Doctrine of Deification in the Greek Patristic Tradition* (New York: Oxford University Press, 2006).

18. Daniel Gimaret, "Mu'tazila," *EI²* 7:783–93; J. van Ess, "Mu'tazilah," *ER* 10:220–29; Richard M. Frank, *Texts and Studies on the Development and History of Kalam,* 3 vols., ed. Dimitri Gutas (Aldershot, UK: Ashgate, 2005); Richard Martin and Mark Woodward, with Dwi S. Atmaja, *Defenders of Reason: Mu'tazilism from Medieval School to Modern Symbol* (Oxford: Oneworld, 1997).

19. See, e.g., Roger Arnaldez, "Ibn Hazm," *EI²* 3:790–99; idem, *Grammaire et théologie chez Ibn Hazm: Essai sur la structure et les conditions de la pensée*

*musulmane* (Paris: J. Vrin, 1956); Ignac Goldziher, *The Zāhirīs: Their Doctrine and Their History; A Contribution to the History of Islamic Theology* (Leiden: Brill, 1971).

20. See, e.g., Christopher Melchert, *Ahmad ibn Hanbal* (Oxford: Oneworld, 2006); Muhammad Abu Zahrah, *The Four Imams: The Lives and Teaching of Their Founders* (London: Dar Al-Taqwà, 2001); Thomas Michel, *A Muslim Theologian's Response to Christianity: Ibn Taymiyya's al-Jawab al-sahih* (Delmar, NY: Caravan Books, 1984).

21. Major proponents include Bāqillānī (d. 1013), Juwaynī (d. 1085), Abū Hāmid al-Ghazālī (d. 1111; on whom, see especially chapter 8), the noted heresiographer Shahrastānī (d. 1153), and Fakhr ad-Dīn ar-Rāzī (d. 1209). See Tilman Nagel, *The History of Islamic Theology from Muhammad to the Present* (Princeton, NJ: Markus Wiener, 2000); Josef van Ess, *The Flowering of Muslim Theology* (Cambridge, MA: Harvard University Press, 2006); idem, *Theologie und Gesellschaft im 2. und 3. Jahrhundert Hidschra: Eine Geschichte des religiösen Denkens im frühen Islam*, 6 vols. (Berlin: Walter deGruyter, 1991–). See also, e.g., R. M. Frank, "Ashʿarī, al-," *ER* 1:445–49; idem, "Ashʿarīyah," *ER* 1:449–55; idem, *Early Islamic Theology: The Muʿtazilites and al-Ashʿarī* (Aldershot, UK: Ashgate, 2007); idem, *Classical Islamic Theology: The Ashʿarites* (Aldershot, UK: Ashgate, 2007).

22. Among Māturīdī's followers are Najm ad-Dīn an-Nasafī (d. 1142), Abū'l-Barakāt an-Nasafī (d. 1310), and Saʿd ad-Dīn at-Taftazānī (d. 1390).

23. See, e.g., Ulrich Rudolph, *Al-Māturīdī und die sunnitische Theologie in Samarkand* (Leiden: Brill, 1996); Mustafa Cerić, *Roots of Systematic Theology in Islam: A Study of the Theology of Abū Mansūr al-Māturīdī* (Kuala Lumpur: International Institute of Islamic Thought and Civilization, 1995); W. Madelung, "Al-Māturīdī" and "Māturīdiyya," *EI²* 6:846–48; Michel Allard, *Le problème des attributs divins dans la doctrine d'al-Ashʿarī et des ses premiers grands disciples* (Beirut: Imprimerie Catholique, 1965); J. R. T. Peters, *God's Created Speech: A Study in the Speculative Theology of the Muʿtazili Qadil-Qudat Abu l-Hasan ʿAbd al-Jabbar ibn Ahmad al-Hamadani* (Leiden: Brill, 1976); Iysa A. Bello, *The Medieval Islamic Controversy between Philosophy and Orthodoxy: Ijmāʿ and taʾwīl in the Conflict between al-Ghazālī and Ibn Rushd* (Leiden: Brill, 1989); Robert Caspar, *A Historical Introduction to Islamic Theology: Muhammad and the Classical Period* (Rome: Pontificio Istituto di Studi Arabi e d'Islamistica, 1998). See also David Thomas, *Christian Doctrines in Islamic Theology* (Leiden: Brill, 2008) for excellent material on theological cross-referencing.

24. See Mohammad Ali Amir-Moezzi, *The Divine Guide in Early Shiʿism: The Sources of Esotericism in Islam*, trans. David Streight (Albany: SUNY Press, 1994); Abdulaziz A. Sachedina, *Islamic Messianism: The Idea of the Mahdi in Twelver Shiʿism* (Albany: SUNY Press, 1981), esp. 56–59, comparing Nawbakhtī to Mufīd; G. Troupeau, "Al-Mufīd," *EI²* 7:312–13; J. L. Kraemer, "Al-Nawbakhtī," *EI²* 7:1044.

25. Two recent detailed studies on the end of Jesus' earthly life are Todd Lawson, *The Crucifixion and the Qur'an: A Study in the History of Muslim Thought* (Oxford: Oneworld, 2009), and A. H. Mathias Zahniser, *The Mission and Death of Jesus in Islam and Christianity* (Maryknoll, NY: Orbis, 2008). A good recent related study is I. Mark Beaumont, *Christology in Dialogue with Muslims: A*

*Critical Analysis of Christian Presentations of Christ for Muslims from the Ninth and Twentieth Centuries* (Colorado Springs, CO: Paternoster, 2005). For other helpful studies of "Islamic Christology," see, e.g., Neal Robinson, *Christ in Islam and Christianity* (Albany: SUNY Press, 1991); Mahmoud M. Ayoub, "Towards an Islamic Christology," *The Muslim World* 66:2 (1976): 163–88; idem, "The Death of Jesus, Reality or Delusion? A Study of the Death of Jesus in *Tafsir* Literature," *The Muslim World* 70 (1980): 91–121; Smail Balic, "The Image of Jesus in Contemporary Islamic Theology," in *We Believe in One God,* ed. A. Schimmel and A. Falaturi (New York: Seabury Press, 1979), 1–8; Suleiman A. Mourad, "A Twelfth-Century Muslim Biography of Jesus," *Islam and Christian-Muslim Relations* 7:1 (1996): 39–46.

5. BENEATH THE BRICK AND MORTAR

1. Bernard Weiss, *The Search for God's Law* (Salt Lake City: University of Utah Press, 1992), 1.

2. Robert Broderick, ed., *The Catholic Encyclopedia,* rev. ed. (Nashville: Thomas Nelson, 1987), 94.

3. See F. A. Sullivan and S. K. Wood, "Bishop (In the Church)," *NCE* 2:411–17; A. J. Quinn, "Bishop, Diocesan (Canon Law)," *NCE* 2:419–22; S. Miranda, "Cardinal," *NCE* 3:103–8. These entries offer some general accounts of the historical development. Thomas J. Reese, *Inside the Vatican: The Politics and Organization of the Catholic Church* (Cambridge, MA: Harvard University Press, 1996), offers a succinct introduction to the contemporary Catholic hierarchy.

4. Since Mormons do not subscribe to any of the historical Christian creeds, many Christian organizations question their claims to "Christian" identity.

5. See D. Michael Quinn, *The Mormon Hierarchy: Extensions of Power* (Salt Lake City: Signature Books, 1997).

6. See Thomas E. Fitzgerald, *The Orthodox Church* (Westport, CT: Greenwood, 1995).

7. See Wilhelm Baum and Dietmar W. Winkler, *The Church of the East: A Concise History* (London and New York: RoutledgeCurzon, 2003).

8. See relevant articles in Michael Prokurat, Alexander Golitzin, and Michael Peterson, *Historical Dictionary of the Orthodox Church* (Lanham, MD: Scarecrow, 1996).

9. See, e.g., John Lynch, "Church: Church Polity," *ER* 3:473–80.

10. See N. Halligan, "Holy Orders," *NCE* 7:35–42.

11. Further see, e.g., James Bill and John Williams, *Roman Catholics and Shi'i Muslims: Prayer, Passion, and Politics* (Chapel Hill: University of North Carolina Press, 2002).

12. "Shaykh al-Islām," *EI²* 9:398–402.

13. For a comparison of scriptural foundations, see, e.g., Edwin B. Firmage, Bernard G. Weiss, and John W. Welch, eds., *Religion and Law: Biblical-Judaic and Islamic Perspectives* (Winona Lake, IN: Eisenbrauns, 1990); Jacob Neusner and Tamara Sonn, *Comparing Religions through Law: Judaism and Islam* (London and New York: Routledge, 1999).

14. The entire following section on canon law is summarized from surveys

of the subject in James A. Brundage, *Medieval Canon Law* (London: Longman, 1995); James Provost, "Canon Law," *ER* 3:69–72; J.E. Lynch et al., "Canon Law, History of," *NCE* 3:37–58; "Canon Law," *ODCC*, 280.

15. See, e.g., Panteleimon Rodopoulos, *An Overview of Orthodox Canon Law,* trans. W.J. Lillie, ed. George Dion Dragas (Rollinsford, NH: Orthodox Research Institute, 2007).

16. See, e.g., Ahmet T. Karamustafa, "Community," in *Key Themes for the Study of Islam,* ed. Jamal J. Elias (Oxford: Oneworld, 2010), 93–103; Patricia Crone, *Medieval Islamic Political Thought* (Edinburgh: University of Edinburgh Press, 2004), esp. chap. 11 ("Hadith Party"); Christopher Melchert, *Ahmad ibn Hanbal* (Oxford: Oneworld, 2006); idem, "The Formation of the Sunni Schools of Law, 9th–10th Centuries C.E.," in *Islamic Law and Society,* vol. 4, ed. Ruud Peters and Bernard Weiss (Leiden: Brill, 1997).

17. See, e.g., Harald Motzki, *The Origins of Islamic Jurisprudence: Meccan Fiqh before the Classical Schools* (Leiden: Brill, 2002); Bernard Weiss, ed., *Studies in Islamic Legal Theory* (Leiden: Brill, 2002); Jonathan Brockopp, *Early Mālikī Law: Ibn ʿAbd al-Hakam and His Major Compendium of Jurisprudence* (Leiden: Brill, 2000); and Knut Vikør, *Between God and the Sultan: A History of Islamic Law* (New York: Oxford University Press, 2005).

18. Weiss, *Search for God's Law,* 2.

19. Summarized from R. Paret, "*Istihsān* and *Istislāh*," *EI²* 4:255–59.

20. For a full discussion of al-Āmidī's defense of the principle, see Weiss, *Search for God's Law,* 660–68.

21. F.E. Vogel, "*Siyāsa:* In the Sense of *siyāsa sharʿīya,*" *EI²* 9:694–96; see also C.E. Bosworth, "Nasīhat al-Mulūk," *EI²* 7:984–88.

22. See G.-H. Bosquet, "ʿĀda: i. General and ii. North Africa"; Shamoon T. Lokhandwalla, "ʿĀda: iii. India"; and J. Prins, "ʿĀda: iv. Indonesia," *EI²* 1:170–74.

23. Augustine of Hippo, *The City of God,* intro. Thomas Merton, trans. Marcus Dodds (New York: Modern Library, 1994). For a general introduction to political theologies, see Peter Scott and William T. Cavanaugh, eds., *The Blackwell Companion to Political Theology* (Malden, MA: Blackwell, 2004); Peter Iver Kaufman, *Redeeming Politics* (Princeton, NJ: Princeton University Press, 1990).

24. See, e.g., J.H. Burns, ed., *The Cambridge History of Medieval Political Thought, c. 350–c. 1450* (Cambridge: Cambridge University Press, 1991).

25. See, e.g., Yves Congar, *Tradition & Traditions* (Dallas: Basilica, 1997); idem, "Church: Ecclesiology," *ER* 3:480–86; M.R.P. McGuire, D.J. Herlihy, and M.J. Havran, "Church and State," *NCE* 3:630–43; F. Schüssler Fiorenza, "Political Theologies," *NCE* 11:459–61; Thomas G. Sanders, *Protestant Concepts of Church and State: Historical Backgrounds and Approaches for the Future* (New York: Holt, Rinehart and Winston, 1964).

26. For texts, analysis, and background on the genre, see Ann K.S. Lambton, "Islamic Mirrors for Princes," in *La Persia nel Medioevo* (Rome: Accademia dei Lincei, 1971); Nizam al-Mulk, *The Book of Government, or Rules for Kings,* trans. Hubert Darke (London: Routledge and Kegan Paul, 1978); Ghazālī, *Ghazali's Book of Counsel for Kings,* trans. F.R.C. Bagley (London: Oxford University Press, 1964); Anon., *The Sea of Precious Virtues: A Medieval Islamic Mirror for Princes,* trans. Julie S. Meisami (Salt Lake City: University of Utah Press, 1991);

Kay Ka'us Ibn Iskandar, *A Mirror for Princes, the Qābūs Nāma,* trans. Reuben Levy (London: Luzac, 1951); Mustafa Ali Gelibolu, *Mustafa Ali's Counsel for Sultans of 1581,* trans. Andreas Tietze (Vienna: Verlag der Österreichischen Akademie der Wissenschaften, 1979); Yusuf Khass Hajib, *The Wisdom of the Royal Glory,* trans. Robert Dankoff (Chicago: University of Chicago Press, 1983); C. E. Bosworth, "Nasīhat al-Mulūk," *EI²* 7:984–88.

27. See, e.g., Patricia Crone, *God's Rule—Government and Islam: Six Centuries of Medieval Islamic Political Thought* (New York: Columbia University Press, 2005); Hanna Mikhail, *Politics and Revelation: Mawardi and After* (Edinburgh: Edinburgh University Press, 1995); Al-Mawardi, *The Ordinances of Government,* trans. Wafaa H. Wahba (Reading, UK: Garnet, 2000); Sherman A. Jackson, *Islamic Law and the State: The Constitutional Jurisprudence of Shihāb Al-Dīn Al-Qarāfī* (Leiden: Brill, 1996); Henri Laoust, *Essai sur les doctrines socials et politiques de Ibn Taymīya* (Cairo: IFAO, 1939); Anne K. S. Lambton, "Khalīfa: In Political Theory," *EI²* 4:947–50; I. R. Netton and F. E. Vogel, "Siyāsa," *EI²* 9:693–96; W. Madelung, "Imāma," *EI²* 3:1163–69; F. Rosenthal, "Dawla," *EI²* 2:177–78; L. Gardet, "Dīn," *EI²* 2:293–96.

## 6. INSTITUTIONS IN ACTION

1. See F. X. Murphy, "Constantine I, The Great, Roman Emperor," *NCE* 4:179–83; "Milan, Edict of," *ODCC,* 1092.

2. See, e.g., Peter Brown, *The Making of Late Antiquity* (Cambridge, MA: Harvard University Press, 1978); F. M. Clover and Stephen Humphries, "Toward a Definition of Late Antiquity," in *Tradition and Innovation in Late Antiquity,* ed. F. M. Clover and Stephen Humphries (Madison: University of Wisconsin Press, 1989), 3–19; Arnaldo Marcone, "A Long Late Antiquity? Considerations on a Controversial Periodization," *Journal of Late Antiquity* 1:1 (2008): 4–19; Edward James, "The Rise and Function of the Concept of Late Antiquity," *Journal of Late Antiquity* 1:1 (2008): 20–30; Clifford Ando, "Decline, Fall, and Transformation," *Journal of Late Antiquity* 1:1 (2008): 31–60.

3. See Sidney Z. Ehler, *Twenty Centuries of Church and State: A Survey of Their Relations in Past and Present* (Westminster, MD: Newman, 1957); Walter Ullmann, *The Growth of Papal Government in the Middle Ages: A Study in the Ideological Relation of Clerical to Lay Power* (New York: Barnes & Noble, 1962); D. J. Herlihy et al., "Church and State," *NCE* 3:630–43, esp. the section on the Middle Ages.

4. See Thomas F. Madden, *The New Concise History of the Crusades* (Lanham, MD: Rowman & Littlefield, 2005).

5. Madden, *Concise History of the Crusades,* esp. the section "The Period of Confessional States."

6. On scripture and the language of power, see, e.g., Eltigani Abdelgadir Hamid, *The Qur'ān and Politics: A Study of the Origins of Political Thought in the Makkan Qur'ān,* 1st English ed. (Herndon, VA: International Institute of Islamic Thought, 2004); on early political developments, see Wilferd Madelung, *The Succession to Muhammad: A Study of the Early Caliphate* (Cambridge: Cambridge University Press, 2008). For broader surveys of Islamic history, see, e.g., Hugh Kennedy, *When*

*Baghdad Ruled the Muslim World: The Rise and Fall of Islam's Greatest Dynasty* (Cambridge, MA: DaCapo, 2004); Ira Lapidus, *A History of Islamic Societies* (New York: Cambridge University Press, 1990).

7. See, e.g., James A. Bill and John Alden Williams, *Roman Catholics and Shi'i Muslims: Prayer, Passion, and Politics* (Chapel Hill: University of North Carolina Press, 2002); Said Amir Arjomand, ed., *Authority and Political Culture in Shi'ism* (Albany: SUNY Press, 1988).

8. For comparative study, see, e.g., George Makdisi, "The Model of Islamic Scholastic Culture and Its Later Parallel in the Christian West," in *Vocabulaire des collèges universitaires (XIIIe-XVIe siècles)*, ed. Olga Weijers (Turnhout: Brepols, 1993), 158–76.

9. Note Cyprian's distinction between "red" and "white" martyrdoms, and Origen's "secret" and "outward" martyrdoms in his "Exhortation on Martyrdom," in *Origen*, trans. Rowan A. Greer (New York: Paulist, 1979), 41–79.

10. For this and the following sections, see, e.g., Marilyn Dunn, *The Emergence of Monasticism: From the Desert Fathers to the Early Middle Ages* (Hoboken, NJ: Wiley-Blackwell, 2003); Mayeul de Druille, OSB, *From East to West: A History of Monasticism* (New York: Herder & Herder, 1999); John W. Binns, *Ascetics and Ambassadors of Christ: The Monasteries of Palestine, 314–631* (New York: Oxford University Press, 1996).

11. See, e.g., J. Gribomont et al., "Monasticism," NCE 9:786–803; William M. Johnston, ed., *Encyclopedia of Monasticism* (Chicago and London: Fitzroy Dearborn, 2000).

12. See, e.g., Richard L. DeMolen, ed., *Religious Orders of the Catholic Reformation* (New York: Fordham University Press, 1994); Michael Mullett, *The Catholic Reformation* (New York: Routledge, 1999); Barbara B. Diefendorf, *From Penitence to Charity: Pious Women and the Catholic Reformation in Paris* (New York: Oxford University Press, 2004).

13. See, e.g., Ahmet T. Karamustafa, *Sufism: The Formative Period* (Berkeley: University of California Press, 2007); Jamil M. Abun-Nasr, *Muslim Communities of Grace: The Sufi Brotherhoods in Islamic Religious Life* (New York: Columbia University Press, 2007); Erik Ohlander, *Sufism in an Age of Transition: 'Umar al-Suhrawardī and the Rise of the Islamic Mystical Brotherhoods* (Leiden: Brill, 2008); Carl W. Ernst and Bruce B. Lawrence, *Sufi Martyrs of Love: The Chishti Order in South Asia and Beyond* (New York: Palgrave MacMillan, 2002); Dina Le Gall, *A Culture of Sufism: Naqshbandis in the Ottoman World, 1450–1700* (Albany: SUNY Press, 2005).

14. See, e.g., John Marenbon, *Early Medieval Philosophy (480–1150): An Introduction*, 2nd ed. (London and New York: Routledge, 1988), esp. 111–47; idem, *Later Medieval Philosophy (1150–1300): An Introduction* (London and New York: Routledge, 1991), esp. 1–92; various essays in *Medieval Philosophy*, ed. J. Marenbon, vol. 3 of *Routledge History of Philosophy*, new ed. (London and New York: Routledge, 2003).

15. See, e.g., Heinz Halm, *The Fatimids and Their Traditions of Learning* (London: I.B. Tauris, 1997); Jonathan Berkey, *The Transmission of Knowledge in Medieval Cairo: A Social History of Islamic Education* (Princeton, NJ: Princeton University Press, 1992), esp. chaps. 2 and 3 (instruction and institutions); see

also Wadad Kadi and Victor Billeh, eds., *Islam and Education: Myths and Truths* (Chicago: University Of Chicago Press, 2007): esp. Sebastian Günther, "Be Masters in That You Teach and Continue to Learn: Medieval Muslim Thinkers on Educational Theory," 61–82; and Indira Falk Gesink, "Islamic Reformation: A History of *Madrasa* Reform and Legal Change in Egypt," 19–39; Joseph E. Lowry, Devin J. Stewart, and Shawkat M. Toorawa, eds., *Law and Education in Medieval Islam: Studies in Memory of Professor George Makdisi* (Cambridge: E. J. W. Gibb Memorial Trust, 2004): esp. Lowry, Stewart, and Toorawa, "Colleges of Law and the Institutions of Medieval Sunni Islam," 1–6; and Christopher Melchert, "The Etiquette of Learning in the Early Islamic Study Circle," 33–44; Maria Eva Subtelny and Anas B. Khalidov, "The Curriculum of Islamic Higher Learning in Timurid Iran in the Light of the Sunni Revival under Shah-Rukh," *Journal of the American Oriental Society* 115:2 (1995): 210–36; Yoginder Sikand, *Bastions of the Believers: Madrasas and Islamic Education in India* (New Delhi: Penguin Books India, 2005); Nenad Filipovic et al., "The Sultan's Syllabus: A Curriculum for the Ottoman Imperial *Medreses* Prescribed in a *Ferman* of Qanuni I Suleyman, Dated 973 (1565)," *Studia Islamica* (2004): 183–218; Claude Gilliot, ed., *Education and Learning in the Early Islamic World* (Aldershot, UK: Ashgate, 2008).

16. See George Makdisi, *The Rise of Colleges* (Edinburgh: Edinburgh University Press, 1981): 35–74; idem, "Muslim Institutions of Learning in Eleventh-Century Baghdad," *Bulletin of the Schools of Oriental and African Studies* 24:1 (1961): 1–56; idem, "On the Origin and Development of the College in Islam and the West," in *Islam and the Medieval West,* ed. K. I. Semaan (Albany: SUNY Press, 1980): 26–49, esp. 37 n. 47; idem, "The *Madrasa* in Spain: Some Remarks," *Revue de l'Occident Musulman et de la Mediteranée* (1973): 153–58; idem, *The Rise of Humanism in Classical Islam and the Christian West: With Special Reference to Scholasticism* (Edinburgh: University of Edinburgh Press, 1990); J. Pedersen and G. Makdisi, "Madrasa," *EI²* 5:1123–35.

17. See, e.g., William R. Jones, "Pious Endowments in Medieval Christianity and Islam," *Diogenes* 109 (1980): 23-36.

18. On this and the following section, see, e.g., L. Michael White, *The Social Origins of Christian Architecture,* vol. 1, *Building God's House in the Roman World: Architectural Adaptation among Pagans, Jews, and Christians,* and vol. 2, *Texts and Monuments for the Christian Domus Ecclesiae in Its Environment* (Valley Forge, PA: Trinity International, 1990).

19. Constantine's mother, Saint Helen, is celebrated for her role in promoting the building of the Church of the Holy Sepulcher in Jerusalem. For other sources on the history of Christian architecture, see, e.g., Richard Krautheimer, *Early Christian and Byzantine Architecture* (New Haven, CT: Yale University Press, 1984); Kenneth J. Conant, *Carolingian and Romanesque Architecture, 800–1200* (New Haven, CT: Yale University Press, 1992); Paul Frankl, *Gothic Architecture* (New Haven, CT: Yale University Press, 2001).

20. See, e.g., R. Kevin Seasoltz, *A Sense of the Sacred: Theological Foundations of Christian Architecture and Art* (New York: Continuum, 2005); Peter Murray, ed., *The Oxford Companion to Christian Art and Architecture* (New York: Oxford University Press, 1996); Richard Kieckhefer, *Theology in Stone: Church Architecture from Byzantium to Berkeley* (New York: Oxford University Press, 2008).

21. See, e.g., Kate Cooper and Julia Hillner, eds., *Religion, Dynasty, and Patronage in Early Christian Rome, 300–900* (Cambridge: Cambridge University Press, 2007); Jeanne Halgren Kilde, *Sacred Power, Sacred Space: An Introduction to Christian Architecture* (New York: Oxford University Press, 2008); Steven J. Schloeder, *Architecture in Communion: Implementing the Second Vatican Council through Liturgy and Architecture* (San Francisco: Ignatius, 1998); Terryl N. Kinder, *Cistercian Europe: Architecture of Contemplation* (Grand Rapids, MI: Eerdmans, 2002).

22. See, e.g., W. Montgomery Watt, *Muhammad at Mecca* (Oxford: Clarendon, 1953), 104–6; idem, *Muhammad at Medina* (Oxford: Clarendon, 1956), 198–204 and passim, on this and related points.

23. See, e.g., Robert Hillenbrand, *Islamic Architecture: Form, Function, and Meaning* (New York: Columbia University Press, 1994), esp. on mosque, mausoleum, and madrasa; John Hoag, *Islamic Architecture* (New York: Rizzoli, 1975), for samples of the regional and dynastic styles; George Michell, ed., *Architecture of the Islamic World: Its History and Social Meaning* (New York: Morrow, 1978).

24. Peter C. Hennigan, *The Birth of a Legal Institution: The Formation of the Waqf in Third-Century A.H. Hanafī Legal Discourse* (Leiden: Brill, 2004).

25. Erwin Panofsky, *Gothic Architecture and Scholasticism* (repr., Latrobe, PA: Archabbey, 2005); Otto von Simpson, *The Gothic Cathedral*, 2nd ed. (Princeton, NJ: Princeton University Press, 1962).

26. Charles Radding and William Clark, *Medieval Architecture, Medieval Learning: Builders and Masters in the Age of Romanesque and Gothic* (New Haven, CT: Yale University Press, 1992), 3. See also Allan Doig, *Liturgy and Architecture* (Aldershot, UK: Ashgate, 2008).

27. See Nader Ardalan, *The Sense of Unity* (Chicago: University of Chicago Press, 1973); T. Burckhardt, *Art of Islam: Language and Meaning* (London: World of Islam, 1976); S.H. Nasr, *Islamic Art and Spirituality* (Albany: SUNY Press, 1987); Lois Ibsen al-Faruqi's chapters on the arts, in *A Cultural Atlas of Islam,* by L. al-Faruqi and R. al-Faruqi (New York: Macmillan, 1986), 162–81, 354 ff.; also L. al-Faruqi, *Islam and Art* (Islamabad: National Hijra Council, 1985); idem, "Islam and Aesthetic Expression," *Islam and Contemporary Society* (London: Longman, Islamic Council of Europe, 1982): 191–212; idem, "An Islamic Perspective on Symbolism and the Arts," in *Art and the Sacred,* ed. Diane Apostolos-Cappadona (New York: Crossroad, 1984), 164–78. For yet another, more philosophical perspective, see Oliver Leaman, *Islamic Aesthetics: An Introduction* (Notre Dame, IN: University of Notre Dame, 2004). By far the most persuasive analysis of the use of symbolism in Islamic architecture appears in various works by Gülru Necipoğlu, including "The Suleymaniye Complex in Istanbul: An Interpretation," *Muqarnas* 3 (1985): 92–117; and "The Dome of the Rock as Palimpsest: 'Abd al-Malik's Grand Narrative and Sultan Suleyman's Glosses," *Muqarnas* 25 (2008): 17–105.

## 7. SOURCES, METHODS, AND SOCIAL VALUES IN THEOLOGICAL ETHICS

1. On Islamic literature, see, e.g., Margaretha T. Heemskerk, *Suffering in Muʿtazilite ʿAbd al-Jabbār's Teaching on Pain and Divine Justice* (Leiden: Brill,

2000); Fauzan Saleh, *The Problem of Evil in Islamic Theology: A Study on the Concept of al-qabāʾih in al-Qāḍī ʿAbd al-Jabbār al-Hamadhānī's Thought* (Ottawa: National Library of Canada [microform], 1993); also Jon Hoover, *Ibn Taymiyya's Theodicy of Perpetual Optimism* (Leiden: Brill, 2007); Eric Ormsby, *Theodicy in Islamic Thought: The Dispute over al-Ghazālī's "Best of All Possible Worlds"* (Princeton, NJ: Princeton University, 1987). For a general discussion on Christian ethics, see, e.g., John Mahoney, *The Making of Moral Theology: A Study of the Roman Catholic Tradition* (New York: Oxford University Press, 1987); Paul L. Lehmann, *Ethics in a Christian Context* (New York: Harper & Row, 1976). For the problem of evil in Christian thought, see, e.g., Peter van Inwagen, *The Problem of Evil: The Gifford Lectures Delivered in the University of St. Andrews in 2003* (New York: Oxford University Press, 2006).

2. See, e.g., Temba Mafico, ""Ethics: Old Testament," *ABD* 2:645–52.

3. See, e.g., Pheme Perkins, "Ethics: New Testament," *ABD* 2:652–55.

4. See, e.g., Daud Rahbar, *The God of Justice: A Study in the Ethical Doctrine of the Qurʾān* (Leiden: Brill, 1960); Toshihiku Izutsu, *Ethico-Religious Concepts in the Qurʾān* (Montreal: McGill University, 1966); idem, *God and Man in the Koran* (Tokyo: Keio University, 1964); Helmer Ringgren, *Studies in Arabian Fatalism* (Wiesbaden: Harrassowitz, 1955); W. Montgomery Watt, *Freewill and Predestination in Early Islam* (London: Luzac & Co., 1948); A. Kevin Reinhart, "Ethics and the Qurʾān," *EQ* 2:55–79.

5. On the various key pre-Islamic virtues, see articles in *EI²* on *dayf* (hospitality), *ḥamāsa* (valor), *ḥilm* (self-control), *ʿird* (personal honor), *kabīla* (tribal loyalty), and *murūwa* (virility). See also David L. Johnston, "Virtue," *EQ* 6:433–36; George F. Hourani, *Reason and Tradition in Islamic Ethics* (Cambridge: Cambridge University Press, 2002).

6. The foregoing sections summarize the argument in John Renard, "Muslim Ethics: Sources, Interpretations, and Challenges," *The Muslim World* 69:3 (1979): 163–77.

7. Muslim, *Ṣaḥīḥ Muslim* (Beirut: Dār Ibn Hazm, 1995), 4:1567–1615 and 4:1670–97.

8. See, e.g., Vigen Guroian, *Incarnate Love: Essays in Orthodox Ethics,* 2nd ed. (Notre Dame, IN: University of Notre Dame Press, 2002).

9. The entire previous section is summarized from a variety of sources: e.g., V. J. Bourke, "Ethics," *NCE* 5:388–92; G. J. Dalcourt, "Ethics, History of," *NCE* 3:392–98; J. M. Ramirez, "Moral Theology," *NCE* 9:848–58; F. X. Murphy, "Moral Theology, History of (to 700)," *NCE* 9:858–61; L. Vereecke, "Moral Theology, History of (700 to Vatican Council II)," *NCE* 9:861–64; J. J. Farraher, "Moral Theology, History of (20th-Century Developments)," *NCE* 9:864–65; N. J. Rigali, "Moral Theology, History of (Contemporary Trends)," *NCE* 9:865–70; M. M. Labourdette and M. Johnson, "Moral Theology, Methodology of," *NCE* 9:870–72; Charles Curran, "Christian Ethics," *ER* 2:340–48; idem, "Moral Theology," *ODCC*, 921–22; Renzo Gerardi, *Storia della morale: Interpretazione teologiche del' esperenza christiana* (Bologna: EDB, 2003); John Mahoney, *The Making of Moral Theology: A Study of the Roman Catholic Tradition* (Oxford: Clarendon, 1987); John A. Gallagher, *Time Past, Time Future: An Historical Study of Catholic Moral Theology* (New York: Paulist, 1990).

10. See, e.g., Alasdair MacIntyre, *After Virtue: A Study in Moral Theory*, 3rd ed. (Notre Dame, IN: University of Notre Dame Press, 2007), as a response to "modernity"; and the more classic Evangelical treatment of Glen H. Stassen and David P. Gushee, *Kingdom Ethics: Following Jesus in the Contemporary Context* (Downer's Grove, IL: Intervarsity, 2003).

11. F. Gabrieli, "Adab," *EI²* 1:175–76.

12. See L. Gardet, *"Kasb:* As theological term," *EI²* 692–94; further on Mu'tazilite ethics, see, e.g., several works by George Hourani: *Islamic Rationalism: The Ethics of ʿAbd al-Jabbār* (Oxford: Clarendon, 1971); "The Rationalist Ethics of ʿAbd al-Jabbār," in *Islamic Philosophy and the Classical Tradition*, ed. S. M. Stern, Albert Hourani, and Vivian Brown (Oxford: Cassirer, 1972), 105–15; "Juwayni's Criticism of Mu'tazilite Ethics," *The Muslim World* 65 (1975): 161–73; "Two Theories of Value in Medieval Islam," *The Muslim World* 50 (1960): 269–78; "Ethics in Medieval Islam: A Conspectus," in *Essays on Islamic Philosophy and Science*, ed. George Hourani (Albany: SUNY Press, 1975), 128–35.

13. Ahmad ibn Muhammad Miskawayh, *The Refinement of Character*, trans. Constantine K. Zurayk (Beirut: Centennial, 1968; repr., Kazi, 2003); see also the editors' entry "Miskawayh," *EI²* 7:143–44.

14. R. Walzer and H. A. R. Gibb, "Akhlāk," *EI²* 1:325–29; see also, on Ghazālī's ethics, Muhammad Umaruddin, *The Ethical Philosophy of al-Ghazzali* (Aligarh, 1951); idem, "Ghazālī on the Ethics of Action," *JAOS* 96 (1976): 69–88; Franz Rosenthal, *The Muslim Concept of Freedom* (Leiden: Brill, 1960). See also Ghazālī, *The Alchemy of Happiness*, trans. Claude Field, rev. Elton Daniel (Armonk, NY: Sharpe, 1991).

15. For a comparative study on environmental stewardship, see David L. Johnston, *Earth, Empire, and Sacred Text: Muslims and Christians as Trustees of Creation* (London: Equinox, 2009).

16. Recent studies on the Islamic side include Amyn Sajoo, *Muslim Ethics: Emerging Vistas* (New York: Tauris, 2008); Th. Emil Homerin, "The Golden Rule in Islam," in *The Golden Rule: The Ethics of Reciprocity in World Religions*, ed. Jacob Neusner and Bruce Chilton (New York: Continuum, 2008), 99–115; Ahmad Hasan, "Social Justice in Islam," *Islamic Studies* 10 (1971): 209–19; Jonathan Brockopp, *Islamic Ethics of Life: Abortion, War, and Euthanasia* (Columbia: University of South Carolina Press, 2003); Mohammad Hashim Kamali, *The Dignity of Man: An Islamic Perspective* (Cambridge: Islamic Texts Society, 2002); idem, *Equity and Fairness in Islam* (Cambridge: Islamic Texts Society, 2005); idem, *Freedom, Equality, and Justice in Islam* (Cambridge: Islamic Texts Society, 2002); Sohail H. Hashmi, *Islamic Political Ethics: Civil Society, Pluralism, and Conflict* (Princeton, NJ: Princeton University Press, 2002); Kecia Ali, *Sexual Ethics and Islam: Feminist Reflections on Qur'ān, Hadith, and Jurisprudence* (Oxford: Oneworld, 2006); Sumner B. Twiss and Bruce Grelle, *Explorations in Global Ethics: Comparative Religious Ethics and Interreligious Dialogue* (Boulder, CO: Westview, 2000); David Joseph Wellman, *Sustainable Diplomacy: Ecology, Religion, and Ethics in Muslim-Christian Relations* (New York: Palgrave Macmillan, 2004); Camille Mansour, *L'autorité dans la pensée musulmane* (Paris: J. Vrin, 1975).

17. Cf. Mt 8:1–4, 9:9–13, 12:1–8, 23:1–36; Mk 1:40–45, 2:13–17, 23–28, 3:1–6, 7:1–23; Lk 5:27–32, 6:1–11, 7:36–50, 11:37–54, 16:19–31, 18:9–14; Jn 4:1–42, 8:1–11.

18. See, e.g., Richard B. Hays, *The Moral Vision of the New Testament: Community, Cross, New Creation; A Contemporary Introduction to New Testament Ethics* (San Francisco: HarperCollins, 1996); Frank J. Matera, *New Testament Ethics: The Legacies of Jesus and Paul* (Louisville, KY: Westminster John Knox, 1996).

19. See, e.g., G.H.A. Juynboll, "Sunna," *EI*² 9:878–81. See also Annemarie Schimmel, "Muhammad the Beautiful Model," in *And Muhammad Is His Messenger* (Chapel Hill: University of North Carolina Press, 1985), 24–55.

20. See Mikel de Epalza, "Los nombres del Profeta en la teologia musulmana," *Miscelanea Comillas* 33:2 (1975): 149–203; Schimmel, "The Names of the Prophet," in *And Muhammad Is His Messenger*, 105–22. On the Hadith of Gabriel, see Sachiko Murata and William Chittick, *The Vision of Islam* (New York: Paragon, 1994).

21. Michael Cook, *Commanding Right and Forbidding Wrong in Islamic Thought* (Cambridge: Cambridge University Press, 2000); idem, "Virtues and Vices, Commanding and Forbidding," *EQ* 6:436–43.

22. Translated from Arabic text in *Sahīh al-Bukhārī* (Beirut: Dār as-Sādir, 1995), 4:1074–75 (no. 5).

23. *Sahīh Muslim, Kitāb al-masāqa,* 3:979 (no. 31).

24. *Sahīh Muslim, Kitāb al-īmān,* 1:109 (no. 204).

25. Translated from Arabic text in *Sayings of Muhammad,* ed. Ghazi Ahmad (Lahore: Sh. Muhammad Ashraf, 1972), 34.

## 8. SOURCES AND MODELS IN TRADITIONS OF SPIRITUALITY

1. For a general introduction, see I. Nowell, "Psalms, Book of," *NCE* 11:794–97. For liturgical use of the Psalms in different Christian traditions, see John Alexander Lamb, *The Psalms in Christian Worship* (London: Faith, 1962); Harold W. Attridge and Margot E. Fassler, eds., *Psalms in Community: Jewish and Christian Textual, Liturgical, and Artistic Traditions* (Atlanta: Society of Biblical Literature, 2003). For christological interpretation of the Psalms, see Hans-Joachim Kraus, *Theology of the Psalms,* trans. Keith Crim (Minneapolis: Augsburg, 1986), 177–203.

2. For an Islamic version, see J. W. T. Allen, trans., "Job's Wife in the Swahili *Epic of Job,*" in *Tales of God's Friends,* ed. John Renard (Berkeley: University of California Press, 2009), 197–206. For Wisdom literature and spirituality, see, e.g., Kathleen M. O'Connor, *The Wisdom Literature* (Wilmington, DE: M. Glazier, 1988).

3. See William Graham, *Divine Word and Prophetic Word in Early Islam* (Hague: Mouton, 1977), for these and many other examples; also J. Robson, "Hadith" and "Hadith Kudsi," *EI*² 3:23–29.

4. Perhaps the most representative classic work is Thomas à Kempis's *Imitation of Christ.*

5. The most representative work is Saint Athanasius's *On the Incarnation,* trans. C.S.M.V., with an introduction by C. S. Lewis (Crestwood, NY: St. Vladimir's Seminary, 1996). For the key role of incarnation in the teachings of the church fathers, see, e.g., Christopher Alan Hall, *Learning Theology with the Church Fathers* (Downers Grove, IL: InterVarsity, 2002).

6. H. E. W. Turner, *The Patristic Doctrine of Redemption: A Study of the Development of Doctrine during the First Five Centuries* (London: Mowbray, 1952).

7. See J. Lewis, "Spiritual Exercises," *NCE* 13:430–33. For the relationship between Ignatian spirituality and Christ, see, e.g., Robert L. Schmitt, SJ, "The Christ-Experience and Relationship Fostered in the Spiritual Exercises of St. Ignatius of Loyola," *Studies in the Spirituality of Jesuits* 6:5 (1974): 217–55.

8. See, e.g., Catholic Church, *Catechism of the Catholic Church,* 2nd ed. (Vatican City: Libreria Editrice Vaticana; Washington, DC: Distributed by United States Catholic Conference, 2000); see part 4 on the theme of the Lord's Prayer.

9. For a further elaboration of this three-part model of Muhammad's spiritual example, see John Renard, *Understanding the Islamic Experience* (Mahwah, NJ: Paulist, 2002); see also Carl W. Ernst, *Following Muhammad: Rethinking Islam in the Contemporary World* (Chapel Hill: University of North Carolina Press, 2003); and Omid Safi, *Memories of Muhammad: Why the Prophet Matters* (New York: HarperOne, 2009).

10. My translation from Arabic text in A. H. Farid, *Prayers of Muhammad* (Lahore: Sh. M. Ashraf, 1974), 217.

11. See "Canonization of Saints (History and Procedure)," *NCE* 3:61–66; see also the following entries: "Saints and Beati," *NCE* 12:607–8; "Beatification," *NCE* 2:177; "Venerable," *NCE* 14:434.

12. See John Renard, *Friends of God: Islamic Images of Piety, Commitment, and Servanthood* (Berkeley: University of California Press, 2008); and Renard, *Tales of God's Friends.*

13. For general background, see, e.g., Lawrence Cunningham, *A Brief History of Saints* (Malden, MA: Blackwell, 2005); Lynda L. Coon, *Sacred Fictions: Holy Women and Hagiography in Late Antiquity* (Philadelphia: University of Pennsylvania Press, 1997), esp. chaps. 1 and 2.

14. See "Polycarp," *EEC,* 2:701; "Perpetua and Felicity," *EEC,* 2:670–71.

15. See "Martyrology," *EEC,* 1:536–37; "Hagiography," *EEC,* 1:370; "Martin of Tours [c. 316–97]," *EEC,* 1:531.

16. See "Paulinus of Nola," *EEC,* 2:660–61; "Ambrose of Milan," *EEC,* 1:28–29.

17. See F. Halkin, "Hagiography," *NCE* 6:613–16; Robert Cohn, "Sainthood," *ER* 13:1–6.

18. *The Life of Muhammad: A Translation of Ibn Ishaq's "Sirat Rasul Allah,"* trans. A. Guillaume (Oxford: Oxford University Press, 1955), 3–4; Lk 3:23–28.

19. *Life of Muhammad,* trans. Guillaume, 181–82.

20. E.g., Ibn Khafīf (d. 982), Abū Ishāq al-Kāzarūnī (d. 1033), and Abū Saʿīd ibn Abī 'l-Khayr (d. 1049).

21. For a global thematic overview and primary texts, see Renard, *Friends of God* and *Tales of God's Friends.*

22. See chapter 11 of Renard, *Friends of God,* for a summary of theological dimensions of the miracle/marvel.

23. Victor Turner and Edith Turner, *Image and Pilgrimage in Christian Culture* (New York: Columbia University Press, 1978), 33.

24. Summarized from *Sir Gawain and the Green Knight, Pearl, and Sir Orfeo,* trans. J. R. R. Tolkien (New York: Ballantine, 1980), 123–68; see also a very accessible translation online at http://www.hccentral.com/eller10/index.html.

25. 'Attār, *The Conference of the Birds* [abridged], trans. C.S. Nott (New York: Samuel Weiser, 1969), 31 and 131. For a more complete verse translation, see 'Attār, *The Conference of the Birds*, trans. A. Darbandi and D. Davis (New York: Penguin, 1984). For a brief analysis of the work, see James W. Morris, "Reading *The Conference of the Birds*," in *Approaches to Asian Classics*, ed. W. de Bary (New York: Columbia University Press, 1990), 77–85.

## 9. THEMES IN PRAYER AND MYSTICAL THEOLOGY

1. See Kenneth Cragg's general comparison of Muslim and Christian prayers in his introductory essay in his *Alive to God: Muslim and Christian Prayer* (New York: Oxford University Press, 1970), 1–55; see also his *Common Prayer: A Muslim-Christian Spiritual Anthology* (Oxford: Oneworld, 1999).

2. See *Catechism of the Catholic Church* (Washington, DC: U.S. Conference of Catholic Bishops, 2003), 247–50.

3. See P. J. Mahoney, "Intercession," *NCE* 7:519–20.

4. My translation of the Latin text from http://the-orb.net/encyclop/culture/music/mather.html (accessed March 21, 2009).

5. My translation of both hymns from the Latin text.

6. Text at http://www.online-literature.com/donne/863/ (accessed March 21, 2009).

7. Text at http://www.poemhunter.com/poem/bitter-sweet/ (accessed March 21, 2009).

8. Text at http://www.bartleby.com/122/34.html (accessed March 21, 2009).

9. My translation from the Persian of Sanā'ī's *Hadīqat al-Haqīqat*, 1:2–11; Persian text in *The First Book of the Hadiqatu'l-Haqiqat, or The Enclosed Garden of the Truth*, ed. and trans. Major J. Stephenson (New York: Samuel Weiser, 1971), 1.

10. My translation from Arabic text in A. J. Arberry, *Mystical Poems of Ibn al-Fārid* (London: Chester Beatty, 1954), 39–40, lines 45–56.

11. Kojiro Nakamura, trans., *Ghazālī on Prayer* (Tokyo: Institute of Oriental Culture, 1973), 109, 117.

12. William Chittick, trans., *The Psalms of Islam* (London: Muhammad Trust, 1988), quoting from p. 245, used with permission of the translator and copyright holder. For a survey of popular traditional prayers, see Constance Padwick, *Muslim Devotions: A Study of Prayer-Manuals in Common Use* (Oxford: Oneworld, 1996).

13. Listen, for example, to any of the many recordings of the late Nusret Fath Ali Khan for samples of the intense affection lavished on the Prophet and scores of South Asian Friends of God.

14. See Kenneth Cragg, *The Mind of the Qur'ān: Chapters in Reflection* (London: Allen and Unwin, 1973), 30–31.

15. This and subsequent sections summarized from Louis Bouyer, *A History of Christian Spirituality*, vol. 1, *The Spirituality of the New Testament and the Fathers* (New York: Seabury, 1963); Jean LeClerq, François VandenBroucke, and Louis Bouyer, *A History of Christian Spirituality*, vol. 2, *The Spirituality of the Middle Ages* (New York: Seabury, 1968); Louis Bouyer, *A History of Christian Spirituality*, vol. 3, *Orthodox Spirituality and Protestant and Anglican Spiritual-*

*ity* (New York: Seabury, 1969); Bernard McGinn, *The Foundations of Mysticism: Origins to the Fifth Century* (New York: Crossroad, 1994); idem, *The Growth of Mysticism: Gregory the Great through the 12th Century* (New York: Crossroad, 1994); idem, *The Flowering of Mysticism: Men and Women in the New Mysticism—1200–1350* (New York: Crossroad, 1998); idem, *The Harvest of Mysticism in Medieval Germany* (New York: Crossroad, 2008); Moshe Idel and Bernard McGinn, eds., *Mystical Union in Judaism, Christianity, and Islam: An Ecumenical Dialogue* (New York: Crossroad, 1996).

16. Especially Basil of Caesarea (d. 379), Gregory Nazianzen (d. 389/90), Gregory of Nyssa (d. 395), Cyril of Alexandria (d. 444), Jerome (d. 420), and Augustine (d. 430).

17. Here we see the development of a distinction and theoretical tension between the science of theology and the ineffable experiential phenomenon of mysticism that began with Clement of Alexandria. See Henny Fiskå Hägg, *Clement of Alexandria and the Beginnings of Christian Apophaticism* (Oxford: Oxford University Press, 2006). For a comparative analysis of apophatic mysticism, see Michael Sells, *Mystical Languages of Unsaying* (Chicago: University of Chicago Press, 1994).

18. See, e.g., John Meyendorff, *St. Gregory Palamas and Orthodox Spirituality* (Yonkers, NY: St. Vladimir's Seminary, 1997); Vladimir Lossky, *The Mystical Theology of the Eastern Church* (Yonkers, NY: St. Vladimir's Seminary, 1997); Sebastian Brock, *Syriac Fathers on Prayer and the Spiritual Life* (Kalamazoo, MI: Cistercian, 1988); and for a comparative view, see James Cutsinger, *Paths to the Heart: Sufism and the Christian East* (Bloomington, IN: World Wisdom, 2004).

19. See, e.g., Robert Fastiggi, *The Mystical Theology of the Catholic Reformation: An Overview of Baroque Spirituality* (Lanham, MD: University Press of America, 2006).

20. Gerhard Böwering, *The Mystical Vision of Existence in Classical Islam: The Qur'ānic Hermeneutics of the Sufi Sahl at-Tustarī* (Berlin: Walter de Gruyter, 1980), 144–60.

21. Summarized from Michael Sells, *Early Islamic Mysticism: Sufi, Qur'ān, Poetic and Theological Writings* (Mahwah, NJ: Paulist, 1996); John Renard, ed. and trans., *Knowledge of God in Classical Sufism: Foundations of Islamic Mystical Theology* (Mahwah, NJ: Paulist, 2004). Other authors of major compendia included Muhāsibī (d. 857, *Book of the Observance of the Rights of God*); Abū Sa'īd al-Kharrāz (d. c. 899, *Book of Spiritual Authenticity*); Kalābādhī (d. 990 or 994, *Exploration of the Teachings of Those Who Subscribe to Sufism*); Abū Tālib of Mecca (d. 996, *Sustenance of Hearts*); Hujwīrī (d. 1072, *Revelation of Realities Veiled*, the first of its kind in Persian); Qushayrī (d. 1072, *Treatise on Sufism*). The last broadly influential work in the genre was Abū Hafs 'Umar as-Suhrawardī's (d. 1234) *Benefits of Intimate Knowledge*.

22. See William Chittick, *The Self-Disclosure of God* (Albany: SUNY Press, 1997); idem, *The Sufi Path of Knowledge: Ibn al-'Arabī's Metaphysics of Imagination* (Albany: SUNY Press, 1989); also Claude Addas, *Quest for the Red Sulphur: The Life of Ibn 'Arabī* (Cambridge: Islamic Texts Society, 1993); James W. Morris, *The Reflective Heart: Discovering Spiritual Intelligence in Ibn 'Arabi's 'Meccan Illuminations'* (Louisville, KY: Fons Vitae, 2005).

23. Yusuf Ibish, "Ibn Arabi's Theory of Journeying," in *Traditional Modes*

*of Contemplation and Action*, ed. Y. Ibish and P.L. Wilson (Tehran: Imperial Iranian Academy of Philosophy, 1971), 441–46.

24. Such poets include Sanā'ī (d. 1131), 'Attār (d. 1221), Rūmī (d. 1274), and Sa'dī (d. 1292).

25. For a brief anthology of mystical lyric, see David Fideler and Sabrineh Fideler, *Love's Alchemy: Poems from the Sufi Tradition* (Novato, CA: New World Library, 2006); for a scholarly approach, see Fatemeh Keshavarz, *Reading Mystical Lyric: The Case of Jalal al-Din Rumi* (Columbia: University of South Carolina Press, 1998); and on contemporary Persian poetry, see idem, *Recite in the Name of the Red Rose: Poetic Sacred Making in Twentieth-Century Iran* (Columbia: University of South Carolina Press, 2006).

26. For interesting approaches to various other texts and authors, see Ayman Shihadeh, ed., *Sufism and Theology* (Edinburgh: University of Edinburgh Press, 2008); see also Toby Mayer, "Theology and Sufism," in *The Cambridge Companion to Classical Islamic Theology*, ed. Tim Winter (Cambridge: Cambridge University Press, 2008), 258–87.

27. Rūmī, *Masnavī-yi Ma'nawī*, ed. M. Estelami (Tehran, 1990), 3:189–97.

EPILOGUE

1. Rūmī, *The Masnavi: Book One*, trans. Jawid Mojaddedi (Oxford: Oxford University Press, 2004), 174–75, lines 2847–64.

2. Robert Cummings Neville, *Behind the Masks of God: An Essay toward Comparative Theology* (Albany: SUNY Press, 1991), 166.

3. A "pluralist" model proposed by John Cobb and Paul Knitter is another important possibility in this context; see, e.g., Paul Knitter, *Introducing Theologies of Religions* (Maryknoll, NY: Orbis, 2002); John B. Cobb, Jr., *Transforming Christianity and the World: A Way beyond Absolutism and Relativism*, ed. Paul Knitter (Maryknoll, NY: Orbis, 1999).

4. Neville, *Behind the Masks of God*, 166–67.

5. N. Ross Reat and Edmund F. Perry, *A World Theology: The Central Spiritual Reality of Humankind* (Cambridge: Cambridge University Press, 1991), 313 [my emphasis] and frontispiece.

6. Ibid., 266; see also Wilfred Cantwell Smith, *Towards a World Theology: Faith and the Comparative History of Religion* (Philadelphia: Westminster, 1981).

7. Reat and Perry, *World Theology*, 266.

8. Ibid., 275.

9. Ibid., 289.

10. Ibid., 302.

11. Neville, *Behind the Masks of God*, 12, 155. Two other programmatic comments by Neville are worth noting: "The contemporary problem in theology is to construct a concept of divinity that functions to organize the multitude of concepts, symbols, images, and referring practices so that the questions of agreement, disagreement, and truth can be formulated" (9); "Any attempt to limit the drive toward a worldwide community of inquirers to which any theological enterprise ought to be responsible makes theology uncritical and hence untheological. The development of theology in our time is thus part of larger forces that may well

transform our economic and military world society into a somewhat richer world culture. Put negatively, the failure of the drive toward world theology is but one of the many demons pushing the accident of world society toward total conflagration" (163).

12. Saʿdī, *Bustān* (The Orchard), 2:37–54, ed. C.H. Graf (Vienna, 1858), 142–43; A.R. Kidwai, "Leigh Hunt's 'Abraham and the Fire-Worshipper': A Possible Source," *N&Q* 43 (1996): 44–45.

13. "Neither on this mountain, nor in Jerusalem will you worship . . . but in spirit and truth" (Jn 4:21–24).

14. "*Nostra Aetate*," in *Documents of the Second Vatican Council,* ed. Walter M. Abbott and Joseph Gallagher (New York: Guild, 1966).

15. Charles S. Peirce, "A Neglected Argument for the Reality of God," in *Values in a Universe of Choice,* ed. Philip Wiener (Stanford: Stanford University Press, 1958), 358–79, quoting from pp. 359, 360, and 361.

16. W.M. Thackston, trans., *Signs of the Unseen: The Discourses of Jalaluddin Rumi* (Putney, VT: Threshold, 1994), 164.

17. Richard McCarthy, *Freedom and Fulfillment* (Boston: Twayne, 1980), lix.

18. Ibid.

# Theological Glossary

A = Arabic, G = Greek, Gm = German, H = Hebrew, L = Latin, P = Persian

*'abd* (A)  servant (or worshipper)

*'adā* (A)  customary law, or *'urf*

*adab* (A)  virtuous behavior

*adab al-manāqib* (A)  literature of extraordinary achievements, hagiography

*'adl* (A)  justice, divine quality acc. to Mu'tazila and Shī'a

*agape* (G)  love

*agnosia* (G)  unknowing

*ahādīth al-fitan* (A)  traditions of discord (a subgenre of Hadith)

*Ahādīth Qudsīya* (A)  Sacred Hadith (God speaks in the first person)

*ahl al-kitāb* (A)  People of the Book (i.e., Jews, Christians, Muslims)

*'ālim* (A)  knowledgeable person, religious scholar (pl. *'ulamā'*)

*al-jāhilīya* (A)  age of ignorance (previous to revelation delivered through Muhammad)

*allegoria* (L)  a spiritual interpretation (one of the four senses of scripture)

*al-qiyāma* (A)  resurrection

*anagogia* (L)  an eschatological interpretation (one of the four senses of scripture)

*aphairesis* (G)  transcendence

*apophasis* (G)  unsaying, or negative (theology)

*apostellein* (G)  to send; root of "apostle"

*'aqā'id* (A)  creedal formulations, creeds (pl. of *'aqīda)*

*'aqīda* (A)  element of belief, doctrine

*'aql* (A)  rational or intellectual approaches

*ar-rahīm* (A)  the Compassionate (divine name)

*ar-rahmān* (A)  the Merciful (divine name)

*asbāb an-nuzūl* (A)  circumstances of the revelation (Qur'ānic analogue to *Sitz im Leben*) *'ashara mubāshara* (A)  Ten Recipients of Good News

*as-sāʿa(h)* (A)  the hour (of judgment)

*āyāt* (A)  signs, verses (sg. *āya*)

*āyatullāh* (A)  sign of God, title of high-ranking Twelver Shiite cleric

*barzakh* (A)  the separation (an intermediate state between death and resurrection)

*basilica* (L)  imperial hall; church architecture (*basileus* = king)

*bātin* (A)  inward, hidden, or esoteric meaning of scripture or law

*bidʿa* (A)  innovation, deviation from right belief/practice, opp. of *sunna*

*bī-lā kayf* (A)  without asking how (in regard to understanding Qurʾan)

*bʾrith* (H)  covenant (key Old Testament concept)

*charis* (G)  divine grace, goodwill, favor

*dajjāl* (A)  Muslim name for Antichrist

*daʿwā* (A)  inviting, apologetics, invitation, proselytizing

*dawla* (A)  political entity, regime, "state"

*derash* (H)  reflection (one of four modes of exegesis)

*dhikr* (A)  remembrance of God, including the repetition of names of God

*dhimmī* (A)  protected minority, Peoples of the Book

*diakonoi* (G)  deacons, early "rank" in Christian church structure

*dīn* (A)  religion

*ekklesia* (G)  assembly, church

*encheiridion* (G)  handbook, classical manual of Christian theology

*episkopos* (G)  overseer, bishop

*extasis* (G)  ecstasy, the obliteration of distinction between knower and Known

*fāsiq* (A)  fabricator, category of theologically errant thinker; corrupter (pl. *fasiqūn*)

*fatwā* (A)  legal advisory indicating level of acceptability of possible acts (pl. *fatāwa*)

*filioque* (L)  and [from] the Son (Western insertion in the Nicene Creed)

*fiqh* (A)  profound comprehension, jurisprudence, positive law

*firqa* (A)  sect, faction (pl. *firaq*)

*fitna* (A)  trial, tribulation (apocalyptic), temptation to apostasy, civil war

*fitra* (A)  innate disposition, original condition of every human being at birth

*fuqahāʾ* (A)  legists, jurisprudents (sg. *faqīh*)

*gnosis* (G)  knowledge, esoteric or saving knowledge

*hadīth* (A)  sayings of, anecdotes about, Muhammad

*hairesis* (G)  choice, theological opinion, later "heresy" as incorrect belief

*hanīf* (A)  seeker after the one God, Abraham being the first

*haqq* (A)  the Truth (name of God)

*henosis* (G)  oneness, unification (with God)

*hijra* (A)  Muslim migration to Medina in 622 C.E.

*historia* (L)  generally literal interpretation (one of the four senses of scripture)

*homoiousios* (G)  of similar substance (term in Christian Trinitarian debates)

*homoousios* (G)  of identical substance (term in Christian Trinitarian debates)

*hypostasis* (G)  substance (technical term in Trinitarian theology)

*ihsān* (A)  doing what is beautiful, or putting *īmān* and *islām* into action

*ihyā* (A)  bringing back to life, revival

*ijmāʿ* (A)  consensus, originally of community, later only of religious scholars

*ijtihād* (A)  exercise of independent investigation and interpretation, juristic method

*ikhtilāf* (A)  divergence of scholarly opinion

*ikhtiyār* (A) freedom of choice
*iktisāb* (A) acquisition of acts (see also *kasb*)
*'ilm* (A) traditional, discursive, acquired knowledge
*imān* (A) faith
*intelligo ut credam* (L) "I seek understanding in service of faith" (Thomistic view)
*irjā'* (A) postponement, deferring to God's judgment regarding another's state
*islām* (A) surrender to God
*isnād* (A) chain of transmitters in Hadith studies
*istihsāb* (A) lit., presumption of a condition's perdurance (legal principle)
*istihsān* (A) seeking the good (legal principle)
*istislāh* (A) seeking *maslaha*, or broader public interest (legal principle)
*jabr/jabrīya* (A) moral compulsion; school that holds this view
*jadal* (A) dialectical discourse/thinking
*jalāl* (A) God's majesty, transcendence
*jamāl* (A) God's attractive beauty, immanence
*jihād* (A) struggle, exertion, including religiously sanctioned warfare
*jihād an-nafs* (A) battle against the ego-soul, spiritual struggle
*kāfir* (A) unbeliever (pl. *kuffār*)
*kalām* (A) discourse, short for *'ilm al-kalām*, dialectical/systematic theology
*karāma* (A) marvel worked through a nonprophetic figure, or Friend of God
*kasb* (A) acquisition, human appropriation of actions created by God
*kataphasis* (G) speaking out, or positive (theology)
*kenosis* (G) emptying (christological concept of divine condescension to human condition)
*kerygma* (G) proclamation (the earliest narrative of Christian belief)
*khalīfa* (A) vice-gerent, successor, caliph
*khawārij* (A) seceders, separatists over identify of true Muslims (sg. *khārij*)
*koinoia* (G) communion, sharing
*kufr* (A) covering over, unbelief, generic for "heresy"
*Logos* (G) Word (of God), title of Christ
*ma'ād* (A) return; eschatology: "resurrection" of bodies and souls at Judgment
*madhhab* (A) way of proceeding, school of legal methodology (pl. *madhāhib*)
*madrasa* (A) place of study, institution of higher learning (medieval)
*mahdī* (A) guided one returning at end of time (Sunnī); twelfth imam (Shī'ā)
*ma'rifa* (A) intimate, experiential, infused, esoteric, mystical knowledge
*masjid* (A) place of prostration, mosque
*ma'sūm* (A) impeccable, beyond reproach, quality of Prophet, Friends, Shi'i imams
*mathētai* (G) learners (i.e., Jesus' disciples)
*midrash* (H) lit., to study; homiletic method of Jewish exegesis (mostly used to denote the compilation of such exegesis)
*mihna* (A) inquisition, theological court of the Mu'tazila (early ninth century)
*mīthāq* (A) covenant, divine-human relationship from creation on
*mu'jiza* (A) miracles worked through a prophet (distinct from *karāma*)
*mujtahid* (A) jurist, one authorized to exercise *ijtihād*
*mulhid* (A) one who deviates from correct path, apostate, heretic
*munāzar* (A) theological disputation
*murji'a* (A) postponers, who argued that only God judges one's eternal destiny

*mutakallimūn* (A) those who engage in *kalām,* systematic theologians

*mutashābihāt* (A) metaphorical or allegorical (open to interpretation especially regarding Qur'ānic texts)

*mu'tazila* (A) those who practice *i'tizāl* (hold themselves aloof), early systematic theologians

*nabī* (A) prophet, divine emissary (more general)

*naql* (A) traditional Islamic disciplines (revelation)

*naskh* (A) abrogation, supersession of one revealed text by a later one

*ordo* (L) ecclesial (clerical) rank

*ousia* (G) substance (term in Trinitarian theology)

*Pantokrator* (G) Creator of All, Orthodox title of Christ

*paraklētos* (G) advocate, name of Holy Spirit

*physis* (G) nature (key term in christological debates)

*pneuma* (G) spirit

*presbyteroi* (G) elders, early term for "priest"

*psyche* (G) spirit, soul

*qadā* (A) immutable and inexorable divine decree

*qadar* (A) power, moral agency, capability to determine events (also *qudra*)

*qadarīya* (A) theological school focusing on centrality of human freedom to act

*qadr* (A) God's dominion over human affairs

*qibla* (A) direction of orientation for Islamic ritual prayer, Mecca-facing wall of mosque

*qiyās* (A) analogical reasoning; *qiyās khafī:* covert analogical reasoning

*rasūl* (A) messenger, prophet sent with universal message

*ra'y* (A) individual judgment

*rūh* (A) spirit

*ru'ya bi 'l-absār* (A) vision of God, ocular sight of God in next life

*sahāba* (A) Companions (of the Prophet), first generation of Muslims

*sarrakenophroni* (G) Saracen-minded, reference to some Middle-Eastern Christian theologians

*sensus fidelium* (L) general understanding of believers

*shafā'a* (A) "to make the odd even," advocacy before God on behalf of another, hence "intercession"

*shahāda* (A) profession of faith (= Islamic "creed")

*sharī'a* (A) revealed law, embracing positive law in practice (*sunna, fiqh*)

*shī'a* (A) party, faction, original supporters of 'Alī's claim to caliphal rule

*shirk* (A) associating partners with God, hence "idolatry"

*sifāt* (A) attributes of God (key term in early Muslim theological debates)

*sirāt al-mustaqīm* (A) straight path, metaphor for core Islamic beliefs and practices

*Sitz im Leben* (Gm) life-situation, context of New Testament text in Jesus' life

*sunna* (A) example of the Prophet, individual requirements of Muslim belief

*sura* (A) segment, chapter

*tābi'ūn* (A) Followers (of the Prophet), second generation of Muslims

*tafsīr* (A) elaboration, ordinary exegesis of Qur'ān

*taghyīr* (A) alleged alteration of content of sacred text by Jews and Christians

*tahrīf* (A) alleged tampering with sacred text by Jews and Christians

*takfīr* (A) pronouncing someone guilty of *kufr,* anathematizing for unbelief *tanzīh* (A)  uniqueness, otherness, transcendence as theological category

*taqlīd* (A)  mere conformity, unquestioning acceptance of authority

*tarīqa* (A)  way, path (especially connected to Sufism)

*tashbīh* (A)  likening, being similar, immanence as a theological category; anthropo-
    morphism as a category of error/heresy

*ta'tīl* (A)  denial of all attributes to God, opp. of *tashbīh* (syn. *tanzīh*)

*tawhīd* (A)  divine transcendent unity

*ta'wīl* (A)  taking back to beginnings; esoteric/mystical, nontraditional, sometimes
    "erroneous," exegesis

*theanthropos* (G)  divine-human

*theosis* (G)  divinization, deification

*theotokos* (G)  God-bearer, title of Mary

*trivium* (L)  three of the seven liberal arts: grammar, rhetoric, logic

*tropologia* (L)  an ethical interpretation (one of the four senses of scripture)

*'ulamā'* (A)  religious scholars generally (sg. *'ālim*)

*umma* (A)  global Muslim community

*ummi* (A)  unlettered (Ummi: title of Muhammad)

*wajd* (A)  finding, being found, and existing; a spiritual process

*waqf* (A)  pious endowment, funding of religious institution

*zāhir* (A)  outer, apparent, or evident meaning; exoteric interpretation

*zandaqa* (A)  heresy, initially indicating dualism, as in Manichaeism

*zāwiya* (A)  corner (humble residence for prayer); sometimes syn. with *ribāt*,
    *khānqāh*

*zindīq* (A/P)  heretic/dualist (originally from *zand,* Zoroastrian commentary on the
    scripture Avesta)

*zuhd* (A)  detachment, asceticism

*zulm* (A)  evil or injustice, deeds of a tyrant

# Selected Bibliography

Abbott, Walter M., and Joseph Gallagher, eds. *Documents of the Second Vatican Council*. New York: Guild, 1966.

Abun-Nasr, Jamil M. *Muslim Communities of Grace: The Sufi Brotherhoods in Islamic Religious Life*. New York: Columbia University Press, 2007.

Ackroyd, Peter, and C. F. Evans, eds. *Cambridge History of the Bible*. Vol. 1, *From the Beginnings to Jerome*. Cambridge: Cambridge University Press, 1975.

Adam, A. K. M., Stephen E. Fowl, and Kevin J. Vanhoozer. *Reading Scripture with the Church: Toward a Hermeneutic for Theological Interpretation*. Grand Rapids, MI: Baker, 2006.

Al Kalby, Kais. *Prophet Muhammad: The Last Messenger in the Bible*. Bakersfield, CA: American Muslim Cultural Association, 2005.

Allard, Michel. *Le problème des attributs divins dans la doctrine d'al-Ash'arī et des ses premiers grands disciples*. Beirut: Imprimerie Catholique, 1965.

Amanat, Abbas. *Apocalyptic Islam and Iranian Shi'ism*. London: I. B. Tauris, 2009.

Amir-Moezzi, Mohammad Ali. *The Divine Guide in Early Shi'ism: The Sources of Esotericism in Islam*. Translated by David Streight. Albany: SUNY Press, 1994.

Anawati, George C., and S. de Beaurecueil. "Une preuve de l'existence de Dieu chez Ghazali et s. Thomas d'Aquin." *Mélanges d'Institut des Études Orientales* (1956): 207–14.

Arjomand, Said Amir, ed. *Authority and Political Culture in Shi'ism*. Albany: SUNY Press, 1988.

Arnaldez, Roger. *Grammaire et théologie chez Ibn Hazm: Essai sur la structure et les conditions de la pensée musulmane*. Paris: J. Vrin, 1956.

Ascha, Ghassan. "The 'Mothers of the Believers': Stereotypes of the Prophet Muhammad's Wives." In *Female Stereotypes in Religious Traditions*, edited by Ria Kloppenborg and Wouter J. Hanegraaff, 89–107. Leiden: Brill, 1995.

'Athamina, Khalil. "Biblical Quotations in Muslim Religious Literature: A Perspective of Dogma and Politics." *Shofar* 16 (1998): 84–103.

Attridge, Harold W., and Margot E. Fassler, eds. *Psalms in Community: Jewish and Christian Textual, Liturgical, and Artistic Traditions.* Atlanta: Society of Biblical Literature, 2003.

Augustine of Hippo. *Four Anti-Pelagius Writings.* Translated by John A. Mourant and William J. Colling. Washington, DC: Catholic University of America Press, 1992.

———. *The City of God.* Introduced by Thomas Merton and translated by Marcus Dodds. New York: Modern Library, 1994.

Ayoub, Mahmoud M. "Towards an Islamic Christology." *The Muslim World* 66:2 (1976): 163–88.

———. "The Death of Jesus, Reality or Delusion? A Study of the Death of Jesus in *Tafsir* Literature." *The Muslim World* 70 (1980): 91–121.

Badawi, Jamal. *Muhammad in the Bible.* Halifax, NS, Canada: International Islamic Publishing House, 1997.

Baghdadi, 'Abd al-Qahir al-. *Moslem Schism and Sects.* Pt. 2. Translated by A.S. Halkin. Tel Aviv, 1935.

Balic, Smail. "The Image of Jesus in Contemporary Islamic Theology." In *We Believe in One God,* edited by A. Schimmel and A. Falaturi, 1–8. New York: Seabury Press, 1979.

Bāqillānī, al-. *Kitāb al-Tamhīd.* Edited by Richard McCarthy, SJ. Beirut: Al-Maktabat ash-Sharqīya, 1957.

Bar-Asher, Meir M. *Scripture and Exegesis in Early Imāmī Shiism.* Leiden: Brill, 1999.

Barlas, Asma. *"Believing Women" in Islam: Unreading Patriarchal Interpretations of the Qur'an.* Austin: University of Texas Press, 2002.

Bateman, Herbert W. *Early Jewish Hermeneutics and Hebrews 1:5–13: The Impact of Early Jewish Exegesis on the Interpretation of a Significant New Testament Passage.* New York: Peter Lang, 1997.

Baum, Wilhelm, and Dietmar W. Winkler. *The Church of the East: A Concise History.* London and New York: RoutledgeCurzon, 2003.

Baumer, Christoph. *The Church of the East: An Illustrated History of Assyrian Christianity.* New York: I.B. Tauris, 2006.

Beaumont, I. Mark. *Christology in Dialogue with Muslims: A Critical Analysis of Christian Presentations of Christ for Muslims from the Ninth and Twentieth Centuries.* Colorado Springs, CO: Paternoster, 2005.

Bellitto, Christopher. *The General Councils: A History of the Twenty-One Church Councils from Nicaea to Vatican II.* Mahwah, NJ: Paulist, 2002.

Bello, Iysa A. *The Medieval Islamic Controversy between Philosophy and Orthodoxy: Ijmā' and ta'wīl in the Conflict between al-Ghazālī and Ibn Rushd.* Leiden: Brill, 1989.

Berg, Herbert, ed. *Method and Theory in the Study of Islamic Origins.* Leiden: Brill, 2003.

Berkey, Jonathan. *The Transmission of Knowledge in Medieval Cairo: A Social History of Islamic Education.* Princeton, NJ: Princeton University Press, 1992.

Bill, James A., and John Alden Williams. *Roman Catholics and Shi'i Muslims:*

*Prayer, Passion, and Politics.* Chapel Hill: University of North Carolina Press, 2002.

Binns, John W. *Ascetics and Ambassadors of Christ: The Monasteries of Palestine, 314–631.* New York: Oxford University Press, 1996.

Bonsor, Jack A. *Athens and Jerusalem: The Role of Philosophy in Theology.* New York: Paulist, 1993.

Bouyer, Louis. *A History of Christian Spirituality.* Vol. 1, *The Spirituality of the New Testament and the Fathers.* New York: Seabury, 1963.

———. *A History of Christian Spirituality.* Vol. 3, *Orthodox Spirituality and Protestant and Anglican Spirituality.* New York: Seabury, 1969.

Böwering, Gerhard. *The Mystical Vision of Existence in Classical Islam: The Qur'ānic Hermeneutics of the Sufi Sahl at-Tustarī.* Berlin: Walter de Gruyter, 1980.

Brinner, William, trans. *Lives of the Prophets as Recounted by . . . Tha'labī.* Leiden: Brill, 2002.

Brock, Sebastian. *Syriac Fathers on Prayer and the Spiritual Life.* Kalamazoo, MI: Cistercian, 1988.

———. *The Bible in Syriac Tradition.* Piscataway, NJ: Gorgias, 2006.

Brockopp, Jonathan. *Early Mālikī Law: Ibn 'Abd al-Hakam and His Major Compendium of Jurisprudence.* Leiden: Brill, 2000.

———. *Islamic Ethics of Life: Abortion, War, and Euthanasia.* Columbia: University of South Carolina Press, 2003.

Brown, Peter. *The Making of Late Antiquity.* Cambridge, MA: Harvard University Press, 1978.

Brundage, James A. *Medieval Canon Law.* London: Longman, 1995.

Bulliet, Richard. *Conversion to Islam in the Medieval Period: An Essay in Quantitative History.* Cambridge, MA: Harvard University Press, 1979.

———. "Conversion to Islam and the Spread of Innovation." *Fathom:* The Source of Online Learning, 2002, http://www.fathom.com/feature/2199/index.html.

———. *The Case for Islamo-Christian Civilization.* New York: Columbia University Press, 2006.

Burckhardt, T. *Art of Islam: Language and Meaning.* London: World of Islam, 1976.

Burns, J.H., ed. *The Cambridge History of Medieval Political Thought, c. 350–c. 1450.* Cambridge: Cambridge University Press, 1991.

Burrell, David, CSC. *Knowing the Unknowable God: Ibn Sina, Maimonides, Aquinas.* Notre Dame: Notre Dame University Press, 1986.

Burrell, David, and Bernard McGinn, eds. *God and Creation: An Ecumenical Symposium.* Notre Dame: Notre Dame University Press, 1990.

Burton, John. *The Collection of the Qur'an.* Cambridge: Cambridge University Press, 1979.

———. *An Introduction to the Hadith.* Edinburgh: Edinburgh University Press, 1994.

Casciaro, J. M. *El dialogo teologico de Santo Tomas con musulmanes y judios: El tema de la profecia y la revelacion.* Madrid: Instituto Francisco Suarez, 1969.

Caspar, Robert. *A Historical Introduction to Islamic Theology: Muhammad and the Classical Period.* Rome: Pontificio Istituto di Studi Arabi e d'Islamistica, 1998.

Cerić, Mustafa. *Roots of Systematic Theology in Islam: A Study of the Theology of Abū Mansūr al-Māturīdī.* Kuala Lumpur: International Institute of Islamic Thought and Civilization, 1995.

Chittick, William, trans. *The Psalms of Islam.* London: Muhammad Trust, 1988.

———. *The Sufi Path of Knowledge: Ibn al-'Arabi's Metaphysics of Imagination.* Albany: SUNY Press, 1989.

———. *The Self-Disclosure of God.* Albany: SUNY Press, 1997.

Clover, F. M., and Stephen Humphries. "Toward a Definition of Late Antiquity." In *Tradition and Innovation in Late Antiquity,* edited by F. M. Clover and Stephen Humphries, 3–19. Madison: University of Wisconsin Press, 1989.

Cobb, John B., Jr. *Transforming Christianity and the World: A Way beyond Absolutism and Relativism,* edited by Paul Knitter. Maryknoll, NY: Orbis, 1999.

Collins, John J., ed. *The Encyclopedia of Apocalypticism.* Vol. 1, *The Origins of Apocalypticism in Judaism and Christianity.* New York: Continuum, 1991.

Conant, Kenneth J. *Carolingian and Romanesque Architecture, 800–1200.* New Haven, CT: Yale University Press, 1992.

Congar, Yves. *Tradition & Traditions.* Dallas: Basilica, 1997.

Cook, David. *Studies in Muslim Apocalyptic.* Princeton, NJ: Darwin, 2002.

Cook, Michael. *Commanding Right and Forbidding Wrong in Islamic Thought.* Cambridge: Cambridge University Press, 2000.

Coon, Lynda L. *Sacred Fictions: Holy Women and Hagiography in Late Antiquity.* Philadelphia: University of Pennsylvania Press, 1997.

Cragg, Kenneth. *Alive to God: Muslim and Christian Prayer.* New York: Oxford University Press, 1970.

———. *The Mind of the Qur'ān: Chapters in Reflection.* London: Allen and Unwin, 1973.

———. "Legacies and Hopes in Muslim/Christian Theology." *Islamochristiana* 3 (1977): 1–10.

———. *The Christ and the Faiths.* Philadelphia: Westminster, 1986.

———. *Common Prayer: A Muslim-Christian Spiritual Anthology.* Oxford: Oneworld, 1999.

———. *The Qur'an and the West.* Washington, DC: Georgetown University Press, 2005.

Creswell, Dennis R. *St. Augustine's Dilemma: Grace and Eternal Law in the Major Works of Augustine of Hippo.* New York: Peter Lang, 1997.

Crone, Patricia. *God's Caliph: Religious Authority in the First Centuries of Islam.* Cambridge: Cambridge University Press, 1986.

———. *Medieval Islamic Political Thought.* Edinburgh: University of Edinburgh Press, 2004.

———. *God's Rule—Government and Islam: Six Centuries of Medieval Islamic Political Thought.* New York: Columbia University Press, 2005.

Cunningham, Lawrence. *A Brief History of Saints.* Malden, MA: Blackwell, 2005.

Daniélou, Jean. *Gospel Message and Hellenistic Culture.* Translated by John Austin Baker. Philadelphia: Westminster, 1973.

Dante. *The Divine Comedy: Inferno, Purgatorio, Paradiso.* Translated by John Ciardi. New York: Norton, 1977.

Davis, Leo Donald. *The First Seven Ecumenical Councils (325–787): Their History and Theology.* Collegeville, MN: Liturgical, 1990.

Dawud, Abdu I. Ahad. *Muhammad in the Bible.* New Delhi: International Islamic Publishers, 1996.

De Epalza, Mikel. "Los nombres del Profeta en la teologia musulmana." *Miscelanea Comillas* 33:2 (1975): 149–203.

DeMolen, Richard L., ed. *Religious Orders of the Catholic Reformation.* New York: Fordham University Press, 1994.

Di Berardino, Angelo, and Basil Studer. *The History of Theology.* Vol. 1, *The Patristic Period.* Collegeville, MN: Liturgical, 1997.

Doig, Allan. *Liturgy and Architecture.* Aldershot, UK: Ashgate, 2008.

Donner, Fred. *Early Islamic Conquests.* Princeton, NJ: Princeton University Press, 1981.

———. *Narratives of Islamic Origins: The Beginnings of Islamic Historical Writing.* Princeton, NJ: Darwin, 1998.

———. *Muhammad and the Believers: At the Origins of Islam.* Cambridge, MA: Harvard, Belknap Press, 2010.

Druille, Mayeul de, OSB. *From East to West: A History of Monasticism.* New York: Herder & Herder, 1999.

Dunn, James D. G. *Unity and Diversity in the New Testament: An Inquiry into the Character of Earliest Christianity.* Philadelphia: Trinity International, 1990.

Dunn, Marilyn. *The Emergence of Monasticism: From the Desert Fathers to the Early Middle Ages.* Hoboken, NJ: Wiley-Blackwell, 2003.

Ehler, Sidney Z. *Twenty Centuries of Church and State: A Survey of Their Relations in Past and Present.* Westminster, MD: Newman, 1957.

Ehrman, Bart D. *The New Testament: A Historical Introduction to the Early Christian Writings.* 3rd ed. New York: Oxford University Press, 2003.

———. *Lost Scriptures: Books That Did Not Make It into the New Testament.* New York: Oxford University Press, 2005.

Elias, Jamal J. *Death before Dying: The Sufi Poems of Sultan Bahu.* Berkeley: University of California Press, 1998.

Ellingson, Mark. *The Richness of Augustine: His Contextual and Pastoral Theology.* Louisville, KY: Westminster John Knox, 2005.

Elwell, Walter A. *Encountering the New Testament: A Historical and Theological Survey.* Grand Rapids, MI: Baker Books, 1998.

Epp, Eldon Jay. *Junia: The First Woman Apostle.* Minneapolis: Fortress, 2005.

Ernst, Carl W. *Following Muhammad: Rethinking Islam in the Contemporary World.* Chapel Hill: University of North Carolina Press, 2003.

Ernst, Carl W., and Bruce B. Lawrence. *Sufi Martyrs of Love: The Chishti Order in South Asia and Beyond.* New York: Palgrave MacMillan, 2002.

Espín, Orlanddo, and James B. Nickoloff, eds. *An Introductory Dictionary of Theology and Religious Studies.* Collegeville, MN: Liturgical, 2007.

Farid, A. H. *Prayers of Muhammad.* Lahore: Sh. M. Ashraf, 1974.

Faruqi, L. al-. "An Islamic Perspective on Symbolism and the Arts." In *Art and the Sacred,* edited by Diane Apostolos-Cappadona, 164–78. New York: Crossroad, 1984.

———. *Islam and Art.* Islamabad: National Hijra Council, 1985.

Faruqi, L. al-, and R. al-Faruqi. *A Cultural Atlas of Islam*. New York: Macmillan, 1986.

Fastiggi, Robert. *The Mystical Theology of the Catholic Reformation: An Overview of Baroque Spirituality*. Lanham, MD: University Press of America, 2006.

Ferguson, Everett. *Baptism in the Early Church: History, Theology, and Liturgy in the First Five Centuries*. Grand Rapids, MI: Eerdmans, 2009.

Fideler, David, and Sabrineh Fideler. *Love's Alchemy: Poems from the Sufi Tradition*. Novato, CA: New World, 2006.

Filipovic, Nenad, et al. "The Sultan's Syllabus: A Curriculum for the Ottoman Imperial *Medreses* Prescribed in a *Ferman* of Qanuni I Suleyman, Dated 973 (1565)." *Studia Islamica* (2004): 183–218.

Firmage, Edwin B., Bernard G. Weiss, and John W. Welch, eds. *Religion and Law: Biblical-Judaic and Islamic Perspectives*. Winona Lake, IN: Eisenbrauns, 1990.

Fitzgerald, Allan D., ed. *Augustine through the Ages: An Encyclopedia*. Grand Rapids, MI: Eerdmans, 1999.

Fitzgerald, Thomas E. *The Orthodox Church*. Westport, CT: Greenwood, 1995.

Flynn, J.G. "St. Thomas and Avicenna on the Nature of God." *Abr Nahrain* 14 (1973–74): 53–65.

———. "St. Thomas Aquinas' Use of the Arab Philosophers on the Nature of God." *Al-Mushir* 16 (1974): 278–86.

———. "St. Thomas and Averroes on the Nature and Attributes of God." *Abr Nahrain* 15 (1974–75): 39–49.

———. "St. Thomas and Averroes on the Knowledge of God." *Abr Nahrain* 18 (1978–79): 19–32.

Ford, David F., ed. *The Modern Theologians: An Introduction to Christian Theology in the Twentieth Century*. 2nd ed. Cambridge, MA: Blackwell, 1997.

Forward, Martin. *Inter-Religious Dialogue: A Short Introduction*. Oxford: Oneworld, 2001.

Frank, Richard M. *Texts and Studies on the Development and History of Kalam*. Edited by Dimitri Gutas. 3 vols. Aldershot, UK: Ashgate, 2005.

———. *Classical Islamic Theology: The Ash'arites*. Aldershot, UK: Ashgate, 2007.

———. *Early Islamic Theology: The Mu'tazilites and al-Ash'arī*. Aldershot, UK: Ashgate, 2007.

Frankl, Paul. *Gothic Architecture*. New Haven, CT: Yale University Press, 2001.

Gardet, Louis. "Deux grands maitres: Al-Bīrūnī et Albert Le Grand; Essai de typologie comparative." *Islamochristiana* 1 (1975): 25–40.

———. "La connaissance que Thomas d'Aquin put avoir du monde islamique." In *Aquinas and the Problems of His Time*, edited by G. Verbeke and D. Verhelst, 139–49. Leuven: Leuven University Press, 1976.

———. *Regards chrétiens sur l'Islam*. Paris: Desclee de Brouwer, 1986.

Geanakoplos, Deno John. *Byzantine East and Latin West: Two Worlds of Christendom in Middle Ages and Renaissance*. New York: Harper, 1966.

Gesink, Indira Falk. "Islamic Reformation: A History of *Madrasa* Reform and Legal Change in Egypt." In *Islam and Education: Myths and Truths*, edited by Wadad Kadi and Victor Billeh, 19–39. Chicago: University Of Chicago Press, 2007.

Ghazālī. *Ghazali's Book of Counsel for Kings.* Translated by F. R. C. Bagley. London: Oxford University Press, 1964.

———. *The Book of Fear and Hope.* Translated by William McKane. Leiden: Brill, 1965.

———. *The Alchemy of Happiness.* Translated by Claude Field and revised by Elton Daniel. Armonk, NY: Sharpe, 1991.

Gilliot, Claude, ed. *Education and Learning in the Early Islamic World.* Aldershot, UK: Ashgate, 2008.

Glei, Reinhold, ed. and trans. *Petrus Venerabilis: Schriften zum Islam.* Altenberge: Corpus Islamo-Christianum, 1985.

Goddard, Hugh. *Christians and Muslims: From Double Standards to Mutual Understanding.* Richmond, Surrey, UK: Curzon, 1995.

———. *A History of Christian-Muslim Relations.* Chicago: New Amsterdam, 2001.

———. *A History of Middle Eastern Theologies.* New York: RoutledgeCurzon, 2003.

Goldingay, John. *Models for Interpretation of Scripture.* Grand Rapids, MI: Eerdmans, 1995.

Goldziher, Ignac. *The Zāhirīs: Their Doctrine and Their History; A Contribution to the History of Islamic Theology.* Leiden: Brill, 1971.

González, Justo L. *A History of Christian Thought.* 3 vols. Rev. ed. Nashville: Abingdon, 1987.

Goppelt, Leonhard. *Typos: The Typological Interpretation of the Old Testament in the New.* Translated by Donald H. Madvig. Grand Rapids, MI: Eerdmans, 1982.

Graham, William. *Divine Word and Prophetic Word in Early Islam.* Hague: Mouton, 1977.

Green, Joel B., and Max Turner, eds. *Jesus of Nazareth: Lord and Christ; Essays on the Historical Jesus and New Testament Christology.* Grand Rapids, MI: Eerdmans, 1994.

Greenslade, S. L. *Cambridge History of the Bible.* Vol. 3, *The West from the Reformation to the Present Day.* Cambridge: Cambridge University Press, 1975.

Gregory of Nyssa. *The Life of Moses.* Translated by Abraham Malherbe and Everett Ferguson. Mahwah, NJ: Paulist, 1978.

Griffith, Sidney. "Faith and Reason in Christian Kalām: Theodore Abū Qurrah on Discerning the True Religion." In *Christian Arabic Apologetics during the Abbasid Period (750–1258),* edited by Samir Khalil Samir and Jørgen Nielsen, 1–43. Leiden: E. J. Brill, 1994.

———. "The View of Islam from the Monasteries of Palestine in the Early Abbasid Period: Theodore Abu Qurrah and the *Summa Theologiae Arabica.*" *ICMR* 7:1 (1996): 9–28.

———. *The Beginnings of Christian Theology in Arabic: Muslim-Christian Encounters in the Early Islamic Period.* Rutland, VT: Ashgate Variorum, 2003.

———. *The Church in the Shadow of the Mosque: Christians and Muslims in the World of Islam.* Princeton, NJ: Princeton University Press, 2007.

Guillaume, Alfred. "Christian and Muslim Theology as Represented by Al-Shahrastani and St. Thomas Aquinas." *Bulletin of the Schools of Oriental and African Studies* 13:3 (1950): 551–80.

Günther, Sebastian. "Be Masters in That You Teach and Continue to Learn: Medieval Muslim Thinkers on Educational Theory." In *Islam and Education: Myths and Truths,* edited by Wadad Kadi and Victor Billeh, 61–82. Chicago: University Of Chicago Press, 2007.

Guroian, Vigen. *Incarnate Love: Essays in Orthodox Ethics.* 2nd ed. Notre Dame, IN: University of Notre Dame Press, 2002.

Hägg, Henny Fiskå. *Clement of Alexandria and the Beginnings of Christian Apophaticism.* Oxford: Oxford University Press, 2006.

Hall, Christopher A. *Reading Scripture with the Church Fathers.* Downers Grove, IL: InterVarsity, 1998.

———. *Learning Theology with the Church Fathers.* Downers Grove, IL: InterVarsity, 2002.

Halm, Heinz. *The Fatimids and Their Traditions of Learning.* London: I.B. Tauris, 1997.

Hambly, Gavin, ed. *Women in the Medieval Islamic World: Power, Patronage, and Piety.* New York: St. Martin's, 1998.

Hamid, Eltigani Abdelgadir. *The Qur'ān and Politics: A Study of the Origins of Political Thought in the Makkan Qur'ān.* 1st English ed. Herndon, VA: International Institute of Islamic Thought, 2004.

Harrington, Daniel J., SJ. *The Church according to the New Testament: What the Wisdom and Witness of Early Christianity Teach Us Today.* Chicago: Sheed & Ward, 2001.

Hasan, Ahmad. "Social Justice in Islam." *Islamic Studies* 10 (1971): 209–19.

Hashmi, Sohail H. *Islamic Political Ethics: Civil Society, Pluralism, and Conflict.* Princeton, NJ: Princeton University Press, 2002.

Hays, Richard B. *The Moral Vision of the New Testament: Community, Cross, New Creation; A Contemporary Introduction to New Testament Ethics.* San Francisco: HarperCollins, 1996.

Heemskerk, Margaretha T. *Suffering in Mu'tazilite 'Abd al-Jabbār's Teaching on Pain and Divine Justice.* Leiden: Brill, 2000.

Heine, Ronald E. *Reading the Old Testament with the Ancient Church: Exploring the Formation of Early Christian Thought.* Grand Rapids, MI: Baker, 2006.

Henderson, John. *The Construction of Orthodoxy and Heresy.* Albany: SUNY Press, 1998.

Hennigan, Peter C. *The Birth of a Legal Institution: The Formation of the Waqf in Third-Century A.H. Hanafī Legal Discourse.* Leiden: Brill, 2004.

Hillenbrand, Robert. *Islamic Architecture: Form, Function, and Meaning.* New York: Columbia University Press, 1994.

Hoag, John. *Islamic Architecture.* New York: Rizzoli, 1975.

Hodgson, Marshall. *The Venture of Islam.* 3 vols. Chicago: University of Chicago Press, 1974.

Hoeberichts, J. *Francis and Islam.* Quincy, IL: Franciscan, 1997.

Homerin, Th. Emil. "The Golden Rule in Islam." In *The Golden Rule: The Ethics of Reciprocity in World Religions,* edited by Jacob Neusner and Bruce Chilton, 99–115. New York: Continuum, 2008.

Hoover, Jon. *Ibn Taymiyya's Theodicy of Perpetual Optimism.* Leiden: Brill, 2007.

Hourani, George. "Two Theories of Value in Medieval Islam." *The Muslim World* 50 (1960): 269–78.

———. *Islamic Rationalism: The Ethics of ʿAbd al-Jabbār*. Oxford: Clarendon, 1971.

———. "The Rationalist Ethics of ʿAbd al-Jabbār." In *Islamic Philosophy and the Classical Tradition,* edited by S. M. Stern, Albert Hourani, and Vivian Brown, 105–15. Oxford: Cassirer, 1972.

———. "Ethics in Medieval Islam: A Conspectus." In *Essays on Islamic Philosophy and Science,* edited by George Hourani, 128–35. Albany: SUNY Press, 1975.

———. "Juwayni's Criticism of Muʿtazilite Ethics." *The Muslim World* 65 (1975): 161–73.

———. *Reason and Tradition in Islamic Ethics*. Cambridge: Cambridge University Press, 2002.

Humphreys, R. Steven. "Qurʾanic Myth and Narrative Structure in Early Islamic Historiography." In *Tradition and Innovation in Late Antiquity,* edited by F. M. Clover and R. S. Humphreys, 271–90. Madison: University of Wisconsin, 1989.

Ibn Ishaq. *The Life of Muhammad: A Translation of Ibn Ishaq's "Sirat Rasul Allah."* Translated by A. Guillaume. Oxford: Oxford University Press, 1955.

Ibn Iskandar, Kay Kaʾus. *A Mirror for Princes, the Qābūs Nāma*. Translated by Reuben Levy. London: Luzac, 1951.

Idel, Moshe, and Bernard McGinn, eds. *Mystical Union in Judaism, Christianity, and Islam: An Ecumenical Dialogue*. New York: Crossroad, 1996.

Iogna-Prat, Dominique. *Order and Exclusion: Cluny and Christendom Face Heresy, Judaism, and Islam (1000–1150)*. Translated by Graham R. Edwards. Ithaca, NY: Cornell University Press, 2002.

İskenderoğlu, Muammer. *Fakhr-al-Dīn al-Rāzī and Thomas Aquinas on the Question of the Eternity of the World*. Leiden: Brill, 2002.

Izutsu, Toshihiku. *God and Man in the Koran*. Tokyo: Keio University, 1964.

———. *Ethico-Religious Concepts in the Qurʾān*. Montreal: McGill University, 1966.

Jabalī, Fuʾād. *The Companions of the Prophet: A Study of Geographical Distribution and Political Alignments*. Leiden: Brill, 2003.

Jackson, Sherman A. *Islamic Law and the State: The Constitutional Jurisprudence of Shihāb Al-Dīn Al-Qarāfī*. Leiden: Brill, 1996.

James, Edward. "The Rise and Function of the Concept of Late Antiquity." *Journal of Late Antiquity* 1:1 (2008): 20–30.

Jenkins, Philip. *The Next Christendom: The Coming of Global Christianity*. New York: Oxford University Press, 2002.

———. *The New Faces of Christianity: Believing the Bible in the Global South*. New York: Oxford University Press, 2006.

Jennings, Theodore W. *Loyalty to God: The Apostles' Creed in Life and Liturgy*. Nashville: Abingdon, 1992.

Johns, Anthony H. "Joseph in the Qurʾān: Dramatic Dialogue, Human Emotion, and Prophetic Wisdom." *Islamochristiana* 7 (1981): 29–51.

Johnston, David L. "An Epistemological and Hermeneutical Turn in Twentieth-Century *Usūl al-Fiqh*." *Islamic Law and Society* 2:11 (2004): 233–82.

———. *Earth, Empire, and Sacred Text: Muslims and Christians as Trustees of Creation*. London: Equinox, 2009.

Johnston, William M., ed. *Encyclopedia of Monasticism*. Chicago and London: Fitzroy Dearborn, 2000.

Jones, William R. "Pious Endowments in Medieval Christianity and Islam." *Diogenes* 109 (1980): 23-36.

Juwaynī, al-. *A Guide to Conclusive Proofs for the Principles of Belief*. Translated by Paul E. Walker. Reading, UK: Garnet, 2000.

Kadi, Wadad, and Victor Billeh, eds. *Islam and Education: Myths and Truths*. Chicago: University Of Chicago Press, 2007.

Kamali, Mohammad Hashim. *The Dignity of Man: An Islamic Perspective*. Cambridge: Islamic Texts Society, 2002.

———. *Freedom, Equality, and Justice in Islam*. Cambridge: Islamic Texts Society, 2002.

———. *Equity and Fairness in Islam*. Cambridge: Islamic Texts Society, 2005.

Karamustafa, Ahmet T. *Sufism: The Formative Period*. Berkeley: University of California Press, 2007.

———. "Community." In *Key Themes for the Study of Islam*, edited by Jamal J. Elias, 93–103. Oxford: Oneworld, 2010.

Kaufman, Peter Iver. *Redeeming Politics*. Princeton, NJ: Princeton University Press, 1990.

Kazhdan, Alexander, et al., eds. *The Oxford Dictionary of Byzantium*. 3 vols. New York: Oxford University Press, 1991.

Keleher, James P. *Saint Augustine's Notion of Schism in the Donatist Controversy*. Mundelein, IL: Saint Mary of the Lake Seminary, 1961.

Kelly, J. N. D. *Early Christian Doctrines*. London: A. C. Black, 1977.

Kennedy, Hugh. *When Baghdad Ruled the Muslim World: The Rise and Fall of Islam's Greatest Dynasty*. Cambridge, MA: DaCapo, 2004.

Keshavarz, Fatemeh. *Reading Mystical Lyric: The Case of Jalal al-Din Rumi*. Columbia: University of South Carolina Press, 1998.

———. *Recite in the Name of the Red Rose: Poetic Sacred Making in Twentieth-Century Iran*. Columbia: University of South Carolina Press, 2006.

Kieckhefer, Richard. *Theology in Stone: Church Architecture from Byzantium to Berkeley*. New York: Oxford University Press, 2008.

Kilde, Jeanne Halgren. *Sacred Power, Sacred Space: An Introduction to Christian Architecture*. New York: Oxford University Press, 2008.

Kinder, Terryl N. *Cistercian Europe: Architecture of Contemplation*. Grand Rapids, MI: Eerdmans, 2002.

Knitter, Paul. "Hans Küng's Theological Rubicon." In *Toward a Universal Theology of Religion,* edited by Leonard Swidler, 224–30. Maryknoll, NY: Orbis, 1987.

———. *Introducing Theologies of Religions*. Maryknoll, NY: Orbis, 2002.

Knysh, Alexander. "'Orthodoxy' and 'Heresy' in Medieval Islam: An Essay in Reassessment." *The Muslim World* 83:1 (1993): 48–67.

Kohlberg, Etan, and Mohammad Ali Amir-Moezzi, eds. *Revelation and Falsification: The Kitāb al-qirā'āt of Ahmad b. Muhammad al-Sayyārī*. Leiden: Brill, 2008.

Kraus, Hans-Joachim. *Theology of the Psalms*. Translated by Keith Crim. Minneapolis: Augsburg, 1986.

Krautheimer, Richard. *Early Christian and Byzantine Architecture*. New Haven, CT: Yale University Press, 1984.

Kritzeck, James. *Peter the Venerable and Islam*. Princeton, NJ: Princeton University Press, 1964.

Küng, Hans. *Christianity and the World's Religions: Paths of Dialogue with Islam, Hinduism, and Buddhism*. Garden City, NY: Doubleday, 1986.

——. *Christianity: Essence, History, and Future*. New York: Continuum, 1995.

——. *Islam: Past, Present, and Future*. Oxford: Oneworld, 2007.

Lampe. G. W. H., ed. *Cambridge History of the Bible*. Vol. 2, *The West from the Fathers to the Reformation*. Cambridge: Cambridge University Press, 1975.

Lapidus, Ira. *A History of Islamic Societies*. New York: Cambridge University Press, 1990.

Latourette, Kenneth Scott. *A History of the Expansion of Christianity*. 7 vols. Grand Rapids, MI: Zondervan, 1970.

Lawson, Todd. *The Crucifixion and the Qur'an: A Study in the History of Muslim Thought*. Oxford: Oneworld, 2009.

Lazarus-Yafeh, Hava. *Intertwined Worlds: Medieval Islam and Bible Criticism*. Princeton, NJ: Princeton University Press, 1992.

Leaman, Oliver. *Islamic Aesthetics: An Introduction*. Notre Dame, IN: University of Notre Dame, 2004.

LeClerq, Jean, François VandenBroucke, and Louis Bouyer. *A History of Christian Spirituality*. Vol. 2, *The Spirituality of the Middle Ages*. New York: Seabury, 1968.

Levtzion, N., ed. *Conversion to Islam*. New York: Holmes & Meier, 1978.

Littell, Franklin H. *The Macmillan Atlas History of Christianity*. New York: Macmillan, 1976.

Logan, F. Donald. *A History of the Church in the Middle Ages*. London and New York: Routledge, 2002.

Lossky, Vladimir. *The Mystical Theology of the Eastern Church*. Yonkers, NY: St. Vladimir's Seminary, 1997.

Lowry, Joseph E., Devin J. Stewart, and Shawkat M. Toorawa, eds. *Law and Education in Medieval Islam: Studies in Memory of Professor George Makdisi*. Cambridge: E. J. W. Gibb Memorial Trust, 2004.

Lubac, Henri de. *Medieval Exegesis*. Vol. 1, translated by Mark Sebanc; vols. 2 and 3, translated by E. M. Macieroweski. Grand Rapids, MI: Eerdmans; Edinburgh: T&T Clark, 1998–2008.

Macdonald, John. "Joseph in the Qur'ān." *Muslim World* 46:2 (1956): 113–31.

MacIntyre, Alasdair. *After Virtue: A Study in Moral Theory*. 3rd ed. Notre Dame, IN: University of Notre Dame Press, 2007.

Madden, Thomas F. *The New Concise History of the Crusades*. Lanham, MD: Rowman & Littlefield, 2005.

Madelung, Wilferd. *The Succession to Muhammad: A Study of the Early Caliphate*. Cambridge: Cambridge University Press, 2008.

Mahoney, John. *The Making of Moral Theology: A Study of the Roman Catholic Tradition*. Oxford: Clarendon, 1987.

Makdisi, George. "Muslim Institutions of Learning in Eleventh-Century Baghdad." *Bulletin of the Schools of Oriental and African Studies* 24:1 (1961): 1–56.

———. "The *Madrasa* in Spain: Some Remarks." *Revue de l'Occident Musulman et de la Mediteranée* (1973): 153–58.

———. "On the Origin and Development of the College in Islam and the West." In *Islam and the Medieval West,* edited by K.I. Semaan, 26–49. Albany: SUNY Press, 1980.

———. *The Rise of Colleges.* Edinburgh: Edinburgh University Press, 1981.

———. *The Rise of Humanism in Classical Islam and the Christian West: With Special Reference to Scholasticism.* Edinburgh: University of Edinburgh Press, 1990.

———. "The Model of Islamic Scholastic Culture and Its Later Parallel in the Christian West." In *Vocabulaire des collèges universitaires (XIIIe-XVIe siècles),* edited by Olga Weijers, 158–76. Turnhout: Brepols, 1993.

Mansour, Camille. *L'autorité dans la pensée musulmane.* Paris: J. Vrin, 1975.

Marenbon, John. *Early Medieval Philosophy (480–1150): An Introduction.* 2nd ed. London and New York: Routledge, 1988.

———. *Later Medieval Philosophy (1150–1300): An Introduction.* London and New York: Routledge, 1991.

———, ed. *Medieval Philosophy.* Vol. 3 of *Routledge History of Philosophy.* New ed. London and New York: Routledge, 2003.

Martin, Richard, and Mark Woodward, with Dwi S. Atmaja. *Defenders of Reason in Islam: Mu'tazilism from Medieval School to Modern Symbol.* Oxford: Oneworld, 1997.

Matera, Frank J. *New Testament Ethics: The Legacies of Jesus and Paul.* Louisville, KY: Westminster John Knox, 1996.

Mawardi, al-. *The Ordinances of Government.* Translated by Wafaa H. Wahba. Reading, UK: Garnet, 2000.

Mayer, Toby. "Theology and Sufism." In *The Cambridge Companion to Classical Islamic Theology,* edited by Tim Winter, 258–87. Cambridge: Cambridge University Press, 2008.

McAuliffe, Jane Dammen. "Qur'ānic Hermeneutics: The Views of al-Tabarī and Ibn Kathīr." In *Approaches to the History of the Interpretation of the Qur'ān,* edited by A. Rippin, 46–62. Oxford: Clarendon, 1988.

———. "Text and Textuality: Q. 3:7 as a Point of Intersection." In *Literary Structures of Religious Meaning in the Qur'ān,* edited by Issa J. Boullata, 56–76. Richmond, Surrey: Curzon, 2000.

———. *Qur'anic Christians: An Analysis of Classical and Modern Exegesis.* Cambridge: Cambridge University Press, 1991.

McCarthy, Richard, SJ, ed. and trans. *The Theology of Al-Ash'arī.* Beirut: Imprimerie Catholique, 1953.

———. *Freedom and Fulfillment.* Boston: Twayne, 1980.

McDermott, Brian O. *Word Become Flesh: Dimensions of Christology.* Collegeville, MN: Liturgical, 1993.

McGinn, Bernard. *The Foundations of Mysticism: Origins to the Fifth Century.* New York: Crossroad, 1994.

———. *The Growth of Mysticism: Gregory the Great through the 12th Century.* New York: Crossroad, 1994.

———. *The Flowering of Mysticism: Men and Women in the New Mysticism—1200–1350*. New York: Crossroad, 1998.

———. *The Harvest of Mysticism in Medieval Germany*. New York: Crossroad, 2008.

Melchert, Christopher. "The Formation of the Sunni Schools of Law, 9th–10th Centuries C.E." In *Islamic Law and Society*, vol. 4, edited by Ruud Peters and Bernard Weiss. Leiden: Brill, 1997.

———. "The Etiquette of Learning in the Early Islamic Study Circle." In *Law and Education in Medieval Islam: Studies in Memory of Professor George Makdisi*, edited by Joseph E. Lowry, Devin J. Stewart, and Shawkat M. Toorawa, 33–44. Cambridge: E. J. W. Gibb Memorial Trust, 2004.

———. *Ahmad ibn Hanbal*. Oxford: Oneworld, 2006.

Meyendorff, John. *Byzantine Theology: Historical Trends and Doctrinal Themes*. 2nd ed. New York: Fordham University Press, 1987.

———. *St. Gregory Palamas and Orthodox Spirituality*. Yonkers, NY: St. Vladimir's Seminary, 1997.

Michel, Thomas. *A Muslim Theologian's Response to Christianity: Ibn Taymiyya's al-Jawab al-sahih*. Delmar, NY: Caravan Books, 1984.

Michell, George, ed. *Architecture of the Islamic World: Its History and Social Meaning*. New York: Morrow, 1978.

Mikhail, Hanna. *Politics and Revelation: Mawardi and After*. Edinburgh: Edinburgh University Press, 1995.

Minkov, Anton. *Conversion to Islam in the Balkans: Kisve Bahası Petitions and Ottoman Social Life, 1670–1730*. Leiden: Brill, 2004.

Mir, Mustansir. "The Qur'ānic Story of Joseph: Plot, Themes, and Characters." *Muslim World* 76:1 (January 1986): 1–15.

Miskawayh, Ahmad ibn Muhammad. *The Refinement of Character*. Translated by Constantine K. Zurayk. Beirut: Centennial, 1968; reprint, Beirut: Kazi, 2003.

Moffett, Samuel Hugh. *A History of Christianity in Asia*. Vol. 1, *Beginnings to 1500*. San Francisco: HarperCollins, 1992.

Moorhead, John. "The Earliest Christian Theological Response to Islam." *Religion* 11 (1981): 265–74.

Morris, James W. *The Reflective Heart: Discovering Spiritual Intelligence in Ibn 'Arabi's 'Meccan Illuminations'*. Louisville, KY: Fons Vitae, 2005.

Moses, Paul. *The Saint and the Sultan: The Crusades, Islam, and Francis of Assisi's Mission of Peace*. New York: Doubleday, 2009.

Motzki, Harald. *The Origins of Islamic Jurisprudence: Meccan Fiqh before the Classical Schools*. Leiden: Brill, 2002.

Mourad, Suleiman A. "A Twelfth-Century Muslim Biography of Jesus." *ICMR* 7:1 (1996): 39–46.

———. *Early Islam between Myth and History: Al-Hasan al-Basrī (d. 110H/728 C.E.) and the Formation of His Legacy in Classical Islamic Scholarship*. Leiden: Brill, 2006.

Mulk, Nizam al-. *The Book of Government, or Rules for Kings*. Translated by Hubert Darke. London: Routledge and Kegan Paul, 1978.

Mullett, Michael. *The Catholic Reformation*. New York: Routledge, 1999.

Munir, Farid. "Sultan al-Malik Muhammad al-Kamil and Saint Francis: Interreligious Dialogue and the Meeting at Damietta." *Journal of Islamic Law and Culture* 10:3 (2008): 307–17.

Murata, Sachiko, and William Chittick. *The Vision of Islam*. New York: Paragon, 1994.

Murray, Peter, ed. *The Oxford Companion to Christian Art and Architecture*. New York: Oxford University Press, 1996.

Muslim. *Saḥīḥ Muslim*. 5 vols. Beirut: Dār Ibn Hazm, 1995.

Myer, M., and Elaine Pagels, eds. *The Gnostic Gospels*. London: Folio, 2008.

Nagel, Tilman. *The History of Islamic Theology from Muhammad to the Present*. Princeton, NJ: Markus Wiener, 2000.

Nakamura, Kojiro, trans. *Ghazālī on Prayer*. Tokyo: Institute of Oriental Culture, 1973.

Nasr, S. H. *Islamic Art and Spirituality*. Albany: SUNY Press, 1987.

———, ed. *Islamic Spirituality: Foundations*. New York: Crossroad, 1987.

Neusner, Jacob, and Tamara Sonn. *Comparing Religions through Law: Judaism and Islam*. London and New York: Routledge, 1999.

Neville, Robert Cummings. *Behind the Masks of God: An Essay toward Comparative Theology*. Albany: SUNY Press, 1991.

Nogales, Salvador Gomez. "Los arabes en la vida y en la doctrina de Sto. Tomas." In *Tomasso d'Aquino nel suo settimo centenario*, 1:334–40. Naples: Edizione Domenicane Italiane, 1975.

———. "Santo Tomas y los arabes: Bibliografia." *Miscelanea Comillas* 63 (1975): 205–50.

O'Grady, John F. *Disciples and Leaders: The Origins of Christian Ministry in the New Testament*. New York: Paulist, 1991.

Ohlander, Erik. *Sufism in an Age of Transition: 'Umar al-Suhrawardī and the Rise of the Islamic Mystical Brotherhoods*. Leiden: Brill, 2008.

Opeloye, Muhib O. "Confluence and Conflict in the Qur'ānic and Biblical Accounts of the Life of Prophet Musa." *Islamochristiana* 16 (1990): 25–41.

Ormsby, Eric. *Theodicy in Islamic Thought: The Dispute over al-Ghazālī's "Best of All Possible Worlds."* Princeton, NJ: Princeton University, 1987.

Osborne, Kenan, ed. *History of Franciscan Theology*. St. Bonaventure, NY: Franciscan Institute, 1994.

———. *The Franciscan Intellectual Tradition: Tracing Its Origins and Identifying Its Central Components*. St. Bonaventure, NY: Franciscan Institute, 2003.

O'Shaughnessy, Thomas J. *Eschatological Themes in the Qur'ān*. Manila: Cardinal Bea Institute/Ateneo de Manila University, 1986.

Otten, Willemien. "Carolingian Theology." In *The Medieval Theologians*, edited by G. R. Evans, 76–80. Oxford: Blackwell, 2001.

Padwick, Constance. *Muslim Devotions: A Study of Prayer-Manuals in Common Use*. Oxford: Oneworld, 1996.

Pagels, Elaine. *Beyond Belief: The Secret Gospel of Thomas*. New York: Random House, 2004.

———. *The Gnostic Gospels*. New York: Random House, 2004.

Panofsky, Erwin. *Gothic Architecture and Scholasticism*. Reprint, Latrobe, PA: Archabbey, 2005.

Peirce, Charles S. "A Neglected Argument for the Reality of God." In *Values in a*

*Universe of Choice*, edited by Philip Wiener, 358–79. Stanford: Stanford University Press, 1958.

Pelikan, Jaroslav. *The Christian Tradition: A History of the Development of Doctrine*. 5 vols. Chicago: University of Chicago Press, 1975–91.

Peters, J. R. T. *God's Created Speech: A Study in the Speculative Theology of the Mu'tazili Qadil-Qudat Abu l-Hasan 'Abd al-Jabbar ibn Ahmad al-Hamadani*. Leiden: Brill, 1976.

Pinault, David. "Zaynab Bint 'Ali and the Place of the Women of the Households of the First Imams in Shi'ite Devotional Literature." In *Women in the Medieval Islamic World: Power, Patronage, and Piety*, edited by Gavin Hambly, 69–98. New York: St. Martin's, 1998.

Pope John Paul II, and John P. Beal. *Theotokos—Woman, Mother, Disciple: A Catechesis on Mary, Mother of God*. Boston: Pauline Books, 1999.

Prokurat, Michael, Alexander Golitzin, and Michael Peterson. *Historical Dictionary of the Orthodox Church*. Lanham, MD: Scarecrow, 1996.

Quinn, D. Michael. *The Mormon Hierarchy: Extensions of Power*. Salt Lake City: Signature Books, 1997.

Rad, Gerhard von. *Old Testament Theology: The Theology of Israel's Historical Traditions*. 2 vols. New York: Harper and Row, 1962.

Radding, Charles, and William Clark. *Medieval Architecture, Medieval Learning: Builders and Masters in the Age of Romanesque and Gothic*. New Haven, CT: Yale University Press, 1992.

Rahbar, Daud. *The God of Justice: A Study in the Ethical Doctrine of the Qur'ān*. Leiden: Brill, 1960.

Reat, N. Ross, and Edmund F. Perry. *A World Theology: The Central Spiritual Reality of Humankind*. Cambridge: Cambridge University Press, 1991.

Reese, Thomas J. *Inside the Vatican: The Politics and Organization of the Catholic Church*. Cambridge, MA: Harvard University Press, 1996.

Reeves, John C., ed. *Bible and Qur'an: Essays in Scriptural Intertextuality*. Leiden: Brill, 2004.

Renard, John. "Muslim Ethics: Sources, Interpretations, and Challenges." *The Muslim World* 69:3 (1979): 163–77.

———. "The Dominican and the Dervish: A Christian-Muslim Dialogue That Might Have Been—Between Thomas Aquinas (d. 1274) and Jalal ad-Din Rumi (d. 1273)." *Journal of Ecumenical Studies* 29:2 (Spring 1992): 189–201.

———. *Seven Doors to Islam*. Berkeley: University of California Press, 1996.

———, ed. *Windows on the House of Islam*. Berkeley: University of California, 1998.

———. *Understanding the Islamic Experience*. Mahwah, NJ: Paulist, 2002.

———, ed. and trans. *Knowledge of God in Classical Sufism: Foundations of Islamic Mystical Theology*. Mahwah, NJ: Paulist, 2004.

———. *Friends of God: Islamic Images of Piety, Commitment, and Servanthood*. Berkeley: University of California Press, 2008.

Rendsburg, Gary A. "Literary Structures in the Qur'ānic and Biblical Stories of Joseph." *Muslim World* 78:2 (April 1988): 118–20.

Reynolds, Gabriel S. "The Ends of *al-Radd al-Jamīl* and Its Portrayal of Christian Sects." *Islamochristiana* 25 (1999): 45–65.

————. "Saint Thomas' Islamic Challenges: Reflections on the Antiochene Questions." *ICMR* 12:2 (April 2001): 161–89.

————, intro. and trans. *The Critique of Christian Origins: Qāḍī 'Abd al-Jabbār's (d. 415/1025) Islamic Essay on Christianity in his Tathbīt dalā'il al-nubuwwa (Confirmation of the Proofs of Prophecy)*, edited by Samir Khalil Samir. Salt Lake City, UT: Brigham Young University Press, 2010.

Robinson, Neal. *Christ in Islam and Christianity*. Albany: SUNY Press, 1991.

Rodopoulos, Panteleimon. *An Overview of Orthodox Canon Law*. Translated by W. J. Lillie and edited by George Dion Dragas. Rollinsford, NH: Orthodox Research Institute, 2007.

Rosenthal, Franz. *The Muslim Concept of Freedom*. Leiden: Brill, 1960.

Rubin, Uri. *The Eye of the Beholder: The Life of Muhammad as Viewed by the Early Muslims—A Textual Analysis*. Princeton, NJ: Darwin, 1995.

————. *Between Bible and Quran: The Children of Israel and the Islamic Self-Image*. Princeton, NJ: Darwin, 1999.

Rudolph, Ulrich. *Al-Māturīdī und die sunnitische Theologie in Samarkand*. Leiden: Brill, 1996.

Rūmī. *The Masnavi: Book One*. Translated by Jawid Mojaddedi. Oxford: Oxford University Press, 2004.

Russell, Norman. *The Doctrine of Deification in the Greek Patristic Tradition*. New York: Oxford University Press, 2006.

Sachedina, Abdulaziz A. *Islamic Messianism: The Idea of the Mahdi in Twelver Shi'ism*. Albany: SUNY Press, 1981.

Sahas, Daniel J. *John of Damascus on Islam: The Heresy of the Ishmaelites*. Leiden: Brill, 1972.

*Saḥīḥ al-Bukhārī*. 4 vols. Beirut: Dār as-Sādir, 1995.

Saint Athanasius. *On the Incarnation*. Translated by C.S.M.V., with an introduction by C. S. Lewis. Crestwood, NY: St. Vladmir's Seminary, 1996.

Saint Cyril, Patriarch of Alexandria. *Against Those Who Are Unwilling to Confess That the Holy Virgin Is Theotokos*. Rollinsford, NH: Orthodox Research Institute, 2004.

Sajoo, Amyn. *Muslim Ethics: Emerging Vistas*. New York: Tauris, 2008.

Sanders, Jack T. *Schismatics, Sectarians, Dissidents, Deviants: The First One Hundred Years of Jewish-Christian Relations*. Valley Forge, PA: Trinity International, 1993.

Sanders, Thomas G. *Protestant Concepts of Church and State: Historical Backgrounds and Approaches for the Future*. New York: Holt, Rinehart and Winston, 1964.

Schick, Robert. *The Christian Communities of Palestine from Byzantine to Islamic Rule*. Princeton, NJ: Darwin, 1996.

Schillebeeckx, Edward. *Christ: The Experience of Jesus as Lord*. Translated by John Bowden. New York: Crossroad, 1980.

Schimmel, Annemarie. *As Through a Veil: Mystical Poetry in Islam*. New York: Columbia University Press, 1982.

————. *And Muhammad Is His Messenger*. Chapel Hill: University of North Carolina Press, 1985.

Schloeder, Steven J. *Architecture in Communion: Implementing the Second Vatican Council through Liturgy and Architecture.* San Francisco: Ignatius, 1998.

Schmitt, Robert L., SJ. "The Christ-Experience and Relationship Fostered in the Spiritual Exercises of St. Ignatius of Loyola." *Studies in the Spirituality of Jesuits* 6:5 (1974): 217–55.

Scott, Peter, and William T. Cavanaugh, eds. *The Blackwell Companion to Political Theology.* Malden, MA: Blackwell, 2004.

Seale, M. S. *Qur'ān and Bible: Studies in Interpretation and Dialogue.* London: Croom Helm, 1978.

Seasoltz, R. Kevin. *A Sense of the Sacred: Theological Foundations of Christian Architecture and Art.* New York: Continuum, 2005.

Sells, Michael. *Mystical Languages of Unsaying.* Chicago: University of Chicago Press, 1994.

———. *Early Islamic Mysticism: Sufi, Qur'ān, Poetic and Theological Writings.* Mahwah, NJ: Paulist, 1996.

Shahrastani, al-. *Muslim Sects and Divisions.* Translated by A. K. Kazi and J. G. Flynn. London and Boston: Kegan Paul International, 1984.

Shihadeh, Ayman, ed. *Sufism and Theology.* Edinburgh: University of Edinburgh Press, 2008.

Shotwell, Willis A. *The Biblical Exegesis of Justin Martyr.* London: S.P.C.K., 1965.

Sikand, Yoginder. *Bastions of the Believers: Madrasas and Islamic Education in India.* New Delhi: Penguin Books India, 2005.

Simpson, Otto von. *The Gothic Cathedral.* 2nd ed. Princeton, NJ: Princeton University Press, 1962.

Slesinski, Robert. "The Doctrine of Virtue in St. Gregory of Nyssa's The Life of Moses." In *Prayer and Spirituality in the Early Church,* edited by Pauline Allen, Raymond Canning, and Lawrence Cross, with B. Janell Caiger, 1:341–52. Everton Park, Qld.: Australian Catholic University, 1998.

Smith, Wilfred Cantwell. *Towards a World Theology: Faith and the Comparative History of Religion.* Philadelphia: Westminster, 1981.

Smulders, P. *The Fathers on Christology: The Development of Christological Dogma from the Bible to the Great Councils.* De Pere, WI: St. Norbert Abbey, 1968.

Speight, R. Marston. "The Function of Hadith as Commentary on the Qur'an, as Seen in the Six Authoritative Collections." In *Approaches to the History of the Interpretation of the Qur'an,* edited by Andrew Rippin, 63–81. Oxford: Clarendon, 1988.

Stassen, Glen H., and David P. Gushee. *Kingdom Ethics: Following Jesus in the Contemporary Context.* Downer's Grove, IL: Intervarsity, 2003.

Stein, Robert H. *Studying the Synoptic Gospels: Origin and Interpretation.* Grand Rapids, MI: Baker Academic, 2001.

Stern, M. S. "Muhammad and Joseph: A Study of Koranic Narrative." *Journal of Near Eastern Studies* 44:3 (July 1985): 193–204.

Stowasser, Barbara F. *Women in the Qur'an, Traditions, and Interpretation.* New York: Oxford University Press, 1994.

Stroumsa, Sarah. *Freethinkers of Medieval Islam: Ibn al-Rāwandī, Abū Bakr al-Rāzī, and Their Impact on Islamic Thought.* Leiden: Brill, 1999.

Tabataba'i, 'Allāmah Sayyid Muhammad Husayn. *Shi'ite Islam*. Translated by Seyyed Hossein Nasr. Albany: SUNY Press, 1977.

Teselle, Eugene. *Augustine the Theologian*. New York: Herder & Herder, 1970.

Thackston, W. M. trans. *The Tales of the Prophets of al-Kisā'ī*. Boston: Twayne, 1978.

———, trans. *Signs of the Unseen: The Discourses of Jalaluddin Rumi*. Putney, VT: Threshold, 1994.

Thomas Aquinas. "Reasons for the Faith against Muslim Objections." Translated by Joseph Kenny, OP. *Islamochristiana* 22 (1996): 31–52.

Thomas, David. "The Bible in Early Muslim Anti-Christian Polemic." *ICMR* 7:1 (1996): 29–38.

———, ed. *Christians at the Heart of Islamic Rule*. Leiden: Brill, 2003.

———, ed. *The Bible in Arab Christianity*. Leiden: Brill, 2006.

———. *Christian Doctrines in Islamic Theology*. Leiden: Brill, 2008.

Thompson, John L. *Reading the Bible with the Dead: What You Can Learn from the History of Exegesis That You Can't Learn from Exegesis Alone*. Grand Rapids, MI: Eerdmans, 2007.

Tolan, John. *Saracens: Islam in the Medieval European Imagination*. New York: Columbia University Press, 2002.

———. *Saint Francis and the Sultan: The Curious History of a Christian-Muslim Encounter*. Oxford: Oxford University Press, 2009.

Turner, H. E. W. *The Patristic Doctrine of Redemption: A Study of the Development of Doctrine during the First Five Centuries*. London: Mowbray, 1952.

Turner, Victor, and Edith Turner. *Image and Pilgrimage in Christian Culture*. New York: Columbia University Press, 1978.

Twiss, Sumner B., and Bruce Grelle. *Explorations in Global Ethics: Comparative Religious Ethics and Interreligious Dialogue*. Boulder, CO: Westview, 2000.

Ullmann, Walter. *The Growth of Papal Government in the Middle Ages: A Study in the Ideological Relation of Clerical to Lay Power*. New York: Barnes & Noble, 1962.

Umaruddin, Muhammad. *The Ethical Philosophy of al-Ghazzali*. Aligarh, 1951.

———. "Ghazālī on the Ethics of Action." *Journal of the American Oriental Society* 96 (1976): 69–88.

Van Ess, Josef. *Theologie und Gesellschaft im 2. und 3. Jahrhundert Hidschra: Eine Geschichte des religiösen Denkens im frühen Islam*. 6 vols. Berlin: Walter de Gruyter, 1991–.

———. *The Flowering of Muslim Theology*. Cambridge, MA: Harvard University Press, 2006.

Veniamin, Christopher, ed. *Mary the Mother of God: Sermons by Saint Gregory Palamas*. South Canaan, PA: Mount Tabor, 2004.

Vidyarthi, Abdul Haq. *Muhammad in World Scriptures: The Parsi, Hindu, and Buddhist Scriptures*. Kuala Lumpur: Islamic Book Trust, 2006.

Vikør, Knut. *Between God and the Sultan: A History of Islamic Law*. New York: Oxford University Press, 2005.

Voll, John O. *Islam: Continuity and Change in the Modern World*. Boulder, CO: Westview, 1982.

Voorhis, John W. "John of Damascus on the Moslem Heresy." *Muslim World* 24 (1934): 391–98.

Vos, A., et. al. *Duns Scotus on Divine Love: Texts and Commentary on Goodness and Freedom, God and Humans*. Aldershot, UK: Ashgate, 2003.

Wadud, Amina. *Qur'an and Woman: Rereading the Sacred Text from a Woman's Perspective*. New York: Oxford University Press, 1999.

Waldman, Marilyn. "New Approaches to the 'Biblical' Materials in the Qur'ān." *Muslim World* 75:1 (January 1985): 1–16.

Waltz, James. "Muhammad and the Muslims in Thomas Aquinas." *Muslim World* 56:2 (1976): 81–95.

Watson, Francis. *Paul, Judaism, and the Gentile: Beyond the New Perspective*. Grand Rapids, MI: Eerdmans, 2007.

Watt, W. Montgomery. *Freewill and Predestination in Early Islam*. London: Luzac & Co., 1948.

————. *Muhammad at Mecca*. Oxford: Clarendon, 1953.

————. *Muhammad at Medina*. Oxford: Clarendon, 1956.

————. *Islamic Creeds: A Selection*. Edinburgh: Edinburgh University Press, 1994.

————. *The Formative Period of Islamic Thought*. Oxford: Oneworld, 1998.

Weiss, Bernard. *The Search for God's Law*. Salt Lake City: University of Utah Press, 1992.

————, ed. *Studies in Islamic Legal Theory*. Leiden: Brill, 2002.

Wellman, David Joseph. *Sustainable Diplomacy: Ecology, Religion, and Ethics in Muslim-Christian Relations*. New York: Palgrave Macmillan, 2004.

Wenham, David. *Paul: Follower of Jesus or Founder of Christianity?* Grand Rapids, MI: Eerdmans, 1995.

Wensinck, A. J. *The Muslim Creed: Its Genesis and Historical Development*. 2nd ed. Cambridge: Cambridge University Press, 1979.

Westra, Liuwe H. *The Apostles' Creed: Origin, History, and Some Early Commentaries*. Turnhout, Belgium: Brepols, 2002.

Wheeler, Brannon M. *Prophets in the Quran: An Introduction to the Quran and Muslim Exegesis*. New York: Continuum, 2002.

White, L. Michael. *The Social Origins of Christian Architecture*. Vol. 1, *Building God's House in the Roman World: Architectural Adaptation among Pagans, Jews, and Christians*. Vol. 2, *Texts and Monuments for the Christian Domus Ecclesiae in Its Environment*. Valley Forge, PA: Trinity International, 1990.

Williams, Thomas, ed. *The Cambridge Companion to Duns Scotus*. New York: Cambridge University Press, 2003.

Winter, Tim, ed. *The Cambridge Companion to Classical Islamic Theology*. Cambridge: Cambridge University Press, 2008.

Wright, Nicholas Thomas. *What Saint Paul Really Said: Was Paul of Tarsus the Real Founder of Christianity?* Grand Rapids, MI: Eerdmans, 1997.

Zahniser, A. H. Mathias. *The Mission and Death of Jesus in Islam and Christianity*. Maryknoll, NY: Orbis, 2008.

Zahrah, Muhammad Abu. *The Four Imams: The Lives and Teaching of Their Founders*. London: Dar Al-Taqwa, 2001.

# General Index

Fount of Knowledge, xix
France, 131, 138, 145
free will (human freedom), xix, 82, 106,
166, 172, 227
Friends of God, 192–94, 196, 200–209, 221
Fustat, 124, 151

Gallicanism, 7
Gemara (Rabbinic commentaries on
Mishna), 122
genealogy, 17, 40, 73
general guardianship (walayat al-'āmma),
45
Gentiles, 50
Ghaza, 19
Gnosis, 51–52, 94, 211–12
God: attributes of, 35, 105–8, 112, 182, 186,
203; deliverance of, 28, 180, 184, 190,
209; Divine-Human relationship, 23,
35, 161, 165, 181–82, 183–84, 188, 200,
202, 205, 210–11, 219; healthy fear of
God, 52, 165, 186; image of, 90–92, 173,
199, 214; immanence of, 103, 110, 187,
202, 203; mercy and forgiveness, xxv,
163, 166, 192, 203; nature of, 5, 9, 101,
106, 107, 109, 182; omnipotence, xix–
xx, 105, 171; ontological argument, 99;
providence of, 54, 82, 87; transcendence
of, 91, 106, 202–3, 207, 218–19; ultimate
reality, 91, 99, 103, 204, 207, 210, 218,
225–27; will of, 101, 169, 172, 181, 189,
198, 214, 226; wisdom of, 81–82, 94, 207
Gog and Magog, 65
gospel, 2, 88, 179; and apocryphal literature, 75; contradictions in, 36; conversion, 38; daily reading, 185; the Day,
62–63; genealogy, 17, 73, 195; Gospel
of Thomas, 75; interpretation, 161, 170;
Jesus of the gospels, 55, 103, 135, 162,
188–89; Mary, 40; origins, 74; and
Qur'ān, 37, 93; variations, 72, 246;
women in, 41. See also synoptic
Gothic, 150, 154
Great Awakening, 8
Greco-Roman, 51, 90
Greece, 4

Hadith, x, 11, 16–20, 190; authenticity and
credibility, 44, 48, 177; "Book of Piety,

Relationships, and Good Comportment," 167; The Book of Repentance,
167; collections, 245, 124; development
of, 47; in education, 147–48, 153; ethics, 166–68, 177, 180, 181; Hadith of
Gabriel, 84, 178, 259; as hagiography,
157, 195–96; and law, 124–25; marvels,
197; mysticism, 215; narrative, 87–88;
as source, 12, 34, 36, 38; spirituality,
187–88, 229; subgenres and themes,
64–65, 77–80; transformation of, 247;
wives of Muhammad, 43
Hagia Sophia, 149
Hagiography, 18, 43, 192–96, 201; Deeds of
the Saints (Acta Sanctorum), Golden
Legend (Legenda Aurea), Greater Life
(Legenda Major) of St. Francis, 195;
adab al-manāqib (literature of amazing feats): Generations of the Sufis,
Ornament of the Friends of God,
Remembrances of God's Friends,
Warm Breezes of Intimacy, 196
hajj (major pilgrimage), 190–91
heaven, 86, 97, 130, 133, 199
Hebrew Bible, 2, 161, 184
hell, 98, 105, 110; in The Divine Comedy, 77;
last things, 10, 26, 97
Hellenist(ic), culture, 50, 51, 90; intellectual
traditions, 21; philosophy, 4, 9, 52, 104,
211; reception of Christian faith, 237
henosis (oneness), 211
heresy (hairesis), xvii, xxi, 51, 195, 247;
heresiography, 10, 23, 85, 109
hesychastic, 214
Hexateuch, 4
Hierarchy, 43, 118, 122, 251
hijra (emigration), 190
historia (what God and Father did), 31, 47
History of Heraclitus, xviii
historical-critical method, 3–4, 8, 33, 36
holiness, 98, 143, 197, 220, 228
Holy Sepulcher, 221, 255
homoousios (of the same substance), 84, 94
House of David, 30, 40; of God, 150; People
of, 118; of the Prophet, 35; of Wisdom,
104
humanity, of Jesus, 5, 9, 94, 182, 190, 244
hujjatolislam (Proof of Islam), 119
hymn, 189, 204, 205

*Revitalization of the Religious Disciplines*
   (*Ihyā' 'ulūm ad-dīn*), 24, 174, 217, 231
*ribāt*, 143
righteousness, 53, 162
Rome, bishop of, 48, 136; as diocese, 116;
   and graves of popes, 221; invaded by
   Huns, 136; and spread of Christianity,
   4; and Uniat churches, 102; Visigoths,
   130
*Rule* (of Benedict), 141–42

*sā'ah, as-* (the hour [of judgment]), 64, 67,
   78, 85
Sabbath, 29, 162
sacrament(s): baptism, 51; confirmation,
   118; general 10, 118, 123, 210; orders, 118;
   reconciliation (penance), 118, 170, 210
sacramental(ity): character, 50; and intercession, 220; language of, 210; theology
   6, 10, 101
sacrifice, 30, 92, 190, 200, 214
Safa and Marwa, 191
saints, canonization of, 122; communion
   of, 83; contrasted to Friends of God,
   200–201; and hagiography, 192, 195;
   and intercession, 203–4, 220; Latter
   Day, 65, 116; as models, 210; tombs of,
   221; veneration of, 193
salvation: and baptism, 51; and church,
   130, 150; and gnosis, 51; and grace, 99;
   history of, 4, 10, 14, 17, 73; individual,
   212; Islamic views of, 174, 227; and
   missionary thrust, 139; and redemption, 110; and repentance, 199
Samaria, 56
Samarqand, 107
*sarrakenophroni* (Saracen-minded), xviii
Satan, 77, 141
*Sayyid*, 119
Scholastic(ism), 6, 8, 9; and architecture,
   154; and baptism, 51; and dialectics,
   101; and dialogue, xxi–xxiii, 224–25,
   229; and ecclesiology, 131; and education, 145; and ethics, 170; and mysticism, 213; and systematics, 32
Science of Hearts, 23, 217
Scribes, 169, 189
Scripture: Christian, canon of, 2; contradictions in, 46–47; and Day of the Lord,

62–63; in early community, 37; and
   ethics, 10, 161–63; and exegesis, 30–32;
   and Jesus' life, 36; and narrative, 72–75;
   senses of, 3, 30–31, 47–48; and spirituality, 183–85
Scripture: Islamic, and contradictions,
   46–47; and creeds, 84; and early community, 37; and ethics, 163–66; and
   exegesis, 32–36; and Hadith, 19; and
   Muhammad, 36; and narrative, 75–76;
   signs in, 14; as source of law, 20, 123–
   24; and spirituality, 185–88
seer, 62, 116
*sensus fidelium* (general understanding of
   believers) 123, 125, 134
Sermon on the Mount, 176, 189
servant (of God), Christ as, 5, 89; and
   God, 181, 187–88, 205; as human
   ideal, 52, 78, 119; Muhammad as, 178;
   prophets as, 63
sexual morality, 168, 174, 206
*shafā'a* (prophetic intercession), 81, 203
*shahāda* (profession of faith), 84–85
*sharī'a* (revealed law), 11, 18–21, 114, 123–
   29, 134
*shaykh* (elder), 67, 120, 143–44, 147–48, 182
*Shaykh al-Islam*, 120
*Shepherd of Hermas*, 169
*shirk* (associating partners with God), 54,
   165
*Shu'arā', ash-*, 13
*shukr* (gratitude), 165
*Simurgh*, 199–200
sin: Crusades and forgiveness for, 138;
   and Islam, 64, 96; original, 98–99, 169;
   repentance for, 194, 199, 212
Sinai, 29, 92, 161
*sīra* (life story), 17
*Sitz im leben* (life-situation), 33
*siyāsa sharʿīya* (rule by sharia standards),
   128
*siyāsat nāma* (work of political theory), 129
Social Gospel, 170
social justice, 52, 174–75, 179–80
soteriology, 190, 220
*Soul's Journey to God, The* (*Itinerarium
   mentis in Deum*), 213
South Asia, 146, 148, 152, 196, 219
Southeast Asia, 24, 55, 61, 126, 144, 152

Tunisia, 57, 124, 151
Turkey, 5, 56, 57, 144, 151

'ulamā', sg. 'ālim (religious scholars), 18,
119–20, 128, 146
Ultramontanists, 7
Umma, 59, 136, 139
ummatology, 96
university, 144–46; curricula, 145; development of, 31, 138, 142, 150; Roman, 123;
students, 145
'urf ( [pre-Islamic] custom, or customary
law), 129
usūl al-fiqh (principles of religious law),
11, 19, 114, 120
uswah (model), 177
'Uthmanic codex, 12
Uzbekistan, 81, 107

veneration, 193
Verse of Light, 35, 186
virtues: cardinal, 31, 169; and charity, 169;
of Companions, 18, 43, 77, 80, 167; and
Jesus, 175; of Muhammad, 77, 80, 167;
in Muslim ethics, 173; pre-Islamic, 164;
of Qur'ān, 77; theological, 169
vision: of divine light, 214; of God, 80, 208,
218, 231; in Hadith, 78–79; of Jesus, 39;
of [apocalyptic] seer, 62–63
voluntarism, 101–2, 105, 182

wad'ī (non-normative or postulative [law]),
127
wajd (ecstasy), 216
wakīl, 45, 108
walāyat al-'āmma (general guardianship),
45
walī, 45, 128
waqf (pious endowment), 152
way of God, 164
wisdom literature, 2, 4, 92, 161, 219
witnesses, cloud of, 194
womb, 94, 185, 205
Word of God, xix, xx, 95, 104, 108, 123,
210, 224
worship: Christian places of, 109, 149, 153;
differs from reverence, 193, 203; and
Jewish Temple, 74; Muslim places of,
153; Muslim practice, 78, 90; of Roman
emperor, 57, 136

Yahweh, 62
York, 145

Zabūr (Psalms), 93, 184
zāhir (outward meaning), 147
zakāt (alms), 180
zāwiyas (corners), 143
Zion(ists), Christian, 62, 65
Zoroastrian, 228
zuhd (piety/asceticism), 78

# Index of Names, Individuals, and Groups

# Index of Scriptural Citations

TEXT
10/13 Sabon

DISPLAY
Sabon

COMPOSITOR
BookMatters, Berkeley

PRINTER AND BINDER
Maple-Vail Book Manufacturing Group